'The world remains plagued with conflict and violence. The contributors illustrate that conflict is not always avoidable but that there are different ways, some more successful than others, to deal with these conflicts through the lenses of agency, socio-economic conditions, culture and human rights. I am personally delighted with the legal pluralistic and interdisciplinary focus of the book.'

Christa Rautenbach, North-West University, South Africa

'This volume is a must-read for anyone interested in the relations between culture and human rights and why positivistic international law does not provide the answers to mediating conflicts in societies populated by hybrid social realities. It brings together a remarkable variety of case studies from Europe, the Middle East and Asia that interrogate conflicts and clashes of values of various kinds that seem unavoidable but not intractable. We learn that in managing pluralities, we must pay attention to alternative social approaches to human rights.'

Tove Malloy, Director of the European Centre for Minority Issues, Flensburg, Germany and Member of the Advisory Committee to the FCNM at the Council of Europe

'In the inherently plural world of the law, universalising human rights norms meet new challenges. These are brilliantly explored in this rich and carefully presented collection of essays by authors who engage with conflicts and disputes in various contexts, and in different places, from India to Austria, from Italy to Israel. The book is an excellent resource for understanding how hybrid normativities work to transform morality, religion and the law in the contemporary world.'

Michele Graziadei, the University of Torino, Italy

Normative Pluralism and Human Rights

The complex legal situations arising from the coexistence of international law, state law, and social and religious norms in different parts of the world often include scenarios of conflict between them. These conflicting norms issued from different categories of 'laws' result in difficulties in describing, identifying and analysing human rights in plural environments.

This volume studies how normative conflicts unfold when trapped in the aspirations of human rights and their local realizations. It reflects on how such tensions can be eased, while observing how and why they occur. The authors examine how obedience or resistance to the official law is generated through the interaction of a multiplicity of conflicting norms, interpretations and practices. Emphasis is placed on the actors involved in raising or decreasing the tension surrounding the conflict and the implications that the conflict carries, whether resolved or not, in conditions of asymmetric power movements. It is argued that legal responsiveness to state law depends on how people with different identities deal with it, narrate it and build expectations from it, bearing in mind that normative pluralism may also operate as an instrument towards the exclusion of certain communities from the public sphere. The chapters look particularly to expose the dialogue between parallel normative spheres in order for law to become more effective, while investigating the types of socio-legal variables that affect the functioning of law, leading to conflicts between rights, values and entire cultural frames.

Kyriaki Topidi is Senior Lecturer and Associate Director of the Centre for Comparative Constitutional Law and Religion at the Faculty of Law of the University of Lucerne in Switzerland. She has undertaken extensive research in the areas of minority rights, human rights law, comparative constitutional law and law and religion issues. Her current research interests focus on religious diversity in public school systems. She is the author and editor of a number of volumes and articles that problematize the use of human rights in plural settings.

Juris Diversitas

Rooted in comparative law, the Juris Diversitas series focuses on the interdisciplinary study of legal and normative mixtures and movements. Our interest is in comparison broadly conceived, extending beyond law narrowly understood to related fields. Titles might be geographical or temporal comparisons. They could focus on theory and methodology, substantive law, or legal cultures. They could investigate official or unofficial 'legalities', past and present and around the world. And, to effectively cross spatial, temporal, and normative boundaries, inter- and multi-disciplinary research is particularly welcome.

For more information about this series, please visit: www.routledge.com/Juris-Diversitas/book-series/JURISDIV

Normative Pluralism and Human Rights

Social Normativities in Conflict

Edited by
Kyriaki Topidi

Routledge
Taylor & Francis Group
LONDON AND NEW YORK

First published 2018
by Routledge

2 Park Square, Milton Park, Abingdon, Oxfordshire OX14 4RN
52 Vanderbilt Avenue, New York, NY 10017

Routledge is an imprint of the Taylor & Francis Group, an informa business

First issued in paperback 2020

British Library Cataloguing in Publication Data
A catalogue record for this book is available from the British Library

Library of Congress Cataloging in Publication Data
Names: Topidi, Kyriaki, editor author.
Title: Normative pluralism and human rights : social normativities in conflict / edited by Kyriaki Topidi.
Description: New York, NY : Routledge, 2018. | Series: Juris diversitas | Includes bibliographical references and index.
Identifiers: LCCN 2018001984 | ISBN 9781138056596 (hardback)
Subjects: LCSH: Human rights. | Cultural pluralism. | Sociological jurisprudence. | Legal polycentricity.
Classification: LCC K3240 .N665 2018 | DDC 342.08/5--dc23
LC record available at https://lccn.loc.gov/2018001984

ISBN: 978-1-138-05659-6 (hbk)
ISBN: 978-0-367-58933-2 (pbk)

Typeset in Galliard
by Taylor & Francis Books

To George

Contents

Figures

Contributors

Tommaso Amico Di Meane is Adjunct Professor at the LUISS University of Rome. He received his PhD in Comparative Public Law from the Seconda Università of Naples (2015). He is Research Assistant in EU Law at the European College of Parma and the SciencesPo University Paris. In 2014, he was Visiting Researcher at the Indian Law Institute of New Delhi and at the Queen Mary University of London. He is editorial member in Naples for the *Associazione di Diritto Pubblico Comparato ed Europeo* and has been recently appointed as expert for the classification of Legal sciences journals at the National Agency for the Evaluation of Universities and Research Institutes ANVUR (2016). Alongside his academic activities, he has served as an expert for international organizations (UNESCO and the Inter-Parliamentary Union), national institutions (Italian Senate and Italian Government) and the non-profit sector (Africa '70 NGO). His main areas of research and teaching are Comparative Public Law, Indian Law, EU Law and Governance and Bio-cultural diversity legal protection.

Domenico Amirante is Professor of Comparative Constitutional Law and Director of the Doctoral Program in Comparative Law and European Integration at Naples II University, Italy. He is also the author of *Lo Stato Multiculturale* (2015), Bologna University Press.

Fabienne Bretscher holds an MLaw and is PhD candidate at the Faculty of Law of the University of Zurich.

Pierluigi Consorti is Professor at the University of Pisa, Department of Law. He teaches 'Law and religion', 'Canon Law', 'Comparative Religious Law' and 'Intercultural law'. He is the Director of the Interdisciplinary Research Center for 'Sciences for Peace' (2009–) and vice President of the School of Law (2011–).

He graduated in law at 'La Sapienza – Università di Roma', obtained his licentiate in Canon Law at the 'Pontificia Università Lateranense', and his PhD in law, religion and canon law. He has been affiliated to the University of Pisa since 1992. He was the Director of the Human Rights Center (1999–2005) and Director of the master's programme in intercultural and interreligious conflict management. He is also the General Secretary of the Foundation Remo Orseri for cultural cooperation, based in Rome. From February 2005 to December 2011, he was the President of the Governmental Committee for 'Civil unarmed and nonviolent defense'. He is also the National Secretary of ADEC (the association that gathers Italian university professors of law and religion). He has been visiting professor in KU Leuven (2014) and Granada (2011, 2013). His recent work focuses on issues of peace and conflict, specifically concerning the role of religion in such contexts. Special attention is devoted in his research to globalization, multiculturalism and legal intercultural dynamics. He has published widely on different aspects of law and religion.

Tanja Herklotz is a research assistant and PhD candidate at the chair for public and comparative law at Humboldt University Berlin. She pursued her studies at the Universities of Heidelberg, Bologna, Münster and SOAS, University of London. Her PhD thesis deals with social movements and the Supreme Court in India. She is affiliated with several women's rights organizations in India.

Peter G. Kirchschlaeger is Professor of Ethics at the Faculty of Theology of the University of Lucerne. He has been visiting fellow at Yale University; senior research fellow at the Faculty of Theology of the University of Lucerne; guest lecturer at the Leuphana University Lueneburg; private lecturer in Ethics at the Faculty of Theology of the University of Fribourg; fellow at the Raoul Wallenberg Institute of Human Rights and Humanitarian Law, Lund University and research fellow at the University of the Free State, Bloemfontein.

In 2013 he was visiting scholar at the University of Technology Sydney, and in 2013–2014 guest professor at the Katholieke Universiteit Leuven. Between 2011–2015, he was chair ad interim, and between 2013 and 2015 dean of research at the Chur University of Theology. He served between 2011 and 2015 as member of the Board of the Swiss Centre of Expertise in Human Rights.

He holds a master's degree in Theology and Judaism from the University of Lucerne, a master's degree in Philosophy, Religious Studies and Political Science from the University of Zurich and a PhD from the Faculty of Theology of the University of Zurich, with his research project supported by the Swiss National Science Foundation. For the period 2005–2006, he obtained a research scholarship from the Swiss National Science Foundation at the University of Chicago Divinity School. In 2012, he obtained his habilitation in Theological Ethics at the Faculty of Theology of the University of Fribourg.

Kalindi Kokal holds a PhD for research undertaken at the Max Planck Institute for Social Anthropology. Prior to that, she obtained a master's in Law from the University of London. Her interdisciplinary research focuses on the dynamics of non-state dispute processing in rural India and its relationship with state law and its systems. Her research interests span the areas of legal ethnography and legal pluralism generally and the connection between religion and law, culture and law and law and society in South Asia specifically.

Chiara Lapi obtained her degree in Law at the Faculty of Law of Pisa University discussing a thesis on Canon Law. She was awarded a scholarship for a PhD in Philosophy of Law (Canon and Ecclesiastical curriculum) at the State University of Milan. She completed her PhD in May 2012 on 'Women and inheritance laws in Hindu law: Paths to gender equality'.

She has also obtained a Post-Graduate Master Degree in Interreligious and Intercultural Conflicts at the 'Sciences for Peace' Interdisciplinary Research Centre (SPIRC), Pisa University. She is the author of a number of publications concerning 'The difficult position of Jehovah's Witnesses in Russia before the Court of Strasbourg', the 'The judgment of the Court of Cassation 4 February 2010, number 2600', the 'Chronicle of the Seminar on Law and Religion' and 'The sexual abuses of children in the Orthodox churches'. She periodically undertook research at the School of Oriental and African Studies in London and at the Centre for Women's Development Studies in New Delhi as well as at the Indian Law Institute in New Delhi.

Presently, she is a scholarship holder at the SPIRC, Pisa University and the issue of her research project deals with 'The accommodation of Hindu law in the contemporary West: The legal position of women within family and society'. She is also a member of the examination board of Canon Law and Ecclesiastical Law at the Law Department of Pisa University.

Werner Menski, MA PhD, is Professor Emeritus of South Asian Laws at SOAS, University of London. He has taught at SOAS since 1980 and was active in legal scholarship on South Asia, teaching numerous law courses at undergraduate and postgraduate level as well as supervising a large number of doctoral students. He was full Professor of South Asian Laws since 2004 until his retirement in 2014. He held many visiting appointments at universities in India, Pakistan, Bangladesh, Japan, Germany and other countries. He still writes extensively on South Asian laws, Hindu law and Muslim law, comparative law and ethnic minority legal issues. Major books are *Comparative Law in a Global Context: The Legal Systems of Asia and Africa* (Cambridge University Press, second edition, 2006); *Hindu Law: Beyond Tradition and Modernity* (Oxford University Press, 2003); *Modern Indian Family Law* (Curzon Press, 2001); *Muslim Family Law* (with David Pearl, Sweet & Maxwell, 1998); *South Asians and the Dowry Problem* (Trentham Books, 1998). He remains editor of *South Asia Research* (New Delhi: SAGE) and acted as area editor for South and Southeast Asia, Africa, Oceania and Latin America for the *Oxford International Encyclopedia of Legal History* (6 volumes, New York: Oxford University Press, 2009).

Kyriaki Pavlidou is a doctoral candidate at the Joint Interdisciplinary Doctoral Program 'Human Rights under Pressure: Ethics, Law and Politics' of Freie University of Berlin and the Hebrew University of Jerusalem. She was a Van Calker Fellow at the Swiss Institute of Comparative Law. She is a practising attorney and legal counsellor in Greece. She obtained her bachelor degree in Law at the Democritus University of Thrace and her postgraduate degree of specialisation in Philosophy of Law at Aristotle University of Thessaloniki and a second master's degree in Human Rights Law at University College London. She has worked at the European Economic and Social Committee in Brussels and was awarded the annual research fellowship of the Lucernaiuris Institute at the University of Lucerne for the year 2015. She has also undertaken additional study visits at the Humboldt University in Berlin, Bahçeşehir University in Istanbul, Birkbeck University London, the Venice Academy of Human Rights and the European University Institute in Florence.

Gopika Solanki is Associate Professor of Political Science at Carleton University in Canada. Her research interests include religion and politics, multiculturalism and legal pluralism, indigeneity and the law, and feminist theory. She is the author of *Adjudication in Religious Family Laws: Cultural Accommodation, Legal Pluralism, and Gender Equality in India* (Cambridge and New York, Cambridge University Press, 2011) and the co-author of *Journey from Violence to Crime: A Study of Domestic Violence in the City of Mumbai.* She is currently working on a book project on legal pluralism and indigenous politics, *The Split Personality of Law: Political Decentralization, Gender, and Adivasi Legal Mobilization in India* that is funded by the Social Sciences and Humanities Research Council of Canada.

Kyriaki Topidi is Senior Lecturer and Associate Director of the Centre for Comparative Constitutional Law and Religion at the Faculty of Law of the University of Lucerne in Switzerland. She has undertaken extensive research in the areas of minority rights, human rights law, comparative constitutional law and law and religion issues. Her current research interests focus on religious diversity in public schools systems. She is the author and editor of a number of volumes and articles that problematize the use of human rights in plural settings.

Melisa Vazquez is a doctoral candidate in Religion and Law at the University of Rome, La Sapienza. With a background in comparative literature and languages, she is interested in intercultural legal translation as a lens through which to assess and explore creative interdisciplinary solutions to contemporary global conflicts within religion and law.

Wolfgang Wieshaider is Professor of Administrative Law, Law of Religion and Culture at the Law School of the University of Vienna. He studied Law in Vienna and Paris. His research topics focus on religion and culture-related legal aspects, thereby including comparative and interdisciplinary approaches. His forthcoming book will be dedicated to the institution of public interest in the realm of the protection of cultural heritage.

Foreword

Normative plurality, that is, the coexistence of different legal logics, is a reality intrinsic to social life. One could say that it is the rule. Perfectly homogeneous societies, if they ever existed, are the exception. And even if one holds to the idea that they exist, they simply confirm the rule. Let us take for example the logic behind kinship: while it is true that it helps explain to a considerable extent and in detail the functioning of certain communities, it is rare for any one system of kinship to enjoy exclusivity in the rules organizing life in society.

Today, in hindsight, we may be surprised that the writings of authors who, in the 1970s and 1980s, introduced the concept of 'legal pluralism' caused such an uproar. In sum, they were doing nothing other than sticking a conceptual label on an empirical observation of universal validity.

Yet it is one thing to observe the undeniable reality of the – more or less peaceful – coexistence of diverse forms of legal logic within a society, and quite another to organize that diversity: how is this simultaneity coordinated in daily life? Is it perceived as a problem, a source of tensions that should thus be kept to a minimum or, on the contrary, is it seen as an added value that benefits not only individuals in their specific situations, but also society as a whole, and which must therefore be maintained, or even encouraged, for the good of all? Between these two extremes, there are of course multiple other, more nuanced, approaches to normative plurality and its optimal regulation. A country's history, its demography, the way relationships evolve over time among groups and communities living on its territory, as well as the influence of international law, are all factors that explain why the way diversity is regulated necessarily differs from one country to the next.

If publications about legal pluralism dating from the 1970s and 1980s were troubling to some, it was because they put their finger on the problem of an overly narrow vision of the law, concentrating exclusively on a body of law produced or recognized by a state and its institutions (also referred to, in legal jargon, as positive law). In fact, and this is what writings on legal pluralism sought to demonstrate, in order to understand how law is inscribed in the daily lives of people and communities, one must take an interest in *all* the different legal registers that mark their lives, and how these are put into practice, negotiated, renewed or, on the contrary, neglected. Some, but by far not all, are directly or indirectly regulated by state law (notably via certain accommodations), while others are ignored or even prohibited by that law, although that does not mean they are not very real. These registers – local laws, customs, clan and/or family loyalties, caste systems, professional codes, contractual commitments, memberships in associations, to name but a few – may be diverse and plural, play out in a concrete situation, overlap to a considerable extent, contradict each other, or be in outright conflict. The law laid down by the state and its institutions plays a more or less intense role in the various registers, but it is far from being the only form of law. It would be a mistake not to take account of this basic observation.

The merit of this work is that it shows how enriching an approach can be that, without falling into the other extreme of providing apologetics for normative pluralism, acknowledges that the only way to shed light on how life in society (large or small) is organized on the ground consists in trying to identify the various registers that play a potential or actual role within a very specific context, and to study as scrupulously as possible what use it is put to by the various protagonists involved in individual situations.

This is no mean effort, as it requires that we take into account all the sources of information available, and that sometimes requires recourse to ancillary disciplines such as sociology, anthropology, history, or psychology. The interdisciplinary approach in a sense serves as a support if one seeks to understand why and how, in a given context, certain rules are given preference while others are avoided and/or rejected, how the prevailing interpretation ultimately emerges, to whom this interpretive exercise is entrusted, etc.

A few years ago, a work like this one might have seemed beyond the pale. Today there are abundant works that demonstrate the complexity of managing normative pluralism in daily life. This is understandable because, with increasingly intense contacts among societies, cultures and communities almost everywhere these days, with the growing number of situations that, in particular in private law, require addressing conflicts of laws, and with the multiplications of identities claimed both by individuals (invoking the protection of individual rights and fundamental freedoms) and by entire communities (some minorities in particular), there are countless situations in which multiple normative systems must be taken into account at *one and the same time* and that demand a concrete and sustainable method to manage this simultaneity (which may be more or less conflictual).

The volume that Kyriaki Topidi has produced distinguishes itself in at least two ways from the many studies published in recent years that focus on the regulation of situations marked by the coexistence of (and often competition between) several legal systems. *On the one hand*, there is a resolutely interdisciplinary openness running through the entire volume, which distinguishes it both from purely social scientific studies and from legal publications in the traditional sense. Several of the contributions by legal scholars start from fieldwork, that is, the observation and documentation of the empirical reality of their subject. They do so not only for purposes of gathering primary source information, but also because the analyses help the reader understand that, without taking into account the multiple factors that can play a role in a given situation of normative pluralism, it is simply impossible to grasp fundamentally what is going on in such a context. The law handed down or validated by the state and its institutions is not wholly absent from the reasoning used by the protagonists involved, but its role is often less important than an analysis based on positive law might suggest; the latter must be seen as interwoven with other legal registers depending on the various potential actors. Werner Menski likes to use the metaphor of the kite to describe this situation: a flying object controlled from the ground by one or more strings. The elegance with which it manages to stay up in the air depends on maintaining a balance of the wind, the sail, the frame and its structure, and of course the strings, by the person who knows how to fly it. The metaphor serves to show that, in the quest for a concrete solution to what is often a complex situation of normative pluralism, positive law is but one of the elements to take into account. Hence, for a good understanding of all the dynamics involved in this quest, it is essential to take an interest in all the parameters at play – not only state law, but also the underlying values (traditions, beliefs, ethical criteria, etc.) that matter to the persons concerned, the socio-economic reality that defines the wider context, the expectations of each party, the relationships among the powers, and the role of international law, to mention but a few.

In his introduction, which sketches out very clearly the content of each contribution as well as the place it occupies in the entire work, Werner Menski does much more than lead the reader into the subject. He demonstrates the importance of a volume such as this one, offering a wide range of convincing illustrations of what can be gained from an approach that seeks to be *contextual*, that is, one that studies each situation in a wider context, that is not exclusively legal, and that is open to interdisciplinarity.

The other way in which this volume distinguishes itself from many recently published studies dealing with the management of normative pluralism is its significant focus on India. No fewer than four contributions, three of them grouped in Part III, are devoted to analyses of managing normative pluralism in Indian societies. In Europe, as Werner Menski mentions in his introduction and as the contributions relating to the 'old world' clearly indicate, normative pluralism, when linked to the long-term effects of post-war migration and the resulting 'new minorities', is seen as a threat, an evil that imperils social cohesion. In India, the context is radically different. Pluralism is in a sense at the root of social identity in India, although that does not mean that there are no problems, but that the cause of certain tensions and the solutions envisaged are cast in very different terms. One must be careful not to catapult societies like those of India from the status of postcolonial society to that of an example to be followed, a 'master' that could teach us how to manage contemporary normative pluralism in a less hostile manner than is the case today in Europe. The attention several authors in this volume pay to the Indian context is not intended to serve as a model or to provide an example; rather, their work examines several ways of managing pluralism that, while not immediately translatable into other contexts, reveal the complexity that plays out within *all* conflicts to do with questions of law, demonstrating clearly that plurality is everywhere, in India and elsewhere, and that it must be recognized as a distinct dimension if one is to understand how a society functions. For European readers interested in the question of normative pluralism, there is much to be gained from taking an interest in the reality of law in contemporary non-European societies which are also plural in makeup but which perceive that plurality in radically different fashions.

Kyriaki Topidi has taken an innovative initiative – inviting early-career researchers to present their work at the Faculty of Law in Lucerne and giving them the greatest possible freedom in their approach – and turned it into this remarkable and refreshing volume. The book is also highly promising, and gives cause for optimism among those who for many years have been interested in questions relating to normative pluralism. The volume attests to the fact that young researchers, by taking an interdisciplinary approach in their work on the law, can produce sophisticated analyses that demonstrate that the quest for justice in plural societies is not the monopoly of a few professionals, but is a constantly evolving process that must be considered within its own context. In the years to come, it would be good to see other works draw inspiration from this very original and stimulating effort.

Marie-Claire Foblets

Acknowledgements

This book, as is the case for edited volumes, is a group achievement: it is based on a series of intensive workshops, conducted for the most in Switzerland, that explored the relation of law to and with religion. But the volume that you have in front of you is more than a group project; it reflects the evolution of the trajectories of a group of scholars at various stages of their careers that share the interest and motivation to understand the inherent pluralities of the law. There is deliberately a variety of voices heard from a variety of disciplinarily perspectives.

As such, this book is the natural continuation of *Religion as Empowerment: Global Legal Perspectives*, also published by Routledge, and represents the next step in the debate on the consequences of acknowledging law as a plural social phenomenon. It focuses on some of the infinite facets of normative conflict, inspired by the daily observation of clashes between state law and religion in our societies. It does not pretend to cover the entire span of scenarios of conflict but instead accounts for situation-specific clashes of rules using human rights on one side and religiously inspired or connected rules on the other to illustrate the types of clashes.

The realization of this rich in perspectives endeavour is, as mentioned, the result of the work of many: first of all, of the contributors who have shared with me their precious work and agreed to reflect on the notion of normative conflict through their individual pieces and intellectual perspectives. In their individual capacities, they have offered fascinating accounts of the workings of normative pluralism in conditions of clash, disagreement and contestation.

I am particularly grateful to Professor Werner Menski who has consistently and tirelessly accompanied this project with his advice, knowledge and own intellectual contribution to the broader discussion. The book in its making has also profited from the advice and suggestions of various individuals, but I would wish to especially highlight the input of Julian Sidoli del Ceno, Lukas Heckendorn and Professors Marie-Claire Foblets and Christa Rautenbach for their insightful, sincere and genuinely supportive suggestions. As crucially, the editorial support of Alison Kirk and Alex Buckley from Routledge has made this book a smooth and pleasant learning experience.

In a world that appears more and more fragmented and super-diverse, our ambition has been to maintain the momentum in the understanding of law as complex, evolving and not homogeneous. This realization alone represents an adequate starting point for one to begin to consider the potential for diversity management that the discipline offers. The discussion is far from settled, the patterns of conflict are still not exhaustively studied (if they will ever be) and at times, we still struggle to draw pertinent conclusions from the empirical observations in front of us. Yet, the ambition of the book is to keep this discussion going while accepting that a conflict is unavoidable but at the same time can be used as a potential opportunity for self-reflection towards more harmonious coexistence.

Kyriaki Topidi

1 Introduction

Conflicts over justice and hybrid social actors as legal agents

Werner Menski

Prologue: a biographical note

More than 70 years after the end of World War II, the world is still suffering much conflict and wanton violence. In fact, chaos looms in the 'trumped' USA and a soon-to-be dis-Mayed UK that misled its voters that it would be feasible, in this globally connected world, to insist on 'sovereignty'. World War II may have ended in 1945, but today the globe has more refugees and displaced people than we have seen at any time in history, as serious disputes flare up on all major continents. In such chaotic conditions, various reverberations of earlier and present conflicts affect how we feel, think, act and react, in many more ways than are immediately obvious. Connected to this, mapping conflicts in relation to human rights remains a huge challenge today, a conundrum in the view of many observers, but that word and/or image does not help take us forward,[1] neither in theory nor in practice. I hope and in fact insist that we can do better than that.

A few years ago, helped by a young Indian historian, I examined Jürgen Habermas as a modern social thinker for an Indian collection of articles (Menski, 2012a). We found that his original theorising was too eurocentric and did not go far enough in critiquing violence in the public sphere. Researching that piece also opened our eyes to the so-called 'accident of birth' affecting how post-War Germans recovered from the disastrous conflict their leaders had caused. Habermas, who was 16 in 1945, could immediately carry on his education to become the international star (Menski, 2012a: 180) he still is today. My father, trained as a village teacher at a young age to replace a schoolmaster drawn into the army in 1943, turned 19 in 1945. But he was not lucky. After having to serve in the army from 1944 onwards, he became a prisoner of war somewhere in Belgium until 1948, in atrocious conditions that he never wanted to speak about. On release, he had nowhere to go, as his home was now in Poland. A stranger in his own country, forced to rebuild his life from scratch, he also did not know the whereabouts of his family, who eventually turned out to be spread all over Germany. That young man, like Habermas shocked to discover what had really happened (Menski,

1 In chapter 6, the image of a giant ball of yarn is mentioned as similarly unhelpful to unravel complexities and find solutions.

2012a: 182), never trusted politicians and the state, which explains to some extent why in due course I became more critical than Habermas about abuses of power and turned into a legal pluralist deeply concerned about conflicts manipulated by individuals in the name of some official law or ideology.

I remember seeing Hamburg in ruins in the early 1950s, never imagining that more than 60 years later I would contribute to a book on conflict. Finding earlier that a major strand running through the work of Habermas is 'fear of violence and abuse of power' (Menski, 2012a: 181), I seem to have reacted to this memorable imprint on my mental map by concluding that Habermas had not gone far enough in his activism of opposing violent conflict. Particularly his insistence on secular rationality had led him to develop a eurocentric blind spot regarding the power of religion and connected normativities. I respect Habermas for admitting this omission, which he famously rectified after 9/11 (Borradori, 2003; Habermas, 2008; 2010). This revised theorising now implicitly endorses the viability of legal pluralism studies as a mapping exercise for better understanding of discourses about the public space and the ubiquitous, multi-layered phenomenon of conflict.

The focus of the current collection of articles

When I was asked earlier to contribute to Topidi and Fielder (2016), in the light of the comments above, it made sense to support the key arguments of that study about religion as a form of empowerment. Similarly, regarding connections of law and 'culture' in relation to human rights protection, I did not hesitate to provide this introduction about the potential for constructive use of 'hybrid social normativities' in efforts to promote and protect human rights. This longish phrase is akin to, and at the same time much more than, the elusive scintillating concept of 'culture', itself a highly pluralistic interdisciplinary entity. In a broadly speaking legal context, 'hybrid social normativities' can evidently mean many different things. It signifies interdisciplinarity, something plural and socio-legal, but is also about values and identity. It is more diverse than 'mixed jurisdictions', a label that stresses the plurality of legal orders, but speaks too little about interdisciplinary overlaps and the impacts of law-related disciplines.[2] As the sphere of hybrid social normativities extends also to values and ethics, 'normativities' are not merely a plethora of 'customs' of various kinds, but also the values and identity markers connected to socio-cultural patterns, structures and processes. Since the socio-cultural sphere partly overlaps with economics and politics, and also extends to the wide field of human rights activism and international law engagement, even prominent phenomena like 'civil society' would fall under this broad label. This deeply hybrid entity is therefore, it appears, composed of all the necessary ingredients for negotiating disputes and, hopefully, balancing agreeable outcomes. It combines elements of the social, the legal and the ethical, in different mixes at different moments, and thus needs to be understood and watched as a chameleon-like entity. It may

2 Farran, Örücü and Donlan (2014: 2) clearly state that '[a]ll modern legal traditions are both mixed and mixing' and suggest different degrees of mixity.

harmoniously blend in at certain times, may even become invisible, but then it may also suddenly change colour, become aggressive, pose risks and enlarge conflicts. Akin in many ways to 'law' itself, then, especially if we do not restrict that label only to a narrow state-centric force, 'hybrid social normativities' either supplement or strengthen any legal order that already exists, or they may seek to oppose, undermine or challenge such law.[3]

All articles in this volume discuss and test the nature and strength of the connections between 'law' in a narrow sense, 'human rights' as an alternative choice of words for 'justice', and the undeniable, often elusive impacts and influences of 'hybrid social normativities', which remain difficult to identify without appropriate lenses or analytical tools. These articles began their life in the laboratory of a series of international doctoral training workshops on legal pluralism and human rights, organised by the editor and the University of Lucerne, with support from several other institutions and individuals, including myself. It is an entirely rational progression that we now cooperate in producing this volume. Composed of highly disparate papers, it needs to contain a clear message to readers, hopefully provided by this introduction.

The doctoral training seminars were advising young researchers that if your project wants to write about everything, you are actually writing about nothing. Aware of that risk, the question arises now what this book is trying to convey. I first provide a comprehensive mapping of the nature and perceptions of conflicts that readers are going to encounter in the various chapters,[4] always with an eye on the core aim of human rights protection and the complications presented by law's inherent plurality. A further section then enlarges the discourse on conflict itself, showing that it need not be perceived as a negative process. Disputes and conflicts arise out of the hybridity of roles and decision-making processes that various actors display, motivated by different values and normativities. These have to be tested in their practical application, always focused on the plurality-conscious key image, as I see it, of law as a kite, outlined below. The continuously cultivated key argument becomes therefore that a variety of social actors and their disparate concerns, voices and values needs to be constantly accounted for if constructive human rights-focused activity is to result in better practice than seen at present. Simply cutting out the 'traditional' voices of 'culture' and 'society' in efforts to introduce 'modern' or 'progressive' laws and safeguard deeper levels of human rights protection is not going to be successful unless we acknowledge that 'law', as a situation-specific, context-dependent and always highly dynamic entity, has to be debated in a plurality-conscious interdisciplinary manner. Whether one calls that 'decentralisation', as Chapter 11 suggests, 'adaptation' (Chapter 12), 'communication' (Chapter 13), or something else, it always seems necessary to allow space

3 Actually, Chiba (1986: 6–7, cited in Menski, 2006: 125) uses the label of the 'legal postulates' in that very same context.

4 As a trained social geographer, I share the interest in spatialisation of social theory discussed in the volume edited by von Benda-Beckmann et al. (2009), but space constraints prevent detailed engagement with this important aspect here.

for competing and conflicting understandings of various voices and their reasons to differ. Rather than ruthless assertions of power, this demands engagement in negotiation and balancing acts, which may result in a partly unsatisfactory compromise for all stakeholders. Simply demanding perfect justice, as we shall see, could itself be toxic. 'Good law', also sensible 'living law' (Menski, 2012b), this means to say, is more than the sum total of state-centric laws, human rights and international law provisions. It needs, which is the key message of this volume, the constructive input of hybrid social normativities to be turned, through well-considered processes of inclusive discourse and practical application, into a lived reality that is sustainable and capable of protecting basic human rights in various specific contexts.

Putting it this way, another important lesson from the doctoral workshops can be added here, related to the theme of limits of law (Allott, 1980). In the seminars leading to this book, we jokingly concluded at some point, on a nice Alm outside Lucerne, that there could not be a viable human right to a Postdoctoral Fellowship for all doctoral students! This indicates the painful realisation that some kind of socio-cultural relativism applies also to basic notions of human rights, which remain subject to multiple limits and constraints in the constantly developing understandings of concepts of justice. This does not make human rights or international law principles irrelevant, redundant or even deficient. It suggests, however, supporting argumentative presumptions backgrounded by history (Sen, 2006), that such competing claims about rights and obligations, about fairness and respect for difference, always need to remain open for debate and adjustments. In that process, they require the constructive input of all law-related entities to become a 'good' lived reality. Equally important, the various human actors involved in such conflicts and discussions need to engage in altruistic abstinence from exploiting majoritarian advantages rather than self-righteous manipulation of power imbalances.

Maps and perceptions of conflict

Current events and developments in the world confirm, however, that self-righteous bullying remains rife, so that the prominent phenomenon of conflict and its (ab)use, in the daily life of individuals, societies, states and the global community, continues to take many shapes, with many competing agenda, multiple purposes and numerous disparate, often disastrous outcomes. Readers who know my recent work, still building on Menski (2006), yet going far beyond it now in a series of articles on law as kite flying (see Menski 2012b, 2013, 2014a, 2014b, 2014c, and much else more recently), will instantly realise that this way of framing conflict relies on complex perceptions of legal pluralism and its practical application, part of ongoing global discourses on justice (Jamal, 2018; Menski, 2016a; Sen, 2009).

Since this volume grew out of a series of international doctoral workshops, partly concerned with different aspects of legal pluralism, all contributors to this volume are familiar with my theorising of law as a kite, yet may of course not endorse it, or simply do not mention it. In fact, as Professor Marie-Claire Foblets has commented on more than one occasion, taking legal pluralism for granted and getting on with the real job of producing world-class literature on how law and anthropology can together create a better world seems to be the real task of legal anthropology today. Yet this knowing silence about an underlying theoretical model or pattern of theorising law as a hybrid plural entity does not help readers who have no mental map of this kite methodology present before them to follow what this volume is trying to say.[5] Hence I must explain here briefly how that map of the kite model works and what its implications for the present study are.

In fact this kite methodology seems as much a matter of common sense than sophisticated legalistic theorising. It seeks to understand the complexities inherent in different manifestations of 'living law' all over the world, testing whether this is 'good law' (Menski, 2012b). In that normative context, it asserts that neither state law nor human rights law or international law, though prominent today, are ever the only form of 'law' needed while searching for the 'right law', as the neo-Kantian legal philosopher Rudolf Stammler (1856–1938) called this long ago. Neither of these may be even the dominant form of law in a specific context, given the highly dynamic nature and culture-specificity of law and the subjective positionality, differential power status and levels of agency of all kinds of individuals as law-related decision-makers. Basically, the kite model shows that there are always four competing types of different kinds of law acting together, in varying relationships of competition and power, explained immediately below and illustrated, if readers can see the wood for the trees, throughout this volume. In brief (see Menski, 2013: 26), at the top, imagine corner 1 representing various forms of traditional natural law, ethics and values, including religion. On the right, envisage corner 2, which signifies various hybrid social normativities as well as economic sustainability. On the left, find corner 3, representing the various familiar forms and manifestations of state law, while corner 4 at the bottom concentrates on the new natural law of human rights and international law.

That is, however, only the first level or layer of legal plurality, resulting in the dynamic image of a kite that flies in the air and needs to be balanced, through application of legal pluralism as a navigating skill, to avoid crashing.[6] For the purposes of plurality-conscious navigation, one needs to imagine a second layer of plurality hidden in this kite model. The first realisation that this may be so is found in the triangular image of law (Menski, 2006: 612) and the accompanying concluding discussion about law's intrinsically plural nature. The 2006 triangle with its intricate numbering system already clarifies that most of socio-legal normativity (in corner 1 of that image), of state law (in corner 2) and of religious, ethical and moral principles (in corner 3) are in fact mixed or hybrid entities and are not

5 As observed by Fikentscher (2016: vii), it is not easy for the social sciences, including law, I would add, to catch up with the pace of the many new developments.

6 The mental image of exciting games with beach kites is a distraction here, as the fun of crashing and then re-floating such kites is merely a nice pastime. In relation to legal systems, the potentially rather boring aim is to achieve plain sailing and as little dramatic and turbulent action as possible.

purely composed of the core ingredient of the respective corner.[7] Elements 11, 22 and 33 (Menski, 2006: 612) are manifestly not the norm and the dominant reality is mixity and hybrid plurality.

When the triangle morphed into a kite, the numbering system was changed and a fourth corner emerged. The subsequent realisation that all these four elements are actually contained in all four kite corners, spread all over the conceptual space of the kite of law, albeit with different characteristics and mixities, led me to graphically represent that every corner contains in itself virtually another kite, comprising each time elements of all the four types of law identified above (see Menski, 2013). This complex dual-level structure, referred to as a power kite, helps to identify conflicts of powers in decision-making between the more ethically focused power from within (corner 1), the more social power exercised with others (corner 2), powers over others in a legal/political sense (corner 3), and finally powers from within and over others as a result of the 'double whammy' or combined authority claims of human rights and international law today. It is really that simple as a basic descriptive structure. However, in practice these kite corners represent also normative entities. Combined in particular sequences of decision-making processes, they always depend on a plethora of contextual parameters that influence the modalities of the use of these various components. All of this, it seems, is not only hybrid, but highly volatile and dynamic,[8] since anything may happen at any time.[9]

Faced with this complex internal plurality of law-related entities, one will certainly not always see the expected results of earlier planning, policy making or mapping, however carefully devised. This is a further aspect of the limits of law, elaborately discussed by Allott (1980). Indeed, the outcome may be further conflict and intensification of disputes rather than settlement. One major reason for this, but not a good enough excuse for tolerating chaos and further abuse, could be that the respective legal navigators work with conceptually difficult and to some extent 'liquid' building blocks.[10] While there simply is no global agreement on what we mean by 'law' (Menski, 2006: 32; Tamanaha, 2008: 391; 2009: 17), 'religion' and 'culture' are also heavily contested basic elements. In the necessarily interdisciplinary discourses about human rights, the term 'human rights' itself, too, 'contains a multitude of meanings that cross many academic disciplines' and is

7 This numbering system is different from that in the kite, as the original triangular model followed the theorising of Chiba (1986), asserting that while unofficial law (corner 1) and official law (corner 2) always co-eisted, both were always connected to the normative entity that Chiba called 'legal postulates' (corner 3).

8 A fuller description of this volatitlity is found in Menski (2014a).

9 I cannot enlarge this point here (see Menski, 2016a), but apparently the fear of more or less sudden chaos, well-documented in the literature on ancient Indic legal systems and the notion of the 'bad age' (*kaliyuga*), including the impressive image of 'shark rule' (*mātsyanyāya*), lurks in the background of older legal orders that then devised ritual and other mechanisms, including deterrrence-focused criminal laws, to help avoid such dreaded chaos scenarios.

10 On the notion of liquity of law, see Menski (2014b) and the other articles in that Special Issue of *Jura Gentium*.

thus 'an inherently interdisciplinary subject' (Gearty, 2008: 553). This means that human rights discourse, everywhere, 'runs a thousand narrative risks' (Baxi, 2002: ix) and has to face the reality, for example, that there are 'as many NGOs as there are human rights' (Baxi, 2002: 50).

It is of course not good enough to state that everything is complex and plural, and then just to move on, for the result can only be further partial theorising, fussy fuzziness and more unproductive conflict. Meanwhile, something else seems to have happened. Partly propelled by widespread frustration that conflicts cannot be avoided, much attention has shifted to the currently fashionable field of post-conflict reconstruction, now a veritable growth industry within the larger domains of law and anthropology, resembling the MILLI phenomenon in relation to Islam.[11] Yet without deeper understanding of the inner nature of 'conflict', which constantly re-appears, despite creation of a UN prevention industry (Mellbourn and Wallensteen, 2008), this all becomes dramatised group dance around hot potatoes, especially 'religion' (Topidi and Fielder, 2016: 2) and 'culture'.

Mapping conflict more precisely thus remains a necessary exercise. It forms the very centre of justice as discourse, focusing on much concern that in this age of human rights, humanity seem to be doing rather badly in implementing what at least some of us, which seems to be part of the problem, have mapped out and declared as desirable agenda for various aspects of development. Today it is claimed, often vociferously and frequently for sound reasons, that some kind of *nirvana*, as peace, justice and protection of human rights principles and standards should, and even shall,[12] be achieved. There is considerable moral force behind such arguments, but also too vague reliance on 'sensible behaviour' (Husa, 2015: 45). At times desperate urgency is felt,[13] but there are also notable risks of self-righteousness for activists, since these issues become matters of belief and resemble strong convictions. Massive disappointment results if the stated ideals and expectations remain unmet, framing such conflicts of expectations as part of the problem. I endorse the apprehensions of Grillo (2015: x) that 'fervent religiosity ... indeed all forms of ideological self-righteousness', which he mentions also in relation to ethnicity and gender, risk causing conflict rather than helping to resolve matters. This does not mean to foreclose or stop debates. I also go along with Grillo (2015: x) that trying to present, as far as possible, an objective account of convoluted discourses does not mean one agrees with everything that is being put forward. In a sense, the kite model of law and its practical application in

11 MILLI stands for 'Muslims, Islam and the Law: A Legal Industry' (Grillo, 2015: 8).

12 I highlight this innocuous little word 'shall' here, as it symbolises the claimed power of positive law, for 'black letter law' seems to dictate or at least suggest that 'shall' means 'must', when in lived reality this is quite often a highly sophisticated legal fiction. The key example (see Menski, 2006: 375–379) is found in Pakistani law, where a positivist reading of 'shall' as 'must' would actually make the state-made Muslim family law un-Islamic and thus unconstitutional.

13 A good example of this is Dhagamwar (1989) and her urgent claims for the need to develop a Uniform Civil Code in India, a topic still vividly debated almost 30 years later.

processes of decision-making, when the legal actor or agent picks up tools from around the kite in particular sequences, merely maps processes of making decisions, step-by-step. It may imply a normatively graded and ordered sequence on the part of the respective legal actor. The observer, however, only records the sequences, in the first place. Evidently, that cognitive process and its connections with normativity need to be examined further.

In this context, it is productive here to scrutinise briefly what bargaining techniques are applied when different kinds of social actors or activist interveners become involved in human rights jurisprudence and discourses, maybe any law-related debate. This closely connects to varying ideas and ideals of 'justice', on which lawyers have had much to say, with Rawls (1971) as one of the major protagonists and many other insightful philosophical interventions. The existing discussions show that scholars and activists may cultivate and operate remarkably different visions of 'justice' and how to achieve it. Sen (2009) highlights this clash in methods of claiming justice by distinguishing basically two strategies of seeking to achieve justice, both generating specific kinds of conflict.

The first strategy identified by Sen (2009: 8) is that '[t]he characterization of perfectly just institutions has become the central exercise in the modern theories of justice', This is broadly based on (one hopes) well-meaning principles of liberalism and Enlightenment, according to which scholars and activists of various kinds claim that desirable developments must be achieved without further delay, mainly by demanding and creating perfect rules. Sen (2009: ix) voices grave doubts about this approach and even calls it 'entirely incorrect', a critique which I endorse (Menski, 2016a: 303). Global demands and hopes for justice suggest that this is in principle a 'good' strategy, because it voices claims that need to be heard and noted. But it is also an aggressive bargaining technique that aims for the full ideal, perhaps unrealistically asking for the moon, as I call this in relation to Indian legal debates (Menski, 2016b). This strategy risks generating tensions, even conflicts and violence, because some of these demands and expectations are simply not practically and rationally realisable in the given contextual circumstances, either instantly, or in the longer term. The lengthy wish lists of such activists and their hybrid social normativities contain many demands for new laws and rules, or appeals seeking to avoid or minimise injustice and conflict: No more world wars! No more ethnic cleansing! No more unemployment! No more hunger and poverty! No more child labour! No more child marriages! No more instant divorces by patriarchy-obsessed men![14] Such wish lists never seem to end, but understanding these as cherished ideals, one can see a specific method involved here,

14 This is a reference to the current drama (*tamāshā*) around triple *talaq* in Indian law and the case of *Sayanara Begum*, decided by the Supreme Court of India on 23 August 2017, seeking to declare such an instant *talaq* legally invalid. The case, framed as concerning the legal validity of a triple *talaq* given by a Muslim husband in India today, is in my view to be understood, and thus mapped, as a purposeful distraction from deeper and quite different issues of conflicts of law and governance in Indian law today. On the concept of *tamāshā* see further below specifically the article by Kalindi Kokal (Chapter 9) and further on talaq Chapter 13 below.

underpinning this frantic action of constantly demanding a better world. While Sen (2009: 8) identifies this strategic focus on ideal rules or perfect scenarios as a prominent bargaining position, he suggests, and most practising lawyers probably know this well, that this is only the beginning of the process of working towards better justice.

The second strategy is much more arduous, as it involves contextually focused working out of sustainable solutions. Calling this the 'comparative route', Sen (2009: 9) identifies the need 'of focusing on actual realizations in the societies involved, rather than only on institutions and rules'. Evidently, this pragmatic path involves hard work, bargaining and conflict management, with outcomes that often do not match the ambitions expressed by the idealistic first strategy of seeking justice.

Unfortunately, humanity as a whole, even in the supposedly developed Western world, often seems confused or disagrees about what it wants to achieve in relation to justice and how it wants to go about securing improvements. While we might say that this is normal, those not belonging to the 'developed world' might retort that desired developments can frequently only be achieved to the detriment of those who do not live in that world. Whether this is an after-effect of colonial memory or evidence of concerns over neo-colonialism, this chain of arguments creates further dispute. Presently, with increasing force, climate change discussions generate such new conflict scenarios, typically over the balances of obligations and rights when countries like Bangladesh voice claims of having to bear the brunt of pollutions caused predominantly by the developed world (Rhaman, 2016). Here again, adversarial patterns of conflict are building up, increasingly sought to be addressed today by international law methods of intervention, while generating yet more law-related industries of considerable attraction, especially for international lawyers. Such claims, then, are often promoted by hybrid social actors raising banners of human rights and international law in barely disguised self-interested efforts to grab a share in yet another growth industry.

Hence, many critical voices about human rights developments are heard among the cacophony of complaints about the continuation of conflicts. What sense does one make of this? While it remains challenging to follow the intricate examinations of the grammar of human rights by Upendra Baxi (2002; 2008), his work contains insightful comments worth building into the current mapping exercise. When Baxi (2002: 143) in his elaborate meditations on the future of human rights crafted the neologism of 'righticidal practices' in the specific context of ecologically violent management by multinational corporations and state governments, this targeted a different range of culprits, however, more along Marxist and anti-establishment lines. Intriguingly, though, in the third edition of his book, Baxi (2008: xxii–xxiii) responds to criticism that his approach lacks anthropological input and recognition of South Asian Studies. Regional cultural relativism appears here, even a shadow of 'Asian values', when Baxi (2008: 8) sets off to critically re-examine the grammar of human rights and correctly, in my view, identifies continuing lack of access to justice as a major bottleneck. However, this revised approach now mainly identifies deficient institutional processes within law and practical attempts to safeguard human rights.

It still bypasses the issue of hybrid social normativities since Baxi remains, also here, deeply distrustful of 'culture' and 'religion', especially regarding India. This rather common 'critical' stance overlooks, and thus fails to examine, the potential of such inputs to contribute to better implementation of human rights, a field which, echoing Gearty (2008) as cited above, is acknowledged also by Baxi (2008: xiii) as displaying a 'fragmented universality'. The cultivation of particular politically motivated blind spots, documented in the sophisticated partiality of the expert commentator writing *ex cathedra*, is of course a hallmark of academia and its cherished freedom of expression, which surely must be protected. But maintaining such blind spots also poses risks of cementing the ongoing persistence of a remarkable mismatch between theory and practice, and between discourse and implementation. The admission that 'there exist different modes of doing anthropology of human rights' (Baxi, 2008: xxiii), notably with a reference to the recent insightful work of Mark Goodale (2007), is thus extremely productive and appears to show a new way for making progress.[15]

While I question purportedly liberal approaches in human rights discourses that simply seek to dismiss 'culture' off-hand as bad for human rights, most aggressively voiced by Okin (1999), the more nuanced approaches of Phillips (2007) and Shachar (2005) receive well-deserved endorsement in recent discussions. Examining modern challenges to Islamic law, Shaheen Sardar Ali (2016: 211) clearly reflects more awareness than earlier writers regarding the hybridity of social normativities, also within Islam (see now also S. Ahmed, 2016; Benkin, 2017). Doubts over progress towards more constructive goodwill and understanding of 'the other' also within a particular tradition resurface, however, when some otherwise insightful recent writing still portrays personal law systems as 'problematic' (F. Ahmed, 2016, see also Chapter 8 below). Deep-running ongoing concerns over the ethics and values connected to certain hybrid social normativities are further identified by Maeso and Araújo (2017) from Portugal. They highlight a barely hidden dismissal of non-European values and 'otherness' in the context of supposedly post-racist societies and related mental frameworks of European scholarship when they observe: 'The boundary between Europeanness and non-Europeanness draws a line between the presumed "democratic and tolerant values" of the majority and the presumed "problematic characteristics" of the minoritized Other' (Maeso and Araújo, 2017: 2). This point, incidentally, verifies the connections of any type of law with values, highlighted earlier by Chiba (1986).

Equally negative, but often more visible and conflictual than scholarly argumentation, and worrying for the whole world, as state practice ought to be 'good law', is the ongoing failure of states to work towards effective implementation of human rights through maintaining 'good governance'. One could raise many examples here of abuse of discretionary spaces, often related to the treatment of migrants and 'others' (Brown, 2017), indeed several contributors (in Chapters 4, 6, 7, 10 and 11) pick this up. There is also much concern that recently, leading

15 How this matches with the theorising in Chapter 13 I shall leave for readers to work out.

Western democracies seem to elect unsuitable leaders, or fall prey to the demagogics of certain claimants to power that promise visions of a future that are completely unrealistic and unsustainable. Instead of serene enjoyment of advanced development, whole nations then experience new turbulences by being 'trumped', struggle over modalities of a clearly conflict-generating BREXIT drama, or elect parliamentarians that, one must fear, could bring back Nazi-inspired nationalism, as now seen in Germany. Such segregationist tendencies carry new risks of complete disaster, with chaotic cliff-edge scenarios.

Conflicts arise also over whom one should then blame for such developments. Behind all these processes of contestation, one finds social/political/legal actors driven by certain normativities, sometimes more concerned about self-interest and pompous deceit, reflecting variations of self-righteousness. Does one then simply criticise those individuals, or is it necessary to question why people elected such leaders and/or voted for their policies? This raises complex questions of political analysis about relationships between various stakeholders. While there is certainly no space to pursue this enquiry here, the connected message for the context of the present book should be reiterated: Conflicts caused by states can often be traced back to specific individual legal/political/social actors playing to a particular, often nationalistic, electorate and pursuing conflict-generating agenda. Sadly, at this point, explicit reference to the current leader of Myanmar shows that even a globally decorated peace campaigner may fail to contain conflict. In fact strategic silence or empty diplomatic promises that offer no sustainable remedies may worsen a conflict. The key lesson here seems to be that individual discretion of legal actors, camouflaged and hidden within the various corners of the kite structure, needs more careful scrutiny.

Such conflicts also concern the right balance between public and private interest. Moreover, it seems to matter what kind of scale is chosen to tackle a specific issue.[16] Is a specific conflict a matter between two individuals, does it arise at the level of social groups, regions or nation states, or the international community? Often, no clear boundaries can be drawn, but skilful choice of scale may help find sustainable solutions (see also Chapters 6 and 9). All such conflicts, evidently, need to be perceived and handled as connected to hybrid social normativities, today prominently visible when a socio-political entity called 'electorate' is asked to participate in decision-making processes within more or less democratic contexts, but may be severely manipulated by those 'in power'. The modalities of such processes confirm such conflicts as a global management predicament, at many levels. Multiple criteria come into play while putting forward certain issues for decision, or specific candidates for leadership, including certain dynastic patterns that generate their own normativities.[17] The complex processes of elections and governance indicate that these, too, are hybrid social, law-related processes, often

16 In this context, the work of Maarten Bavinck (see chapter 10 of von Benda-Beckmann et al., 2009), is highly significant.

17 On the so-called 'battle of the Begums' in Bangladesh as a dangerous example of adversarial politics and conflicts, see Khan (2017) and Menski (2015).

empowering and emboldening ambitious individuals with specific agenda. Notably, recent fieldwork-based studies from South Asia show that common people are increasingly aware of their voting power (Kumar, 2017; Philip, 2017; Rai, 2017). The legal implications of such socio-political insights into voting patterns are undeniable. In principle, this has long been known (Hayden, 1999: 138–40), and remains deeply relevant.

Today's globally interconnected world is increasingly well-informed about multiple conflicts, but do we have sufficient tools to assess the boundaries of tolerable deficiencies in striving for human rights? Constantly revised criteria seem needed to ascertain what is, in line with the plural kite structure of law, either (1) ethical, authentic or credible in terms of basic values, (2) sociable, feasible or doable regarding socio-cultural and socio-economic expectations and criteria, (3) legal in the sense of being in accordance with 'the law' (which as we know from bitter experience is no insurance whatsoever that everything will be 'good'), or (4) tolerable in terms of human rights and international law principles. This list of benchmarks and indicators, a burgeoning research area, needs to be fine-tuned with specific regard to the limits of legal pluralism, maybe following the conclusions of Twining (2009: 218) concerning what is 'intolerable' in the context of elaborate plurality-conscious human rights debates. On the contested subjectivities involved in justice as discourse, especially in the highly conflictual interface of liberalism and Muslim law, Jamal (2018) will be instructive reading.

Recent research demonstrates how technological advances may today be transported into the most remote villages as part of claimed developmental efforts. For Bangladesh, Ullah (2017) shows how introducing computer-based technology at village level among the most disadvantaged sections does not address disadvantage, but seems to reinforce it. In fact, state involvement at village level may generate new conflicts, disturbing and replacing traditional structures of patronage, without change to the predicament that some people remain less resourceful than others. They will then have lesser chances of full equality, whatever that means in the first place. Indeed, whether a demand of total equality is even sustainable as part of a viable human rights discourse remains doubtful, particularly in the light of the already discussed critique by Sen (2009: 9) of 'the transcendental route' of seeking to achieve justice.

Regarding what may be the most important aspect in this mapping of conflicts in relation to human rights protection, the articles in this book seem to suggest collectively, and the editor of this volume wants to convey, I think, that conflicts of various kinds, including clashes of values, seem unavoidable but may be tackled by constructive discourse, for which our contributors chose different names. Hence, there is simply no way to decree or even lobby that there should be no more conflict. But there should be discourse, since better human rights protection remains something worth arguing about, a message entirely in line with the second strategy of seeking justice identified by Sen (2009). But, and this is probably the central heuristic result of this wide-ranging mapping exercise, human rights activists, coming mainly from corner 4 of the kite of law, cannot achieve their objectives effectively by putting themselves in conflict with all other corners of the kite. Nor can state actors on their own, or state law, coming from corner 3, simply decree justice in top-down fashion. In all such scenarios, the sub-kite level of the 'power kite' suggests that a truly empowering approach to human rights protection needs not only to recognise the potential of 'religion' to be an agent of empowerment rather than an obstacle (Topidi and Fielder, 2016). It also has to acknowledge the potentially positive energies and inputs of the various hybrid social normativities encountered in day-to-day experience, accounts of which need to be shared as widely as possible.

The precariousness of conflict and the key role of human agency

As there are already many books on conflicts, one needs to ask what this book may add to the archive and whether, collectively, we can offer some useful guidance for how to manage conflicts of law and culture in relation to hybrid social normativities. There has been some preliminary reviewer comment that this collection is rather much focused on South Asian evidence. While that is partly a reflection of the range of contributors, it also arises because South Asia is one of the major regions of the world, marked by intense diversity, that is generating many conflicts. In addition, there was also a collective aim to counter eurocentrism, even a dose of countering anglo-centrism in the literature and in some thought patterns, with sustained efforts being made to include perspectives from many different angles and locations.

The elaborate mapping exercise of the previous section has confirmed that if lawyers and legal scholars want the cacophonous voices of hybrid social normativities, including their regional manifestations, to be heard more fully, they would be well-advised to listen carefully not only to scholars, but also to common people as legal agents. That this is methodologically and practically challenging is beyond question. It is insufficient to only consider the views of 'systems' or of leader figures, whether politicians or stakeholders of international law and human rights activism. Here, too, anthropological methods are crucial tools. However, the modernising process of the creation of neoliberal states worldwide, inspired by the political principles of democracy, human rights and the rather general and 'liquid' concept of 'rule of law', reflects ample efforts to capture and control power by those who put themselves forward to lead, not only in academia. It also reflects continued efforts to carry on earlier colonising and 'civilising' missions. Globally, this includes determined efforts to push back and extinguish local forms and patterns of dispute management (Hayden, 1999) and to spend much energy on developing uniform structures that systematically privilege the state and its law-related powers (Fitzpatrick, 2001: 212–215).

Through an anthropological lens, though, considering law also as a social fact and connected to values, two important observations arise. First, most disputes, anywhere, do not reach formal state fora, and societies that seem to live without formal law are not thereby 'lawless' (Allott, 1980). Secondly, law itself is so internally diverse that various kinds of conflicts constantly arise. Yet though use of law so evidently generates conflict, it is neither fair, nor sensible scholarship, to blame legal pluralism for the predicament of ubiquitous plurality. This stance basically resents lack of legal certainty as a presumed infringement of a major hallmark of 'law'. The constant process of elastic discursive engagement and inclusion, always respectful of difference, needs to be conducted in cautious circumspection about the risks of self-righteous bullying on the part of any type of excessive 'fundamentalist' reasoning (Benkin, 2017). Moore (1978: 9) showed convincingly that even formal legal reform always occurs in piecemeal steps, since no legal code is ever going to be fully comprehensive. Law making, too, is then potentially a precarious activity for certain stakeholders, as the well-documented ethnography and cartographic work of Wacquant (2014) confirms. Given that law itself can cause trouble and is so difficult to define, it seems unproductive to reject the concept of 'law' itself as a useful building block, preferring instead to discuss 'order' and 'dispute' (Roberts, 1979). Lawyers are evidently stuck with 'law'. Changing labels seems pointless. Instead one should learn better to address, in a responsible manner, the internal differences of the domains lawyers are claiming to focus on. What one calls these processes seems itself disputed, though, as the chapters in Part IV confirm.

The early literature on dispute prominently stresses that life itself inevitably generates disputes and tensions at all levels of existence. While conflicts are often seen as a pathology of troubled and contested relations, this is certainly not the whole story. Roberts (1979: 45) refers to the pioneering work of Simmel, originally written in 1908 in German. This provided insights into the potentially constructive attributes of dispute and '[b]oth in his association of conflict with the normal and inevitable in social life, and in his insistence on its necessary and constructive side, Simmel has been widely followed by other sociologists' (Roberts, 1979: 45).

Similarly, Rouland (1994: 167) observes as a general principle, which may be called the traditional paradigm of justice, that, '[g]lobally, traditional justice is concerned less with applying existing norms than with achieving social equilibrium following disorder'. A re-reading of Roberts (1979: 44–79), which typically focuses on disputes rather than the more recent terminology of 'conflict', is highly instructive. The way in which Roberts (1979) indexes 'conflict' further suggests that this category has today become a fashion item in the legal wardrobe, focused on states and international relations, while earlier writing (see Allott, 1980; Rouland, 1994) tended to focus more on dispute.

Looking back at such earlier literature, the recognition of a critical role for the individual actor or agent in relation to generating and handling disputes and/or conflicts remains remarkable. Conflict may result not only from human interaction, but may already arise within the individual human mind. The mapping exercise of this introduction must therefore include that arguing with oneself is also a frequent form of conflict. Though this book is not a study on conflicts within persons or on psychology, the close connections of law and psychology are undeniable. Focus on conflicts of law and culture should therefore not overlook that the internal map of individual minds is already normatively hybridised by different allegiances, desires, phobias and everything else within that one mind. Discussing such kinds of conflicts as psychological, ethical, or philosophical does not normally allow them to be framed as legal conflicts, yet interdisciplinarity and connectedness are found also here, and at various levels.

Several articles in this book depict the self as a law-related actor, offering instructive examples of how persons living under conditions of legal pluralism, and being conscious of this, react to such challenges. They will not be merely passive recipients of various forms of legal regulation, but also claim the capacity – and seize the chance – to become active agents by using the discretionary spaces opened up by consciousness of legal plurality. Ballard (1994: 8) has clearly shown with specific reference to Asian settlers in Britain how this then occurs 'on their own terms', which is likely to generate further conflict, especially in conditions of ethnic and religious plurality and cultural competition. Conflict here, as many contributors to this book observe, arises over the right and authority to determine aspects of one's own life on one's own terms, not dictated to by others. This reflects fierce competitions over authority and agency in decision-making, a basic issue that arises everywhere and at all times.

Regarding the handling of disputes, Roberts (1979: 53) wrote that 'societies differ widely as to the light in which trouble is viewed by the members and as to the amount of quarrelling which is seen as acceptable'. He continued:

> In some societies peace and quiet is seen as essential and members cannot bear the least argument or disruption; in others there is constant shouting and noise, and people seem to relish a quarrel. Consistent with this, the reaction of individuals to trouble varies greatly from one society to another.

While much of the observable drama may seem entirely pointless, or completely unnecessary and superfluous, much conflict serves important purposes (see Rouland, 1994: 255–290). It may be a device to gain clarity over specific contested matters or issues, it solidifies relationships, or shows that they are not repairable, so that parting ways is better than struggling on. It confirms or modifies power relationships, it secures entitlements, or may simply be a strategy to get heard (Roberts, 1979: 52). Conflict may intend disruption, even desire chaos, but may also be entertainment and drama (*tamāshā*), shown especially here in Chapter 9. Notably, Roberts (1979: 54) makes the important observation that whether conflicts originate from cultural or biological foundations,

> they tend at any rate to be closely related to the values and beliefs held in the societies concerned. In some, physical violence and aggression represent dominant values, whereas restraints and attempts to avoid controversy are equally representative of others ... A response representing the minimum which 'honour' demands in one society may thus seem as inconceivable over-reaction in another.

Evidently, this leads to considerable variation in handling disputes and conflicts. Hayden (1999: 132–134) shows how a changed context, in this case the increased consumption of pork by one particular community, generated more and stronger conflicts, highlighting the dynamic nature of such processes. At the community level, addressing conflicting values through different mechanisms of resistance may be one way to manage conflicts. This may mean keeping any disputes out of state-centric processes, while not being totally unaware of which normative patterns and structures influence state-centric manifestations of law. One will thus need anthropological, sociological, psychological, and not just legal toolkits to address any troubles experienced in law-related management.

Thinking of societies as states, we may find imagined communities of citizens and groups of people tied together, often unwillingly, by bonds of nationality, citizenship or common application of the respective legal order of a state. There is also huge potential for conflicts of interest between those who claim to rule, or have been elected to lead, and those who are being ruled and led. In every group, there will be numerous differentiations and more pluralities with law-related relevance. All of this gives rise to multiple conflict scenarios, particularly since also at this level, absolute equality and uniformity is not normally even a cherished social ideal, since states themselves discriminate and distinguish between various stakeholders based on various rational or irrational criteria (see Chapters 7 and 10). Finally, the global community seems today more seriously fragmented than ever, despite many efforts to devise binding instruments of 'soft law' or even increasingly strong rules of international criminal law.

At all these levels of legal mapping, idealised notions of equality and uniformity can be depicted as argumentative devices to move towards a better future. But they could also constitute a misleading set of words to describe the human predicaments of competing ambitions over what it means to lead a 'good life'. If one individual, group, society or nation wants to take over the neighbour's property or a neighbouring nation's territory, or seeks to expel an undesirable 'other' from close proximity, multiple conflict scenarios arise, variously labelled as robbery, boundary dispute, ethnic cleansing or, even at the global level, the declaration that the presence of some hated 'other' is simply intolerable. What then does one do? We see some current answers in action when terrorists are shot on the spot.

There are, however, also less aggressive and more inclusive models. From the perspective of some 'traditional' cultures or religions, and I suggest this approach is more common today than we care to accept, for example when people are encouraged to think holistically, the categories of 'us' and 'them' do not merely include all humans, but potentially all living or created beings. This would, for example, be practised in the minority religion of Jainism (Rankin and Shah, 2008), based on strong principles of non-violence. Such traditions, in themselves hybrid social normativities, offer reflections and practical guidance on how humans manage themselves and various relationships, wrapped into a wider discourse on justice and the strong South Asian cultural theme of avoidance of chaos (Menski, 2016a). Fear of chaos, confirmed by much of the anthropologically focused writing on conflict in 'traditional' African and Asian contexts, becomes a motivating factor to rebalance existing relationships, often ritually. Ameliorative strategies may also include simply moving away as long as there is enough space, preferring exile rather than death penalty, as in traditional African laws. In more crowded conditions today, it appears that 'modern' notions of conflict often concern conflicts over shared resources, framed as reflecting or involving challenges to a contested status quo perceived as intolerable or unjust. Whatever the factual context, the need to understand better how to manage conflicts remains quite apparent worldwide. It constitutes a constant challenge not only for institutions and structures, but also – and probably mainly – for individual legal actors, wherever on the kite of law they may be found.

The practical test

This penultimate section attempts to deepen understanding of how conflicts in law and society with a specific eye on human agency related to basic rights protection may be matched with more theoretically focused discourses about justice (Jamal, 2018; Sen, 2009). Such an undertaking involves reference to the current state of play in comparative law, which has become a huge field (Husa, 2015), and particularly to comparative public law, still growing vigorously, too. For evident space reasons, this introduction cannot discuss comparative law in relation to conflicts in any depth but notes that all these comparative gymnastics involve many competing actors, involving thereby legal pluralism, its methods of theorising and practical applications. Here, two major irritants remain, firstly that pluralism studies reflect multiple battles about accepting plurality, diversity and difference, related to trouble with 'comparison', selective mental processes or a sort of *mentalité*,[18] which many humans continue to struggle with as law-related actors. Secondly, there is a notable tendency among participants in these forms of communication to treat law as a market of opportunities for self-profiling, an arena of claims and competition, with remarkable unwillingness to use the same language to describe what is, if we envisage the kite model of law, after all a silent journey. The core concept of 'hybrid social normativities', introduced earlier, may motivate various stakeholders to promote or oppose, as the case may be, different suggestions and projects for better human rights protection or any other measure related to law. The resulting cacophonies seem to silence the key issue on whose terms this journey is actually conducted. Indeed, I am often asked who holds the strings of the kite. But as these strings are actually connected to all corners of the kite, the critical issue is that the kite navigator is always some human actor who exercises agency by making decisions through picking tools for legal navigation from around the kite.

Plurality-conscious legal analysis thus provides solid evidence that so-called conflicts arise and seem to be managed by individuals as legal agents or actors, often hiding behind institutions or other structures that grant power and offer discretionary spaces for decision-making (Brown, 2017), which may be easily abused. One realises this as soon as one drops standard legal positivist blinders and

18 On this concept see Fikentscher (2016: 85), earlier Pierre Legrand (see Menski, 2006: 66–70).

classroom-induced state-centric legal analysis, including the excessive focus of Rawlsian theorising on institutions (Sen, 2009: xi). Instead, it is necessary to acknowledge not only the reality of ubiquitous plurality, but the horrible reality that multiple acts of individual human nastiness (Sen, 2009: 32) pose constant risks for justice, basic rights, peace and harmony. Moreover, Sen (2009: xvii) diagnoses 'the prevalence of unreason in the world' as well as 'the unrealism involved in assuming that the world will go in the way reason dictates'. Since there is also a need to allow 'for the possibility that there may exist several reasonable positions' (Sen, 2009: xix), the urgency of solid reasoning as a form of pluralist navigation stands firmly established.

It is easy to write that, but how does one manage this in practice? Various social cacophonies are not normally analysed as legal conflicts. Yet as soon as one begins to scrutinise interactions between groups of people, i.e. various manifestations of 'society', including that fashionable entity of 'civil society', we involve the domains of anthropology and sociology, and other related social sciences, becoming embroiled in fussy discourses over legal and law-related conflicts with ever more diverse dimensions of human rights activism. The challenge then becomes to analyse the specific nature of the respective competition, which may fall between corners 2 and 4 of the kite, but (following Chiba's guidance) is also always connected to corner 1, often with the state in corner 3 as arbiter. The 'hybrid social' component thus also includes the 'civil society' that several contributors discuss (see especially Chapter 8). Partly located in corner 2 of the power kite, as social actors dressed in human rights banners, so to say, civil society is probably more accurately characterised as an element of sub-corner 2 within corner 4, or an element of sub-corner 4 found in corner 2. Here again, the analyst's perspective, and the voice of the respective legal agent, are critical parts of the evidence in situation-specific contexts.

To analyse the inner structure of this entity of 'hybrid social normativities' in more depth, I constantly refer back to what Chiba (1986: 6) was apparently forced to call 'legal postulates', by which he meant a huge collection of value principles or a whole value system, 'specifically connected with a particular official or unofficial law, which acts to found, justify and orient the latter'. This assertion of the close connection of all forms of law with morality and values meant that no legal rule can ever be value-neutral. The triangle of law (Menski, 2006: 612) was therefore devised in accordance with Chiba's methodological guidance. That specific triangular image, however, was actually hiding rather than showing the gradually intensifying conflicts of our times between traditional and modern values, more specifically between various forms of 'old natural law' and 'new natural law', as we now see it. We know from Chiba's later work that this was a deliberate strategic silence about the always latent, growing potential for conflicts between national laws and human rights/international law and the different sets of 'legal postulates' attached to them.

These multiple clashes of values became visible once the 2006 triangle of law turned into the kite model with its four interconnected corners (Menski, 2013: 26). This immediately pluralised the concept of 'hybrid social normativities' even further. Now there were always four, and not just three, types of competing laws to balance. The separate representation of corner 4 on the kite provided the key to analyse such hybrid normative conflicts in more depth. In this regard, it is relevant to recall what Chiba (1989: 177–178) identified as three dichotomies or conflicts, between (1) official law and unofficial law; (2) legal rules (in effect both official and unofficial laws together) and legal postulates; and (3) indigenous law and transplanted law (see Menski, 2006: 128). Once the triangle had developed into the kite, a fourth dichotomy appeared. This explicitly global form of conflict identifies significant tensions between 'old natural law' and the 'new natural law' of human rights principles and international law normativities.

This cleared the path for the already discussed double-decker mapping of the kite of law as a dual-level power kite. This has meanwhile become a useful device to show how virtually all law-related decision-making processes seem to be operated by picking up tools and principles from the various corners and sub-corners of the kite structure, literally the tool boxes of legal pluralist navigation. The kite model of law, as a practice-focused model, acknowledged by Jamal (2018), provides hands-on guidance either for repairing leaks or deficiencies of justice, or for constructing or at least proposing and negotiating better protection of human rights and international law principles. But it cannot fully do this without respect for the hybridity of social normativities. Given the requirement to account at all times for context-specificity in legal decision-making, it is however not possible to offer any binding or general guidance on how to manage competing or conflicting scenarios. Specifically, there cannot be a global directive for where the starting point on the kite for decision-making ought to be. That is a question of agency, situatedness and elastic exercise of power. All we know from this way of presenting the whole field, as observed earlier, is that the deliberate cutting off or omission of any one element of the kite will result in injustice, bad law, deficient policy and further violence.

A decision-making sequence thus always has to contain four elements, with the most hated one put last. Even when all components are included, conflict is not completely avoided. It may become more manageable, but may also result in new conflict scenarios. The various hybrid social normativities that the present book seeks to focus on may be prominently located in corner 2 of the kite of law. But it is crucial to reiterate that these normativities, in different situation-specific manifestations, are always also located within all other corners of the kite. Their spread all over the kite structure arises directly from the realisation, discussed earlier, that the four main corners of the kite are themselves each in turn composed of the same four legal or law-related elements, now at the sub-kite level.

There are thus two stages of the kite management process involved in this exercise. Stage 1 demands of all law-related stakeholders to self-identify from which corner of the kite they wish to start the discursive process. For example, in judicial training seminars we find that judges, within seconds, realise that through their official position they are located in corner 3 of the kite, anchored as part of state law. There is really no escape. It does not matter whether these judges are religiously connected or not, whether they have a family or not and/or feel attachments to any specific social group, and what precisely their stances on human rights and international law may be. From the start, their decision-making process is located within kite corner 3, which now becomes the focus of attention and then opens up this sub-kite for focused further navigation, while the overarching global kite model recedes into the conceptual background. Next, this legal actor now has to choose in a second-stage process which of the four available sub-entities should be employed, and in what sequence, for a specific decision-making process. In other words, the judge now needs to decide in what sequence the four sub-elements of the kite in corner 3 are to be employed to reach a fair decision. Clearly, then, skilful judges cannot rely only on their knowledge of state law, as they have to assess and account for the other three elements involved here, too. At the second stage of tool selection, they may not even start with corner 3 again, given that they already made a firm commitment to be located in that corner.

Similarly, human rights activists have probably already predetermined through adopting that label that their decision-making process will be focused on the sub-kite in corner 4, which now becomes the main kite structure to focus on. It becomes now an interesting challenge to trace whether in any decision-making process such activists will then again start from sub-corner 4 or not. This may depend on what kind of human rights or other law-related entity the activist wants to protect. For example, a Muslim human rights activist may be more concerned at this moment of choice-making about connecting to Islamic principles. In the same manner, socio-legal actors locating themselves in corner 2 will face the same choice-making predicament. As Chapter 9 confirms, a local wise man or woman in an Indian village cannot totally ignore what state law has to say on certain aspects of a conflict. Yet for this legal actor, the expectations and pressures coming from sub-corners 1 and 2 are likely to be more powerful and persuasive than the competing concerns of sub-corners 3 and 4. Finally, an individual legal agent who perceives himself or herself as an ethical entity, for example as a deeply religious person, will again be faced with this pluralist dilemma of having to account for all other sub-corners. Failure to do so, in this specific case, would not just be an act of epistemic violence, but would most likely result in what today we are constantly seeing as aggressive and ultimately self-destructive acts of 'fundamentalist terrorism'.[19]

Thus, whatever the starting point of the respective legal agent on the whole surface of the kite structure may be, there is no escape from choice making and, consequently, a conflicts scenario, inherent in the presence of these competing corners in every space of this globally present structure. What matters therefore in terms of managing conflict is not whether or not a conflict exists, but how this conflicting scenario is handled and addressed. We see here confirmation that 'law' as a complex field is indeed not only composed of rules, regulations and

19 Several studies in Benkin (2017) illustrate how Balochi or Pathan Muslims in Pakistan will self-identify as members of their local communities first, and as Muslims next, but then encounter conflict with other Muslims who demand primary adherence to corner 1, rather than corner 2.

institutions, but also of processes of how to manage these rules, apart from values. In a way, this position comes close to the Hartian distinction between 'primary rules' as rules of obligations between entities and 'secondary rules' as 'rules about rules', or procedural components. However, the ubiquitous link with values, precisely Chiba's 'legal postulates' in their dual manifestation, always makes itself felt, even if eurocentric discourse seeks to silence this. This perception expresses a key expectation of an intensive activity of argumentative inclusion, existing not only in South Asia as heterodox traditions since ancient times (Sen, 2006: xii). Importantly, this always also includes elements, perspectives and normativities that a particular stakeholder may not be in agreement with. All one is asking for, then, is that in this process of interaction, the 'other', no matter how hated and despised, should be acknowledged as present and having a voice, however disagreeable. Banning or silencing any of the perspectives from the outset is likely to be perceived by the excluded entity or element as an act of violence. It is also a matter of common sense, and even of physical reality, that if any element of the kite of law is simply and quite literally cut out, the whole structure will crash to the ground and ceases to be viable.

Seeking to combine all four corners of the kite in specific choreographies to devise some kind of movement, even if inch by inch and painfully slow, towards progress in achieving better human rights protection, this collection of papers hopes to convey the message that pluralist engagement is not just conflict-generating, but can and should be discourse-inducing. It forces all legal actors to reflect, not just to react to emotions, including a sense of superior power. Realising the virtue of 'relative justice' and engaging in respectful debate with 'the other' without preconditions or expectations of absolute agreement helps reduce the heat of conflicts. When there is willingness to engage with all components, even the most obnoxious or odious ones have a space within this discourse. Chapter 13 shows brilliantly how quickly such irrational legal actors may then lose public credibility if they insist that their decision or stance is the right one. Several contributors confirm that if states refuse to engage in a responsible manner, non-state processes will be preferred. The state has then only limited scope for supervision, or may deliberately stand apart (typically, Chapter 6 for Italy). Refusal to engage, as a form of epistemic violence, one now sees more clearly, could generate further violence and conflict. This reinforces realisations that ignoring the various voices of hybrid social normativities is simply not a viable form of managing diversity and difference in the deeply plural contexts we now encounter all over the world. My interdisciplinary and intercultural theorising identifies such conflict scenarios literally as kite turbulences and kite crashes. When the subtle structure of a kite flying in the sky loses its balance and crashes to the ground, this indicates failure in navigation or deficiencies in balancing.

It is no use blaming nature, for the fault lies mostly with more or less deliberate human failures to manage life's challenges regarding pluralities by not paying due attention to hybrid social normativities. While the terror of a *tsunami* does not discriminate on the basis of gender, age, religion or status, human acts of terror, more often than not, follow an agenda of hostility, even blind rage, simply to cause maximum havoc, even if it kills one's own people and frequently the perpetrators of such atrocity themselves. In explicitly anthropomorphic contexts, looking closely at the actions of individual humans, this then points to systemic deficiencies in practices of integrated, self-controlled ordering, connected to abuses of power and discretion. Such precarious stress scenarios affect not only many individuals, but also socio-cultural and other institutions, impact on the (mal)functioning of whole states and affect entire domains of the international legal order. All of this is bad news for human rights, because such acts of nastiness do not respect the ubiquitous existence of hybrid social normativities. In such scenarios, there is no meaningful discourse, only aggression and overstepping of limits that generate conflict and chaos. No amount of 'rule of law' effort, it seems, can completely prevent that. Regrettably, the next acts of human nastiness are going to appear at any time on our media screens.

The individual articles

Despite such depressing news, this book projects overall a hopeful trajectory regarding the theme of conflict, moving from efforts to prevent, to articulation of conflict, its processing, and its resolution. However, nobody should imagine that such hope-inspiring presentation resolves anything forever, as conflict will remain part of the human experience. Sadly, there is often no rational reason for this, just a desire to cause trouble, so that one could argue that extreme forms of atrocities are not really 'conflicts', but evidence of deliberate chaos.

Part I: Preventing conflict

Part I of this book contains two chapters considering methods of preventing conflict. In Chapter 2, Tommaso Amico di Meane argues that conflict, like disorder and even chaos, can be studied through comparative law approaches, which offers many tools to examine contextualised, interdisciplinary fields. However, significant inadequacies in methodology are diagnosed, as well as clashes of ignorance, bias and even malice, as much depends on the lens that one adopts. For example, declaring 'the other' as problematic is itself problematic, leading to conflictual dichotomies, which do not account for the liquidity and elasticity of law as a global phenomenon. This is so particularly regarding non-Western legal cultures, where state law plays a less important role compared with religious, social and cultural paradigms. The chapter argues elaborately that a new methodology for handling disputes is required, including avoidance of eurocentric 'hegemonic' organisations of reality, more focus on non-Western legal traditions and deeper general analytical rethinking of law's plurality. Without explicitly acknowledging recognition of 'hybrid social normativities', the key argument is that comparative law methodology needs to be strengthened by a new approach based on dynamism, tolerance for ambiguity, interdisciplinarity and flexibility. Its current two major standard approaches, functionalism and contextualism, are not necessarily mutually exclusive, but may be complementary, provided there is a will to lessen conflict.

Chapter 3 by Domenico Amirante confirms through the practical example of India's management of socio-legal plurality, with specific reference to linguistic diversity, that sustained sensibility to pluralism and respect for difference can yield conflict-reducing outcomes, even in a vast and highly diverse nation. Exploring the role of the linguistic dimension in (trans)-formation processes of the Indian federal state, which by now has 29 state units, Amirante depicts Indian federalism as an illustration of successful policies of recognition of hybrid cultural identities, and thus social normativities. Though not always readily agreed, and often achieved after much negotiation, this facilitates reduction of conflicts between regional, ethnic or linguistic groups and state institutions at various levels. Amirante explains how language, as a potential source of conflict, given its status as a key component of cultural identity, has been increasingly linked recently to the rise of social transformation phenomena within a globalisation framework. He finds that acknowledgement of language pluralism, as an important aspect of the recognition of community and groups rights, may actually strengthen new forms of belonging of citizens within an 'open' multicultural state. This depicts a modern cohesion policy as a modified continuation of the older 'unity in diversity' model. It indicates that the state's self-interested respect for hybrid social normativities, manifested also in flexible constitutional procedures, together with skilled institutional bargaining, has succeeded in playing a crucial role in conflict management in this hyper-diverse multicultural state.

Ultimately, this endorses as viable what Chapter 2 advised as a theoretical model, namely that within liberal states, plurality-conscious governance of the multicultural state, acting as a medium of communication between the various stakeholder groups within a broader frame of negotiation of difference, can achieve successful balancing of competing claims. The characterisation of India as a 'liberal' state, a classification that is probably counter-intuitive for most readers, is made on the basis of solid research and sound evidence. It shows, confirming Chiba's theoretical presuppositions, that non-Western states are indeed less focused on state-centric laws and thus have learnt, for a variety of reasons, including self-interest, to respect plural voices and hybrid social normativities in the shadow of globalising pressures. When outsiders fail to see this because of blurred vision or preconceived notions, conflict scenarios arise in constructed discourses that sometimes bear little resemblance to the lived experience of the people concerned.

Part II: Articulating conflict

Part II contains four chapters on the articulation of conflict, focusing on Europe and Israel. These contributions illustrate how conflicts, often centred on religion rather than culture, and thus on ethical values (corner 1 of the kite of law) rather than social norms (corner 2), are subjectively framed by legal and law-related decision-makers. This largely confirms the observations by Maeso and Araújo (2017: 2), cited above, that something seems deeply wrong when in Europe today, the non-European 'other' is problematised, even to the extent of being banned, framed as 'religious', while European manifestations of religion are treated as part of 'culture'.

In Chapter 4, Kyriaki Pavlidou considers this conflict in relation to religious symbols, asking whether these are religious or cultural manifestations. Discussing the headscarf controversies in Turkey and Switzerland and the famous Crucifix cases in Italy, she offers a reading based on identity and legitimacy. Her analysis, rather than engaging with wider theoretical debates over identity of the 'subject' at the constitutional level, demonstrates how in practice the terms of a conflict tend to be set and articulated by formal legal entities. She finds specifically that the European Court of Human Rights, through a basically incoherent approach, constructs the identity of the 'subject' in question in such a way that conflict is generated and perpetuated, indeed by declaring 'the other' as problematic.

Pavlidou's critical assessment of these decisions also brings out the contrast of an essentialist approach of the 'subject' as homogeneous and motionless, constituted exclusively as religious when it comes to the headscarf, but notably as socio-cultural in the Italian crucifix conflict. She suggests a contextual, relational understanding of identity as socially constructed and always in transformation. Her discussion identifies the paradox of liberal anti-pluralism in the rationale of the cases, since the real conflict is not 'religious', but is found in the dialectic between law and culture, expressed in dualistic terms like 'us versus them' and conflict between power and agency. This chapter, thus, critiques how the ideological and legal concealment of the socially constructed subject occurs through imposition of a static, predetermined, essentialist concept of identity, using the (pre)-text of constitutional protection. For Pavlidou, the formation of a legitimate identity of the subject can only happen in conformity with the principle of respect for diversity and individual autonomy, premised on equal dignity and value. In any case, European identity, in her analysis, cannot be reduced to religious characteristics and the alleged cultural roots of a 'European essence' premised on religion. Outlawing the 'religious other', as shown here, bans certain aspects of hybrid social normativities in a highly questionable, discriminatory manner that generates conflict.

In Chapter 5, Fabienne Bretscher similarly identifies the problem of official non-recognition of certain hybrid social normativities when she scrutinises the conformity of imposing limitations of religious practices on new socio-cultural groups, formed in Europe by recent immigration. Her analysis focuses on international bodies, such as the United Nations Human Rights Committee and also the European Court of Human Rights. Comparing this restrictive approach to the more favourable treatment of old-established minorities, Bretscher identifies discrepancies that would need to be addressed, both in the global literature on minority protection and in official legal practice regarding the right to freedom of religion and wider questions regarding the right to culture. She also finds that different perceptions of these groups' position in society, particularly whether they are seen as immigrants or minorities, have led to a conflict in the interpretation of such persons' right specifically to freedom of religion.

Regarding possible ways to resolve the conflict of legal norms between the international and European level, Bretscher favours a clearer legal minority perspective for claims of groups formed by recent immigration towards the accommodation of religious belief. This argument confirms that respect for 'hybrid social normativities' should include consideration of people's value systems and ethical foundations, a position entirely in line with Chiba (1986).

Melisa Vazquez addresses in Chapter 6 one specific law-related moral conflict, the handling of claims regarding conscientious objections by trained medical personnel to abortion in Sweden and Italy. A Swedish midwife who objected to taking part in abortions, in a country that endorses them as an aspect of women's human rights protection, did not succeed in having her claims recognised. In the Italian scenario, where abortion is also legalised, but large numbers of medical personnel get away with objecting to it, such conflicts are managed in completely different ways. The difficult balancing act in either case identifies direct contradictions between conscientious objectors and the respective public declarations and conceptions of the state legal system.

Observing that secular European states seem to be particularly adept at packaging righteous-sounding proclamations of neutrality and 'justice', Vazquez highlights the potential role of 'intercultural translation' (similar to Chapter 11) as a means of exploring possible solutions for current struggles within legal pluralism, secularism, protection of freedom and defense of human rights. She questions the laws regulating reproductive issues as 'objective ground' for rights and presents the problem as an example of the hidden rules of behaviour underlying the fabric of both democracies in question. Vazquez argues against semantic stiffness and in favour of situation-specificity, flexibility and fluidity, echoing several other contributions in this volume. Awareness that the categories we choose to establish are always fluid and liquid suggests that the translational path to pluralism can be a viable method for dialoguing among differences. The conclusion puts forward a vision of law as a means of self-actualisation that extends beyond the mission to control human behaviour. Respect for 'hybrid cutlural normativities', acccording to Vazquez achievable through intercultural translation, is ultimately presented as the most productive path forward in bringing together a priori irreconcilable identities, also when no non-European 'other' is involved in the conflict.

Kyriaki Topidi in Chapter 7 scrutinises the workings of legal pluralism in public education in Israel, a country operating a multicultural system that experiences significant conflict, mainly because of efforts to impose a patriarchal minority culture, based on the 'religious primordiality' of the state, on the liberal majority. Examining the potential for empirical variations in the analysis of human rights in their socio-legal dimension, Topidi focuses on freedom of education and religion and considers accounts of how religious diversity challenges public education. While the formal authority to regulate this field belongs to governments, political parties and courts, voices are also heard from various religious communities and from within hybrid social contexts, exploring the potential for adaptation and reconciliation with modernity in a concrete setting, including increasing diversification of educational services.

The ambiguous framework of Israel as a Jewish and democratic state means that in the field of education, the role of religion in state affairs and the state's establishment of religion find an expression in the diversified public education system. In practice, this ambiguous legal framework allows for state funding of religious institutions, particularly orthodox-Jewish ones, risking an imbalanced weighting in favour of this particular minority's right to religious freedom, against rights to equality and education. Within a model of cultural pluralism based on cultural enclaves, managing four different segments of the education system is obviously a huge challenge, also in terms of constructing a mandatory 'core curriculum' for primary and secondary education.

Topidi's analysis shows the high degree of impact of the right to education on inter-group societal relations. It explores specifically how legal and policy responses to religious diversity in education are balanced (or not) with the exercise of other fundamental rights within a multicultural society, showing also the implications that these clashes of rights produce. In practice, the basis of each conflict involving religion in the public sphere relates to the broader conflictual dilemma whether the preservation of a specific form of cultural identity should take priority over the enforcement of shared citizenship values or vice versa. This happens differently here than reported in Chapter 3 for India. Yet here again, while 'religion' is considered as a 'parallel' and competing form of legal system, with conflicts occurring at the legal, political and social levels, hybrid social normativities are making themselves heard through the intricate conflictual struggles between rights to freedom of religion and obligations not to discriminate. The challenge, as elsewhere, remains to find an appropriate balance. This article indicates, by reference to the work of Joseph Raz, the need for more explicit articulation of what 'diversity liberals', as Richard Shweder has called them, may contribute to this debate (see also Jamal, 2018).

Part III: Processing conflict

This Part contains three chapters that examine how conflicts are handled at different levels. In Chapter 8, Tanja Herklotz considers conflict management through the lens of religion and gender equality in the Indian personal law system, according to which individuals are normally governed by the family laws of their religious community. She unpacks the gender dimension of the hybrid social normativities of such personal laws in relation to interconnected arguments of identity, nationality, modernity and secularism.

Applying the concept of intersectionality, Herklotz juxtaposes two feminist approaches towards the engagement with personal laws. The first focuses on state-led reforms and prominent calls for a Uniform Civil Code, while the second considers community-led reforms which compromise on the final outcome but are more embedded in the 'real world'. The chapter first outlines the controversies around personal laws in India and then analyses the internal plurality of the manifold conflicting feminist positions in Indian scholarship regarding personal law debates. Herklotz innovatively combines her analysis with Amartya Sen's distinction of 'arrangement-focused' and 'realisation-focused' views of justice (Sen, 2009: 5–12), highlighting the search for the 'choices that are actually on offer' (Sen, 2009:

106), instead of merely speculating what a perfectly just society would look like. She argues that gender equality in India needs to be considered in the context of the larger discourse on socio-economic discrimination against women, occurring at different levels of law, policy and society. This contribution, neatly identifying the liberal dilemma of Western feminist models and including a contextualising critique of different ways to approach gender discrimination, thus presents a nuanced call for more diligent acknowledgement of hybrid social normativities, even from within the sector of feminism-focused civil society. It concludes that constant reassessment, dialogue and negotiations can bring an advancement of justice for women also in personal law systems.

In Chapter 9, Kalindi Kokal approaches conflict pointedly as a social phenomenon. She accounts for dispute processing methods as they happen, in accordance with a community's sense of order and religious and cultural background. In her analysis, dispute processing as an articulation of conflict is observed as a space of resistance and performance, but also as a test for the resilience for the norms that are being challenged and negotiated.

Through intriguing ethnographic data from two specific Indian communities, Kokal presents and analyses the processing of conflict as a kind of dramatic spectacle (*tamāshā*). She shows how this element of *tamāshā*, despite its various forms, at times almost comparable to street theatre, and often ritualised, remains important to understand the significance of disputes for conflict studies, particularly the choice of dispute processing mechanisms. The study emphasises the element of interconnectedness originating from the religious and cultural background as well as the social bonds within the communities observed. Fights between women over access to water, and claims by newly married women of being possessed by some spirit, are shown to be used as conflict management strategies. They depict *tamāshā* as an element of exercise of agency towards the protection of individual interests, always within a broader framework of circles of solidarity, and often wishing to challenge a certain behavioural protocol. At the same time, this drama opens up new spaces for continued co-existence and exercise of agency, ideally more on one's own terms. In a further case study where one *tamāshā* is employed to curtail another dramatic action, it transpires that the interlinkages of state and non-state legal orders may also become an aspect of such skilful navigation of hybrid social normativities.

Chapter 10 is another contribution from Italy in which Chiara Lapi focuses on conflict of legal orders in scenarios where difference and identity clash and where fear to lose one's identity induces rejection of difference. Law, in the light of recent immigration movements, has increasingly the task of addressing difference, particularly through claims that are not compliant with the official legal principles. This tells us that there is a problem but, somewhat typical for Italian processes of conflict management regarding non-European minorities, we do not learn to what extent such conflicts are actually being handled by recourse to state law.[20]

20 On discretionary spaces in the shadow of the law, see especially Sona (2016), not cited by Lapi, but referred to in Chapter 11. Further confirmation of 'the Italian way' to

The focal question for Lapi's analysis is how Sikh Indian migrants living in Italy handle questions of inheritance law, since it was observed in fieldwork that Sikh women, also in Italy, often renounce their inheritance in favour of males. This identifies conflicts over the (non)-application of the state law's inheritance rules among the large Indian communities in Italy, who seek to adhere to Indian values. The discussion centres on whether and how, in such contexts, state law can sustain cultural diversity. This assumes, in the first place, that state law is perceived as an appropriate tool to manage social conflicts, and is able to do so without neglecting the cultural dimension of such conflicts. In that sense, this Chapter continues the important discussion in Chapter 9 about managing competing legal orders on one's own terms within the non-state sphere.

In Italy, too, the extent to which such conflicts are allowed to become public, with state-centric rules being applied, would become important. Lapi illustrates the potential for conflicts between Indian family values and the Italian legal system by detailing the provisions of Indian Hindu succession law that also apply to Sikhs. This identifies, from a European and feminist perspective, that the individual woman's commitment to joint family principles may disadvantage her in terms of gender equality if she renounces her inheritance in favour of male relatives. Lapi argues that in such conflict scenarios the Italian legal system should take account of the 'cultural codes' of minorities, endorsing legal action 'on their terms'. This is supported by evidence that the Italian legal system has at its disposal the necessary tools to manage cultural diversity of this type among other minorities. Hence, Lapi argues that Italian law has a duty, and the capability, in terms of processing such disputes to pay attention to these new types of hybrid social normativities. She therefore proposes an accommodative solution to address any conflicts that may arise for Sikhs living in Italy.

Part IV: Resolving conflict

In this Part, four chapters seek to discuss how conflicts may be resolved. In Chapter 11, Pierluigi Consorti contributes a sceptical approach to state-based multiculturalism-focused methods regarding resolution of conflicts and argues that interculturalism is a preferable approach. Based on law's ontologically social structure, he accepts that law is also a social and cultural phenomenon and comprises not only rules of state law. Yet, with reference to Huntington's prophecy of clashes of civilisations, which sees social and legal pluralism as problematic and latently dangerous, Consorti speaks of 'cultural shock' if one assumes that certain positions are simply too far apart. He also identifies the potential for 'legal shock', however, in scenarios where the law discriminates and becomes bad through abuse of power. It appears (somewhat contrary to Chapter 3 and the evidence on India) that multiculturalism in Europe is perceived as related to a static assessment of plurality, accompanied by mutually exclusive assertions of claims. It then becomes

manage potential or actual conflict is provided in the amazingly informative picture collection titled *Hidden Islam* (Degiorgis, 2014).

a battle of power, which official state law is likely to win. However, as is also indicated in Chapter 13, if a self-righteous strategy is adopted by state law, despite liberal statements, multicultural approaches reflect lack of communication and generate conflict. Consorti thus distinguishes between state-centric multiculturalism, which he considers flawed as too static and failing in practice, and interculturalism, which he prefers, because of its potential for 'decentralisation' and flexible navigation, trying to understand the perspective of 'the other'.

However, this theoretical distinction uses questionable premises when one considers how this works in practice. The key issue is not whether one privileges state law or not, but rather whether and how participants in the communicative process account for plurality and difference. Consorti's critique of the ideology of multiculturalism seems based on presumptions that law, claiming to know best what is 'right' and 'just', may accept plurality as a social fact, but then proceeds to decide arbitrarily, effectively on its own terms, what is legal and what is not. One must ask whether this problem would not occur also in intercultural approaches, where the pluralised potential for insisting that any specific position is non-negotiable becomes even more precarious. To presume that interculturalism always means acceptance of 'decentralisation' seems too optimistic. In practice all conflicts, even the village *tamāshā* depicted in Chapter 9, involve some kind of unspoken connection to state laws, while discretionary spaces for self-righteous abuse of power for strategic advantage may be exploited by any law-related actor or agent. Success in conflict management depends on balanced curtailment of ill-will, which lurks everywhere. The key difference appears to be whether a particular position of power is simply asserted, allegedly dominant in state-centric multiculturalism, or whether one negotiates difference by selecting with more circumspection from 'the choices that are actually on offer' (Sen, 2009: 106) in any given context of conflict, as also identified by Herklotz in Chapter 8. According to Consorti, interculturalism is a more viable method in structuring political dialogue in cosmopolitan and/or multicultural democracies than multiculturalism, as it implies a relational approach and a dialogical method to reconcile differences of identity related to ethnic, cultural or religious conflicts within society. It avoids the precarious structural consequences of establishing separate spaces ('bird cages') for different communities in efforts to protect the right to diversity, while the general public space remains occupied by a majority or dominant minority (as in Israel, see Chapter 7) that demands cultural and ethical assimilation.

Despite Consorti's persuasive arguments for interculturalism, a form of multiculturalism that avoids illiberal liberalism could also recommend itself. While indeed presently in Europe rigidifying resistance to social change on the part of legal systems occurs when society changes through immigration of 'others', in both methods discussed here, and not just in interculturalism, better communicative procedures and transformative mediation could make the full picture visible and could help to reduce conflict, which like justice itself remains always work in progress.

In Chapter 12, Peter Kirchschlaeger's ethical perspective on human rights explores viable conditions for the study of conflicts, emphasising the multi-layered awareness building process that leads to the recognition of human vulnerability and a sense of solidarity of the conscious self with others and their claims to rights. In order to understand better how normative conflicts related to human rights may arise and how to address and maybe resolve them, this Chapter discusses, as a first step, the legitimacy of human rights as individual rights of all humans and explores parameters for the justification of the universality of human rights. This first step pays respect to the autonomy of all humans, embracing the right to know the reasons why his or her freedom is restricted.

Human rights find themselves at the centre of the discussion of normative conflicts in this Chapter because they represent a catalogue of norms with a strong claim of universality, implying a corresponding controversial potential, but enjoying at the same time, it is claimed here, more global acceptance than any other system of moral or legal norms. With the help of a wide range of select criteria, Kirchschlaeger explains how to identify the elements and spheres of human existence that need to be protected by human rights, both within and outside religious and worldview-based communities. In a second step, the legitimacy of the impact of the universality of human rights within religious and worldview-based communities is elaborated. This part also critically outlines the patterns of argumentation that these communities use when relating to human rights, taking the example of the right for women to vote in Switzerland, which was only fully secured in 1990.

For Kirchschlaeger, human rights serve as preconditions and a framework for religious and worldview-based diversity because they ensure that plurality can be realised and legitimised. In a third step, the patterns of argumentation of different religious and worldview-based communities, or respectively some groups within these communities, against human rights, are assessed from an ethical perspective. In a fourth step, the model of 'adaptation' is examined as a possible way forward in understanding the correlation between religious and worldview-based communities and human rights dialogically and as a tool to address normative conflicts in a way which could contribute to resolving such conflicts. Adaptation embodies an approach proposed to preserve the identity of human rights while translating them into the language of one's own religion and avoiding normative conflict because of the bridge-building effects of this method. Kirchschlaeger ultimately conceptualises this specific approach as a means to counter intolerance encouraged by competitive pluralism and to promote a culture of human rights instead of a globalised culture.

What may be questioned, though, is how this adaptation process is supposed to work in practice. Who is expected to adapt to whom, and on whose terms are the joint outcomes to be constructed? Kirchschlaeger suggests that human rights as inalienable components would need to be granted superior standing, given that they are more widely shared than any other normative structures. Yet what if this was challenged or abused? Here, too, enormous goodwill to engage in meaningful constructive and altruistic discourse rather than to insist on any specific stance or expectation(s) would appear to be a precondition for successful processes of adaptation. Kirchschlaeger appears to indicate much room for overlapping consensus regarding key-concepts, main principles and core values of one's own religion and worldview overlapping with human rights. In a way, then, this Chapter, too, argues that hopefully various kinds of hybrid social normativities can be creatively engaged in securing better human rights protection, given that the culture of human rights is in itself so diverse and plural, and not uniform.

Gopika Solanki in Chapter 13 proposes a legal pluralist reading of normative conflict and scrutinises the hierarchy of laws, as well as their enforcement, focusing on conflicts over gender equality in India with specific reference to Muslim divorce law and the infamous triple *talaq*. She asks which dynamics shape the interactions between multiple and often contradictory sources of law and authority. To answer this question, she uses her rich ethnographic data to throw light on the map of interchanges between various legal authorities in the governance of Muslim marriage and divorce law in India. Solanki first explains the Indian model of legal pluralism, portraying power-sharing arrangements between state and religio-cultural communities that her earlier work has called the 'shared adjudication model', a skilful management strategy in a situation of legal plurality. However, one could question, raising the same issue of relative authority as was identified in Chapter 12, whether it is actually the state that allows this sharing, or whether the state has had to adapt to the strongly present hybrid social normativities.

Based on detailed fieldwork, Solanki critiques assertions by Okin (1999) and others that inherently patriarchal religious and customary laws not only violate international law principles, but also conflict with constitutional provisions that guarantee equality and freedom in law. Moreover, do formal state laws such as India's constitutional provisions really guarantee such rights, in the form of ideal laws? Or do they rather promise guarantees that would still need to be turned into lived reality, as identified by Sen (2009: 9), through 'focusing on actual realizations in the societies involved'? Solanki's experience relates to this arduous route, as she highlights how the governance of Muslim family law takes place in a socio-legal sphere with multiple sources of authority and competing narratives, some of them resembling the *tamāshā* identified in Chapter 9, about law, Islam, gender and rights.

To capture these interactions between various laws and centres of authority, Solanki puts forward the notion of communication.[21] Various normative legal orders may conflict, but can also result in cooperation and harmonisation, containing promises of a potential for securing and advancing rights. Solanki sees communication also as a public arena, akin to a Habermasian space, that handles incommensurabilities as well as identification, similarities and overlap between different actors. A cacophony of competing interests, ideologies and agendas allows a range of possible outcomes, illustrated through two case studies of Muslim women who suffered a triple *talaq* but resisted this. Such disputes, negotiated at multiple levels among extended families, feminist organisations, local NGOs, state courts, the police and different Muslim scholars (*qazis*) brings to light the politics, but also the transformative potential, of communication in affecting localised change.

21 She borrows this from Luhmann's social theorising, which implies that unless thought is communicated, we cannot know what 'the other' thinks (Nobles and Schiff, 2013: 28), if indeed we can ever know.

Observing, rightly, that many scholars and activists have failed to highlight such evidently plural positive countertrends, Solanki states that the social costs of such asymmetric information and misinformation around triple *talaq* are evident. In plainer language, this might be called misusing 'alternative truths'. This Chapter demonstrates how various tensions within hybrid social normativities, between religious law, customs, moral notions of justice and state law are constantly rethought, renegotiated and reformulated. Relationships are at times confrontational, with severe moral disagreements. At other moments they become cooperative, searching for new components that may be built into the complex grammar of communicative interaction. Concluding that such communication between competing sources of authority, namely laws, social norms, values and specific actions and processes, captures this interaction in a political as well as legal sense, Solanki confirms the vast scope for acknowledging hybrid social normativities.

Finally, in Chapter 14 Wolfgang Wieshaider briefly deals with the disposal of objects classified as belonging to cultural heritage in Austria, when conflicts between the right to ownership and the right to religious freedom occurs for some of those objects that serve religious purposes. The discussion explores the mode of simultaneous decision-making by two sets of actors, the state and religious authorities, aiming at a common result in such contexts, laid out in Austrian law. The implications of this procedure suggest a kind of negotiation that emerges as a flexible prototype to consider and accommodate changes within a given religious society.

Wieshaider further provides a comparative analysis on the same question with evidence from the Czech Republic, Slovakia, Hungary, Switzerland as well as Italy and Germany. The findings of such comparison confirm the Austrian model as a procedure of creative development for the sake of the preservation of common living heritage that may be useful for broader purposes. While this chapter identifies skilful navigation of the balance between private and public interest, which is a useful addition, it seems to indicate, without saying it, that Austrian law also employs the notion of 'eminent domain', through which the state claims property rights over entities that others may lay claims to, too. Wieshaider does not discuss, however, whether all this acclaimed and successful navigation might break down in scenarios where religious 'others' are involved. It is probably relatively easy to harmonise the competing interests of the Austrian state and various churches. But what would happen to competing claims over Muslim (or Jewish) objects of cultural heritage, especially when such conflicts raise questions over how soon an object may become 'heritage'. This chapter thus raises more questions than it addresses and answers, especially in light of the Italian evidence in Chapters 10 and 11, but also in view of how Italy handles tensions of religious and cultural fragmentation and diversification when faced with 'ethnic implants' and their – at least initially – informal manifestations (Degiorgis, 2014).

Conclusions

Everywhere in multicultural or intercultural Europe, current significant challenges relate to how strongly, in connection with hybrid social normativities, the influence of various values and normativities arising from corners 2 and 1 of the kite of law may be officially accepted in the secular, human rights-focused spaces of a purportedly liberal Global North. Similar conflicts, in different combinations and contexts, arise everywhere on the globe. These are battles over various aspects of justice which often concern the extent of authority and the role of social actors as legal agents. However, human as law-related actors appear throughout the conceptual space of the internally plural kite of law. By showing the conceptual and argumentative confusions about whether such activism regarding justice is 'social', 'cultural', 'legal', or more a matter of traditional morality or of modern understandings of 'human rights', the present volume hopes to have made a useful advance in understanding the complexities inherent in the negotiations of law and its multiple normative spaces.

One central element of these reflections has been emphasis on the need for constant discourse and communication, reinforced by plurality-conscious realisation that despite conflict, people will need to live together not only right now, but also tomorrow and hopefully in the longer term. Hence, as especially the contributions in Parts III and IV indicate, various intense and at times highly dramatic (and thus potentially not only entertaining but also healing and calming) negotiations, navigations and balancing acts are needed, named and framed in remarkably different ways.

There is still considerable grudging reluctance among lawyers, in particular, to accept that the field of law is inevitably internally plural, which means that conflict over the need for pluralist or intercultural navigation, conceptually connected to a Rawlsian 'overlapping consensus', is inevitable and demands, as all contributions to this volume endorse, intensive interaction. The latently conflictual internal connectedness of law as a hybrid field can be imagined and illustrated in various ways, of course. The image used here, of a kite of law flying in the air, suggests that this subtle structure is only able to keep flying and to move safely as long as all the various interconnected – and indeed overlapping – components of that structure are kept engaged in cooperative, potentially stressful, but remarkably often inaudible actions of communication. Law as a vast hybrid field of law-related and hence also social and moral normativities will always be encountering conflict, but all contributions to this book seem to agree that where there is a will to carry on engaging in discourses over justice and rights, there may be a way forward.

Compared to Topidi and Fielder (2016), this volume provides a more accurate snapshot, particularly regarding the role of social actors, in managing these various competing pluralities. This extended introduction has sought to fine-tune perceptions and understanding of the limited role of positivist law by demonstrating how elastic and fluid, to the point of sometimes being irrelevant and invisible, state law may become when certain conflicts occur. Similarly, human rights law and international law, themselves hugely hybrid fields, cannot claim to be the sole or even dominant agent and motor in seeking to provide and protect basic human rights and dignity. They always need the other elements of the kite.

In the present study, the use of hybrid social normativities as a key concept to theorise this interactive pattern and its practical consequences has been asserted and is richly illustrated in the following chapters. The deliberate plurality and multiple forms of agency with which various kinds of social actors navigate between their multiple roles is brought out in these contributions. Readers will encounter legal actors not only as legal personnel, but also as individuals, members of society and cultural and religious entities, as social workers, members of 'civil society', or explicitly as human rights protectors. In any specific role or combination, such legal or law-related actors are seen to push specific 'agendas', taking advantage of the elasticity and fluidity of 'the law'. At times, this generates conflict, at other times the same process may result in harmony and some form of 'adaptation', as Chapter 12 suggests. Everywhere, one sees complex kite journeys that speak loudly, yet largely inaudibly, of various processes of communication. If this introduction has opened the readers' eyes to this highly complex picture, the book as a whole will have succeeded in its ambition to advance global discussions about how to manage difference and legal plurality in sustainable ways.

References

Ahmed, Farrah (2016) 'Remedying Personal Law Systems', *International Journal of Law, Policy and the Family*, 30(3): 248–273.

Ahmed, Shahab (2016) *What is Islam? The Importance of Being Islamic*. Princeton: Princeton University Press.

Ali, Shaheen Sardar (2016) *Modern Challenges to Islamic Law*. Cambridge: Cambridge University Press.

Allott, Antony (1980) *The Limits of Law*. London: Butterworths.

Ballard, Roger (ed.) (1994) *Desh Pardesh: The South Asian Presence in Britain*. London: Hurst & Company.

Baxi, Upendra (2002) *The Future of Human Rights*. New Delhi: Oxford University Press.

Baxi, Upendra (2008) *The Future of Human Rights*. Third edition. New Delhi: Oxford University Press.

Benkin, Richard L. (ed.) (2017) *What is Moderate Islam*?Lanham: Lexington Books.

Borradori, Giovanna (2003) *Philosophy in a Time of Terror: Dialogues with Jürgen Habermas and Jacques Derrida*. Chicago and London: University of Chicago Press.

Brown, Kevin J. (2017) 'The Hyper-regulation of Public Space: The Use and Abuse of Public Spaces Protection Orders in England and Wales', *Legal Studies*, 37(3): 543–568.

Chiba, Masaji (ed.) (1986) *Asian Indigenous Law in Interaction with Received Law*. London and New York: KPI.

Chiba, Masaji (ed.) (1989) *Legal Pluralism: Towards a General Theory through Japanese Legal Culture*. Tokyo: Tokai University Press.

Degiorgis, Nicoló (2014) *Hidden Islam: Islamic Makeshift Places of Worship in North East Italy, 2009–2013*. Bolzano: Rorhof.

Dhagamwar, Vasudha (1989) *Towards the Uniform Civil Code*. Bombay: N.M. Tripathi.

Farran, Sue, Esin Örücü and Seán Patrick Donlan (eds) (2014) *A Study of Mixed Legal Systems: Endangered, Entrenched or Blended*. Ashgate: Farnham.

Fikentscher, Wolfgang (2016) *Law and Anthropology*. Second edition. München: C.H. Beck.

Fitzpatrick, Peter (2001) *Modernism and the Grounds of Law*. Cambridge: Cambridge University Press.

Gearty, Conor (2008) 'Human Rights'. In Peter Cane and Joanne Conaghan (eds), *The New Oxford Companion to Law* (pp. 553–554). Oxford: Oxford University Press.

Goodale, Mark (2007) 'Introduction: Locating Rights, Envisioning Law Between the Global and the Local'. In M. Goodale and Sally Merry Engle (eds), *The Practice of Law: Tracking Law Between the Global and the Local* (pp. 1–38). Cambridge: Cambridge University Press.

Grillo, Ralph (2015) *Muslim Families, Politics and the Law: A Legal Industry in Multicultural Britain*. Farnham: Ashgate Publishing.

Habermas, J. (2008) *Between Naturalism and Religion*. Cambridge: Polity Press.

Habermas, J. (2010) *An Awareness of What is Missing: Faith and Reason in a Post-Secular Age*. Cambridge: Polity Press.

Hayden, Robert M. (1999) *Disputes and Arguments amongst Nomads*. New Delhi: Oxford University Press.

Husa, Jaakko (2015) *A New Introduction to Comparative Law*. Oxford and Portland: Hart Publishing.

Jamal, Arif (2018) *Islam, Law and the Modern State*. London: Routledge (forthcoming).

Khan, Sonia Z. (2017) *The Politics and Law of Democratic Transition: Caretaker Government in Bangladesh*. London: Routledge.

Kumar, Ashutosh (2017) 'Electoral Politics in Indian Punjab: A New Phase?', *South Asia Research*, 37(1): 37–57.

Maeso, Silvia Rodríguez and Marta Araújo (2017) 'The Semantics of (Anti) Racism in the Governance of Non-Europeanness: An Introduction', *Patterns of Prejudice*, 51(1): 1–8.

Mellbourn, Anders and Peter Wallensteen (eds) (2008) *Third Parties and Conflict Prevention*. Brussels: Madariaga European Foundation.

Menski, Werner (2006) *Comparative Law in a Global Context: The Legal Systems of Asia and Africa*. Second edition. Cambridge: Cambridge University Press.

Menski, Werner (2012a) 'Jürgen Habermas: Post-Conflict Reconstruction, Non-hegemonic Modernity, Discourse about Spaces and the Role of Religion'. In Pradip Basu (ed.), *Modern Social Thinkers* (pp. 180–198). Kolkata: Setu Prakashani.

Menski, Werner (2012b) 'Plural Worlds of Law and the Search for Living Law'. In Werner Gephart (ed.) *Rechtsanalyse als Kulturforschung* (pp. 71–88). Frankfurt am Main: Vittorio Klostermann.

Menski, Werner (2013) 'Law as a Kite: Managing Legal Pluralism in the Context of Islamic Finance'. In Valentino Cattelan(ed.), *Islamic Finance in Europe: Towards a Plural Financial System* (pp. 15–31). Cheltenham: Edward Elgar.

Menski, Werner (2014a) 'Legal Simulation: Law as a Navigation Tool for Decision-making'. In *Report of Japan Coast Guard Academy*, 59(2.1): 1–22. Available at: http://harp.lib.hiroshima-u.ac.jp/jcga/metadata/12172?l=en.

Menski, Werner (2014b) 'The Liquidity of Law as a Challenge to Global Theorising'. *Jura Gentium*, Vol. XI: *Pluralismo Giuridico* (Annuale 2014): 19–42. [http://www.juragentium.org].

Menski, Werner (2014c) 'Remembering and Applying Legal Pluralism: Law as Kite Flying'. In Séan Patrick Donlan and Lukas Heckendorn Urscheler (eds), *Concepts of Law: Comparative, Jurisprudential, and Social Science Perspectives* (pp. 91–108). Farnham: Ashgate.

Menski, Werner (2015) 'Bangladesh in 2015: Challenges of the Iccher Ghuri for Learning to Live Together', *Journal of Law and Politics* (University of Asia-Pacific, Dacca), 1(1): 9–32.

Menski, Werner (2016a) 'Justice, Epistemic Violence in South Asian Studies and the Nebulous Entity of Caste', *South Asia Research*, 36(3): 299–321.

Menski, Werner (2016b) 'Still Asking for the Moon? Opening Windows of Opportunity for Better Justice in India', *Verfassung und Recht in Übersee*, Special Issue 49(2): 125–147.

Moore, Sally Falk (1978) *Law as Process: An Anthropological Approach*. London: Routledge & Kegan Paul.

Nobles, Richard and David Schiff (eds) (2013) *Observing Law through Systems Theory*. Oxford and Portland: Hart Publishing.

Okin, Susan M. (1999) 'Is Multiculturalism Bad for Women?'. In J. Cohen, M. Howard and M.C. Nussbaum (eds), *Is Multiculturalism Bad for Women?* (pp. 9–24). Princeton: Princeton University Press.

Philip, Jessy K. (2017) '"Though He is a Landlord, that Sarpanch is My Servant!" Caste and Democracy in a Village in South India', *Contemporary South Asia*, 25(3): 270–284.

Phillips, A. (2007) *Multiculturalism without Culture*. Princeton: Princeton University Press.

Rai, Praveen (2017) 'Women's Participation in Electoral Politics in India', *South Asia Research*, 37(1): 58–77.

Rankin, Aidan and Atul K. Shah (2008) *Social Cohesion: A Jain Perspective*. Colchester: Diverse Ethics Ltd.

Rawls, John (1971) *A Theory of Justice*. Cambridge, MA: Harvard University Press.

Rhaman, Mofizur (2016) 'Climate Justice Framing in Bangladeshi Newspapers, 2007–2011', *South Asia Research*, 36(2): 186–205.

Roberts, Simon (1979) *Order and Dispute: An Introduction to Legal Anthropology*. Harmondsworth: Penguin Books.

Rouland, Norbert (1994) *Legal Anthropology*. London: The Athlone Press.

Sen, Amartya (2006) *The Argumentative Indian*. London: Penguin.

Sen, Amartya (2009) *The Idea of Justice*. London: Penguin.

Shachar, Ayelet (2005) *Multicultural Jurisdictions: Cultural Differences and Women's Rights*. Cambridge: Cambridge University Press.

Sona, Federica (2016) 'Defending the Family Treasure Chest: Navigating Muslim Families and Secured Positivistic Islands of European Legal Systems'. In Prakash Shah, Marie-Claire Foblets and Mathias Rohe (eds), *Family, Religion and Law: Cultural Encounters in Europe* (pp. 115–142). London: Routledge.

Tamanaha, Brian Z. (2008) 'Understanding Legal Pluralism: Past to Present, Local to Global', *Sydney Law Review*, 30(3): 375–411.

Tamanaha, Brian Z. (2009) 'Law'. In Stanley N. Katz (ed.), *The Oxford International Encyclopedia of Legal History*, Vol. 4 (pp. 17–23). New York: Oxford University Press.

Topidi, Kyriaki and Lauren Fielder (eds) (2016) *Religion as Empowerment: Global Legal Perspectives*. Abingdon and New York: Routledge.

Twining, William (ed.) (2009) *Human Rights, Southern Voices*. Cambridge: Cambridge University Press.

Ullah, Mohammad Sahid (2017) 'Empowerment, Asymmetrical Power Relations and Impacts of Information Technology in Rural Bangladesh', *South Asia Research*, 37(3): 315–334.

von Benda-Beckmann, Franz, Keebet von Benda-Beckmann and Anne Griffiths (eds) (2009) *Spatializing Law: An Anthropological Geography of Law in Society*. Farnham: Ashgate.

Wacquant, Loïc (2014) 'Marginality, Ethnicity and Penality in the Neo-Liberal City: An Analytic Cartography', *Ethnic and Racial Studies*, 37(10): 1687–1711.

Part I

Preventing conflict

2 Beyond the pedagogical beauty of dichotomy

Comparative law methodology in liquid times

Tommaso Amico di Meane[1]

Re-thinking (over and over again) comparative law

The following reflections grapple with the theme of methodology in the global age, which has been gaining momentum together with comparative law itself.[2] 'Over the last few decades', in fact, 'the world has witnessed the rapid spread of constitutionalism [and Comparative law] has developed into one of the most fashionable subjects' (Hirschl 2014: 2). The underlying dynamic appears somewhat clear: Law as discipline has become 'more cosmopolitan in response to the process loosely labelled as globalisation'. Accordingly, comparative law as a subdiscipline has been moving 'from a relatively marginal role to a much more central role' (Twining 2007: 88), shifting from being considered as the 'Cindarella' to the 'Queen' of legal sciences (Frankenberg 2016: 3–4, slightly ironically).

Academia is by no means unanimous in celebrating this 'renaissance' of comparative law (Riles 2005: 149 et seq.),[3] although the discipline has arguably gained relevance at least in quantitative terms. Before such responsibility, prominent academics gathered together in order to 'take up the challenge' posed by this fast evolving scenario (Bussani, Mattei 2012: 3). They have been dealing with an intriguing but also quite complex mission, considering the shifting theoretical scenario where their academic speculations have to be grounded. Indeed 'almost everything' that was more or less consolidated in the area of comparative law has been systematically criticized over the last decades, including the possibility of comparison itself (Van Hoecke 2015: 1). A proper *re-thinking period* started in the 1980s (seminal 'Re-thinking Comparative Law', Frankenberg 1985) and does

1 Università degli Studi della Campania Luigi Vanvitielli, and LUISS Guido Carli Università di Roma.

2 Adams, Heirbaut (eds) 2014; Amirante 2016; Bussani, Mattei (eds) 2012; Frankenberg 2016; Hage 2014; Jackson 2012; Muir Watt 2006; Kennedy Duncan 2006; Menski 2006; Ponthoreau 2017; Husa 2015; Samuel 2004, 2014; Valcke 2012; Van Hoecke 2015; Van Hoecke (ed.) 2013; Van Hoecke (ed.) 2011; Van Hoecke (ed.) 2004; Vimborsati 2008.

3 'As many comparative lawyers have commented in recent years, at this very moment of intense globalization, comparative law ironically is a field in decline, if not outright crisis' (Riles 2015: 149).

not seem to have stopped, after having covered every single aspect of comparative law (again Frankenberg 2016).[4]

Despite such a radical re-thinking, I would argue that comparative law appears still deeply anchored to a *dichotomous mindset* that tends to reduce any scenario into a contrast between two options: irreducible and often conflicting alternatives. *Sovereigns* or *universalists; similarity* or *diversity; Legal culture* or *Legal tradition*. Not to mention the irreproachable passion that comparative lawyers seem to nourish for the classic 'duels' between its charismatic scholars.[5] I then propose to consider the issue of comparative law methodology as a suitable example of this tendency, notably in the way it has been traditionally proposed as a choice between *functionalist* or *contextualist* methods. Such a dichotomous approach is arguably fascinating and effective from a pedagogical viewpoint. Nevertheless, a collateral effect may include a misperception about the described scenarios, in case they do not correspond to a perfectly 'black' or 'white' picture, but rather to a largely 'grey' one.

Hence, I would suggest considering the latter as the 'colour' of the methodological proposals of comparative law, which are clearly neither functionalist nor contextualist. Indeed they represent a third 'hybrid' option that could be defined as 'Late modern' (or 'Liquid modern'), whose main feature would be its intrinsic *flexibility*. It is precisely on this ground that the parallelism with Zygmunt Bauman arises. The Polish intellectual identifies the essence of *modernity* in a 'compulsive research' to build up geometry and order (Bauman 2011, VIII) flowing into a trend to 'obsessively order chaos reality' into taxonomies (Bauman 2015: 139). Such an attitude generates *conflict*, since there are 'redundant' identities (ideas or people) that inevitably do not fit the image prescribed by modernity itself (Bauman 2015: 139). However, 'Solid modernity' – continues Bauman – has been replaced by current 'Liquid modernity' that changed the consistency of our desires, fears, and passions resulting in a general *sense of uncertainty*. Within this 'liquid' context, 'everything is possible, but nothing can be done with certainty' (Bauman 2011: XIII). Consequently, the analytical structures that are 'solid' – and as such aim to merely produce 'control' – result inadequate to grasp current reality (Bauman 2011: VIII).

After all, a consolidated Western tradition that have contrasted the hypocrisy of rationalistic *perfection*, ultimately celebrating *imperfection, does exist*. From Albert Einstein and his observation of nonlinear phenomena as 'Gravitational waves', to Werner Karl Heisenberg 'Uncertainty principle' and Edward Lorenz's 'Chaos theory'. Arts and literature have somehow followed similar paths, just reading for example *Infinite Jest* by David Foster Wallace or contemplating *Number 5* by Jackson Pollock. As well the discipline of Law seems to have progressively encompassing this intellectual challenge, aiming to develop *entropic* forces; that is

4 Furthermore (among others) Baxi 2003, 2013; Choudhry 2006; Yu 2013; Kennedy David 1997; Riles 2007.

5 Such as the saga of Alan Watson *vs* Pierre Legrand on legal transplants (see Frankenberg 2010 on this point).

analytical and methodological tools able to measure the degree of disorder. The chaos 'can be studied' (Ianni 2016: 152), although the Western traditional categories – from Social Sciences (Balagangadhara 2012) to Economics and beyond (Pettini, Ventura 2014) – seem to offer 'lenses' that are too limited in order to grasp today's kaleidoscopic dynamics.

Comparative law appears particularly attuned with these reflections, considering indeed the *sense of uncertainty* (Zumbansen 2012: 75) caused by the *inadequacy* of its methodological equipment (Amirante 2015: 20; Menski 2006; Örücü 2003: 489; Palmer 2004: 1; Samuel 2004: 35) together with the mentioned over-simplification attitude.[6] Within this context, there are two main re-thinking exercises that comparative lawyers are currently deepening in order to globalize their discipline: (a) *geographical* and (b) *thematic*.

(a) The first stems from the growing awareness that the 'majority of Western academia' has relegated legal traditions of non-Western countries (mostly Asia and Africa) to a marginal role, seen at best as transplants of Western legal traditions (Menski 2007: 192). Scholars have been thus making efforts in order to refocus the *geographical* borders of comparative law by elaborating 'world legal atlases' (Ferrari 2010; Siems 2014). This is a much needed re-thinking if we consider that '90% of comparative work in English language covers the same ten (Western) countries' (Dixon, Ginsburg cit. in Hirschl 2014: 213), albeit Western legal countries barely represent 25% of the planet.[7] In wider terms, globalization has definitively overcome the era of cultural imperialism, according to which there is only *one* truth (Bauman 2015: 143). Nuanced in the sphere of law, this corresponds to moving away from the perspective that a sort of 'McDonald's Law' would have inexorably expanded from West to the *rest* (Bussani 2012).[8]

(b) Giving back dignity to non-Western legal traditions undoubtedly represents an meaningful achievement. However, it could not be sufficient if it did not come with a *thematic* (that is analytical and methodological) re-thinking process. In fact there is a pitfall in reasoning 'too much in geographical terms', considering that 'talk of maps and levels of law is a spatial metaphor that it is not always appropriate' (Twining 2007: 73).[9] 'Going to places and gazing at a strange world' – in

6 Such a precariousness, according to some literature, stems from the lack of 'core work that clarifies the essence of the term "comparative" as a project and a method', which therefore leads to a 'fuzzy and rather incoherent epistemological and methodological matrix' (Hirschl 2014: 5). A methodological deepening appears hence to be 'urgent and necessary' (Amirante 2015: 20) as much as 'indisputable and crucial' to the greatest extent (Palmer 2004: 1).

7 Choudhry 2008: 8. In the view of some academics this 'bizarre' dyspraxia would thus require a 'reintegration' that includes 'Islamic, Hindu, African, Indian, Chinese law' – just to make few examples – as part of the 'mainstream rather than as exotic out-posts in our discipline' (Twining 2007: 84· On similar lines Amirante 2015; Baxi 2003 and 2013; Bussani 2012; Frankenberg 2016; Hirschl 2014; Menski 2006; Twining 2007).

8 Landmark pages by Menski 2006: 3–81; and Cassese 2009.

9 A bit less indulgently, other academics have labelled the 'world legal atlases' as mere exercises of a 'comparative bricolage', that would just epitomize 'the futility rather than the utility of reaching out and comparing the laws of all countries at all times

other words – 'does not automatically open up new horizons. More often than not, even exotic trips turn out to be vain attempts to escape from everyday life and to re-invent the travellers' world-view' (Frankenberg 1985: 412).

In other words, comparative lawyers today still resemble 'tourists' who are not yet able to finalise the information gathered during their 'journeys', due to the lack of proper 'equipment': that is a guiding methodology (Van Hoecke 2015: 8). 'What if the central problem of Comparative law', asked Annelise Riles, 'shifted from how to describe foreign legal systems to how to elucidate interest, commitment and respond [creating empathy] to things foreign and unfamiliar?'. What is very clear is that these speculations can be framed within the broader reflection of the *legal education* in global times (see for example Husa 2009).

This methodological 'inadequacy' has thus various nuances and I would propose to consider two of them: (a) *equipment* constraints; (b) *narration* constraints. Addressing these issues will turn out in a set of conclusions.

(a) Firstly, it will be shown that at the origins of 'equipment constraints' there is essentially a monistic understanding of the concept of 'law', combined with the already mentioned taxonomic attitude towards reality. Both aspects surface as typically Western and originally they prevented us from understanding foreign non-Western legal cultures; however, today they do not allow us to understand even 'ourselves' as part of this liquid society.

(b) The mentioned taxonomic and dichotomous approach will then clearly spring from the analysis of 'narration constrains', after having considered how this dichotomous matrix emerged and produced an over-simplified *black or white* methodological landscape (*in books*), leaving in the shade a more complex but realistic methodological landscape (*in action*) made by *shades of grey*. Nevertheless, it is notably in this chromatic complexity and liquidity – I finally argue – that precious methodological answers for global times can be encountered.

Methodological limits

Equipment constraints

The word 'method' derives from ancient Greek and is the combination of the words *metà* and *odòs*: it can be roughly translated as 'a way to go along the road' (Glanert 2013). By using a method, a researcher interprets the *object* and the *aim* of comparison (Lasser 2003: 235), and defines himself as *subject* (Basedow 2014: 837). Each method thus refers to a specific manner for systematically organizing reality (Husa 2006: 109), a distinct way to collect and process information

[...] getting lost in its maze of indeterminacy and global reach' (Frankenberg 2016: 16). On the same path, yet others recognize a 'still-prevalent thread of taxonomic scholarship', that would result in 'multi-tome legal genealogies that resemble 19th-century expositions of newly discovered flora and fauna, some of which focus on pseudo-exotic settings' (Hirschl 2014: 196).

(Frankenberg 2016: 8) and – first of all – a way to select available material through a specific cognitive process (Örücü 2007: 48).

In this light, the methodological rumination offers an opportunity for comparatists to define their *identities* as academics. This appears to be even more crucial in a period where comparative global journeys shift towards faraway and 'exotic' legal systems, but – paradoxically – this is exactly the field where methodology is even more inadequate (Amirante 2015: 15). Nonetheless, what are the characteristics of equipment constrains?

Much of the 'canonical contemporary scholarship', observes Ran Hirschl, replicates the 'formalistic encyclopaedic', 'intellectual cul-de-sac' and largely 'descriptive' approach to comparative legal studies carried out 'a century ago' (Hirschl 2014: 195). 'Little has changed' with respect to the basic epistemology and methodology of comparative law (Hirschl 2014: 195). In this respect, William Twining has described comparative law as a 'long-running and unsatisfactory debate about how major systems, tradition, or families of law should be classified' (Twining 2007: 78). On similar lines, Upendra Baxi pinpointed the tendency of the 'predominant tradition' of comparative law to mainly focus on 'highlighting binary contrasts' *ad nauseam* (Baxi 2003: 49).

Such a taxonomic approach, argues Werner Menski, is typical of the Western approach to legal studies. However, it might be conversely 'meaningless' when applied to non-Western contexts (Menski 2007: 196), that often go beyond *rigidity* and *dichotomies*, offering inherently *elasticity* and *syncretism* (Chiba 1989; Kavanagh 2016). The result is that radically different legal traditions are forced inside 'our' dichotomies (for example the *common law* and *civil law* one), enhancing a brutal simplification that is a 'hegemonic' organization of reality (Frankenberg 1985: 422)[10] in line with the culturally specific Western practice of claiming for its categories 'universality' (Riles 2015: 161).

In other words, it seems that the 'hardware' of comparative law is mainly Western-made, corresponding to a *way of plotting* cultures through familiar labels and, more generally, in a specific way of structuring their own experience towards alterity.[11] Besides this taxonomic attitude, another component of this 'hardware' seems to be represented by a traditional Western understanding of the *concept of law*. Notably a rationalistic approach to law as a typical product of Western modernity (Van Hoecke, Warrington 1998: 504), which does not stand out so firmly in other parts of the globe (Glenn 2010: 2). Indeed 'Western legal culture' is

10 Western matrix, wrote Frankenberg more recently, '[is] anything but neutral' [representing] the non-Western law and traditions as subaltern to the West – as same, similar or derived from or with differences in detail compared to Common or Civil law' (Frankenberg 2016: 76). This would explain, further speculates Esin Örücü, why the interest towards different regions – with the sole exception of the regions (forcibly) seen as an extension of the two families – is usually addressed by regional scholars or anthropologists and not by comparative law scholars (Örücü 2007: 60).

11 These reflections should give credits also to some interesting considerations made by S.N. Balagangadhara, although he does not specifically refer to the field of comparative law (2012).

defined by the predominance of rationalism seen as 'the belief in the infinite possibilities available to the human spirit to know, structure and master reality in an objective manner' (Van Hoecke, Warrington 1998: 503; De Vergottini 2015). Within this framework, 'law' is considered – especially for Europeans – as a *form of equilibrium* to look up and more precisely: 'a form of logic, a geometry, a coherent assembly where everything can be reduced to principles, to concepts, to categories' (Van Hoecke, Warrington 1998: 504–505; see also Ponthoreau 2017: 55 et seq.).

Such an organized and *rational* force might feel itself deeply challenged by a metaphysical one that appears as intrinsically *irrational.* Western scholars 'favour clarity' as an 'almost perfect form of transparency and formal regularity', hence they might find particularly laborious to analyse and understand the solutions offered by non-Western countries that are often seen as 'dystrophic universes' (Harding 2008, 19). Indeed for non-Western cultures, African and Asian *in primis*, 'law' as a set of rules 'plays a less important role' in comparison with religious, social and cultural paradigms (Van Hoecke, Warrington 1998: 504). In such cultures the transmission of knowledge traditionally takes place orally (Menski 2006: 9) and the context is more important than written laws (Van Hoecke 2015: 2). At a deeper level, as illustrated by Massimo Fagioli, *written* tradition has been considered as a fundamental characteristic of Western and-ultimately human *identity*, identified as 'rational' and denying what is 'irrational' (Fagioli 1980/2013: 9 et seq.).

Through this culturally distorted lens, non-Western legal cultures are therefore often erroneously labelled as 'less sophisticated' (Menski 2006: 6) simply because they foster *intangible* forms of normativity which are far from a positivistic concept of law (Donlan, Heckendorn Urscheler 2014, 3). Such an approach can be read as a form of 'conceptual colonialism' that does not understand the main fact that law and legal regimes are not intrinsically superior to other normative orders, and that 'a place without law simply manages its norms differently' (Donlan, Heckendorn Ursheler 2014: 3).

At the roots of such misperception, there is a sort of evolutionistic image of modern law associated to a 'saga of the idea of progress' and whose 'copyright' is clearly Western (Baxi 2003: 50). This reflection has been encompassed by academic literature in terms of *Legal orientalism*, describing 'some prevailing cultural prejudices that inform the interpretation of comparative scholarship' on non-Western law, which is the Western interpretation of legal otherness (Ruskola 2002: 185; see also Ruskola 2013).[12] From this standpoint, concepts as the 'bill of rights', the 'doctrine of separation of powers', rather than 'democracy' itself have been offered 'as moral invention of Euro-American political and legal theory without any lineage elsewhere' (Baxi 2003: 50).[13] The corollary of this approach is that there is 'nothing worthy to learn' from the other (non-Western cultures), incidentally the

12 The reference is clearly Edward Said 'Orientalism' (1978/2003).
13 See Amico di Meane (2015).

latter has been considered irrelevant within the theoretical constructions (see Habermas, Rawls or Dworkin) of the 20th century (Baxi 2003: 50, 53).

Legal orientalism and *concept of law* are therefore two sides of the same coin (two components of the mentioned 'hardware') that have impoverished the academic debate on comparative law and its methodology. By having a methodology 'substantially incapable of understanding cultures that are structurally pluralistic' (Amirante 2015: 15),[14] Western comparative lawyers are reasonably wondering if their research is not 'perhaps meaningless' when 'the object of comparison does not exist in the national positive law' (Ponthoreau 2016: 65), thus deciding to avoid 'the comparison between apples and pears' (Donlan and Heckendorn Ursheler 2014: 8). After all, giving equal dignity to non-Western systems by taking into account an 'understanding of the law within a global perspective' represents an activity that 'greatly complicates the tasks of Comparative law' (Twining 2007: 71).

It seems mandatory to put in place a quite substantial change of the method and a re-imagining of 'analytical and methodological categories of Western' thought (Vimborsati 2008: 7). Such re-thinking is driven by the need to find a 'different conceptual framework' which is able to adapt to specific legal contexts, thus being able to recognize the role and the different forms that the 'law' takes within both Western and non-Western societies (Donlan, Heckendorn Ursheler 2014: 7).[15] This conceptual framework could for example be *Legal pluralism* (LP), which at any rate is everything but 'new', being part of the academic debate for at least a few decades.[16] Within comparative law itself, there is a minority but vibrant tradition that carries such sensibility. It is sufficient to mention relevant collective works (Reimann, Zimmermann 2008; Bussani, Mattei 2012; Donlan, Heckendorn Ursheler 2014) or even individual authors who have developed methodologies designed to 'fly' from one side to another of the law (Menski's 'kite', 2006, 2011, 2014), or to grasp its most 'profound' aspects (Van Hoecke's 'deep' comparison, 2015) exploring the various 'slices' of legal systems (Frankenberg's 'layered narrative', 2011).

The question then flowing would be: why does it seem that comparative law is so inevitably stuck in inappropriate methodologies and that no equipment is available for exploring legal 'exotic' lands? I would argue that the answer could be found considering a further limit that concerns the 'perception' about methods in addition to equipment constraints.

14 The monistic methodology results inappropriate not only for decoding the pluralistic non-Western cultures, but also 'more attuned' for understanding Western European ones especially if we consider today's intrinsic nature of multiculturalism (Menski 2007: 189).

15 This does not mean, Amirante clarifies, that 'dogmatic categories of Western comparison [...] must "necessarily be abandoned". Indeed their "applicability" in non-Western contexts' should be re-discussed in light of the empirical results of academic research, thus allowing scholars to promote a re-thinking of Western categories (Amirante 2015: 27).

16 Starting from Griffiths 1986, to Chiba 1989, Tamanaha 2000 and Menski 2006 – just to mention few representative authors.

Narration constraints

If 'we comparatists would take our head out of the method-debate-bush', observes Jaakko Husa, 'we might realize that our discussions may look really strange to the uninitiated who may be interested in comparative study under different circumstances' (Husa 2006: 1111). Following this line, I have tried to identify three main paradoxes within the narration of methods that may contribute in keeping this issue away from the core discussions of the discipline.

(a) Any serious comparison – as experienced scholars tell us – *must* follow a method.[17] However, this mantra may sound quite paradoxical if we count the number of pages or hours dedicated to the methodological debate within treaties, books or courses on comparative law. Numbers – someone observes – that are certainly growing, but still somewhat slowly (Scarciglia 2015: 1015; Husa 2006: 918). Others – in a less lenient way – have noted how 'some of the most widely read books on Comparative law have virtually nothing to say about methodology and, perhaps consequently, classifications may be described as naive and unaware of methodological questions and issues' (Palmer 2004: 2).

The effect of this slightly schizophrenic tendency is that, in turn, there are scholars who dedicate their entire careers on methodological research. They publish single-issue volumes and develop theories which might be intellectually correct, but that are likely to be limited to a dialogue between ultra-specialists (the 'methodists'). 'Sometimes too theoretical methodology', continues Husa, 'may be counterproductive and it may scare people away from comparing law and lead to a situation in which even high quality methodological constructions have very limited practical value' (Husa 2006: 1114, note 89). Quoting an article from 1988 that expressed the thesis that methodological discussions are a 'good cure for insomnia', Vernon Valentine Palmer noted that sometimes the 'general message from academic circles' is that comparative law 'is a difficult and forbidding field reserved for special few' (Palmer 2004: 1–5–7).

(b) The second paradox arises from the above considerations. In fact, the typical attitude of comparative lawyers would be to speculate on *how not* to compare rather than *how* to compare. Methodological debates often lack 'explanation or concrete guidelines' (Hoecke 2015: 8). In fact, comparative researchers 'many times do not present any clear approach (i.e. a systematic manner as how to proceed in research) in a methodological sense', and prefer to accumulate 'academic aggression' (Husa 2006: 1105). This 'nihilist' attitude is often referred to a specific methodological paradigm. Nevertheless, comparatists cannot avoid the criticism of not being 'very practical' within their methodological advice (Husa 2006: 1105). Needless to say that within this picture the choice of method could be a challenging task.

(c) No standard methodology is available within comparative law. On the contrary, there are different methodological schools that offer a panoplia of approaches to

17 This is true for most comparatists although some propose to adopt the 'non-method' as a method (Feyerabend 1978 and, from the legal field Adams and Griffiths 2012 and partially Glenn 2014).

reality showing different *lenses* that comparative lawyers may adopt in their path (Örücü 2007: 48; Ponthoreau 2005: 23). There are no 'easy answers' as each different methodology was designed and developed 'by different people and in different times and places'; therefore, the idea that a specific theory 'might yield transculturally valid results flies in the face of all the misunderstandings that comparatists observe, produce, decry and consume on a daily basis' (Lasser 2003: 221). After all, there is no 'one true tradition of comparative law ... but *many* traditions', that may have set numerous 'partly incompatible but yet *legitimate* standards of comparative research in law' (Husa 2006: 1112). Different legal minds and cultures seem to enhance 'unconscious methods' and 'models' for comparative law (Palmer 2004: 2), thus comparative lawyers 'should be deeply sceptical of the idea that there could be a comparative methodology ... that could be safely applied in historically variable circumstances' (Lasser 2003: 221).[18]

Hence, there is a 'plurality of methods' and each corresponds to a different focus 'on issues having little in common except that they are addressed in a comparative way' (Graziadei 2003: 101). Many techniques have acquired 'the status of separate methods' and their number depends on the specific taxonomy adopted: functional, structural, historical, evolutionary, thematic, empirical or statistical, represent some options.[19] The possibilities are endless (Palmer 2004: 2). However, as mentioned, there is a common tendency of describing the methodological scenario in either black or white terms: functionalism vs contextualism.[20]

The first (f-method) has been traditionally considered as the *mainstream* approach in contemporary law methodology (Jackson 2012: 62),[21] that 'began to flow' at the end of 19th century (Frankenberg 2016: 5). Despite the existence of different types of functionalism (Michaels 2008), this approach 'in general begins with a question or a feeling' (such as immigrants' rights, or youth's disaffection about politics) that 'spurred on by the intuition that other legal systems may have produced something *better*' (Frankenberg 1985: 436 emphasis added, see also Van Hoecke, 2004: 172). The comparison begins by comparing institutions or functionally equivalent standards of legal systems and ends by identifying the 'most efficient rule' (Cotterrell 2007: 136). Functionalism method is guided by a *praesumptio similitudinis*, which implies that all societies essentially address the same problems but tackle them in different ways (Zweigert, Kötz 1978/1987: 25, 39).

18 The methodological debate can assume a 'multifaceted' order depending on the observer's point of view (Scarciglia 2015: 1012). The latter can have both a *geographical* connotation: *West* (Amirante 2015, although there are sensible differences between US and Europe, Kennedy 1997); East (Menski 2006; Ruskola 2002); South (Africa) (Vimborsati 2008); and a *thematic* connotation, such as the Islamic legal world (Arasani 2014) or even single events like Arab Springs and methodological implications in comparative law (Sbailò 2015).

19 Among the ones offered by Palmer, 2004: 2; Samuel 2014: 64; Van Hoecke 2015; 8.

20 See Dann 2011; Frankenberg 2016; Husa 2006; Ponthoreau 2017; Van Hoecke 2004; Jackson 2012;

21 On functionalism, De Cornick (2010), Michaels (2008); Graziadei (2003); more briefly, Samuel (2004) 38–43].

Functionalism received widespread criticism. Some argue that it simplifies the very notion of 'problem', which would be (too) simplistically associated with a 'solution' (Nelken 2007: 22). This methodological approach would undermine the very concept of 'law' by reducing it to a mere set of rules, procedures and institutions (Husa, 2006: 1110) without considering the specific legal, historical, social and cultural context (Donlan, Heckendorn Urscheler 2014: 8). A 'Kafkaesque' vision of the world that would present the 'law' as 'ideal', 'rational' and 'optimal', thus denying its nature as an 'equivocal' and 'fluid' phenomenon (Frankenberg, 1985: 445–447, widely Samuel 2004: 61–64). Not surprisingly, this approach would prove inappropriate for describing 'other' legal systems such as those of non-Western jurisdictions (Amirante 2015; Menski 2006; Frankenberg 1985: 445).

Functionalism clearly was the dominant method used in the first part of the 20th century. However, in the second part of the century, *contextualism* (c-method) gained relevance and acquired the status of *anti-mainstream* approach (Husa, 2006: 1106). The latter method is based upon the idea that 'law' is not limited to 'a series of discrete legal events' or to the analysis of laws, procedures and institutions – without taking into account the historical, legal, cultural and social context (Frankenberg 1985: 423).

The boundaries of c-method are perhaps even less clear than those of functionalism. Nevertheless, each of them has a wide range of methodological approaches. Indeed, many c-method currents are labelled as 'non-orthodox', 'deconstructionist', 'culturalist', 'post-modern' (Husa 2006: 1105, for a more detailed analysis see Jackson 2012: 67). '[W]hatever you chose to call them', as some sceptical scholars underline, it 'is a difficult task to try to say in a general way what they are about', however 'one main strand in non-mainstream comparative law has been the idea to stress difference in a very pronounced and profound manner' (Husa 2006: 1105–1106). 'Let's take a painting', proposes Legrand, one of the greatest scholars of contextualism, '[l]et us take, specifically, a painting from 1812 by the French painter, Jacques-Louis David … depicting Napoleon in his study drafting the French civil code by candlelight. In my view, this painting offers the comparatist at least as much understanding of the French legal mind as any article of the French civil code' (Legrand: 1996: 235).

The core idea of this approach is that 'each law is a unique spiritual creation' thus requiring a 'call for a new paradigm for comparative law' (Palmer, 2004: 11). While admitting that the meaning of 'law' is fundamentally related to a specific socio-cultural context, it undoubtedly implies a wider perspective that shifts its focus away from purely regulatory aspects (Graziadei 2003: 110). The entrance of 'culture' in legal grammar, says Glenn, responds to both the growing influence of Social Sciences (anthropology in particular) and the dissemination of terms that exist in common usage (Glenn 2010: 8). Within this specific context, elucidates Graziadei, the notion of 'culture' comes across 'as the best opportunity for comparative legal studies to modernize itself' and to distance itself from concepts as 'uniformity', 'positivism', 'law as rules' (Graziadei 2003: 114). These concepts are replaced by an 'intellectual posture' whose *mantras* became 'diversity', pluralism', 'law-as-culture' (Graziadei 2003: 108, 114).

'All legal scholars will agree that comparative research cannot be limited to pure black-letter comparison of legal rules, concepts or systems', underlines Van Hoecke, but the 'next question is what is the relevant context for fully and correctly understanding (foreign) rules? ... Here the comparative lawyer is lost (Van Hoecke 2004, 167). 'What sources should the comparatist actually seek to study? Perhaps she should approach assorted 'high' and 'low' cultural forms, such as architecture, the visual arts, public-opinion polls, novels, newspaper accounts, oral histories, films and/or television. I strongly suspect, for example', continues a more sceptical M. de S.-O.-l'E. Lasser, 'that a detailed study of assorted forms of legal iconography' cannot help despite being fascinating and suggestive (Lasser 2003: 228).

On this topic, Michele Graziadei argues that 'despite the energy put in challenging the functionalist canon through the appeal to the cultural dimension of legal phenomena', [critics] of functional comparisons have made little progress in discussing' new methodological proposal (Graziadei 2003: 110). In this vein, Husa claims that *contextualism* tends to place itself in opposition to functionalism. This results in 'an anti-strategy' or 'nihilist' story which is simply 'turning the conviction of orthodoxy upside down translating the black and white, without taking into account all the other colours' (Husa 2006: 111).

It therefore seems that such a 'love-hate' debate has monopolized the academic discussions on the methodology of comparative law (Husa 2011: 250). *Functionalism* and *contextualism* indeed represent two 'existential tensions' that have marked 'comparative constitutional studies from the dawn of the 20th century onward' (Hirschl 2014: 193). Two 'contrasting tracks' (Frankenberg 2016: 5), with deep 'implications for core methodological considerations such as case selection and research design' (Hirschl 2014: 193). Two 'main strands within comparative study of law' (Modeér),[22] whose 'grouping' has been crucial for the formation of modern comparative law schools. Rule-oriented, on one side (f-method); contextual approach (c-method) on the other (Husa 2006: 1098).

In the shadow of such a polarization, new paths of legal experiences classification have been crafted, as shown by the shift from *legal system/legal family* to *legal culture/legal tradition*. This is not a mere lexical speculation. Indeed between *comparative law* and *comparative legal studies*, as David Nelken reports, a real 'territorial war' took place over the last decades (Nelken 2007: 13). Anti-mainstream methodology (notably in its anti-formalist dimension) became 'the dominant professional vocabulary' after WW2. It replaced 'legal method' with a more pragmatic 'thinking like a lawyer' and fostered a sort of 'methodological eclecticism' (Kennedy 2003: 347). Nevertheless this was a rather 'odd' sequence, David Kennedy continues, because after a while anti-mainstream 'became mainstream common sense' (Kennedy 2003: 352). How could that happen?

22 Quoted in Husa 2006: 1098.

Frankenberg has a fairly accurate idea about this and explains that

> [e]ach phase or era, dominant school or trend was characterized by a paradigm of legal comparison privileging a specific tool-kit (method/theory), distinct goals and a peculiar interpretive framework. Justified by the prevailing discourse, each paradigm shaped the nature, style and purpose of 'good comparative practices' and congealed into an orthodox or mainstream. (Frankenberg 2016: 14–15)

After all, the author continues, 'the disciplinary identity provides the criteria for defining who is in and who is out and, if reified, forms the core around which the orthodoxy of practice though and may crystallize'. Within this context, '[o]rthodoxy tells its followers (and also curious various) that, at a time, only one method or theory or an established set of them is considered legitimate. It mandates a (serial) kind of intellectual monogamy that looks down upon pluralism and mandates for eclecticism to be integrated, as to as possible, in a unitary framework' (Frankenberg 2016: 9).

Jaakko Husa himself, quoting Paul Feyerabend's well-known volume on methodological rigidity, argues that 'he clearly has a point when he warned against unanimity of methodological option that would be fitting for a rigid *church*, for the frightened or greedy victims of some (ancient, or modern) myth, of for the weak and willing followers of some tyrant' (Husa 2006: 1117 emphasis added). Other authors strongly underline the presence of 'methodological *faiths*' in comparative law (Graziadei 2003, emphasis added). This debate seems to be driven by an 'existential' tone if we take into account its declination as 'naïve epistemological optimism' (f-method) *versus* 'strong epistemological pessimism' (c-method) (Van Hoecke, 2004: 172).[23]

After all, the progressive classification of the two methodological paradigms appears to have taken a clear *political* significance starting 'from the beginning of the twentieth century (Kennedy 2003: 349), by feeding itself of 'ad hominen attacks' (Palmer, 2004: 22).[24] Within this canvas of strong opposition between methodological monogamies and their ideological constructions, we can definitely start to understand why this debate has been fuelled by reciprocal descriptions in 'hyperbolic terms' (Hirschl 2014: 16). Accounts on methodological opponents are often instrumental and are forcibly seen as either 'total black' or 'total white'. In other words, both traditional descriptions of f-method and/or c-method seem to

23 On one hand, a naïve epistemological optimism (f-method): this means comparing without posing the problem that there might be implications in epistemological terms whatsoever. Assuming that 'comparing is just a natural activity [that does not need any method]: you look and listen, and you automatically see the commonalities and divergences' (Van Hoecke 2004: 172). On the other hand, a strong epistemological pessimism (c-method), that 'has led to a simple denial of any possibility of comparing [considering that foreigners] in this reasoning never will be able to understand "really" foreign law, because of the cultural differences' (Van Hoecke 2004: 172).

24 Frankenberg points out that 'there is nothing virginal, natural, and inevitable about the ways and means of comparative laws' [...] 'how we deal with and understand foreign laws and foreign legal cultures is not only a matter of theory and method but has ethical and political implications' (Frankenberg 2016: IX–X).

denote a certain degree of superficiality[25] turning out in an ultimately 'misleading and exaggerated dichotomy' (Ponthoreau 2017: 58).

In conclusion, this black or white storytelling seems to be 'at the heart' of today's 'epistemological and methodological matrix inadequacy' (Hirschl 2014: 197). Indeed it produced both 'weak theories and weak theorists' who are more committed to build simplified images and escape 'the need for working out an adequate methodology for comparative law' (Van Hoecke 2004: 172; on similar lines Husa 2006: 1112). This *hyperbolic* understanding of the adversary did not allow scholars to realize that *functionalism* and *contextualism* would actually be *similar* or even *complementary*.[26] Such perceptions are grounded on the fact that both paradigms share a similar awareness of the complexity of the context.

However, they draw very different operational consequences. Functionalism, in fact, 'suggests a practical approach' to the problem. It promises simplified paths, which allow – in any case – to compare all similarities (Frankenberg 1985: 439–440). On the other side, contextualism focuses on the examination of the context. However, it does not always find a way forward and often concludes that 'the comparison is not possible' (Dann 2011: 164). In other words, 'to put crudely ... functional theory (not practice, however) says basically the same: one must look beyond law, and see also the context' (Husa 2006, 1110). Other authors go even beyond and propose that 'some kind of reconciliation could be possible between functionalism and contextualism' (Samuel 2004: 64 et seq.) as demonstrated by the prototype of 'contextualized functionalism' (Jackson 2012: 73).[27] However, what emerges very clearly again is that the methodological debate can be addressed also by avoiding the conflicting vision between f-method and c-method, offering either a new path or reciprocal cross-fertilization.

Beyond the dichotomy: a flexible approach

Among the effects of the dualistic storytelling about methods, there is the 'squeezing [of] the plethora of scholarship into binary positions' (Husa 2006: 1097). As consequence a 'lot of published, but largely unnoticed, research outside rule and case-oriented comparative law offers different approaches,

25 Graziadei has shown, for example, that the narrative which blames functionalism of carrying a law-as-rule approach can be misleading. Moreover, the same comparative lawyers often do not exclusively use one methodology (Graziadei 2003: 101).

26 Husa has no doubts about it. 'I would like to argue that if one looks at contextually oriented studies and compares them with the so-called mainstream studies there do not seem to be many that differences. Different vocabulary, yes. Different point of stress, yes. But incommensurability, no [in fact] there are crucial similarities in epistemic basic-ideas of studying law comparatively' (Husa 2006: 1110). Not far from this, Samuel observes that 'if conceived carefully enough from an epistemological and methodological point of view it might as well be that the contradiction [between f-method and c-method will reveal itself as unreal' (Samuel 2004: 64).

27 After all, on one hand 'the functional method has to be complemented by other methods' (Van Hoecke 2015: 11[3]); on the other hand, 'law-in-context as a method cannot be isolated from the other methods' (Van Hoecke 2015: 16[4]).

Figure 2.1 Methodology landscape in books

Figure 2.2 Methodology landscape in action

which could be usefully applied in comparative research, remains at the borders of methodological ruminations' (Van Hoecke 2015: 1). Building on that, we could also say that following the 'pedagogical beauty' of the *black and white* picture (Husa 2006: 1097) results in a methodological landscape *in books*, that seems however very far from the methodological *in action* that shows the reality for what it is: *shades of grey*.

It is precisely this 'grey' area that I would suggest to explore in search for interesting methodological hints for global times. A chromatic complexity that could be difficult to navigate if compared to the *black or white* picture, but nevertheless offers some tools that should be carefully considered before claiming the lack of methods in comparative law. I am alluding to a bouquet of proposals that have been developed in rather different regions (Asia, US, Europe) and periods (from the 1980s onward) that here are labelled as 'late modern' (or 'fluid modern') options. These approaches can be distinguished by a number of specific and not conflicting features – (i) *dynamism*, (ii) *tolerance for ambiguity* and (iii) *interdisciplinarity* – that are all held together ultimately by a common characteristic: (iv) *flexibility*.

i One of the most common characteristics is arguably *dynamism*. It is Rodolfo Sacco who during the 1990s developed his well-known 'dynamic approach to comparative law' (Sacco 1991). The latter was linked to a specific methodological proposal that focused on the 'comparability of the legal systems of people that have or do not have a written language' (Sacco 1991: 7, emphasis added). Today, a dynamic methodology appears by then 'more and more necessary' to analyse the transformations of legal phenomena involved in globalization (Scarciglia 2015: 1018) and such a sensibility is now shared by many authors.[28]

ii Liquid times have modified the borders and the scopes of legal investigation and its concepts – just thinking about 'citizenship' or 'foreigner' – are now changing and being constantly disputed (Zonca 2016: 23). This is the ground where the second methodological characteristic originates: tolerance for ambiguity. The latter contrasts a comparative law attitude (and expression of modern 'solidity', as Bauman explained us) based on 'forcing data into controllable cognitive categories' with their many dichotomous nuances (Frankenberg 1985: 522; on this point see also Panthoreau 2017: 55 et seq.). As mentioned, there is a consolidated tendency in Western tradition to conceive the concept of 'hybridity' as a source of 'ambiguity' itself. Such attitude has been to some extent challenged by legal pluralism (LP) and perhaps more directly by global legal pluralism (GLP). Paul Schiff Berman, for example, suggests to apply 'a pluralist framework to the global arena', trying to approach 'legal hybridity' not just in a descriptive manner as LP does, but as a desirable condition, as GLP proposes. Indeed, there are normative lessons that would be drawn from the spaces for contestation among multiple, overlapping legal systems that should be deliberately created and preserved (for deepening see Schiff Berman 2007, 2009, 2012, 2013, 2015).

iii Interdisciplinarity describes the third set of features that are present among the 'late modern' methods. A skill that has become 'necessary' nowadays (Amirante 2015: 27, Scarciglia 2015: 1017) and methodologically 'preferable' (Hirschl 2014: 13). Furthermore some authors take this to the point of proposing 'a step away from soloist type of comparativism', moving towards 'research based comparative study of law' with the participation of historians, sociologists, linguists, anthropologists and political scientists (Husa 2006: 1116).[29]

However such a 'collaborative' research method – someone reflects – could result in a marginalization of comparative lawyers, in fact '[w]ho needs to read a

28 See Adams, Amirante, Bussani, Mattei, Menski Muir Watt, Ponthoreau, Scarciglia.

29 These teams, others stress, should provide 'some rough understanding of differences and similarities between legal systems, and of the relevant context for explaining them' (Van Hoecke 2015: 7). For example, when comparing banking law, 'one may assume that economics is most relevant for explaining similarities and differences, but maybe history and/or psychology would eventually appear to be even more relevant for the specific research question' (Van Hoecke 2015: 7).

scholarly comparison of legal institutions in India and the United States when one can simply incorporate an Indian legal thinker into one's project collaboratively?' (Riles 2015: 155).

i These characteristics – dynamism, tolerance for ambiguity, interdisciplinarity – have been taking shape over the last decade by pushing the borders of the discipline, enhancing a change in the understanding of method itself: from fixed to flexible. Indeed a mechanical consideration of method, that is 'A type of law requires X method' – we have learned – seems not to fit anymore in today's legal fluidity (Husa 2006: 251). Such flexibility seems to offer twofold nuances: (a) *between* and (b) *within.*

  a Methodology should not be seen as a clear road map – someone argues – but as a 'toolbox' offering proposals that will be determined on the basis of the aim and the research question that lies at the heart of the comparative project (Van Hoecke 2015: 1). In this light, method represents nothing else than 'a function of variables', that 'should be adapted to the purpose of the project and the individual circumstances' (Palmer 2004: 6). In conclusion, flexibility *between* methods represents the exigency to shift from the one-method beginning with capital 'M', to a plurality of methods beginning with a lowercase 'm' (Husa 2011: 252) appears to be gaining relevance in today's comparative legal studies.[30]
  b A method in liquid times cannot be pictured as a conflict between monotheisms, but rather as a pragmatic choice in a *polytheistic* scenario, where there is not a *definitive* and *ultimate* method. This would lead us to a second level of awareness that is *within* flexibility, according to which methods should be considered 'complementary and not mutually exclusive', thus they 'may be combined' together (Van Hoecke 2015: 1). Seminal projects of 'mixed methodology' have been experimented (i.e. the 'Common Core' of European Private law)[31] and continue to be referred to in the works of brilliant academics (Graziadei 2003,) relying also on a growing awareness about the *interdependence* of legal traditions (Glenn 2010).[32]

This brief overview of 'late modernity' demonstrates that comparative law, despite the general precariousness, already has some useful methodological itineraries that nevertheless have been at times shadowed by the mentioned dualistic narrative. At the roots of these proposals, there is essentially the awareness that the nature of 'law' – which is *plural, flexible, changing* – cannot be disconnected from

30 Amirante 2015; Husa 2006, 2015; Jackson 2012; Menski 2006; Ponthoreau 2017; Scarciglia 2015, 2016).
31 See Common Core Private Law official website: http://www.common-core.org/.
32 The interdependence theory argues that it is impossible to insulate one country's legal tradition without taking into consideration that of other countries, as actually already observed at the beginning of the 20th century (Romano 1918).

the nature of its methods. No doubts that further work on this field could and should be developed, as it is important to not stop the methodological research in order to address the ever-changing complexities of our global scenario.

After all, the characteristic of 'liquid' modernity is the 'ever stronger belief' that the only constant element is represented by change and that the only certainty is uncertainty. Being modern in 'Solid' times used to mean pursing 'the state of definitive perfection', while now (in 'liquid' times) it alludes to an infinite improvement 'without any prospective of aspiration to become definitive' (Bauman 2011; VII; Bauman 1999: 12). Hence, what appears ultimately crucial is to re-thinking also the *expectations* that we place on methodology itself, which should not include the possibility of organizing reality within a coherent ('solid') system. This process do not have to discourage scholars from embracing with enthusiasm journeys towards unexpected destinations, by offering their imperfect but nevertheless generous and vital descriptions that will crucially nourish comparative law in our global age.

Bibliography

AA. VV. (2016) *Ricerca sulla verità della nascita umana. 40 anni di Analisi collettiva*, Roma, L'Asino d'oro edizioni.

Adams, M. and J. Bomhoff (2012) *Practice and Theory in Comparative Law*, Cambridge, Cambridge University Press.

Adams, M. and D. Heirbaut (2014) *The Method and Culture of Comparative Law: Essays in Honour of Mark Van Hoecke*, Oxford and Portland, Hart Publishing.

Amico di Meane, T. (2015) La forma di governo dell'India alla luce delle elezioni politiche del 2014: profili costituzionali, in *Rivista di Diritto Pubblico Comparato ed Europeo*, 2, 555–570.

Amirante, D. (2010) (ed.) *Altre democrazie. Problemi e prospettive del consolidamento democratico nel sub-continente indiano*, Milano, Franco Angeli.

Amirante, D. (2015) *Lo Stato multiculturale. Contributo alla teoria dello Stato dalla prospettiva dell'Unione Indiana*, Bologna, Bononia University Press.

Amirante, D. (2015) Al di là dell'Occidente. Sfide epistemologiche e spunti euristici nella comparazione 'verso Oriente', in *Rivista Diritto Pubblico Comparato ed Europeo*, 1, 11–46.

Arasani, H. (2014) Islamic Law as a Comparable Model in Comparative Legal Research, *Global J. Comp. Law*, 3, 186 et seq.

Balagangadhara, S.N. (2012) *Reconceptualizing India Studies*, Oxford, Oxford University Press.

Balagangadhara, S.N. (2013) *What Do Indians Need, a History or the Past? A Challenge or Two to Indian Historians*. Available at http://ichr.ac.in/snb_lec.pdf.

Balagangadhara, S.N. and J. De Roover (2008) John Locke, Christian Liberty and the Predicament of Liberal Toleration, *Political Theory: an International Journal of Political Philosophy*, 36(4), 523–549.

Balagangadhara, S.N. and J. De Roover (2009) Liberty, Tyranny and the Will of God: The Principle of Toleration in Early Modern Europe and Colonial India, *History of Political Thought*, 30(1), 11–139.

Barton, J.H. and J.L. Gibbs (1983) *Law in Radically Different Cultures*, St. Paul, MN, West Publishing Company.

Basedow, J. (2014) Comparative Law and Its Clients, *American Journal of Comparative Law*, 4, 837 et seq.

Basu, D.D. (1984) *Comparative Constitutional Law*, New Delhi, Prentice-Hall India.

Basu, D.D. (2014) *Comparative Constitutional Law*, New Delhi, (first edn 1984), Gurgaon, LexisNexis.

Bauman, Z. (1999) *La società dell'incerteza*, Milano, il Mulino.

Bauman, Z. (2011) *Modernità Liquida*, Roma/Bari, Editori Laterza.

Bauman, Z. and E. Mauro (2015) *Babel*, Roma/Bari, Editori Laterza.

Baxi, U. (1985) *Courage, Craft and Contention*, Bombay, Tripathi.

Baxi, U. (2003) The Colonialist Heritage, in Legrand, P. and Munday, R. (eds), *Comparative Legal Studies: Traditions and Transitions*, Cambridge, Cambridge University Press, 46–75.

Baxi, U. (2013) 'Ordering' Constitutional Transfers: A View from India, in Frankenberg, G. (ed.), *Comparative Constitutional Design and Legal Culture*, Cheltenham and Northampton, Edward Elgar.

Bussani, M. and M. Mattei (2012) (eds) *The Cambridge Companion to Comparative Law*, Cambridge, Cambridge University Press

Cassese, S. (2009) *Il diritto globale. Giustizia e democrazia oltre lo Stato*, Torino, Einaudi.

Chakrabarty, D. (2000) *Provincializing Europe*, Princeton, Princeton University Press.

Chiba, M. (1989) *Legal Pluralism: Towards a General Theory through Japanese Legal Culture*, Tokyo, Tokai University Press.

Choudhry, S. (2006) Migration as a New Metaphor in Comparative Constitutional Law, in Choudhry, S. (ed.), *The Migration of Constitutional Ideas*, Cambridge, Cambridge University Press.

Choudhry, S. (2008) Bridging Comparative Politics and Comparative Constitutional Law: Constitutional Design in Divided Societies, in Choudhry, S. (ed.), *Constitutional Design for Divided Societies: Integration or Accommodation?*, Oxford, Oxford University Press, 3–31.

Cotterrell, R. (1997) The Concept of Legal Culture, in Nelken, D. (ed.), *Comparing Legal Cultures*, Aldershot, Dartmouth, 13–31.

Cotterrell, R. (2002) Seeking Similarity, Appreciating Difference: Comparative Law and Communities, in Harding, A. and Örücü, E. (eds), *Comparative Law in the 21st Century*, London, The Hague and New York, Kluwer.

Cotterrell, R. (2007) Is it so Bad to be Different? Comparative Law and the Appreciation of Diversity, in Örücü, E. and Nelken, D. (eds), *Comparative Law: A Handbook*, London, Hart Publishing, 133–155.

Cotterrell, R. (2014) A Concept of Law for Global Legal Pluralism?, in Donlan, S.P. and Heckendorn Urscheler, L. (eds), *Concept of Law: Comparative, Jurisprudential, and Social Science Perspectives*, Farnham, Ashgate, 193–208.

Dann, P. (2011) Federal Democracy in India and the European Union: Towards Transcontinental Comparison of Constitutional Law, in *Übersee/Law and Politics in Africa, Asia and Latin America*, 44, 160–176.

Di Martino, A. (2010) *Il territorio: dallo Stato-Nazione alla globalizzazione. Sfide e prospettive dello Stato costituzionale aperto*, Milano, Giuffrè.

De Vergottini, G. (2015) Tradizioni costituzionali e vincoli alla comparazione, in *Diritto pubblico comparato ed europeo*, 4, 853–986.

Donlan, S.P. (2010) Comparative Law and Hybrid Legal Traditions: An Introduction, in Donlan, S.P. (ed.), *Comparative Law and Hybrid Legal Traditions*, Zurich, Shulthess.

Donlan, S.P. (2011) Remembering: Legal Hybridity and Legal History, *Comparative Law Review*, 2, 1 et seq.

Donlan, S.P. and L. Heckendorn Urscheler (eds) (2014) *Concept of law: Comparative, Jurisprudential, and Social Science Perspectives*, Farnham, Ashgate.

Eberhard, C. (2005) Beyond Legal pluralism: A Dynamic and Intercultural Approach to Law in India, *Indian Socio-Legal Journal*, 31, 131–148.

Eberhard, C. and N. Gupta (2005) Legal Pluralism in India: An Introduction, *Indian Socio-Legal Journal*, 31 (special), 1–10.

Fagioli, M. (1973/2013) *Bambino, donna e trasformazione dell'uomo*, Roma, L'Asino d'oro edizioni.

Ferrari, G.F. (2010) *Atlante di diritto pubblico comparato*, Torino, Utet.

Ferrari, S. (2008) (cur.) *Introduzione al diritto comparato. Ebraismo, islam e induismo*, Milano, il Mulino.

Frankenberg, G. (1985) Critical Comparisons: Re-thinking Comparative Law, *Harvard International Law Journal*, 26, 411–455.

Frankenberg, G. (2010) Constitutional Transfer: The IKEA Theory Revisited, *I.CON*, 8(3), 563–579.

Frankenberg, G. (2013) Constitutions as Commodities: Notes on a Theory of Transfer, in Frankenberg, G. (ed.), *Comparative Constitutional Design and Legal Culture*, Cheltenham and Northampton, Edward Elgar, 1–28.

Frankenberg, G. (2016) *Comparative Law as Critique*Cheltenham and Northampton, Edward Elgar.

Glanert, S. (2013) Method?, in Monateri, P.G. (ed.), *Methods of Comparative Law*, Cheltenham and Northampton, Edward Elgar, 61–82.

Glenn, P.H. (2004) Legal Culture and Legal Tradition, in Van Hoecke, M. (ed.), *Epistemology and Methodology of Comparative Law*, Oxford and Oregon, Hart Publishing, 7–20.

Glenn, P.H. (2007) Comparing, in Örücü, E. and Nelken, D. (eds), *Comparative Law: A Handbook*, London, Hart Publishing, 91–108.

Glenn, P.H. (2010) *Legal Traditions of the World: Sustainable Diversity in Law*, Oxford, Oxford University Press.

Graziadei, M. (2003) The Functionalist Heritage, in Legrand, P. and Munday, R. (eds), *Comparative Legal Studies: Traditions and Transitions*, Cambridge, Cambridge University Press, 100–130.

Graziadei, M. (2009) Legal Transplants and the Frontiers of Legal Knowledge, *Theoretical Inquiries in Law*, 10(693), 694–714.

Griffiths, J. (1986) What Is Legal Pluralism, *J. Legal Pluralism & Unofficial Law*, 24, 1, 1–55.

Habermas, J. (1998) Legittimazione tramite diritti umani, in Habermas, J., *L'inclusione dell'altro. Studi di teoria politica*, Milano, Feltrinelli.

Habermas, J. (1999) *La costellazione postnazionale. Mercato globale, nazioni e democrazia*, Milano, Feltrinelli.

Habermas, J. and C. Taylor (1998) *Multiculturalismo: lotte per il riconoscimento*, Milano, Feltrinelli.

Hage, J. (2014) Comparative Law as Method and the Method of Comparative Law, in Adams, M. and Heirbaut, D. (eds), *The Method and Culture of Comparative Law: Essays in Honour of Mark Van Hoecke*, Oxford and Portland, Hart Publishing.

Hirschl, R. (2014) *Comparative Matters: The Renaissance of Comparative Constitutional Law*, Oxford, Oxford University Press.

Husa, J. (2006) Methodology of Comparative Law Today: From Paradoxes to Flexibility?, *Revue Internationale de Droit Comparé*, 58(4), 1095–1117.

Husa, J. (2009) Turning the Curriculum Upside Down: Comparative Law as an Educational Tool for Constructing Pluralistic Legal Mind, in *Comparative Research in Law &*

Political Economy, Research Paper No. 35. Available at http://digitalcommons.osgoode.yorku.ca/clpe/147.

Husa, J. (2015) *A New Introduction to Comparative Law*, Oxford, Hart Publishing.

Jackson, V.C. (2012) Comparative Constitutional Law: Methodologies, in Rosenfeld, M. and Sajó, A. (eds), *The Oxford Handbook of Comparative Constitutional Law*, Oxford, Oxford University Press.

Kavanagh, C. (2016) *Can Religion be Based on Ritual Practice without Belief?*, in *aeon.com.*

Kennedy, D.W. (1997) New Approaches to Comparative Law: Comparativism and International Governance, *Symposium Utah Law Review*, 2, 255–663.

Kennedy, D.W. (2003) The Method and the Politics, in Legrand, P. and Munday, R. (eds), *Comparative Legal Studies: Traditions and Transitions*, Cambridge, Cambridge University Press, 345–436.

Khilnani, S. (1999) *The Idea of India*. New York: Straus and Giroux, Farrar.

Khilnani, S. (2010) Politics and National Identity, in Jayal, N.G. and Mehta, P.B. (eds), *The Oxford Companion to Politics in India*, New Delhi, Oxford University Press.

Khilnani, S., V. Raghavan and A.K. Thiruvengadam (2013) *Comparative Constitutionalism in South Asia*, Oxford, Oxford University Press.

Krisch, N. (2011) *Beyond Constitutionalism: The Pluralist Structure of Postnational Law*, Oxford, Oxford University Press.

Kymlicka, W. (1999) *La cittadinanza multiculturale*, Bologna, Il Mulino, 1999.

Lasser, M. (2003) The Questioning of Understanding, in Legrand, P. and Munday, R. (eds), *Comparative Legal Studies: Traditions and Transitions*, Cambridge, Cambridge University Press, 197–239.

Legrand, P. (1996) How to Compare Now, *Legal Studies*, 16(2), 232–242.

Legrand, P. (2003) The Same and the Different, in Legrand, P. and Munday, R. (eds), *Comparative Legal Studies: Traditions and Transitions*, Cambridge, Cambridge University Press, 240–311.

Lijphart, A. (1996) The Puzzle of Indian Democracy: A Consociational Interpretation, *American Political Science Review*, 90(2), 258 et seq.

Menski, W. (2006) *Comparative Law in a Global Context: The Legal Systems of Asia and Africa*, Cambridge, Cambridge University Press.

Menski, W. (2007) Beyond Europe, in Örücü, E. and Nelken, D. (eds), *Comparative Law: A Handbook*, London, Hart Publishing, 189–217.

Michaels, R. (2008) The Functional Method of Comparative Law, in Reimann, M. and Zimmermann, R. (eds), *The Oxford Handbook of Comparative Law*, Oxford, Oxford University Press, 339–382.

Monateri, P.G. (ed.) (2013) *Methods of Comparative Law*, Cheltenham and Northampton, Edward Elgar.

Morrison, A.S. (2013) *The Law is a Fractal: The Attempt to Anticipate Everything*, University of Michigan Public Law Research paper n. 292

Mortati, C. (1976) *Istituzioni di diritto pubblico*, Padova, Cedam, 1976.

Muir Watt, H. (2006) Globalization and Comparative Law, in Reimann, M. and Zimmermann, R. (eds), *The Oxford Handbook of Comparative Law*, Oxford, Oxford University Press.

Nelken, D. (2007) Comparative Law and Comparative Legal Studies, in Örücü, E. and Nelken, D. (eds), *Comparative Law: A Handbook*, London, Hart Publishing, 3–40.

Nobles, R. and D. Schiff (eds) (2014) *Law, Society and Community: Socio-Legal Essays in Honour of Roger Cotterrell*, London, Ashgate.

Örücü, E. (2003) Comparatists and Extraordinary Places, in Legrand, P. and Munday, R. (eds), *Comparative Legal Studies: Traditions and Transitions*, Cambridge, Cambridge University Press, 467–492.

Örücü, E. (2004) Family Trees for Legal Systems: Towards a Contemporary Approach, in Van Hoecke, M. (ed.) *Epistemology and Methodology of Comparative Law*, Oxford and Oregon, Hart Publishing, 1–6.

Örücü, E. (2007) Developing Comparative Law, in Örücü, E. and Nelken, D. (eds), *Comparative Law: A Handbook*, London, Hart Publishing, 43–66.

Örücü, E. and D. Nelken (eds) (2007) *Comparative Law: A Handbook*, London, Hart Publishing.

Peters, A. and H. Schwenke (2000) Comparative Law beyond Post-modernism, *International Comparative Law Quarterly*, 49, 800–834.

Pettini, A. and A. Ventura (eds) (2014) *Quale crescita. La teoria economica alla prova della crisi*, Roma, L'Asino d'oro edizioni.

Ponthoreau, M.-C. (2005) Le droit comparé en question(s). Entre pragmatisme et outil épistémologique, *RIDC*, 1, 7–27.

Ponthoreau, M.-C. (2017) Le pluralism méthodologique dans l'enquête comparative à l'heure de la globalisation, in *Diritto pubblico comparato ed europeo*, 1, 53–68.

Riles, A. (2005) From Comparison to Collaboration: Experiments with a New Scholarity and Political Form, *Law and Contemporary Problems*, 78, 147–183.

Riles, A. (2007) *Rethinking the Masters of Comparative Law*, Lake Mary, FL, Vandeplas Publishing.

Romano, S. (1918) *L'ordinamento giuridico*, Pisa.

Ruskola, T. (2002) Legal Orientalism, *Michigan Law Review*, 101(1), 179–234.

Ruskola, T. (2013) *Legal Orientalism: China, the United States and Modern Law*, Cambridge, MA, Harvard University Press.

Sacco, R. (1991) Legal Formants: A Dynamic Approach to Comparative Law, *The American Journal of Comparative Law*, 39, 1–31.

Sacco, R. (2000) Il diritto indiano, in Gambaro, A. and Sacco, R. (eds), *Sistemi giuridici comparati*, Torino, pp. 485 et seq.

Said, E. (1978/2003) *Orientalism*, London, Penguin.

Sbailo', C. (2015) Diritto comparato e 'Primavera araba'. Spunti metodologici, in *Diritto pubblico comparato ed europeo*, 1, 247–253.

Scarciglia, R. (2016) *Metodi e comparazione giuridica*, Wolters Kluwer / Cedam.

Scarciglia, R. (2015) Diritto globale e metodologia comparativa: verso un approccio verticale?, in *Diritto pubblico comparato ed europeo*, 4, 1011–1026.

Schiff Berman, P. (2007) Global Legal Pluralism, *Southern California Law Review*, 80, 1155–1237.

Schiff Berman, P. (2009) The New Legal Pluralism, *Annual Review of Law & Social Science*, 5, 225 et seq.

Schiff Berman, P. (2012) *Global Legal Pluralism: A Jurisprudence of Law beyond Borders*, New York, Cambridge University Press.

Schiff Berman, P. (2013) Jurisgenerative Constitutionalism: Procedural Principles for Managing Global Legal Pluralism, *Indiana Journal of Global Legal Studies*, 20, 665–695.

Schiff Berman, P. (2015) Non-State Law Making through the Lens of Global Legal Pluralism, in Helfand, M.A. (ed.), *Negotiating State and Non-State Law: The Challenge of Global and Local Legal Pluralism*, New York, Cambridge University Press.

Sen, A. (2004) *La democrazia degli altri. Perché la libertà non è un'invenzione dell'Occidente*, Milano, Mondatori, trad. it. a cura di A. Piccato.

Sen, A. (2005) *Lo sviluppo è libertà*, Milano, Mondadori, trad. it. a cura di G. Rigamonti.

Sen, A. (2005) *L'altra India. La tradizione razionalistica e scettica alle radici della cultura indiana*, Milano, Mondatori, 2005, trad. it. a cura di G. Rigamonti.

Taylor, C. (1971) Interpretation and the Sciences of Man, *The Review of Metaphysics*, 25, 3–51.

Twining, W. (2007) Globalization and Comparative Law, in Örücü, E. and Nelken, D. (eds), *Comparative Law: A Handbook*, London, Hart Publishing, 69–90.

Valcke, C. (2012) Reflections on Comparative Law Methodology: Getting Inside Contract Law, in Adams, M. and Bomhoff, J. (eds), *Practice and Theory in Comparative Law*, Cambridge, Cambridge University Press, 22–48.

Van Hoecke, M. (2004) (ed.) *Epistemology and Methodology of Comparative Law*, Oxford and Portland, Hart Publishing.

Van Hoecke, M. (ed.) (2013) *Methodologies of Legal Research: Which Kind of Method for What Kind of Discipline?*, Oxford and Portland, Hart Publishing.

Van Hoecke, M. (2015) *Methodology of Comparative Legal Research*, paper at *Law and Method*, at http://rem.tijdschriften.budh.nl/tijdschrift/lawandmethod/2015/12/RENM-D-14-0000.

Van Hoecke, M. and M. Warrington (1998) Legal Cultures, Legal Paradigms and Legal Doctrine: Towards a New Model for Comparative Law, *The International and Comparative Law Quarterly*, 47(3), 1–41.

Vimborsati, A.C. (2008) *Teoria del costituzionalismo africano. Metodo-linguaggio-istituzioni*, Torino, Giappichelli Editore.

Yu, G. (2013) *Rethinking Law and Development*, New York, Routledge.

Zaumbansen, P. (2012) Carving out Typologies and Accounting for Differences across Systems: Towards a Methodology of Transnational Constitutionalism, in Rosenfeld, M. and Sajó, A. (eds), *The Oxford Handbook of Comparative Constitutional Law*, Oxford, Oxford University Press.

Zonca, E.V. (2016) *Cittadinanza sociale e diritti degli stranieri. Profili comparatistici*, Milano, Wolters Kluwer/CEDAM.

Zweigert, K. and H. Kötz (1987) *Introduction to Comparative Law*, 2nd revised edition (transl. T. Weir), Oxford, Clarendon Press.

3 Managing language in multicultural societies

Learning from the Indian experience

Domenico Amirante

Preventing conflicts and managing language in multicultural societies

In contemporary multicultural States language constitutes a potential (and in many cases an actual) source of conflict. The "linguistic divide", as a component of cultural identity, is manifestly linked to social diversity and often to ethnic conflicts, but States and public policies normally address it as a specific problem. Language conflicts arise from different causes: the imposition of a dominant (or leading) language in large States, the presence of historical linguistic minorities, the settlement of "new minorities" of migrants and more recently the advent of "superdiversity"[1] in globalized societies, to quote a few. Indeed, in recent decades the rise of social transformation phenomena resulting from globalization has concerned language in a very significant dimension. Today, the increase in linguistic diversity characterizes not only the historically multicultural and polyethnic States (the US, Canada, Switzerland, India, and China) but also most of the relatively small European States, affected by relentless waves of immigration.

Legal science cannot disregard such changes concerning the relationship between law, language and society in several respects, although it should be noted that the current acceleration of such phenomena only accentuates concealed dynamics, previously existing in the modern and in the contemporary State. In recent times, interesting research works regarding the relationship between "law and language" (touching various aspects, from the philological dimension to, philosophical, historical and sociological perspectives) have been developed. However, these studies have predominantly tried to analyse language as an "instrument of law" rather than as an element guiding and determining legal choices (thus, as a "subject" of the legal game). In the field of comparative law,

1 Socio-anthropological studies describe "superdivesity" as a phenomenon characterizing various social areas and specifically affecting the linguistic aspects. This would result in the need for a reversal of the traditional socio-linguistic approach because, according to these guidelines, the relevant analysis to the relationship between social and language phenomena today "piuttosto che lavorare in termini di omogeneità, stabilità e certezza dei confini, partono oggi da fenomeni quali la mobilità, la commistione, le dinamiche politiche ed il radicamento storico". J. BLOMMAERT and B. RAMPTON, *Language and Superdiversity*, in *Diversities*, Vol. 13, n. 2, 2011, p. 3.

for instance, while it is properly stated that "the language appears an essential tool in the process of knowledge ...",[2] the most significant contributions mainly concern the so-called "traductology". This is especially true in Europe where it is necessary to "manage" a common political and legal space (notably the European Union) where multilingualism appears to be a stable feature.

In this context, an area in which the language question requires more insights is certainly constitutional law. Until now, constitutional lawyers have addressed this issue primarily in terms of the protection of the so-called "language rights" with special focus on minorities. This is undoubtedly a relevant aspect, but it is not adequate to analyse comprehensively the role that the linguistic dimension has played in the processes of formation of the State and in its transformation.

In the occurrence of a tangible "crisis of the Nation-State", it is important to enquire if the acknowledgement of language pluralism can possibly broaden the social base of consensus and strengthen new forms of belonging of citizens to a constitutional perspective of an "open" and multicultural State. Starting from this hypothesis, constitutional comparative law can receive new inputs from some recent theoretical proposals that come from political science studies and from some relatively new Constitutions of the "Global South". I refer, on the one hand, to the State-Nation theory, which postulates the consolidation of a new model of State (an alternative to the Nation-State based on monocultural and political-institutional approach) "that recognizes and protects multiple socio-cultural identities but complementary".[3] On the other hand, interesting developments are coming from the galaxy of the post-colonial States, where frequently the State is no longer built on strictly monocultural bases but on multicultural and multilingual ones.[4]

Therefore, in the contemporary State, the language question is today one of the essential elements to address in practice the problems of coexistence in social contexts often characterized by strong diversifications (divided societies). This consideration will also help redefine the very concept of a multicultural State theoretically. To achieve this result it is necessary to adopt a methodological turn, by analysing the role played by language in the formation and in the transformation of the State (from the State-building process to constitutional reforms). In other words, the already existing literature on the "rights to language" (the legal guarantees granted to individuals or to linguistic communities) needs to be contextualized into the "national dimension".

In fact, the protection of language and the management of the language issue are highly dependent on the internal organization (i.e., from the territorial distribution of power within the State structure) and from the legal and constitutional ethos of national States. It is for this reason that the protection of languages in international and supranational context, while representing an inescapable point

2 B. POZZO, Traduzione giuridica, in *Digesto delle discipline privatistiche*, UTET, Torino, 2013, p. 709.

3 A. STEPAN, J. LINZ AND Y. YADAV, *Crafting State-Nations: India and Other Multinational Democracies*, The Johns Hopkins University Press, Baltimore, 2011.

4 On this aspect see E. DARIAN-SMITH, Postcolonial Theories of Law, in R. BANAKAR and M. TRAVERS (Eds.), *Law and Social Theory*, Hart, London, 2013, pp. 247–264 .

of comparison, cannot claim to represent the exclusive source for the solution of the language issues.

The "rights approach" must therefore necessarily be framed in an institutional perspective, paying attention to the constitutional and linguistic policies of the national States, and using a comparative approach to identify new paths for research and innovative constitutional practices.

Indian federalism: institutional tools to manage cultural and language conflicts

An interesting case to discuss, in the comparative perspective mentioned above, is contemporary Indian federalism, considering its successful policies of recognition of cultural identities that has allowed reducing conflicts between regional/ethnical and linguistic groups and the State. Such policies have not undermined the consolidation of an Indian identity; on the contrary, they have consolidated it. For Annamalai, the Indian language politics allows "an understanding of the nature of the Indian nation and its differences from the neighbouring countries, whose national integrity was broken or threatened on the issue of language dominance".[5] What is important to underline here is that India avoided the conflicts which have arisen in countries like Pakistan and Sri-Lanka, where language determined unrest and civil wars, by "managing linguistic nationalism through constitutional design".[6]

The Indian constitutional design rests on several elements: firstly on structural and institutional features ("asymmetric" and "dynamic" federalism) and secondly on a legal recognition of languages, and of the related language rights, in different ways. Evidently, the Indian situation is particularly intricate, because regional identities are intermingled with the religious factor and with social inequalities (backwardness and caste). This scenario was often considered unpropitious both to democracy and to the setting up a viable federal state. According to Bhattacharyya,[7] since the first post-independence years "the resurgence of regionalism in many parts of India baffled the observers of Indian politics and offered as the basis of prediction of the country's imminent balkanization (Harrison)".[8] Today the Indian federal model is rather considered a "success story".[9] Nevertheless the debate is still open between the advocates of Indian federalism, considering it an

5 E. ANNAMALAI, Politics Language in India, in P. R. BRASS (Ed.), *Routledge Handbook of South Asian Politics*, Routledge, London and New York, p. 213.

6 S. CHOUDHRY, Managing linguistic nationalism through constitutional design: Lessons from South Asia. *Int J Const Law* 7 (4), 2009, pp. 577–618, p. 577.

7 H. BHATTACHARYYA, *Federalism and regionalism in India. Institutional strategies and political accommodation of identity. Working Paper n. 27*, South Asia Institute, University of Heidelberg, 2005, p. 2.

8 H. BHATTACHARYYA, *Federalism and regionalism in India. Institutional strategies and political accommodation of identity. Working Paper n. 27, supra* note n. 7.

9 S. K. MITRA, Federalism' Success, in S. GANGULY, L. DIAMOND, M. F. PLATTNER (Eds.), *The State of India's Democracy*, The Johns Hopkins University Press, Baltimore, 2007, pp. 89–106.

example of successful political accommodation of identity[10] or a model for "containing ethnic conflict through internal reorganization",[11] and those who, on the basis of the Kashmir divide and other border problems, consider that "India as Nation-State remains a deeply contested fact".[12]

Introducing this topic, I would like to assert that, in the Indian constitutional design, federalism has represented, right from the independence period, a very effective technique for managing diversity and solving the related conflicts using democratic tools. As it has been noted, federal policies to face cultural and ethnic conflicts are strictly related to democracy "which stipulates that the political association or institution (whether statehood, sub-statehood, or tribal or regional councils) that ethnic groups may demand as the fulfilment of their identity needs … must be democratically based and formed by the consent of the 'ethnic' electorate and not to be something 'naturally' given".[13] The centrality of the democratic method and the far-sighted vision of the founding fathers, trying to combine a federal structure with a strong centre, explain the first structural feature: the "dynamic nature" of Indian federalism. As I have said in another context,[14] it has received many labels and definitions, from "quasi-federation" to "unitary state with subsidiary federal principles" (in the classical definition by Wheare), to "centralised federalism", all of them showing some discomfort with the traditional criteria of identification and classification of federal States. Without insisting too much on the nature of the Indian State, whose federal character has been authoritatively demonstrated by D. D. Basu,[15] a realistic definition could be "a federal State with centripetal tendencies", indicating the multiple possibilities of the federal system to function alternatively as a more decentralized or centralized system, according to the evolution of historical conditions. This view is also in tune with the idea of federalism as a continuous bargaining process between different levels of government ("flexible federalism" in the definition of B. Arora).[16]

Coming back to the language issue, we must underline a quite distinctive feature of the Indian Union: its attitude to cultural and social diversity as the central issue upon which to build the entire constitutional architecture. Isolated institutional arrangements to cope with cultural minorities have been taken in Western countries even before the period of elaboration of the Indian Constitution, but the discourse on multiculturalism as a doctrine and an articulate State policy has developed quite

10 H. BHATTACHARYYA, Federalism and Competing Nations in India, in M. BURGESS AND J. PINDER (Eds.), *Multinational Federations*, Routledge, London and New York, 2007, pp. 50–67.

11 M. CHADDA, Integration through internal reorganization: containing ethnic conflict in India, *The Global Review of Ethnopolitics*, 2 (1), 2002, pp. 44–61.

12 G. SINGH, Critical reflections on celebrating success: a response to Maya Chadda, *The Global Review of Ethnopolitics*, 2 (2), 2003, p. 52.

13 H. BHATTACHARYYA, Multiculturalism in Contemporary India, *International Journal on Multicultural Societies* (IJMS), 5 (2), 2003, p.158.

14 D. AMIRANTE, *India. Si governano così*, Il Mulino, Bologna, 2007, p. 63.

15 D. DAS BASU, *Comparative Federalism*, Wadhwa, New Delhi, 2008, pp. 144–145.

16 B. ARORA and D. V. VERNEY (eds.), *Multiple Identities in a Single State: Indian Federalism in a Comparative Perspective*, Konark Publishers, New Delhi, 1995.

recently, initially in the West and then in the international debate.[17] This is why the Indian Constitution, as noted, can be said to be a multicultural document "in the sense of providing for political and institutional measures for the recognition and accommodation of the country's diversity",[18] but it should be defined, in my view, as an "anticipatory multicultural Constitution".

This distinctive character of the Indian Constitution and polity is claimed by several Indian scholars contributing to the international debate on the topic, with different approaches. From one side, G. Mahajan proudly asserts "at a time when Western liberalism advocated neutrality and difference-blind approach, India acknowledged the rights of minorities and valued cultural diversity".[19] From a slightly more critical angle, Subrata K. Mitra speaks of fortuitous or "fuzzy" multiculturalism. According to this author the Indian State, in the attempt to combine *sarva darma samabhava* (equal attitude towards religion) and *dharma nirapekshata* (religious neutrality), "made effort to acknowledge the salience of individual rights to freedom of religion and equality before the law, and group rights to cultural and religious practices in its charter of fundamental rights".[20]

In this perspective, we can describe the Indian multicultural approach as a mixed and ongoing multiculturalism based on both the recognition of community and group rights in a democratic constitutional framework and a peculiar structure of the State based on asymmetrical federalism and grassroots self-government. In the following pages I will discuss the Indian approach to the language question, describing initially the institutional federal organization (namely the formation of "linguistic States"), and furthermore the recognition of language rights in the fundamental charter.

Preventing language conflicts through institutional arrangements: the linguistic States

Coming to the "dynamic" aspect of Indian federalism, we must consider the successful constitutional design of inclusion of cultural identities through a cautious and cooperative use of institutional instruments, such as the recognition of languages and the concession of different forms of autonomy (namely of Statehood) to linguistic minorities.

I have already mentioned how relevant the linguistic issue is in contemporary India, both for the choice of the official language of the Union and for the

17 On this aspects it is sufficient to refer to a recent overview by W. KYMLICKA, Liberal Multiculturalism: Western Models, Global Trends and Asian Debates, in W. KIMLYCKA, B. HE (Eds.), *Multiculturalism in Asia*, OUP, Oxford, 2005, pp. 22–55.

18 H. BHATTACHA RYYA, *supra* note 13, p. 152.

19 G. MAHAJAN, Indian Exceptionalism or Indian Model: Negotiating Cultural Diversity and Minority Rights in a Democratic Nation-State, in W. KIMLYCKA, B. HE (Eds.), *supra* note 17, p. 288.

20 S. K. MITRA, *Constitutional design, democratic vote counting and India's fortuitous multiculturalism, Working Paper n. 4*, South Asia Institute, University of Heidelberg, 2001, p. 7.

relation among the Union and its member States, considering the presence of numerous linguistic minorities scattered over a vast territory. The focus on the linguistic challenges has its roots in the *humus* of South Asian cultures[21] and in the gentrification of the Indian civilization – as thoroughly described by the literature on these topics.[22] We must consider also the historical role of language in the process of building regional and national identities and of shaping the Indian political and social structures.[23]

The language question acquired a central position in the movement for independence since the end of the nineteenth century. Then, the Constituent Assembly[24] held a fervent debate that ended up with the approval (for just one vote) of *Hindi* with the *Devanagari* alphabet as the "official language of the Union" (art. 343 of the Constitution). Together with Hindi, other 14 official languages were added as listed in the Eighth Annex ("Scheduled languages", extended to 22 languages now). English was not in this list; nonetheless it had to represent the official language for official purposes of the Union for a period of 15 years (art. 343). This deadline was then extended *sine die* by the Official Language Amendment Act of 1967 and therefore it results still today an "auxiliary" official language. The Indian Constitution recognizes the possibility for each Member State to adopt one or more languages for official purposes, by choosing among the official languages and the one spoken (literally "used") in the region (art. 345). Practically, the constituent Fathers of India acknowledged territorial rights to a group of minority languages and assigned a sort of status of *primus inter pares* to Hindi, without giving in to a pragmatic use of English.

These choices reflect a profound awareness of the political establishment of the time but, more broadly, of the Indian political culture, that was conscious of the importance of the language issue within the architecture of a complex social structure in a multicultural context ("a composite society" as defined in the constituent age). Incidentally, in 1937 Nehru already supported with strength that "our great provincial languages are no dialects or vernaculars, as the ignorant

21 A. CONSOLARO, *Cultura linguistica, politica linguistica e democrazia in India*, in D. AMIRANTE (Ed.), *"Altre" democrazie. Problemi e prospettive del consolidamento democratico nel sub-continente indiano*, FrancoAngeli, Milano, 2010, p. 37.

22 See among others, K. S. SINGH, S. MANOHARAN, *People of India: Languages and Scripts (Anthropological Survey of India)*, Oxford University Press, Delhi, 1997; C.A. FERGUSON, J.J. GUMPERZ (Eds.), *Linguistic Diversity in South Asia: Studies in Regional, Social and Functional Variation*, Indiana University Research Center in Anthropology, Folklore and Linguistics, Bloomington, Ind. 1960; C. SHAPIRO, H.F. SCHIFFMAN, *Language and Society in South Asia*, Motilar Banarsidas, New Delhi, 1981. For an historical perspective, M. DESHPANDE., *Socio Linguistic Attitudes in India: An Historical Reconstruction*, Ann Arbor, Karoma Publishers, 1979.

23 On linguistic policies in India, V.C. GROFF, *Status and Acquisition Planning and Linguistic Minorities in India*, working paper presented at Conference on Language development, language revitalization and multilingual education in minority communities in Asia, 6–8 November 2003, Bangkok, Thailand, www.sil.org/asia/ldc/parallel_papers/cynthia_groff.pdf (last access June 2017).

24 R. GUHA, *India after Gandhi: The History of the World's Largest Democracy*, Picador India, London, 2008, p. 107.

sometimes call them. They are ancient languages with a rich inheritance, each spoken by many millions of people, each tied up inextricably with the life and culture and ideas of the masses as well as the upper classes".[25]

However, the leaders of the Congress Party (as most of the Indian political class) recognized the high political content of the different languages present in the country and the difficulty of creating a unified and cohesive State. At that time, like today, the language issue could not be reduced "simply to the problem of language planning, policy, and programmes, but should take into account the ideological power of language(s) and its various forms of domination and subordination".[26]

This is why, globally, the Constitution reserves to the language issue more than 10 articles and an entire Schedule (notably articles 120, 210, and 343 to 351, plus the Eight Schedule). This also demonstrates how important the linguistic aspects are for the organization of a multicultural State.[27]

In our perspective, the most interesting Indian policy in the field of language politics is the recognition of the cultural and political relevance of regional languages, through the creation of the so-called "linguistic States", which characterized the process of territorial allocation of power within the Union since the mid-1950s. Concerning the number of States or the criteria to legitimate their creation, the Constituent Assembly did not take any operational decision but established a clear procedure for the incorporation of new territories into the Union or for the creation of new States within the Union itself. Article 2 disposes that a law approved by the Union Parliament can admit new States acquired from outside the territory of the Union.[28] Article 3 empowers the Union Parliament to carve out a new State by separation of a part of territory of an "old" State or to merge two or more States.[29] It also clarifies that

25 R. GUHA, *India after Gandhi: The History of the World's Largest Democracy, supra* note 24, p. 181.

26 A. SARANGI, *Introduction: Language and Politics in India*, A. SARANGI (Ed.), *Languages and Politics in India*, Oxford India Paperbacks, New Delhi, 2010, p. 2. According to Sarangi, the choice to pluralize the official languages can be explained on the basis of considerations of both opportunities and identity. Under the first profile, the author underlines how the language communities without recognition of their language in the Eighth Annex of the Indian Constitution do lose a number of economic, political and social opportunities (for example, the inability to use their own language in public competitions). Concerning the second profile, Sarangi notes that not being recognized linguistically may involve isolation of the communities themselves, deprived of a channel of dialogue with the political level, whether state or national.

27 Articles 343 to 351 address the issue of "Official Language": *Language of the Union* (Chapter I), *Regional Languages* (Chapter II), *Language of the Supreme Court, High Courts, etc.* (Chapter III), *Special Directives* (Chapter IV). Adding to that, artt. 29–30 on "Cultural Rights" and art. 120 on the language of the Parliament.

28 The text of article 2 (entitled "Admission or establishment of new States") establishes that: "Parliament may by law admit into the Union, or establish, new States on such terms and conditions as it thinks fit". Under this article Sikkim was admitted as a state in Indian union on 26 April 1975.

29 According to article 3: "Parliament may by law- (a) form a new State by separation of territory from any State or by uniting two or more States or parts of States or by

> no Bill for the purpose shall be introduced in either House of Parliament except on the recommendation of the President and unless, where the proposal contained in the Bill affects the area, boundaries or name of any of the States, the Bill has been referred by the President to the Legislature of that State for expressing its views thereon within such period as may be specified in the reference or within such further period as the President may allow and the period so specified or allowed has expired.[30]

Article 4 (2) specifies that none of such laws "shall be deemed to be an amendment of this Constitution for the purposes of article 368". Summing up, this procedure gives the final word for the creation of new States to the Union Parliaments, but involves both the President of the Union (that has the exclusive power of making the initial proposal) and the legislative Assemblies of the State (or the States) involved in the territorial variations. The decision will not be taken with the special majorities required for the constitutional amendments (art. 368), but will follow the rules of the ordinary legislative process, making the recognition of the recognition of the new linguistic state a more viable (although sometimes very long) procedure.

The provisions written by the constituent fathers represent the beginning of a process that a few years later would bring a territorial reorganization of the internal boundaries of India according to linguistic differences. One of the most convincing periodizations of this territorial and political reorganization articulates the process of the creation of the Indian States into three successive "waves" (1952–56; 1971–1987; 1999–2000 to the present day).[31] For M. Chadda "each phase was guided by a master theme". Notably in the first wave, the coherence of India as a State and its territorial cohesion were at stake, while in the second phase "the twin problems of governance and security shaped the rival perspectives of what the India federation should be".[32] The third phase, stretching until today, is centred less on the federal perspective and more on various economic and political considerations about the "weight" of territories and about the political parties' territorial map.

In my opinion, the most important challenge for the Indian Union, after the partition from Pakistan, was the integration of the Dravidian region (the Southern States and Provinces, covering one fifth of the Union territory), having a common culture, similar languages and a shared historical tradition. This challenge was addressed by the creation of "linguistic States", realized by the State Reorganization Act in 1956, based on the work of the State Reorganization Commission (SRC). This Commission concluded its proceedings in 1955 with the publication of a

uniting any territory to a part of any State; (b) increase the area of any State; (c) diminish the area of any State; (d) alter the boundaries of any State; (e) alter the name of any State."

30 Article 3 of the Constitution.

31 M.CHADDA, Integration through internal reorganization: containing ethnic conflict in India, *supra* note 11, p. 45

32 *Supra*.

Report proposing the division of India in 14 States, based on "ethno-linguistic communities". The leading idea of the reform, approved by the Parliament with the State Reorganization Act of 1956, was to balance the recognition of cultural identities with a good governance of the States and the safeguard of the unity of the Nation. For these reasons, the newly designed States were not mono-linguistic (although they all contained a linguistic majority) and insisted on territories of large dimensions. According to Chadda "the first reorganization created a unique design for governance" able to handle Indian heterogeneity. The main aspect of this design was the setting up of a system of "interlocking balances" between the diverse nationalities based on three features. The first one implied the corroboration of the role of the Central State as an "impartial pan-Indian agency", through strong constitutional powers. The second one brought the establishment of a "layered order" (through decentralization within the member States). The third feature was the reinforcement of regional autonomy at the Member State level, where "the central government was forced to yield linguistic States that would thereafter organize politics on the basis of their distinctive cultural and political identity".[33]

The creation of a relevant political and institutional space at the Member State level is probably the most important result of this first reform because it paved the way the transformation of the Indian political system through the emergence of the "regional parties" as political units capable to influence even federal politics. From a legal point of view, it demonstrates the viability of the constitutional procedural arrangements (article 2–4 mentioned above) to manage the claims.

The second and third waves of reorganization, resulting in the present 29 States and 7 Union Territories, confirmed substantially this trend, although they took place in different political periods and contexts. Some critical voices assert that, after the first period, the successive waves of creation of new States just used the language question to pursue other interests, mainly political or even electoral benefits for ruling parties (the Congress, or BJP). In other words the creation of new States was due "to the conjunction of political processes unfolding according to different yet often overlapping timetables".[34]

We cannot comment on these developments here, but the lesson to learn from this experience is that flexible constitutional procedures for internal reorganization are able to play a crucial role in managing conflicts in a very diverse multicultural State by a gradual and piecemeal recognition of cultural minorities through institutional bargaining.

Preventing language conflicts through rights

Within the Indian Constitution, the recognition of language rights to individuals and communities goes along with the institutional and territorial recognition of languages, mentioned in the previous paragraph. In general terms the

33 M. CHADDA, *supra*, pp. 49–50.

34 L. TILLIN, *Remapping India: New States and Their Political Origins*, C. Hurst & Co., London, 2013, p. 200.

Constitution aims at granting the broadest linguistic pluralism, taking into consideration the number of languages and dialects currently spoken, but, at the same time, it targets the "linguistic cohesion" though the use of an official language. According to a widespread classification of language rights, what is mostly guaranteed by the Indian Constitution are the so-called language rights of the first species (guarantees for the use minority languages in public documents and trials, if so required) and of the second species (guarantees of a public space for minority language groups, through the recognition and enhancement of their languages).[35]

The declaration of the official language (art. 343) opens the section dealing with the language question. The (contested) choice of Hindi as the official language cannot be depicted as a success, both from the standpoint of official purposes and for its diffusion as a common language among the linguistic communities of the Union. Although solemn proclamations were made for the indigenous languages, today English is still in place as the auxiliary official language. Practically, in the institutional and political Indian life, at the Union level mostly, English is the most spoken language and its use in the Parliament and in the Courts is required by the Constitution (art. 348). A long debate has been going on about the reasons that hindered the possibility for Hindi to affirm itself as the unifying language of the whole Indian territory. Here it is important to stress that the safeguard tools provided by the Constitution were not sufficient to reach that goal, including the institutional structure set out in article 344. This provision establishes two different bodies, a Parliamentary Commission to represent the official languages of the Union and a Commission to investigate and assess proposals for supporting the diffusion of Hindi and the reduction of the use of English. Both of them have proved inefficient up to the present day.

Highly interesting are the provisions concerning regional languages that represent a key element in Indian federalism. The Constitution grants member States the possibility to adopt one or more spoken languages inside their territory as official languages within the State (article 345). It is one of the privileges that the Member State have used extensively, fostering the organization and the establishment of sizable "regional" political parties. Article 347 guarantees a broader protection of language and minority pluralism, inside the member States, allowing the possibility that a language spoken by a section of the population could be recognized as a further official language, if the Member State files a formal request to the President of the Union.

With regard to the inter-State communications and the Union–States communications, the Union official language is used. Currently, the member States still communicate among themsleves using English (the de facto official language), but the Constitution provides a possibility to sign bilateral treaties allowing member States to use Hindi.

35 G. POGGESCHI, I diritti linguistici in India fra pluralismo, nazionalismo e pragmatismo, in D. AMIRANTE, C. DECARO, E. PFÖESTL (Eds.), *La Costituzione dell'Unione Indiana. Profili introduttivi*, Giappichelli, Torino, 2013, p. 169.

Finally, it is important to remember that linguistic issues are not limited to the use of the official languages but include education and more generally the safeguarding of minorities. There are currently hundreds of local mother-tongue languages and dialects still alive and spoken and these needs have to be addressed by the public institutions. For example, many tribal languages are severely disadvantaged when it comes to being acknowledged in the Schedule Eight, because they do not have a proper alphabet or a written form. Around 30 million people, prevalently with tribal origins, express themselves using non-offical languages that are not taught at school, do not have any sort of recognition at an administrative level and are excluded by the contemporary media and cultural scene.[36] Today, some of the States have up to 20% of their overall population (*Bengali* in Assam, *Garo* in Meghalaya or *Dogri* in Jammu and Kashmir). In this situation, it is not suitable to express, at a national level, an univocal criterion for the selection of official languages, because it must refer to criteria that diverge from one State to another.[37] It is not surprising that such a territorial reorganization fostered the growth of regional parties that could have great influence at the Union level.[38] It is hard separating *Urdu* and *Punjabi* linguistic claims from the conflicts that arise in the related communities, specifically Muslims and Sikhs against the majority Hindus.[39] Urdu as well as *Sindhi* represent nowadays languages that are included in Schedule Eight but that are not able to assert themselves as official languages in any Indian State. Those who speak these languages (about 60 million people) constitute what are defined as "absolute minorities". We have also to consider 90 million Indian citizens, belonging to "relative minorities", whose mother tongue is recognized in a State that is not the same where they reside.[40]

The Constitution does not provide a detailed definition of "language minority", but some criteria for the assessment of the status of a minority have been identified by the Supreme Court in its case-law and conform to those used to assess the status of minorities in general. For example, in *D.A.V. College Etc. v. State of Punjab*, the Court specifies that not only the religious minorities but also the linguistic ones must be determined on a case by case ratio, adding that in the circumstance of a State law, the minorities are determined based on the State's population itself.[41]

These considerations are similar to the elements used to define and recognize *Scheduled* and *Non-Scheduled* languages to which the *Official* and *Non-Official* languages are added at a State level (art. 343). Such an articulated system for the

36 T. BENEDIKTER, The protection of linguistic rights in India: India's language policy toward linguistic minorities, in *European Yearbook of Minority Issues*, 8, 2009, p. 465.

37 This seems to be the conclusion reached by T. BENEDIKTER, The protection of linguistic rights in India: India's language policy toward linguistic minorities, *supra*, p. 461.

38 D. AMIRANTE, *Nation building through constitutionalism: lessons from the Indian experience*, in *Hong Kong Law Journal* 42 (1), 2012, pp. 23–42.

39 G. POGGESCHI, *I diritti linguistici in India fra pluralismo, nazionalismo e pragmatismo*, *supra* note 35, p. 234.

40 T. BENEDIKTER, The protection of linguistic rights in India: India's language policy toward linguistic minorities, *supra* note 36, p. 456.

41 On this point, see A. CONSOLARO, Cultura linguistica, politica linguistica e democrazia in India, *supra* note 21, p. 5.

acknowledgement of languages has created, in the opinion of some Indian academics, a hierarchical and pyramidal structure of languages and dialects in India, according to their respective socio-economic importance.[42] As stressed by Arora and Mukherjee "asking ethno-linguistic groups to prove that they were important enough to be institutionally recognised" may not have been the best method to promote national cohesion.[43] Nonetheless, N. Chandhoke underlined the fact that such a counter-productive risk for national unity did not materialize for different reasons.[44] The main reason was probably the responsible behaviour of the governments of the Union, which demonstrated a clear sensibility towards linguistic political movements, by establishing institutions that reflect the cultural diversity. This permitted also the development of bilingualism, very common nowadays in India, whose affirmation can be considered as a consequence of the acknowledgement of linguistic pluralism.[45]

Comparative conclusions: suggestions from a post-colonial experience

The Indian experience of prevention and management of language conflicts, illustrated above, demonstrates the viability of a pluralist and multicultural approach to face diversity in contemporary societies. It also underlines the preference for a structural and constitutional approach, through territorial design and institutional bargaining, illustrated by the creation of the "linguistic States". In India, the recognition of linguistic pluralism through the "language rights" approach has played only a subsidiary role, showing the inadequacy of the traditional liberal approach to the language question. In spite of globalization and of the undeniable "crisis of the State", constitutional arrangements and institutional bargaining within the framework of the State (declined as a multicultural State) represent the main solution to face language conflicts and, more broadly, cultural conflicts. Choudhry underlines the success of the linguistic federalism, stating that: "from the perspective of constitutional design, the Indian solution is the desirable one".[46] In this area, the Indian experience is able to offer many hints and suggestions to both the Asian and the global debate on multicultural constitutionalism. An important recognition of this role is offered by Kymlicka, asserting that India is not only "one of the few countries outside the West to have voluntarily federalized to accommodate minority nationalist claims for autonomy", but also "seems to

42 More in A. ABBI, Vanishing diversities and submerging Identities: An Indian case, in A. SARANGI (Ed.), *Language and Politics in India, supra* note 26, pp. 303–304.

43 B. Arora and N. Mukherjee (Eds.), Introduction, in *Federalism in India: Origins and Development*, Vikas, New Delhi, 1992, p. 9.

44 N. CHANDHOKE, Negotiating Linguistic Diversity in Democratic States: A Comparative Study of India and the USA, in K. S. BAJPAI (Ed.), *Democracy and Diversity: India and the American Experience*, Oxford University Press, New Delhi, 2007, p. 126.

45 N. CHANDHOKE, Negotiating Linguistic Diversity in Democratic States: A Comparative Study of India and the USA, *supra*, pp. 126–127.

46 S. CHOUDHRY,*supra* note 6 p. 614

have had much less difficulty accepting the principle of asymmetry than many Western multinational federations".[47]

In conclusion, it must be recalled that in the liberal State the language question has often been hidden under the veil of national sovereignty. The liberal state postulated in fact a sort of "monolingualism" that was functional to the internal cohesion of the State through a "simplified" national identity. But such an homologation policy proves inadequate for the evolution of the democratic State, in particular due to the intensification of its multicultural composition. As it was rightly pointed out, "cultural pluralism determines today an institutional organization which can be defined as the antithesis of the Nation-State ... and of the monolingual State".[48]

The language question therefore assumes a central role in the process of emergence of the multicultural State, considered as an evolution of the democratic and social State. In this perspective, the recognition of the multilingual components of the State can be a resource of great importance, because of the objective nature of the linguistic phenomenon. In other words, language can play the role of a medium of communication between the various social groups present in the multicultural State. Through the recognition of minority languages and the diversified use of a vehicular language, a balanced use of the linguistic discipline can contribute to the construction of a "constitutional identity", able to overcome the potential conflicts between linguistic communities in a multicultural State.

In this perspective, we should not underestimate the possibility of using the pragmatic Indian model in other multilingual contexts (both in national and supranational situations). This involves, however, for comparative law, the overcoming of barriers considered until now insurmountable, such as the postulated gap between the Western tradition and post-colonial legal experiences. This implies, also, embracing the perspective of a "methodological pluralism", a vital tool to confront the challenges of "hyperdiversity" of our contemporary society.

In the perspective of the multicultural State, we must consider that "given the massive mobilization over identity the world over, democrats have increasingly come to terms with categories that they have spurned as pre-modern, such as religion, caste, gender and language".[49] Thus, the Indian experience teaches us that democrats have "to apprehend that democracy in complex societies is not about the *transcendence* or *bracketing* but about the *negotiation* of difference".[50]

47 W. KYMLICA, *supra* note 17, pp. 39–40.

48 R. TONIATTI, Pluralismo e autodeterminazione delle identità negli ordinamenti culturalmente composti: osservazioni in tema di cittadinanza culturale, in E. CECCHERINI, M. COSULICH (Eds.), *Tutela delle identità culturali, diritti linguistici e istruzione: dal Trentino-Alto Adige/Südtirol alla prospettiva comparata*, CEDAM, Padova, 2012, p. 12.

49 N. CHANDHOKE, *supra* note 44, p. 142.

50 *Idem*, p. 143.

Part II

Articulating conflict

4 De-religionising religion

The European Court of Human Rights and the conflict of definition

Kyriaki Pavlidou[1]

Introduction

On 28 February 2005 the cover of *Time* magazine featured a portrait of the *Mona Lisa* covered in veils under the title "Europe's Identity Crisis".[2] More than ten years after, this article is added to the long-standing debate revolving around the issue of identity and religious symbols in Europe. From politicians using aggressive slogans such as "Multiculturalism is dead"[3] and mouthing platitudes about how Muslims have led to the weakening of a clear, collective cultural identity[4] to the

1 The present chapter is the outcome of part of the research conducted with the support of the Van Calker Scholarship of the Swiss Institute of Comparative Law. I thank the Director of the SICL Professor Dr. iur. Christina Schmid and the Vice-Director Dr. Lukas Heckendorn Urscheler, my mentor Ms. Johanna Fournier, and all the scientific staff at the Institute for their feedback on my paper, as it was presented during the *Rencontres informelles de l'Institut suisse de droit comparé*. Sincere thanks to Mrs. Christiane Serkis for her endless and much appreciated support at the Institute. I am indebted to Dr. Kyriaki Topidi, Senior Lecturer and Associate Director of the Center for Comparative Constitutional Law and Religion at the University of Lucerne for her support, insightful remarks and all the constructive talks on various drafts of this chapter. An earlier version of the paper was presented during the UNILU Workshops on Global Approaches to Law and Culture of the Network of Transnational Doctoral Research; many thanks to all the participants for their comments and lively discussions. Special thanks to Dr. Liav Orgad for his valuable comments and criticisms on the final draft of the paper. I greatly benefited from the comments on previous versions by Professor Drucilla Cornell and Professor Susanna Mancini, each of whom has considerably inspired me on this topic. Responsibility for the views presented herein rests solely with the author.

2 Atakav, A., 2007. Mona Lisa in Veils: Cultural Identity, Politics, Religion and Feminism in Turkey. *Feminist Theology*, 16(1), p. 11.

3 See the reference in Augenstein, D., 2012. Religious Pluralism and National and Constitutional Traditions in Europe Chapter 11, pp. 261–280 in Zucca, L., Ungureanu, C. (eds), *Law, State and Religion in the New Europe: Debates and Dilemmas*. 1st ed. Cambridge University Press, p. 264.

4 Wintour P., 2011. David Cameron Tells Muslim Britain: Stop Tolerating Extremists. *The Guardian*. [online] Available at: https://www.theguardian.com/politics/2011/feb/05/david-cameron-muslim-extremism [Accessed 16 July 2012].

actual measures taken, such as the banning of the burqa in France and Italy,[5] the identity question emerges as one of preeminent concerns in the European public sphere.

The contribution of the European Court of Human Rights[6] appears to be critical in this direction. The chapter analyses in juxtaposition some highly disputable religious symbols cases, which were brought before the ECtHR, with a particular focus on the *Sahin v. Turkey*,[7] the *Dahlab v. Switzerland*[8] and the *Lautsi v. Italy*[9] cases. There is a vast amount of academic literature written on these decisions. The present analysis offers a different reading, by asking the question about these cases as a question of identity and legitimacy. The headscarf controversies around Europe as well as the crucifix case in Italy, all within public educational establishments, serve as the point of departure and as the substrate throughout the analysis. The significance of these cases lies in their construction of the subject,[10] which is demarcated by competing notions of collective identities through religious means.

It is beyond the scope of this analysis to make a comprehensive assessment of the concept of subjectivity or to engage with the problematic of the ill-defined and fragmented notion of the 'legal subject' under the mainstream positivistic understanding. For one, the 'legal subject', in traditional positivistic terms, is usually equated with individuality[11] and hence with non-objective parameters and is considered to stand outside the scope of law and to be excluded from jurisprudential study. The analysis takes issue with this premise and argues that the cases at hand evaluate these parameters in order to construct and define individuality. 'Subjectivity' and the 'subject' are understood in this sense as referring to the individual and individuality in a critical, inter-subjective manner. The analysis does not engage with the debate over the identity of the subject at a constitutional level either. It addresses the identity of the 'constitutional subject',[12] but does not go into depths about the background or justification of this term.

The chapter examines which legal doctrines and arguments the Strasbourg Court uses; how the Court employs these in constructing the identity of the subject; what type of identity is the subject constructed into, and why this type of identity does not fall within the purview of the legitimate aim concerned. First, there is a

5 Nussbaum, M., 2012. *The New Religious Intolerance: Overcoming the Politics of Fear in an Anxious Age*. 1st ed. Belknap Press Harvard University, p. 104.
6 ECtHR or Strasbourg Court or Court hereinafter.
7 *Sahin v. Turkey* [2004] Application No. 44774/98 (ECtHR).
8 *Dahlab v Switzerland* [2001] Application no. 42393/98 (ECtHR).
9 *Lautsi v. Italy* [2009] Application No. 30814/06 (ECtHR, Chamber); Lautsi v. Italy [2011] Application no. 30814/06 (ECtHR, Grand Chamber).
10 Vakulenko, A., 2007. Islamic Dress in Human Rights Jurisprudence: A Critique of Current Trends. *Human Rights Law Review*, 7(4), p. 739.
11 Balkin, J., 1993. Understanding Legal Understanding: The Legal Subject and the Problem of Legal Coherence. *The Yale Law Journal*, 103(1), p. 3.
12 For a comprehensive analysis see Rosenfeld, M., 2009. *The Identity of the Constitutional Subject: Selfhood, Citizenship, Culture, and Community*. 1st ed. London: Routledge.

brief overview of the facts and the Court's rulings. Thereafter, the chapter explores in more detail the judgments delivered by the ECtHR and identifies certain patterns, which are common in the assessed cases. In light of the parallels drawn between the cases in question, the analysis seeks to illustrate an incoherent approach of the Court in delivering its judgments.

It stands against an essentialist approach[13] that conceives the identity of the subject as natural, homogeneous and motionless elevating religion as the exclusive constituent of it. By contrast, a more contextual and relational understanding of an identity that is socially constructed and is always in transformation is put forward[14] and an anti-essentialist view is adopted and strengthened. In assessing the legitimacy challenges that arise, the discussion focuses on the paradox of liberal anti-pluralism in the cases' rationale. The latter echoes the dialectic between law and culture as an identity conflict expressed in the dualistic terms of 'us-versus-them'. It further reflects on the process of constructing and defining the subject, as being a conflict between power and agency. The analysis is interested in the ideological and legal concealment of the subject[15] within the terms of their social construction, whose content is formatted by a certain understanding of the role and reason of the state. This results in the positioning of the individual in relation to the state within a hierarchical and asymmetrical relationship and further translates in the construction and imposition of static, predetermined, essentialist conceptions of the identity of the subject under the seal of constitutional protection. In this respect, the chapter further looks at state neo-liberalism in the context of the specific cases by drawing parallels between the underlying power structure of the neo-liberal state and the concept of unsocial sociability that grips the fabric of the society.

The Gioconda in veils crystallizes the *Mona*-lithic and polarized identities that shape today's identity talks in the intercultural discourse in Europe. This chapter stands opposite such monolithic interpretations and defends the formation of a legitimate identity of the subject in terms of both process and substance, in conformity with the principle of respect to diversity and to individual autonomy premised on equal dignity and value.

13 Ringelheim J., 2002. Identity Controversies before the European Court of Human Rights. *German Law Journal*, 3(7), p. 2.

14 Gutwirth, S., 2008. Beyond Identity? *IDIS – Identity in the Information Society*, 1(1), p. 130 [online] Available at: http://works.bepress.com/serge_gutwirth/15/ [Accessed 12 June 2012].

15 For an insightful analysis see Balkin (1993) and particularly p. 4, which reads: '… our inquiry into the contributions of 'the legal subject' does not imply that the object of legal interpretation has no existence independent of a particular subject's comprehension of it. Our subjectivity contributes to, but does not create the cultural objects we comprehend. This is the dialectic between the subjective and objective aspects of social life – between individual thought, belief, and action on the one hand, and language, ideology, culture, conventions, and social institutions on the other. Culture and cultural objects have meaning only when they are understood by subjects, but their meaning is not dependent on the view of any particular subject.'

The selected cases of the Strasbourg Court

The facts and the judgments

The cases at hand concern the right of the applicants to display religious garments in the public sphere. When referring to the headscarf jurisprudence the focus turns to two of the most prominent and much cited cases, that of *Sahin v. Turkey*[16] and *Dahlab v. Switzerland.*[17] In brief, in the *Sahin* case the Court upheld the ban of the headscarf in Turkish universities, contrary to the claims of the applicant, who argued that the ban interfered with her right to manifest her religious beliefs; the ban was held to be prescribed by law, had the legitimate aim of protecting the rights and freedoms of others and was necessary in a democratic society.[18] Prior to this, in *Dahlab v. Switzerland*, a teacher in a state-run primary school converted to Islam and started wearing the headscarf while teaching. After a lapse of five years during which she wore the garment with no complaints recorded, the Swiss Director General of Public Education demanded that she cease wearing the headscarf at work. Mrs. Dahlab refused to comply with the direction issued and complained in domestic courts about the school authorities' decision to prohibit her from wearing the religious garb. The decision was eventually upheld by the Swiss Federal Court and was subsequently brought by Mrs. Dahlab before the ECtHR where the Court declared the application inadmissible holding that the teacher's right of Article 9(2) of the European Convention on Human Rights[19] to manifest her religious beliefs "was outweighed by the state's interest in protecting the rights and freedoms of others and preserving public order and safety".[20]

In the infamous case *Lautsi v. Italy*,[21] that lasted nearly a decade, the applicant opposed the fact that her children had to attend a public school where all classrooms had a crucifix on the walls and as a member of the Italian Union of Atheists, Agnostics and Rationalists[22] she considered the presence of crucifixes contrary to the philosophical convictions by which she wished to bring up her children. The applicant complained in domestic courts, though unsuccessfully, and took her case to the ECtHR. Before the Strasbourg Court Mrs. Lautsi claimed that the display of the crucifix in the educational arena was held in breach of Article 9 in conjunction with Article 2 Protocol 1 of the ECHR. In her argumentation she claimed that the display of the cross in public schools interfered with her right of freedom of religion and infringed upon the principle of secularism[23] by placing

16 *Sahin v. Turkey* [2004].
17 *Dahlab v Switzerland* ibid [2001].
18 Marshall, J., 2006. Freedom of Religious Expression and Gender Equality: Sahin v Turkey. *Modern Law Review*, 69(3), p. 453.
19 ECHR hereinafter.
20 Calo, Z. R., 2011, Pluralism, Secularism and the European Court of Human Rights. *Journal of Law and Religion*, 26. *SSRN Electronic Journal*, p. 104.
21 *Lautsi v. Italy* [2009].
22 Lobeira, P., Cristóbal P., 2011. Veils, Crucifixes and Public Sphere: What Kind of Secularism? Rethinking Neutrality in a Post-Secular Europe, p.2.
23 *Lautsi v. Italy* [2009] para.32.

Christianity in a "privileged position".[24] On the other hand, the Italian Government maintained that the presence of crucifixes in classrooms was "natural"[25] and necessary among the other equipment[26] and that the cross was bearing a cultural symbolization.[27]

The Court in its first judgment in 2009 ruled in favour of Lautsi, arguing that the "display of crucifixes in Italian classrooms violates religious and educational freedoms".[28] In the Court's assessment, the religious significance of the cross prevailed over the plethora of meanings, while the treatment of it as an integral part of the school environment was particularly contested. The decision caused uproar in the Italian society and this post-ruling controversy, which escalated into unprecedented magnitudes,[29] led to the Government's appeal to the ECtHR's Grand Chamber[30] with the support of multiple European states. The Court in its final judgment in 2011 reversed the Second Chamber's ruling; that is, it found no violation of Article 2 Protocol 1 of the ECHR, while it held that no separate issue arose under Article 9 either.

The common patterns

I suggest that the cases at hand share basic common ground; in line with this I identify the following recurrent patterns in terms of i) the *process*, i.e. the legal doctrines and arguments used; ii) the *method* employed by the Strasbourg Court and iii) the *context of* the cases within which they are positioned.

As far as the legal doctrines are concerned, the Strasbourg Court resorted mainly to the margin of appreciation doctrine and referred the matter to the concerned state in order to support its claim for the legitimate purpose of the restrictions of human rights. In upholding the imposition of bans it handed a wide margin of discretion to the state for implementing these in order to support the claim for serving the public interest of society. It further interpreted the Islamic symbols at the relevant cases as if these symbols were objectively endangering democratic values and as if they were posing a threat to the public order and thus manifested distrust[31] towards the Islamic headscarf itself.

24 Ibid, para. 30.
25 Ibid, para. 11.
26 Ibid, para. 20.
27 Ibid, para. 35, 40.
28 Pavone, T., 2011. Redefining Religious Neutrality: Lautsi vs. Italy and the European Court of Human Rights. *SSRN Electronic Journal*, p. 13.
29 Mancini, S., 2010. The Crucifix Rage: Supranational Constitutionalism Bumps Against the Counter-Majoritarian Difficulty. *European Constitutional Law Review*, 6 (01), p.7: '[C]rucifixes were distributed in the village's main squares, and bylaws were enacted to compel even shopkeepers to display the crucifix. In one case a two-meter-tall crucifix was posted at the gate of a municipality. The judges who took part in the decision were subject to personal attacks.'
30 *Lautsi v. Italy* [2011].
31 Rorive I., 2009. Religious Symbols in the Public Space: In Search of a European Answer. *Cardozo Law Review*, 30:6, p. 2680.

With respect to the significance of the contested symbols the judges characterized the Islamic garb as a "powerful external symbol"[32] and ascribed to it solely a religious connotation[33] that was held irreconcilable with Western values.[34] By contrast, in the *Lautsi* case the cross was depicted as an "essentially passive symbol"[35] whose presence was found 'natural' within public classrooms. Although the Court stated in its main reasoning that the crucifix is above all a religious symbol[36] in the side-lines of the judgment it vigorously appraised its cultural significance and emphasized its importance as a cultural mainstay and momentous historical emblem of Europe that embodies the liberal democratic ideals.[37]

However, behind the shield of the margin of appreciation the Court delivered a peremptory and one-sided interpretation of the religious meaning of the headscarf and acted as "an authentic interpreter of religion"[38] under the public interest and secularism pretext. On the other hand, in the crucifix case the judiciary trivialized the religious importance of the cross by using the margin of appreciation doctrine. By doing so, the Court made use of the procedural legitimacy of legal doctrines in order to naturalize the cultural significance of the cross "as the end point of religion's logical development".[39] Thus, the Court by de-religionising the religious

32 *Lautsi v. Italy* [2011] para.72; It is interesting to note that in *Dahlab v. Switzerland* [2001] the Swiss Government referred to 'conspicuous religious symbols', see under Law, par.1, which reads: 'At that time she had been a member of the Catholic faith and had not manifested her religious beliefs by wearing any conspicuous religious symbols' and to look at the use of 'ostentatious' religious symbols at Judge Tulkens' dissenting opinion in *Sahin v. Turkey* [2004] para. 8: 'As regards the first condition, this could have not been satisfied if the headscarf the applicant wore as a religious symbol had been *ostentatious* or aggressive ...' [emphasis added]. To this respect, see the sharp observation of Rorive, n. 33 as above, p. 2686 'It is striking to note the borrowing from the French debate of the term "ostentatious" (signes ostentatoires), which was largely used during the 1990s by the Administrative Supreme Court (Conseil d'Etat) and which was replaced by "conspicuous" (signes religieux ostensibles) in official documents subsequent to the work of the Stasi Commission (named after the former Republic Mediator) on the question of the laïcité.'

33 *Dahlab v Switzerland*, ibid n.7: 'a powerful external symbol such as the wearing of the headscarf ... appears to be imposed on women by a precept which is laid down in the Koran'; *Sahin v. Turkey* [2004] para. 115.

34 Mancini, S., 2011. The Free Exercise of Exclusion: On Veils, Enemies and Militant Democracy. *SSRN Electronic Journal.* [online] Available at: < http://dx.doi.org/10.2139/ssrn.1784786> [Accessed 20 June 2012], p. 5.

35 *Lautsi v. Italy* [2011] para.72.

36 Ibid, para.66.

37 Ibid; see in particular the concurring opinion of Judge Bonello.

38 Custos, D., 2006. Secularism in French Public Schools: Back to War? The French Statute of March 15, 2004. *The American Journal of Comparative Law*, 54 (2), p. 389.

39 Danchin, P., 2011. Islam in the Secular Nomos of the European Court of Human Rights. *Michigan Journal of International Law*, 32, pp. 663–2011; *University of Maryland Legal Studies Research Paper* No. 2010–41. *SSRN Electronic Journal*, p. 26. [online] Available at: <http://ssrn.com/abstract=1670671> [Accessed 17 March 2012].

symbolism of the cross and transforming the sacred to the secular[40] managed to downplay religion, while still securing the public display of the majoritarian religious symbols. Moreover, the juxtaposition of the crucifix as the symbol of the 'true' insignia of the European culture against the misleading and threatening Islamic headscarf negated the concept of 'state neutrality' understood as the state's incompetence "to pronounce on the truth or falsity of a religious dogma or a moral belief".[41] Christianity bereft of its religiosity was thus presented as if it were the means to the preservation of the core values of the liberal society and not as the endpoint of the discourse on the right to religious expression that it actually is.

Turning to the question of method the Court resorted to the use of binary logic. This plays an important role in the framing of the debate; for that, method, as it has been eloquently stated in theory, "... shapes each theory's vision of social reality";[42] it "organizes the apprehension of truth; it determines what counts as evidence and defines what is taken as verification".[43] Whatever the public dilemma is, so long as it is presented in dualistic terms serves to manipulate public perception. When resorting to polar oppositions, these embody a sort of logic of dominance or privilege;[44] that is to say, binary thinking "gives priority to the first term of the dyad, while subordinating the second".[45] With binary constructions, one term is given a positive value, while the other signifies the lack of the positive attributes that characterize the first.[46] Therefore, the construction of a debate in terms of opposites unavoidably favours one side at least in principle. Applying the above claims in the disputes at hand, translates that as long as the matter is presented as a West versus Islam controversy one shall prevail. In deciding who will, stereotypical generalizations of Islam as illiberal, autocratic and patriarchal that have been established in the public imagination point at the 'liberal, democratic, Christian, West' as the one to preponderate.

Last but not least, in terms of the *context*,[47] the common denominator in the case law at hand was that these concerned women and children and that they took

40 McGoldrick, D., 2011. Religion in the European Public Square and in European Public Life–Crucifixes in the Classroom? *Human Rights Law Review*, 11(3), p. 479.
41 Martínez-torrón, J., 2012. The (Un)protection of Individual Religious Identity in the Strasbourg Case Law. *Oxford Journal of Law and Religion*, 1(2), p. 375.
42 MacKinnon C. A., 1982. Feminism, Marxism, Method, and the State: An Agenda for Theory. *Feminist Theory, Signs*, 7 (3), p.527.
43 Ibid, p. 527.
44 Elbow P., 1993. The Uses of Binary Thinking. *Journal of Advanced Composition*, 13 (1), p. 51.
45 Volpp, L., 2001. Feminism versus Multiculturalism. *Columbia Law Review*, 101(5), p.1204.
46 Yeğenoğlu, M., 2005. *Colonial fantasies: Towards a Feminist Reading of Orientalism*. 1st ed. Cambridge University Press, p.7.
47 For an assessment of the relevance of context when a religious claim is grounded in a Christian context (majority religion) or in a non-Christian context (minority religion) in a given constitutional setting see also the analysis of Topidi, K., 2016. Public Education and Religious Rights: A Comparative Analysis, Chapter 12, pp. 278–281 in Topidi K., Fielder L. (eds), *Religion as Empowerment: Global Legal Perspectives*. Routledge.

place in the public sphere, mainly in public educational establishments. This casts new light in terms of the Court's paternalistic stance. Paternalism being primarily educational[48] is not found only in the headscarf case, but in the crucifix case as well. Within public schools, pupils are supposedly introduced to a robust ideal of autonomy founded in equality, reciprocal respect and tolerance towards difference. Detached from cultural or religious influences students are encouraged to exercise their critical capacity,[49] make choices on their own and think for themselves. This liberal notion of autonomy is what Muslim women are thought to be lacking as they are imprisoned within the stifling bounds of their religiously dictated culture. And it is this type of autonomy that stands in compliance with the liberal legal edifice so as to derive from it its societal legitimation.

Taking into account the crucifix case, the Court's paternalism is susceptible to a re-interpretation. Allowing the cross to hang in public classrooms under the pretext of its cultural significance, which nonetheless looks back upon its Christian heritage and historical background, admits to only one understanding of what kind of choices are left to be made; those that lead to the recognition of Christianity as the exclusive identity-marker of the European self. Conditioned upon the status of reduced agency and minority, Christianity thus becomes a one-way choice for children in order to establish their autonomy within the confines of European state-run schools.

Looking at Muslim women and assuming, *ex hypothesi*, that they are not autonomous by virtue of their cultural lineage and equating them with children, who *ex lege* have a reduced agency,[50] implies that the 'lesson' of the *right-type of autonomy* that is taught to children is the same for Muslim women, too. Therefore, the abstract paternalistic stance taken in the headscarf cases became concrete with the crucifix case. By rejecting the Islamic veil and by tacitly accepting the crucifix, the Court not only expressed a "negative value judgment on the culture of a religious minority",[51] but simultaneously pointed at the majoritarian Christian religion as capable of preserving traditional values of liberalism.

But why schools? Why are schools so different?[52] That is because state schools are "the bedrock of a nation's values and the means by which it helps to form

48 Ibid, p. 400.

49 See *Lautsi v. Italy* [2011], §7 of the dissenting opinion of Judge Malinverni joined by Judge Kalaydjieva of the Grand Chamber judgment which reads: '… As the Chamber rightly pointed out, in schools "the compelling power of the State is imposed on minds which still lack the critical capacity which would enable them to keep their distance from the message derived from a preference manifested by the State"' (see § 48 of the Chamber judgment).'

50 Guerrero, M., 2011. International Women's Rights and the 'War of Cultures': Avoiding the 'Westernization' Debate. *Vienna Journal on International Constitutional Law*, 5 (3), p. 396.

51 Mancini, S., 2009. The Power of Symbols and Symbols as Power: Secularism and Religion as Guarantors of Cultural Convergence, *Cardozo Law Review*, p. 2656.

52 Regina (Shabina Begum) v. Governors of Denbigh High Sch. [2006] UKHL 15, [2007] 1 AC 100, para. 96, 97; In the Begum case, Lady Hale of the House of Lords underlined: 'If a woman freely chooses to adopt a way of life for herself, it is not for

good citizens";[53] they are the "laboratories of the future"[54] through which control of the public sphere can be achieved. The expression of religious beliefs contributes through the medium of education to the formation of identity,[55] since the "content of education cannot be easily separated from that of the identity of the pupils".[56] And yet why women and children? If women contribute to the transmission of collective identity[57] through childbirth, it is schools where first collectivities are nurtured and shaped. As follows, the headscarf and crucifix decisions can quickly move from the milieus of education to the general public sphere and drastically influence public treatment of social phenomena. It is also that within schools the embryonic perceptions of individuals about the world are starting to form and slip into their social unconscious becoming thus difficult to dismantle afterwards.[58] Ultimately the liberal 'lesson' extends beyond children and Muslim women to all individuals within the European liberal legal system where power relations and public morals take place. Hence, the bodies of women and children are used as a canvas for the societies to inscribe their moral and political aspirations.[59]

Debating conceptions of identity of the subject

Against an essentialist identity

The establishment of a homogeneous collective identity anchored in secularized Christianity[60] renders religion as the basic constituent of European identity and imprisons the individuals to monolithical, non-negotiable, predetermined notions

others, including other women who have chosen differently, to criticise or prevent her ... *But schools are different ... Like it or not*, this is a society committed, in principle and in law ... Young girls from ethnic, cultural or religious minorities growing up here *face* particularly *difficult choices: how far to adopt or to distance themselves from the dominant culture.*' [emphasis added].

53 Hunter-Hénin, M., 2012. *Law, Religious Freedoms and Education in Europe (Cultural Diversity and Law)*, Ashgate Publishing Group, p. 8.

54 Laborde, C., 2005. Secular Philosophy and Muslim Headscarves in Schools. *Journal of Political Philosophy*, 13 (3), p. 317.

55 Topidi, K., 2012. Religious Diversity in Public Education. A Comparative European Perspective, p. 109 in Roux, C., 2012. *Safe Spaces: Human Rights Education in Diverse Contexts* (Critical Issues in the Future of Learning and Teaching). 1st ed. Sense Publishers.

56 Topidi, K. (2016), p. 277.

57 Mancini, S., 2012. Patriarchy as the Exclusive Domain of the Other: The Veil Controversy, False Projection and Cultural Racism. *International Journal of Constitutional Law*, 10 (2), p.417.

58 Bottici, Ch. and Challand, B., 2012. Islam and the Public Sphere: Public Reason or Public Imagination, Chapter 5, p. 120 in Zucca, L., Ungureanu, C. (eds), *Law, State and Religion in the New Europe: Debates and Dilemmas*. 1st ed. Cambridge University Press.

59 Mancini (2012), p. 412.

60 Ibid, p. 413.

of an identity. Religious symbols, by virtue of their capacity to evoke "absolute and therefore reassuring truths",[61] are further used to legitimize this artificial divide. That is to say, religious symbols being able to unite and erect barriers, they are used at the same time[62] to affirm identitarian claims of natural belongingness and to endorse assertions of a shared cultural history among members of each community.

In turn, the appeal to identity appears to be some kind of a "self-evident naturalistic fact",[63] something like a given, by reason of an inherited culture. This essentialist conception of identity conceives collective identity as "based on some 'essence' or set of core features shared by all members of the collectivity and no others".[64] Puppnick's argument, who has participated in the defence of the *Lautsi* case and stood in favour of the display of the cross in public classrooms, is characteristic of that essentialist approach; as he bluntly argues with respect to the Italian state's neutrality obligation, this "concerns State action, not the State's nature in itself (its essence). The Court does not judge the States for what they *are* but for what they *do*".[65] The way in which the argument is framed itself, does not aim only for the state, but it is rather a way of promulgating national identity. The state's 'essence' is taken to be its citizen's essence and the crucifix on the wall – elevated to a common cultural attribute – is the essential feature of the collective identity that citizens share. It is illogical and disingenuous though that the Court would judge a person (Mrs. Dahlab) for what she is and not what she does, and yet refrain from doing so when it comes to a State (Italy, in the Lautsi case). States do not have a being as individuals do, in the same sense that "classrooms do not have human rights, while individuals do".[66]

Therefore, the cross on the wall as a cultural tradition suggests a "unified, singular social experience, a single canvas"[67] against which individuals construct a common sense of self. For that reason, Christianity falls off its religious pedestal and is gauged in a contextual manner, where culture, tradition and history appear to be determinants of the European identity. On the other hand, Muslim identity is understood only on the basis of a single affiliation, that is, the religious one,[68] while the headscarf controversies are not examined in their context-dependent

61 Mancini, S., Rosenfeld, M., 2010. Unveiling the Limits of Tolerance: Comparing the Treatment of Majority and Minority Religious Symbols in the Public Sphere. *Cardozo Legal Studies Research Paper* No. 309, p.4.

62 Ibid, p. 4.

63 Plant, R., 2011. Religion, Identity and Freedom of Expression. *Res Publica*, 7, p.6.

64 Ringelheim J. (2002), p. 2.

65 Emphasis added by the author; See Puppinck, Gr., 2011. Lautsi v. Italy. The leading case on majority religions in European Secular states. *European Centre for Law and Justice*, p.14 [online] Available at: <http://eclj.org/pdf/ECLJ-LAUTSIvITALY-secular-states-20110315.pdf> [Accessed 25 March 2012].

66 Ronchi, P., 2011. Crucifixes, Margin of Appreciation and Consensus: The Grand Chamber Ruling in Lautsi v Italy. *Ecclesiastical Law Journal*, 13, p. 291.

67 Cerulo, K.A., 1997. Identity Construction: New Issues, New Directions. *Annual Review of Sociology*, 10 (23), p. 387.

68 Mancini, S. (2009), p. 2666.

merits. Thus, with the subject being abstracted from its own cultural and historical framework,[69] Muslim identity tends to be interpreted in the abstract through "sterile monologues"[70] without the voices of those concerned to be heard.

In order for a collective identity to be affirmed, the individual differences between members of the same group and other groups must be trivialized and smoothed out. Seen that way, complex human conduct is analysed in terms of its simple components[71] and headscarf bans are justified as a means to restore normalcy.[72] In other words, the more "collective identities become affirmative, the more they have a flattening effect: they normalise, they reduce diversity and complexity".[73] In both the crucifix and the headscarf cases the collective identities set forth reduce the individuals to one and only of their characteristics, i.e. the religious one, and limit individuals' freedom of self-determination. Respectively, the concept of identity becomes something static and pre-existing that entraps individuals[74] to uni-dimensional identity models; while this practice reflects the desire of the majority to "re-establish clear boundaries between the self and the other, to avoid dialogue and compromise with the other, and to reduce the visibility of the latter, in order to guard the (supposedly) homogeneous character of the public sphere".[75]

In line with this, the identity of oneself is taken to be first and foremost a given identity that is presumably specified in wholly factual terms and includes normative characteristics that put others under the obligation to recognize and respect that particular identity.[76] What is more, these normative characteristics provide a strict account of certain behaviours and expressions that are thought to be mandated by this empirical and fixed type of identity.[77] Being a Muslim or a European is equated to speaking and thinking like a Muslim or European and to acting as a Muslim or European. But in order for this value judgment to be made, moral ethics and moralising are brought forward. Thus, the fixed identity of that sort proves to be a matter of value and belief rather than fact. In turn, beliefs are evaluated as right or wrong, true or false, satisfactory or unsatisfactory and are judged upon a particular set of values.[78]

69 Malik, M., 2009. Feminism and its 'Other': Female Autonomy in the Age of Difference. *Cardozo Law Review*, 30, p. 2661.
70 Mancini, S (2009), p. 2666.
71 Malik, M. (2009), p. 2661.
72 Mancini, S. (2012), p. 413.
73 Gutwirth, S. (2009), p. 127.
74 Ibid, p. 132.
75 Mancini, S., 2013. The Tempting of Europe, the Political Seduction of the Cross: A Schmittian Reading of Christianity and Islam in European Constitutionalism, in Mancini, S. and M. Rosenfeld (eds), *Constitutional Secularism in an Age of Religious Revival.* Oxford University Press, p. 29.
76 Plant, R. (2011), p. 14; Gutwirth (2009), p. 128.
77 Plant, R. (2011), p. 14.
78 Weber, M., Ed.A.Shils, Finch, H.A., eds. and transl., 1949. *The Methodology of the Social Sciences.* Free Press, p. 1.

Within the case law at hand the Court while formally relying on the supposedly neutral legal doctrine of the margin of appreciation interprets the Islamic gear as incompatible with Western values. By doing so the ECtHR puts forth a value judgment,[79] finding that that Islamic gear is wrong and not the least useful for the purposes of liberal democracy. In accord with this, Muslim practices are evaluated within the majoritarian moral values while Muslim identity becomes equivalent to Islam and the values that it allegedly stands for. Hence what emerges is a type of moralism that "tends to conflate persons with beliefs";[80] that is to say "persons are equated with subject positions which are equated with identities, which are equated with certain beliefs and values".[81]

However, in the crucifix case the Western values that are sought to be protected do not conflict with the morals of the majoritarian Christian religion; hence, the law does nothing but to conform to the ethical values of the dominant majority church.[82] The immediate effect is that once Muslim culture, which in itself is not homogeneous and should therefore not be treated as such, is cast as irreconcilable with Western identity it is then that "Muslims can only choose to either assimilate, by renouncing to their (inferior) identity or leave".[83] Thus the "moral burden is placed upon the shoulders of these people, as they must choose between disobedience to the law and disobedience to their conscience".[84]

Towards a socially formatted identity

The notion of a preordained and motionless collective identity as part of a homogeneous society appears to be very problematic and poses a threat to democracy. The collective meaning of identities is neither predetermined nor fixed[85] and what are considered as the essential requirements of an identity are the outcome of social constructions and social contestation within the group.[86] The content of identities is the product of processes embedded in personal choice, culture and historical and political circumstances.[87]

In this respect treating oneself as an *object* "defined in terms of one's essential nature"[88] goes opposite the 'social constructionist approach'[89] that has been

79 Mancini, S. (2009), p. 2643.
80 As cited in Vakulenko, A. (2007), p. 737.
81 Ibid.
82 Martínez-Torrón, J. (2012), p. 7.
83 Mancini, S. (2012), p. 415.
84 Martínez-Torrón, J. (2012), p. 10.
85 Abdelal, R. H., Yoshiko, M. J., Alastair, I., and McDermott R., 2006. Identity as a Variable. *Perspectives on Politics*, 4 (4), p. 700.
86 Ringelheim, J. (2002), p. 2; See also Abdehal (2006).
87 On the content of identity as being the product of contestation that occurs through this process within groups see the analysis with an empirical focus of Abdelal et al. (2006), pp. 700–701.
88 Ibid, p. 13.
89 For the 'social constructionist approach' to identity see Cerulo, K.A., 1997. Identity Construction: New Issues, New Directions. *Annual Review of Sociology*, 10 (23),

gaining momentum in social and legal theory. According to this approach identities are considered to be fragmented and contested; they are the outcome of an interminable process where identities are "constantly reinterpreted or renegotiated through interactions between groups and individuals".[90] Social constructionists scholars draw attention to the collective's struggle to self-name and to self-characterize[91] and challenge the unbalanced power relations within the society and the subaltern positioning of some groups compared to other. This anti-essentialist view charts also collective national identity as a product of both "natural" continuity and conscious manipulation.[92] As it has been shown in the case law examined here, natural continuity emerges from the invocation to a pre-existing identity, while conscious manipulation is achieved both via commemoration of common history and cultural tradition and via symbolism, i.e. by the use of the crucifix.[93]

Furthermore, the guise under constitutional protection entraps the individual in predefined notions of identity within spheres of prescribed actions and expectations[94]. Speaking for a legitimate constitutional subject as the product of a collectivity of persons is quite arbitrary, since these individuals might not necessarily share the same definition of their group identity.[95] Groups on the other hand are not pre-existent entities that remain identical and impervious to change; on the contrary they are shifting in meaning and are "permanently in a state of flux".[96] Imposing thus a single collective identity on individuals as something natural for homogenizing purposes undermines plurality and diversity.[97] Imposing further a homogeneous identity as the product of courts and legal mandates through the polarity of friend and enemy of 'us' and the 'other', i.e. the 'stranger', calls for serious criticism on what type of theory of justice is put forward in a democratic society.

In light of this, constitutional and critical theorists' voices raise the alarm that anti-veil measures and pro-crucifix decisions pursue an understanding of the subject according to Carl Schmitt's theory.[98] That is to say, it is claimed that these

pp. 385–409 and the assessment of the constructionist approach and the postmodern and deconstruction approach to identity; see also Anderson, B., 1991. *Imagined Communities: Reflections on the Origin and Spread of Nationalism*, revised edition. London: Verso.

90 Ibid, p. 2.

91 p. 393.

92 Cerulo, K. A. (1997), p. 390.

93 Ibid, p. 391.

94 See also Cerulo, K.A (1997), p. 388.

95 Ringelheim, J. (2002), p. 2.

96 Gutwirth, S. (2009), p. 128.

97 Ibid, p. 128.

98 See also for an analysis of Carl Schmitt's theory in relation to contemporary constitutional discourse in Mancini, S., Rosenfeld, M. (eds), 2014. *Constitutional Secularism in an Age of Religious Revival.* Oxford University Press; Dyzenhaus, D., 2006. *The Constitution of Law, Legality in a Time of Emergency.* Cambridge University Press; and in Bellamy, R., Baher, P., 1993. Carl Schmitt and the Contradictions of Liberal Democracy. *European Journal of Political Research*, 23, pp. 163–185.

practises "draw on an essentialist and idealized notion of the people, and aim at artificially reinforcing the cultural and religious homogeneous character of the European public sphere, thus pursuing a Schmittian 'identitarian' model of democracy".[99] This practice, as theory has already stressed,[100] points at a Schmittian understanding of constitutionalism, where the polarity of friend/enemy stands out and the democratic state is not based on equality any longer, but on homogeneity instead.[101] However, if the way people reach unity is through an artificial homogeneity and a legally imposed collective identity rather than by means of integration and equal respect of diversity and pluralism, this not only undermines the legitimacy but also raises serious concerns for the liberal legal order itself.

Challenging the legitimate aim

The unsocial sociability of illiberal liberalism

It would have been assumed that the religious cases concerning the Islamic garb fall outside the perimeter of the restrictive line taken by the Court reformulated in the language of public interest and legitimate aim in a democratic polity. Especially, since as it has been stressed by scholars "Article 9 serves mainly ***an individual end***, while Articles 10–11 (and Article 3 of Protocol 1) serve ***a purpose that is political***, in that it pertains to need for debate on issues of public interest".[102] It would have been equally assumed that the limitations 'necessary-in-a-democratic-society' namely, in terms of public safety, protection of public order, health, or morals, and protection of the rights and freedoms of others in articles 8–11 of the ECHR, "which implicitly invoke John Stuart Mill's 'harm principle' as a benchmark for legitimate state intervention in a liberal society",[103] do not possibly pertain to individual belief, since this is in itself "socially inconsequential"[104] and irrelevant to the public phenomena and thus falls outside the law's regulation and the state's radar.

However, contrary to this assumption, the ECtHR allowed the state by deference to the margin of appreciation to define and dictate the proper content of religious liberty, even in situations where no harm[105] to others or to the concerned human beings themselves existed.[106] To justify this, it has been argued that the Court

99 Mancini, S., Rosenfeld, M., eds., ibid (2014), Introduction, xxvi.
100 Mancini, S. (2013).
101 Ibid, p. 27.
102 Begum, B. and Zysset, A., 2013. Personal autonomy' and 'democratic society' at the European Court of Human Rights: friends or foes? *UCL Journal of Law and Jurisprudence* 2(1) p. 238; emphasis added in the text by the author.
103 Joppke, Chr, 2016. Pluralism vs. Pluralism: Islam and Christianity in the European Court of Human Rights, Chapter 4 p. 91, in Cohen, J.L., Laborde, C. (eds), *Religion, Secularism, and Constitutional Democracy*. Columbia University Press.
104 Ibid, p. 91.
105 Tourkochoriti, I., 2012. The Burka Ban: Divergent Approaches to Freedom of Religion in France and in the U.S.A. *William & Mary Bill of Rights Journal*, 20, p. 804.
106 See Mill, J. St., first publ. 1859, 2001. *On Liberty*. Batoche Books, p. 13 on the 'Harm Principle': 'The only purpose for which power can be rightfully exercised over

adopted in relation to Muslim communities a mode of reasoning, which was coined with the term '*liberal anti-pluralism*'.[107] Drawing inspiration from the international legal discourse where the above term is encountered, liberal anti-pluralism refers to the capacity of the state to determine its standing in the family of nations, while the focus is placed on the internal characteristics of the communities, upon which distinction is carried out.[108] This type of neo-liberalism, seen through an absolutist, fixed and dogmatic prism of the liberal way of life and values, is "endowed with a sort of moralistic fervour, a conviction and intolerance of the illiberal"[109] and often resorts to profoundly illiberal conformity tactics and confrontations with the preserved as the illiberal 'Other'. The state is thus the only "*competent agent par excellence*"[110] to assure that liberty is real and to define the proper meaning and content of religious symbols.

A dilemma and an irony though arise in this self-reflexive paradox of liberalism itself; that is to say, "liberal states, in order to preserve what they perceive as a liberal regime, are resorting to illiberal means to guarantee liberal values".[111] This paradox further reflects on the ECtHR's jurisprudence; a prohibition, which is the opposite of 'tolerance', is justified by reference to 'tolerance' in the Court's reasoning in the relevant Islamic symbol cases.[112] Liberalism then needs either to tolerate illiberal practices, "or turn to illiberal means in order to "liberate" the illiberal".[113] Tolerance in this sense is considered legitimate within the justificatory framework of this 'liberalism of certainty' or 'liberal anti-pluralism', which is "exclusive and illiberal in its effects".[114] Excluding though is "only legitimate when there is an actual threat to individual freedoms".[115] On the contrary excluding in order to re-include under the proper accepted liberal prerequisites, manifests an arbitrary bias and betrays the concept of political liberalism understood as the state's neutrality of aim[116] and neutrality towards conceptions of the

any member of a civilized community, against his will, is to prevent harm to others. His own good, either physical or moral, is not a sufficient warrant ... We may still argue, entreat, and remonstrate with people who seem bent on doing themselves harm (as we judge it) or are simply acting in a way we don't like. But we should not use either the law or moral condemnation to alter their behaviour, unless they are causing harm to other people.'

107 Tyulkina, S., 2011. *Militant Democracy: Undemocratic Political Parties and Beyond.* Routledge, p. 200.

108 Simpson, G., 2001. Two Liberalisms. *European Journal International Law* 12 (3), p. 541.

109 Ibid, p. 541.

110 Tourkochoriti, I. (2012), p. 826.

111 Orgad, L.,2010. Illiberal Liberalism: Cultural Restrictions on Migration and Access to Citizenship in Europe. *American Journal of Comparative Law*, 58 (1), p. 92.

112 Joppke, Chr. (2016), p. 92.

113 Orgad, L. (2010), p. 92.

114 Simpson, G., (2001), p. 539.

115 Ibid, p. 89.

116 Kyritsis, D., Tsakyrakis, St., 2013. Neutrality in the Classroom. *International Journal of Constitutional Law* 11 (1), p. 207.

good.[117] As a result, this leads towards what has been phrased in theory as '*illiberal liberalism*'.[118]

This 'illiberal liberalism' or 'liberal anti-pluralism' upon which liberal societies are constructed, traces back, I suggest, to the Kantian concept of '*unsociable sociability*'.[119] As it has been stressed in theory unsociable sociability can be considered as a way of assessing the inherent antagonism and conflicting viewpoints within the neo-liberal state model and a way of indicating the deeply ambivalent moral function in the dynamics both of personal conduct and of social relationships.[120] State-Neoliberalism then as "a theory of relentless competition"[121] and antagonism requires at an outcome level the preponderance and dominion of the most robust set of values within the society and implies that the stronger liberal ideal will come to dominate weaker concepts that are perceived as illiberal. Having described how the religious symbols controversy was built and portrayed on the basis of culture essentialism and clash of values between different value systems, the bans were thereby used to defuse this tension and to reinstate public order according to State's preference.

In this respect, the Court by resorting to this mode of reasoning in the Islamic garb cases, failed to acknowledge and value the subjects in their capacity to judge

117 Orgad L. (2010) as above, p. 95.

118 See Orgad, L. (2010), pp. 53–106, where Orgad frames the term 'Illiberal Liberalism' to assess the legitimacy of culture-based criteria for regulating migration and access to citizenship and to raise criticisms towards liberalism for the disqualification of people from citizenship and their exclusion from political equality. For an interesting comparison of different contexts accommodating the same term, see also Phillips, A., 2001. Feminism and Liberalism Revisited: Has Martha Nussbaum Got it Right. *Constellations,* 8 (2), p. 252 how the term 'Illiberal Liberalism' is used within the feminist discourse to assess the liberal understanding of autonomy, to criticize unjust social power and to explore the relation of liberalism with feminism. Comparing these two theoretical analyses it is interesting to notice how the 'illiberal liberalism' term is used in both cases to raise valid and serious concerns about liberalism and its structural deficiencies from the angle of equally marginalized categories of the society, i.e. of immigrants (men and women) – in Orgad's analysis – or of women only – in Phillip's criticism.

119 In the essay 'Idea for a Universal History with a Cosmopolitan Purpose' in the fourth proposition, Kant had described humanity's 'Unsociable Sociability' (*Ungesellige Geselligkeit*) as follows: '*The means which nature employs to bring about the development of innate capacities is that of antagonism within society, in so far as this antagonism becomes in the long run the cause of a law-governed social order.* By antagonism, I mean in this context the *unsocial sociability* of men, that is, their tendency to come together in society, coupled, however, with a continual resistance which constantly threatens to break this society up.' [emphasis kept according to the source]; See Kant, I, Reiss, H. S. ed., Nisbet, H. B. transl., 1991. *Kant: Political Writings* (Cambridge Texts in the History of Political Thought). 2nd ed. Cambridge University Press, p. 44.

120 Rossi Philip, J., 2006. *The Social Authority of Reason: Kant's Critique, Radical Evil, and the Destiny of Humankind.* Suny Series in Philosophy, pp. 78, 79.

121 Michaels, R., 2014. On Liberalism and Legal Pluralism p. 142, in Maduro M., Tuori K. and Sankari S., (eds), *Transnational Law: Rethinking European Law and Legal Thinking.* Cambridge University Press.

for themselves and by themselves[122] and to self-characterize themselves. It failed to recognize the individual's right to self-definition,[123] as Tourkochoriti brilliantly captures in her analysis, i.e. the persons' right to decide and define by themselves the meaning of their choices and to act as rational agents. By considering individuals as not capable of exercising practical reason and by casting their condition as being irreconcilable with the liberal cultural norm, the negation of differences was imposed in a top-to-bottom fashion[124] by the state all the way down to the individuals.

The arbitrary advancement of Christianity by the ECtHR as the cultural emblem of Europe and as the personally chosen cultural narrative of individuals is problematic in other ways, as well. This is because the liberal discourse of modernization and tolerance denies its own involvement with cultural norms[125] and encourages plurality of positions and autonomous choices over traditional ascriptive identities and deep attachment to cultural groups.[126] The pairing of liberal secularism with Christianity flags thus an interesting moment of anxiety and incoherence within the liberal model,[127] which ends up as patronizing and illiberal. Put differently, the primary commitment of classic liberalism to freedom of choice and to the equal worth of persons as choosers[128] is violated in two ways. On the one hand the Court's practice interferes with one's capacity to self-reflection on their own cultural practices[129] and with one's liberty to self-determination, i.e. one's freedom "to be and become the person one chooses".[130] The choice to interpret what religious symbols mean seems to belong exclusively to the Court and the state by deference to the margin of appreciation doctrine but not to the individuals.

However, this lack of recognition of a "symmetrical relationship between rational agents, which is engendered by respect for practical reason"[131] leads to the alarming observation that "coercion will be the modus operandi and the state of unsocial sociability will reign".[132] This contorted logic entails a lack of recognition of the human dignity and an unwillingness to include and engage individuals as free and equal interlocutors in the public sphere. Coercion is then used as the tool for order and control, an order though "which is not rational and thus

122 Tourkochoriti, I. (2012), p. 830.
123 Ibid, p. 846.
124 Ibid, p. 795.
125 Vakulenco, A., 2007. Liberalism, Civilisation and the (Non-) Oxymoronic Limits of Tolerance. *International Journal of Law in Context* 3 (4), p. 330.
126 Kymlicka, W., 1997. *States, Nations and Cultures.* Van Gorcum, p. 21.
127 Vakulenko, A. (2007), p. 325.
128 Nussbaum, M., 1999. *Sex& Social Justice.* Oxford University Press, p. 70.
129 Lépinard, E., 2011. Autonomy and the Crisis of the Feminist Subject. *Constellations,* 18 (2), p. 207.
130 Marshall, J., 2008. Women's Right to Autonomy and Identity in European Human Rights Law: Manifesting One's Religion. *Res Publica* (14), p. 185.
131 Erlewine, R., 2009. *Nation of Devils: Monotheism and Tolerance; Recovering a Religion of Reason.* Indiana Series in the Philosophy of Religion, p. 104.
132 Ibid.

not ultimately legitimate in its most foundational grounds"[133] and in favour of the universal interest of humanity.[134]

State reasoning and the question of agency and human dignity

It has been argued that the religious symbols in dispute were interpreted according to the "majoritarian cultural parameters"[135] so as to endorse a particular form of religious identity and to recreate cultural homogeneity[136] "permeated by Christian values".[137] By resorting to the margin of appreciation the Court tacitly affirmed the superiority of the European cultures over the non-European ones[138] and safeguarded the culturally homogeneous character of Europe at the expense of religious heterogeneity.

Within this framework, Muslim women were further portrayed as victims of their culture, who were unconditionally subdued to a number of restrictions, imposed by men and thus were depicted as being deprived of agency. In line with this, their culture was found to restrict those women from realizing what their 'true' freedom is.[139] What was needed according to this rationale was an intervention from the liberal state that would help women realize their predicament and assist them in reaching 'true' equality and liberty.[140]

For intervening the liberal society was criticized because it was considered to submit women to another form of tutelage[141] and oppression only so as to act as the women's saviour and champion of their emancipation from their own communities.[142] By pointing towards the lack of agency of women, the state challenged the authenticity of their will[143] and elevated itself to the proper expression of reason for individuals, who were not capable of realizing it themselves. By using women as the pretext to reflect upon the illiberal nature of another society the liberal state back lashed, though, on its own illiberal practices and affirmed its intrinsic paternalistic stance.

This rationalistic fallacy that runs through the examined ECtHR's jurisprudence reflects further on the paternalistic role of the state towards not only women but all individuals and on the relation that the persons maintain with each other and

133 Ibid.
134 Ibid.
135 Mancini, S. (2009), p. 2642.
136 Malik, M., 2012. The 'other' citizens: religion in a multicultural Europe, Chapter 4, p. 97 in Zucca, L., Ungureanu, C. (eds), *Law, State and Religion in the New Europe: Debates and Dilemmas*. 1st ed. Cambridge University Press.
137 Augenstein, D. (2012), pp. 264, 261.
138 Malik, M. (2012), p. 98.
139 Marshall, J., 2009. *Personal Freedom through Human Rights Law?* Martinus Nijhoff, p. 151.
140 Ibid, p. 152.
141 Dawn, L., Spini, D., 2004. Unveiling the Headscarf Debate. *Feminist Legal Studies* (12), p. 342.
142 Marshall, J. (2009), p. 189.
143 Tourkochoriti, I. (2012), p. 825.

with themselves that is mediated through the state.[144] The way this happens is manifold; in the cases at hand, the people within the polity are viewed as 'a political community of fate',[145] i.e. they are viewed as "a community of character"[146] bound together by the power of shared fate and belonging. The identity and rationalism[147] of the individual is absorbed in this sense by the collective identity, which is presumed to be one single, static and predetermined identity incarnated by the state.

The Court by allowing the state to define both religious liberty and the relation that individuals have with themselves, and by permitting the state to "impose the 'proper' use of reason" attests to essentialist conceptions of one's identity. Interestingly enough, this *fascination*, in Tourkochoriti's strong words, towards the exercise of collective state power is expressed through the legislative branch.[148] In practical terms, the margin of appreciation that the Court hands to the state translates into the discretionary power that the democratic legislator has within the borders of the nation-state. That is to say, the legislator has the prerogative to transform the meaning of law by allowing the state a wide margin of discretion and by evoking the public interest argument. However, the legislator may remove in this way some interests from the calculation by defining them a priori as of lesser importance within an overriding scheme of moral values and can promote the general interest of the state in an abstract and moralistic way. This practice then violates individual and collective autonomy premised on human dignity and free and equal agency, and brings forward issues of essentialism, paternalism and moral relativism.[149] It also makes possible that the majority identifies its own interests with interests of the public by ignoring minority claims, like religious minorities in our case.

Looking at the cases at hand, the advancement of the narrow interests of the powerful majoritarian religion reduced reason to 'instrumental reason' and turned "the means of Enlightenment against its ends".[150] The Court, devoid of its neutralist pretentions forsook the Enlightenment promise to religious diversity.[151] In other words, the recourse to claims of nature and essence in articulating one's

144 For a brilliant analysis on the matter see Tourkochoriti, I. (2012), pp. 795, 804, 806, 830.

145 Phrase accommodated for the purposes of the present context; for the original context see article of Benhabib, S., 2012. On Michel Rosenfeld's The Identity of the Constitutional Subject. *Cardozo Law Review*, 33 (5), p.1907.

146 For the use of term see Orgad, L. (2010), p. 88.

147 Toukochoriti, I. (2012), p. 831.

148 Ibid; p. 797.

149 See also McHarg, A., 1999. Reconciling Human Rights and the Public Interest: Conceptual Problems and Doctrinal Uncertainty in the Jurisprudence of the European Court of Human Rights. *The Modern Law Review*, 62 (5), pp. 671, 675; see also Moller, K., 2009. Two Conceptions of Positive Liberty: Towards an Autonomy-based Theory of Constitutional Rights. *Oxford Journal of Legal Studies*, 29 (4), pp. 758, 761, 765, 773.

150 Mancini, S. (2010), p. 3.

151 Augenstein, D. (2012), p. 268.

identity negated the "program of Enlightenment", understood as the "disenchantment of the world" through the prevalence of reason and the dissolution of myths.[152] Thus, the initial disenchantment of the world was reduced to a "disenchantment of reason",[153] understood as the supreme reason of the state, which was further attuned to the interests of religious Christian institutions that hold considerable political power in the European public sphere.[154] For doing so, the Court has been criticized for adopting a highly political positioning in the matter and for being motivated by political concerns more than by legal arguments.[155] On the other hand this approach was partly justified on the basis that the Court needs to have "political antennae"[156] and to adjust to the convictions and perceptions of the people in the public sphere; perceptions, though, to whose formation the Court has conduced in vicious and not virtuous circles.

Bearing in mind the dualist reasoning[157] that the Strasbourg Court specifically developed in dealing with the religious symbols jurisprudence, it endorsed legal centralism in the sense of state supremacist reasoning contrary to a pluralistic and contextual one. The Court acted in this sense in a counter-pluralistic manner by prioritising the State over the individual in balancing the competing rights examined. By legitimizing a degree of state interventionism and a certain conception of state reasoning, it rather conceded to a system of political rather that judicial oversight of the law for safeguarding any abuses against it. That is to say, the Court neglected its once proclaimed task for European supervision. This could be understood as the necessary judicial review of state discretion handed through the margin of appreciation in matters that are of importance to all member States, so that supervision cannot be overstepped or escaped simply by invoking this doctrine.[158] The Court by transferring its right and duty for judicial control of the state power to the state itself, negated its anticipated role to safeguard the constitutional equilibrium and the rule of law in a democratic liberal society, while it raised further questions as to why the illegitimate majority is always the one that defines and justifies the width of the margin.

The aim is thus far from being considered legitimate. Looking at the legitimacy aspect of the discourse, this is usually exhausted in normative legitimacy leaving aside the social legitimacy element. Normative legitimacy being considered an

152 Horkheimer, M., Adorno, Th. W., 2002. *Dialectic of Enlightenment*. Stanford University Press, p. 3.
153 Mancini, S. (2010), p. 22.
154 Raday, F., 2012. Sacralising the Patriarchal Family in the Monotheistic Religions: To no Form of Religion is Woman Indebted for One Impulse of Freedom. *International Journal of Law in Context*, 8 (2), p. 212.
155 Ibid Rorive, I. (2009), p. 2697; see also Nigro, R., 2010. The Margin of Appreciation Doctrine and the Case-Law of the ECtHR on the Islamic Veil. *Human Rights Review*, 11 (4), p. 543.
156 McGoldrick, D. (2011), p. 49.
157 On the dualist reasoning of the Strasbourg Court under articles 8–11 of the ECHR, see Begum, B. and Zysset, A. (2013) and particularly pp. 232–246.
158 See *Sahin v. Turkey* [2004]; Dissenting Opinion of Judge Tulkens, para.3.

objective measure,[159] which is based on reason, is identified with the concept of legality. The latter requires vigilance since the substantive principles of legitimacy should be reasons that reflect the values that the law serves in the name of the people and not in the name of the state in spite of the people. That is to say, when deciding issues of constitutional importance the Court rather than simply applying normative principles to legal problems it employs, public reasons,[160] i.e. reasons that reflect the values of a democratic society and process.[161] In this sense the judgments that the Court delivers are the expressions of the values that the law serves in the name of the people, fulfilling in this way the procedural and the social aspect of the legitimacy discourse. This is crucial since in the liberal post-Enlightenment traditions the State is considered to be "invested with the task of realising the reason of the citizens, because they are considered incapable of realizing it by themselves".[162]

In line with this, the aim should not be considered legitimate because of its believed legitimacy[163] in procedural terms, stemming from an undisputed supremacy of majoritarian state reasoning that the Court concedes. Instead, it needs to reflect, on a procedural level, on the reason of individuals for themselves, while on a substantial one it requires the equal standing of individuals as persons,[164] who are respected on the basis of their free and equal agency and human dignity. This further calls for the protection of the autonomy of individuals as private persons, while it also creates the conditions for their participation as public agents.[165] If the aim sought in order to protect the public order and rights and freedoms of others[166] is the homogeneous character of the public order by means of an essentialist conception of the identity of the subject, then the aim is not legitimate. This is flawed not only because of what is considered a reasoned order but also because of the instrumentalist use that renders the subject of judicial interpretation an object; however, the subject cannot be considered a means towards any end, as it is an end in itself.

159 Weiler, J.H.H. (2012). In the Face of Crisis: Input Legitimacy, Output Legitimacy and the Political Messianism of European Integration. *Journal of European Integration*, 34 (7), p. 826.

160 Rawls, J., 1993. *Political Liberalism*. Columbia University Press, pp.216, 231.

161 Bellamy, R. (2013). The Democratic Qualities of Courts: A Critical Analysis of Three Arguments. *Representation*, 49 (3), pp. 333–346 in C Parau, R. Bellamy, eds. Special Issue: Courts and Representative Democracy, p. 336.

162 Tourkochoriti, I. (2012), p. 830.

163 See also Balkin, J. (1993), p. 4, which reads: '... *The beholder is not fully in control of what she sees; she is part of a larger legal and political culture that shapes the very forms of her understanding*. She does not choose the terms of her ideology or social construction. *Rather she chooses through them*; they form the framework within which her choices are understood and made.' [emphasis added].

164 Garthoff, J., 2010. Legitimacy is Not Authority. *Law and Philosophy*, 29 (6), p. 689.

165 Benhabib S. (2012), p. 1897.

166 See *Sahin v. Turkey* [2004], paras. 99, 154, 158, 165 and *Dahlab v. Switzerland* [2001], pp. 8, 10.

By way of epilogue

Assessing the religious symbols controversy in order to untangle the Ariadne's clue of the narrative, the analysis has turned to the jurisprudence of the ECtHR and to the juxtaposition of the Christian crucifix and the Islamic veil. This comparison was found to be mandated by a persistent 'us vis-à-vis them' binary logic that aimed to secure cultural homogenization within the European public space and to advance Christianity as the majority religion of Europe.[167]

The chapter has further taken a critical stance at the reduction of the European identity to religious characteristics and vigorously underscored the alleged cultural roots of a 'European essence' premised on religion,[168] which were put forward in the assessed cases. This essentialist concept of European identity was further criticized for promoting fixed and static forms of identity conceptualised within competing notions of collective identities.

This led to the assessment of the legitimacy of the constructed constitutional subject at the Court's jurisprudence. In doing so, the analysis delved to the justificatory line of the Court, which fell well within what has been termed as liberal anti-pluralism. The paradoxical and anti-nomical nature of this ascertainment was emphasized as the analysis sought to illustrate how behind the realization of the true and proper content of one's identity and liberty, the agent of this realization is indeed the structure and "reason of the state".[169] The practice described as 'liberal anti-pluralism' was identified as being an illiberal liberalism, premised upon the hierarchical idea of antagonism and supremacy between competing systems of values.

The rationale underlying state neo-liberalism was suggested to trace back to the concept of unsocial sociability by means of inherent antagonism, supremacist dominion and potential coercion in the society. Debating the concept of legitimacy and legality the analysis further stressed that the Strasbourg Court in deciding upon issues of importance did not simply apply normative principles to the legal problems in question. It challenged the Court's stance for endorsing the state as the one having a superior reason to the reason of the individual[170] and as being the interpreter of the will of people.

As the analysis sought to prove, the Court has sanctioned a double standard[171] approach in delivering its judgments in the cases at hand by demonstrating

167 See also Topidi, K. (2016), p. 280, where Topidi suggests as a solution to this clash of negative and positive qualifications to embrace a narrower approach to religious rights, which allows for the concretization of competing interests in the spirit of diversity and tolerance; this *doctrine of reasonable accommodation* appears to still largely missing from the European settings, while it is deemed essential in non-European ones. [emphasis added].

168 Challand, B., 2009. From Hammer and Sickle to Star and Crescent. The Question of Religion for European Identity and a Political Europe. *Religion, State and Society*, 37 (1), p. 67.

169 Tourkochoriti, I. (2012), pp. 826, 830.

170 Ibid, p.826.

171 Joppke, Chr. (2016), p.96.

"laxness for Christianity and an unforgiving stance toward Islam".[172] By citing legitimacy aims in justifying its decisions, the analysis stressed that the Court handled the cases in an uneven and escapist way. In addition, the Court with its 'value judgments' on the rightness or wrongness of cultural practices has transformed itself into a "conscience of Europe",[173] while it imposed itself in this way upon individual consciences because of its prestige.[174]

In this respect, attention was drawn to the fact that these essentialist conceptions of subjectivity, which are premised on the incapability of the individual to exercise practical reason and free agency, bring forward a Schmittian understanding of the society where the individual is considered as being part of a homogeneous society and not of a society of equals. In line with this, emphasis was laid on how the Court struggled to take into account the autonomous interests of the affected persons.

What has been suggested instead was a socially constructed understanding of the identity of the subject seen through an anti-essentialist approach. It was stressed that homogeneity leads to cultural essentialism and reinforces binaries between Western and non-Western cultures and that essentialist pictures of culture[175] depict collective and individual identities as static and unsusceptible to transformation. The use of void legal concepts, unsubstantiated claims, populist images[176] and blanket stereotypes to replace legal arguments raise serious concerns in terms of law. Respecting an undisputed yet imaginable principle of constitutional identity that safeguards the sovereign and homogeneous character of the public sphere over the rule of law leads to the alarming ascertainment that legitimacy prevails over legality.[177]

Away from these static binaries, it was highlighted that identities should be considered fluid, be periodically challenged and rearticulated in the public sphere. In light of this, the cited legitimate aim needs to fall in step with democratic values and provide for respect for the equal value and protection of the best interests of all individuals. It further needs to safeguard the autonomy and human dignity of the person, the latter being an intrinsic concept to autonomy understood as "equal attention and equal respect on behalf of the government".[178] In line with this the analysis underscored the importance of defending the right of individuals to define themselves as opposed to the concession of this right to the state, as the one incarnating practical reason.

In that respect, it was stressed that the Court needs to perform its task of European supervision and demonstrate increased judicial review so as to protect individuals from excessive and improper use of state power. It needs to promote the

172 Ibid, p. 96.
173 Puppinck, Gr. (2011), p.15.
174 Ibid.
175 Narayan, U., 1998. Essence of Culture and a Sense of History: A Feminist Critique of Cultural Essentialism. *Hypatia*, 13 (2), p.92.
176 Rorive, (2009), p. 2685.
177 Mancini, S. (2014), pp.2, 29.
178 Tourkochoriti, I. (2012), p. 846.

construction of a democracy of human beings, and not that of the collective of the nation and needs to safeguard the democratic values that democratic procedures express. It further needs to safeguard that the legitimate aim for restrictions on religious expression within intricate webs of understandings[179] is held accountable to the affected communities and to the persons themselves and that it ensures that individuals are not subject to forced reconciliation, arbitrary state will and eventually domination. As long as the issues around religious symbols and expression are presented as an identity controversy, identities will be meant structurally to clash rather than to dialogue with each other[180] and they will stay mired in this battle. Unless we assess the subjectivity and legitimacy questions that arise at a conceptual level, and the relevant issues of who has the power to define the contested subject and what type of definition this is formulated into, we are only but doomed to remain mired in this controversy as if it were a conflict of 'us versus them' or a conflict of values, while it is in fact a conflict of definition.

References

Abdelal, R. H., Yoshiko, M. J., Alastair, I., and McDermottR., 2006. Identity as a Variable. *Perspectives on Politics*, 4(4), pp. 695–711

Atakav, A., 2007. Mona Lisa in Veils: Cultural Identity, Politics, Religion and Feminism in Turkey. *Feminist Theology*, 16(1), pp. 11–20

Augenstein, D., 2012. Religious Pluralism and National and Constitutional Traditions in Europe, chapter 11, pp. 261–280 in Zucca, L., Ungureanu, C. (eds), *Law, State and Religion in the New Europe: Debates and Dilemmas.* 1st ed. CambridgeUniversity Press

Balkin, J., 1993. Understanding Legal Understanding: The Legal Subject and the Problem of Legal Coherence. *The Yale Law Journal*, 103(1), pp. 105–176

Begum, B., Zysset, A., 2013. 'Personal Autonomy' and 'Democratic Society' at the European Court of Human Rights: Friends or Foes?. *UCL Journal of Law and Jurisprudence*, 2(1), pp. 230–249

Bellamy, R., 2013. The Democratic Qualities of Courts: A Critical Analysis of Three Arguments. *Representation*, 49(3), pp. 333–346 in Parau, C. and Bellamy, R. eds. Special Issue: Courts and Representative Democracy, p. 336

Bellamy, R., Baher, P., 1993. Carl Schmitt and the Contradictions of Liberal Democracy. *European Journal of Political Research*, 23, pp. 163–185

Benhabib, S., 2012. On Michel Rosenfeld's The Identity of the Constitutional Subject. *Cardozo Law Review*, 33(5), pp. 1889–1906

Bottici, Ch., Challand, B., 2012. Islam and the Public Sphere: Public Reason or Public Imagination, chapter 5, pp. 115–134 in Zucca, L., Ungureanu, C. (eds), *Law, State and Religion in the New Europe: Debates and Dilemmas.* 1st ed. CambridgeUniversity Press

Calo, Z. R., 2011. Pluralism, Secularism and the European Court of Human Rights. *Journal of Law and Religion*, 26. *SSRN Electronic Journal*, p. 104

179 See also in Topidi, K. (2016), p. 281, which reads: 'It is indeed true that a state's authority to draw a line and designate the space where religious rights can be exercised is no longer exclusive: courts, constitutions and transnational bodies contribute to the exchange of norms and concepts creating webs of understandings that become decreasingly easy to study in isolation'.

180 Mancini, S. (2009), p. 2666.

Cerulo, K. A., 1997. Identity Construction: New Issues, New Directions. *Annual Review of Sociology*, 10(23), pp. 385–409

Challand, B., 2009. From Hammer and Sickle to Star and Crescent: The Question of Religion for European Identity and a Political Europe. *Religion, State and Society*, 37(1), pp. 65–80

Custos, D., 2006. Secularism in French Public Schools: Back to War? The French Statute of March 15, 2004. *The American Journal of Comparative Law*, 54(2), pp. 337–399

Danchin, P., 2011. Islam in the Secular Nomos of the European Court of Human Rights. *Michigan Journal of International Law*, 32, pp. 663–2011; University of Maryland Legal Studies Research Paper No. 2010–2041. *SSRN Electronic Journal*, p. 26. [online] Available at: <http://ssrn.com/abstract=1670671> [Accessed 17 March 2012]

Dawn, L., Spini, D., 2004. Unveiling the Headscarf Debate. *Feminist Legal Studies*, 12(3), pp. 333–345

Dyzenhaus, D., 2006. *The Constitution of Law, Legality in a Time of Emergency*. Cambridge University Press

Elbow, P., 1993. The Uses of Binary Thinking. *Journal of Advanced Composition*, 13(1), pp. 51–78

Erlewine, R., 2009. *Nation of Devils: Monotheism and Tolerance; Recovering a Religion of Reason*. Indiana Series in the Philosophy of Religion

Garthoff, J., 2010. Legitimacy is Not Authority. *Law and Philosophy*, 29(6), pp. 669–694

Guerrero, M., 2011. International Women's Rights and the 'War of Cultures': Avoiding the 'Westernization' Debate. *Vienna Journal on International Constitutional Law*, 5(3), pp. 379–399

Gutwirth, S., 2008. Beyond Identity?. *IDIS – Identity in the Information Society*, 1(1), pp. 122–133. [online] Available at: http://works.bepress.com/serge_gutwirth/15/ [Accessed 12 June 2012]

Horkheimer, M., Adorno, Th. W., 2002. *Dialectic of Enlightenment*. Stanford University Press

Hunter-Hénin, M., 2012. *Law, Religious Freedoms and Education in Europe (Cultural Diversity and Law)*. Ashgate Publishing

Joppke, Chr., 2016. Pluralism vs. Pluralism: Islam and Christianity in the European Court of Human Rights, chapter 4, pp. 89–109 in Cohen, J. L., Laborde, C. (eds), *Religion, Secularism, and Constitutional Democracy*. Columbia University Press

Kant, I, 1991. *Kant: Political Writings*, Reiss, H. S. ed., Nisbet, H. B. transl. (Cambridge Texts in the History of Political Thought). 2nd ed. Cambridge University Press

Kymlicka, W., 1997. *States, Nations and Cultures*. Van Gorcum

Kyritsis, D., Tsakyrakis, St., 2013. Neutrality in the Classroom. *International Journal of Constitutional Law*, 11(1), pp. 200–217

Laborde, C., 2005. Secular Philosophy and Muslim Headscarves in Schools. *Journal of Political Philosophy*, 13(3), pp. 305–329

Lépinard, E., 2011. Autonomy and the Crisis of the Feminist Subject: Revisiting Okin's Dilemma. *Constellations*, 18(2), pp. 205–221

Lobeira, P., CristóbalP., 2011. Veils, Crucifixes and Public Sphere: What Kind of Secularism? Rethinking Neutrality in a Post-Secular Europe. *Journal of Intercultural Studies*, 35(4), pp. 385–412

McGoldrick, D., 2011. Religion in the European Public Square and in European Public Life–Crucifixes in the Classroom?. *Human Rights Law Review*, 11(3), pp. 451–502

McHarg, A., 1999. Reconciling Human Rights and the Public Interest: Conceptual Problems and Doctrinal Uncertainty in the Jurisprudence of the European Court of Human Rights. *The Modern Law Review*, 62(5), pp. 671–696

MacKinnon, C. A., 1982. Feminism, Marxism, Method, and the State: An Agenda for Theory. *Feminist Theory, Signs*, 7(3), pp. 515–544

Malik, M., 2009. Feminism and its "Other": Female Autonomy in the Age of Difference. *Cardozo Law Review*, 30, pp. 2613–2628

Malik, M., 2012. The 'Other' Citizens: Religion in a Multicultural Europe, chapter 4, pp. 93–114 in Zucca, L., Ungureanu, C. (eds), *Law, State and Religion in the New Europe: Debates and Dilemmas*. 1st ed. CambridgeUniversity Press

Mancini, S., 2009. The Power of Symbols and Symbols as Power: Secularism and Religion as Guarantors of Cultural Convergence. *Cardozo Law Review*, 30(6), pp. 2629–2668

Mancini, S., 2010. The Crucifix Rage: Supranational Constitutionalism Bumps against the Counter-Majoritarian Difficulty. *European Constitutional Law Review*, 6(01), pp. 6–27

Mancini, S., 2011. The Free Exercise of Exclusion: On Veils, Enemies and Militant Democracy. *SSRN Electronic Journal*. [online] Available at: <http://dx.doi.org/10.2139/ssrn.1784786> [Accessed 20 June 2012]

Mancini, S., 2012. Patriarchy as the Exclusive Domain of the Other: The Veil Controversy, False Projection and Cultural Racism. *International Journal of Constitutional Law*, 10(2), pp. 411–428

Mancini, S., 2013. The Tempting of Europe, the Political Seduction of the Cross: A Schmittian Reading of Christianity and Islam in European Constitutionalism, pp. 111–136 in Mancini, S., Rosenfeld, M. (eds), *Constitutional Secularism in an Age of Religious Revival*. Oxford University Press

Mancini, S., Rosenfeld, M. eds., 2014. *Constitutional Secularism in an Age of Religious Revival*. Oxford University Press

Mancini, S., Rosenfeld, M., 2010. Unveiling the Limits of Tolerance: Comparing the Treatment of Majority and Minority Religious Symbols in the Public Sphere. Cardozo Legal Studies Research Paper No. 309

Marshall, J., 2006. Freedom of Religious Expression and Gender Equality: Sahin v Turkey. *Modern Law Review*, 69(3), pp. 452–461

Marshall, J., 2008. Women's Right to Autonomy and Identity in European Human Rights Law: Manifesting One's Religion. *Res Publica*, 14, pp. 177–192

Marshall, J., 2009. *Personal Freedom through Human Rights Law?*. Martinus Nijhoff

Martinez-Torron, J., 2012. The (Un)protection of Individual Religious Identity in the Strasbourg Case Law. *Oxford Journal of Law and Religion*, 1(2), pp. 363–385

Michaels, R., 2014. On Liberalism and Legal Pluralism, pp. 122–142, in MaduroM., TuoriK., Sankari, S. (eds), 2014. *Transnational Law: Rethinking European Law and Legal Thinking*. Cambridge University Press

Mill, J. St., first publ. 1859, 2001. *On Liberty*. Batoche Books

Moller, K., 2009. Two Conceptions of Positive Liberty: Towards an Autonomy-based Theory of Constitutional Rights. *Oxford Journal of Legal Studies*, 29(4), pp. 757–786

Narayan, U., 1998. Essence of Culture and a Sense of History: A Feminist Critique of Cultural Essentialism. *Hypatia*, 13(2), pp. 86–106

Nigro, R., 2010. The Margin of Appreciation Doctrine and the Case-Law of the ECtHR on the Islamic Veil. *Human Rights Review*, 11(4), pp. 531–564

Nussbaum, M., 1999. *Sex & Social Justice*. Oxford University Press

Nussbaum, M., 2012. *The New Religious Intolerance: Overcoming the Politics of Fear in an Anxious Age*. 1st ed. Belknap Press Harvard University

Orgad, L., 2010. Illiberal Liberalism: Cultural Restrictions on Migration and Access to Citizenship in Europe. *American Journal of Comparative Law*, 58(1), pp. 53–106

Pavone, T., 2011. Redefining Religious Neutrality: Lautsi vs. Italy and the European Court of Human Rights. Available at https://www.strasbourgconsortium.org/content/blurb/files/Pavone%20-%20Redefining%20Religious%20Neutrality%20-%20Lautsi%20v.%20Italy%20and%20the%20ECtHR.pdf

Philip, J., 2006. *The Social Authority of Reason: Kant's Critique, Radical Evil, and the Destiny of Humankind*. SUNY Series in Philosophy

Phillips, A., 2001. Feminism and Liberalism Revisited: Has Martha Nussbaum Got it Right?. *Constellations*, 8(2), pp. 249–266

Plant, R., 2011. Religion, Identity and Freedom of Expression. *Res Publica*, 7, pp. 7–20

Puppinck, Gr., 2011. Lautsi v. Italy: The Leading Case on Majority Religions in European Secular States. *European Centre for Law and Justice*, p. 14 [online] Available at: <http://eclj.org/pdf/ECLJ-LAUTSIvITALY-secular-states-20110315.pdf> [Accessed 25 March 2012]

Raday, F., 2012. Sacralising the Patriarchal Family in the Monotheistic Religions: To no Form of Religion is Woman Indebted for One Impulse of Freedom. *International Journal of Law in Context*, 8(2), pp. 211–230

Rawls, J., 1993. *Political Liberalism*. Columbia University Press

Ringelheim, J. (2002). Identity Controversies before the European Court of Human Rights. *German Law Journal*, 3(7), pp. 167–175

Ronchi, P., 2011. Crucifixes, Margin of Appreciation and Consensus: The Grand Chamber Ruling in Lautsi v Italy. *Ecclesiastical Law Journal*, 13, pp. 287–297

Rorive, I., 2009. Religious Symbols in the Public Space: In Search of a European Answer. *Cardozo Law Review*, 30(6), pp. 2669–2698

Rosenfeld, M., 2009. *The Identity of the Constitutional Subject: Selfhood, Citizenship, Culture, and Community*. 1st ed. London: Routledge

Simpson, G., 2001. Two Liberalisms. *European Journal International Law*, 12(3), pp. 537–572

Topidi, K., 2012. Religious Diversity in Public Education: A Comparative European Perspective, pp. 109–128 in Roux, C. (ed.), *Safe Spaces: Human Rights Education in Diverse Contexts* (Critical Issues in the Future of Learning and Teaching). 1st ed. SensePublishers

Topidi, K., 2016. Public Education and Religious Rights: A Comparative Analysis', chapter 12, pp. 269–302 in Topidi, K., Fielder, L. (eds), *Religion as Empowerment: Global Legal Perspectives*. Routledge

Tourkochoriti, I., 2012. The Burka Ban: Divergent Approaches to Freedom of Religion in France and in the U.S.A. *William & Mary Bill of Rights Journal*, 20, pp. 791–852

Tyulkina, S., 2011. *Militant Democracy: Undemocratic Political Parties and Beyond*. Routledge

Vakulenco, A., 2007. Liberalism, Civilisation and the (Non-) Oxymoronic Limits of Tolerance. *International Journal of Law in Context*, 3(4), pp. 323–341

Vakulenko, A., 2007. Islamic Dress in Human Rights Jurisprudence: A Critique of Current Trends. *Human Rights Law Review*, 7(4), pp. 717–739

Volpp, L., 2001. Feminism versus Multiculturalism. *Columbia Law Review*, 101(5), pp. 1181–1218

Weber, M., Shils, Ed. A. and Finch, H. A., eds. and transl., 1949. *The Methodology of the Social Sciences*. Free Press

Weiler, J. H. H., 2012. In the Face of Crisis: Input Legitimacy, Output Legitimacy and the Political Messianism of European Integration. *Journal of European Integration*, 34(7), pp. 825–841

Yeğenoğlu, M., 2005. *Colonial Fantasies: Towards a Feminist Reading of Orientalism*. 1st ed. CambridgeUniversity Press

European Court of Human Rights

Dahlab v. Switzerland [2001] Application no. 42393/98 (ECtHR)
Lautsi v. Italy [2009] Application No. 30814/06 (ECtHR, Chamber)
Lautsi v. Italy [2011] Application no. 30814/06 (ECtHR, Grand Chamber)
Regina (Shabina Begum) v. Governors of Denbigh High Sch. [2006] UKHL 15, [2007] 1 AC 100, para. 96, 97
Sahin v. Turkey [2004] Application No. 44774/98 (ECtHR)

Newspaper articles

Wintour, P., 2011. David Cameron Tells Muslim Britain: Stop Tolerating Extremists. *The Guardian*. [online] Available at: www.theguardian.com/politics/2011/feb/05/david-cameron-muslim-extremism [Accessed 16 July 2012]

5 Immigrants or new religious minorities?

Conflicting European and international perspectives

Fabienne Bretscher

Introduction

While for a long time being a society of emigrants, Europe has some difficulties in coping with its new status as an immigrant-receiving continent. In particular the religious differences between groups formed by recent immigration and the majority population seems to be a hot topic today. Motivated by fear for social cohesion or democratic values such as gender equality, religious practices of such immigrant groups, for instance the wearing of turbans or headscarves, are restricted. This contribution looks at limitations of these practices from a human rights perspective and inquires on the conformity of such measures with the right to freedom of religion. It is based on the premise that the evaluation of such human rights conformity strongly depends on the position given to groups formed by recent immigration in today's society, namely whether they are seen as immigrants who need to assimilate to majority society or as minorities in need of protection.

In a first section, this contribution elaborates thus on the special legal protection granted to such minorities and the conflicting approaches taken at the level of the United Nations (UN) and the Council of Europe (CoE) in the debate on the inclusion of so-called new minorities, that is groups formed by recent immigration, in the scope of such minority protection instruments. A second section is then dedicated to inquiring whether these different perspectives have also led to conflicts in the practice of the two respective bodies, which can receive individual complaints for violations of the right to freedom of religion, namely the UN Human Rights Committee (UNHRC) and the European Court of Human Rights (ECtHR). Lastly, a third section is dedicated to possible ways to resolve the conflict arisen between the international and European level.

Religious diversity in Europe: minorities and immigrants

Many perceive that European society has become multi-religious due to recent immigration, for example from Turkey, Morocco, Former Yugoslavia, but also from India or Bangladesh. Yet, religious diversity has been present on the European continent for a long time and many states have been hosting various religions. This does not only include Catholics and Protestants, but also Jews or Muslims for some countries. Most European states thus define themselves as secular and consequently constitutionally detached from religious institutions. Yet, this did not prevent that conflicts between the different religious groups arose, for example with regard to the definition of religious holidays[1] or controversial religious practices such as kosher butchering.[2] In order to guarantee the rights of persons, which do not adhere to the majority's religion, legal instruments were drafted on the international level for the protection of these so-called minorities.[3] Their principal features are presented in the first section. Only in a second step the question of a definition of the term minority and the inclusion of religious groups formed by recent immigration in the personal scope of these instruments is addressed in detail. This is done so because it is important to know the content of existing guarantees before entering in the discussion of the potential right holders.

A brief overview of the legal protection of religious minorities

This contribution focuses on the legal framework specifically designed to protect religious and other minorities in European states; this includes the Council of Europe (CoE) Framework Convention for the Protection of National Minorities (FCNM)[4] and the so-called UN Minority Declaration.[5] Both instruments developed from the idea that minorities are in need of special protection on the international level in addition to the already existing, so-called general human rights instruments, such as for example the International Covenant on Civil and Political Rights (ICCPR).[6] This can be linked to the end of the Cold War, which showed that in order to guarantee stability and cohesion as well as effective protection of minority groups, specific state obligations for the protection of minorities were necessary.[7] Minority instruments thus aim at creating a feeling of national cohesion that should protect the minorities from repression by the majority and guarantee the full realization of their human rights.[8] The current existing minority protection regime foresees

1 See for example *Sessa v Italy* ECHR 2012-III 165 (extracts).
2 See for example *Cha'are Shalom Ve Tsedek v France* [GC] ECHR 2000-VII 231.
3 It needs to be noted that these instruments do not only aim at religious minorities, but also include national, linguistic or ethnic minorities.
4 ETS No 157, 1 adopted on 1 February 1995, entered into force on 1 February 1998.
5 Declaration on the Rights of Persons Belonging to National or Ethnic, Religious and Linguistic Minorities, United Nations General Assembly (UNGA) Res 47/135 (18 December 1992).
6 999 UNTS 171, adopted on 16 December 1966, entered into force on 23 March 1976. It needs to be noted that Art 27 ICCPR grants religious minorities a right to profess their own culture. As this provision is significantly less specified than the instruments specifically drafted for minorities, this section focuses on the latter.
7 Asbjørn Eide, 'The Rights of "New" Minorities: Scope and Restrictions' in Kristin Henrard (ed) *Double Standards Pertaining to Minority Protection* (Brill 2010) 169.
8 Anna Meijknecht, 'Minority Protection System between World War I and World War II' *Max Planck Encyclopedia of Public International Law* (MPEPIL 2010) para 6.

> … obligations to prevent discrimination and to take measures to ensure full and effective equality, and … to promote conditions for diversity and to abstain from assimilationist policies, while recognising the justification of the state to promote integration in society.[9]

For example, the FCNM in its Article 5 obliges states to "promote the conditions necessary [for minorities] to maintain and develop their culture, and to preserve the essential elements of their identity". Furthermore, it puts forward that states "shall refrain from policies or practices aimed at assimilation of [minorities] against their will". As an example, numerically small minorities in Poland can be named. According to the Advisory Committee on the FCNM (ACFC) they lack "funding necessary for the establishment of cultural centres, libraries or similar institutions, without which their communities face rapid and full assimilation with the majority".[10] This shows that minority instruments take an explicit stand against assimilation and for the preservation of religious (and other) diversity. Moreover, all minority instruments also contain a specific guarantee of freedom of religion for minorities.[11]

Differing from general human rights instruments, minority instruments explicitly impose on states the responsibility to take special positive measures to promote full and effective equality of minorities in all domains of the economic, social, political and cultural life.[12] This follows an understanding of substantive and not just formal equality and entails that it may sometimes not be enough to treat everyone in the same way, but to achieve effective equality, special measures for certain disadvantaged groups may be necessary.[13] This ideal of equality for all can also be seen in Article 15 FCNM, which obliges states to "create the conditions necessary for the effective participation of persons belonging to national minorities". This shall be realized with measures, which

> encourage a spirit of tolerance and intercultural dialogue and … promote mutual respect and understanding and cooperation among all persons … irrespective of those persons' ethnic, cultural, linguistic or religious identity.[14]

Nevertheless, according to minority instruments, this does not mean that minorities' rights cannot be restricted. Article 19 FCNM states that this is possible, permitting however "only those limitations, restrictions or derogations which are

9 Eide (*supra* n 7) 167; Julie Ringelheim, *Diversité Culturelle et Droits de l'Homme – La Protection des Minorités par la Convention Européenne des Droits de l'Homme* (Bruylant 2006) 4.
10 ACFC, '3rd Opinion on Poland' (28 November 2013) ACFC/OP/III(2013)004, para 62.
11 Art 8 FCNM; Art 27 ICCPR; Art 2(1) UN Minority Declaration.
12 For example Art 4(2) FCNM.
13 Kristin Henrard, *Devising an Adequate System of Minority Protection: Individual Human Rights, Minority Rights and the Right to Self-Determination* (Brill 2000) 13.
14 Art 6(1) FCNM.

provided for in international legal instruments ... in so far as they are relevant to the rights and freedoms flowing from the said principles". Furthermore, members of minorities also have certain obligations. For example, Article 20 FCNM states that "any person belonging to a national minority shall respect the national legislation and the rights of others, in particular those of persons belonging to the majority or to other national minorities". Also the UN Minority Declaration limits the rights of minorities and excludes practices, which are "contrary to international standards",[15] from its protection. Hence, it can be summarized that although minority instruments pursue the integration of minorities in society, they aim at ensuring their equal enjoyment of rights by accommodating minorities' diversity and preventing assimilation.

Immigrants as new minorities: divergent approaches

'Traditional' religious diversity has in recent decades been expanded to include 'new' religious diversity due to immigration movements. Religious beliefs of groups originating from recent immigration are often restricted. This may be in a direct way, for example by passing legislation, which prohibits the construction of minarets[16] or the wearing of the Burqa in public places;[17] it can, however, also happen in an indirect or systemic way, for example by forcing children wearing religious headgears to abstain from this religious practice or to attend private schools.[18] This situation raises the question how social cohesion can be maintained and how members of groups formed by recent immigration, who are adhering to minority religions, can be protected. Considering the similarity of these concerns with the issues touched upon by the already existing minority protection regime, some argue that groups formed by recent immigration should be included as so-called new minorities in its scope of protection.[19] A precondition for the application of this minority protection regime is the definition of a group as a minority. Yet, as this is a very controversial topic, in international law, no generally agreed-upon definition of the term minority could be reached until now and consequently, these legal instruments do not contain a definition of their personal scope, i.e. the individuals or groups they are applicable to.[20] Although international bodies and legal scholars put forward several definitions, there is none, which can be seen as established.[21]

15 Art 4(2) UN Minority Declaration.
16 In Switzerland in 2009, a popular initiative introduced the prohibition of the construction of minarets in the Constitution (Art 72(3) of the Swiss Constitution of 1999), undoubtedly aiming at restricting the freedom of religion of the Muslim minority in Switzerland (see UN Working Group, Universal Periodic Review, Report for the Second Cycle, Switzerland (7 December 2012) UN Doc A/HRC/22/11).
17 *SAS v France* [GC] ECHR 2014-III 341 (extracts).
18 See section III.A.
19 For example Perry Keller, 'Rethinking Ethnic and Cultural Rights in Europe' (1998) 18 *Oxford Journal of Legal Studies* 29.
20 Eide (n 7) 170f.
21 Henrard, *Minority Protection* (n 13) 18ff.

Confronted with this situation, international bodies have thus developed different approaches to the question as to whether groups formed by recent immigration should be included in the definition of the term minority. Among the instruments applicable to European countries, two main perspectives can be distinguished: the United Nations Human Rights Committee (UNHRC) opts for a wide scope of application of Article 27 ICCPR and defines minorities as all persons "who belong to a group and who share in common a culture, a religion and/or a language"; this includes even migrant workers or visitors. Minorities thus have "the right, in community with members of their group, to enjoy their own culture, to practise their religion and speak their language".[22] One could argue that such a wide definition is only appropriate because of the limited rights guaranteed by Article 27 ICCPR, yet, also for the UN Minority Declaration, which contains more extensive rights, a similar approach is adopted. New minorities are generally included in the personal scope of relevant guarantees at the UN level. Nevertheless, the Commentary to the Declaration recognizes "that in the application of the Declaration the 'old' minorities have stronger entitlements than the 'new'".[23] Taking a rather practical approach, the Commentary puts forward that states are required to take the measures necessary to ensure

> peaceful and constructive group accommodation based on equality in dignity and rights for all and which allows for the necessary pluralism to enable the persons belonging to the different groups to preserve and develop their identity.[24]

What such measures should consist of needs to be determined in the concrete circumstances. This means that so-called old minorities may have "stronger rights than those who have recently arrived",[25] for example with regards to language rights. This needs to be determined in the application and interpretation of the respective provision.[26]

Contrary to this, in the practice of the Advisory Committee on the FCNM (ACFC), a more restrictive approach to the issue of definition can be found. Similar to the UN instruments, the FCNM failed to include a definition of its personal scope because no agreement on the characteristics of a minority could be found.[27] Nevertheless the Explanatory Report to the FCNM clearly dissociates the

22 UNHRC, 'General Comment No 23 on Article 27 ICCPR' (8 April 1994) UN Doc CCPR/C/21/Rev.1/Add.5, paras 5.1.f; see also Henrard, *Minority Protection* (n 13) 21.
23 Economic and Social Council (ESC), 'Commentary of the Working Group on Minorities to the United Nations Declaration on the Rights of Persons Belonging to National or Ethnic, Religious and Linguistic Minorities' (4 April 2005) UN Doc. E/CN.4/Sub.2/AC.5/2005/2, para 11.
24 Ibid, para 13.
25 Ibid, para 10.
26 Ibid, para 7.
27 Rainer Hofmann, 'Introduction' in Marc Weller, *The Rights of Minorities in Europe* (OUP 2005) 16ff.

interpretation of the concept of minority adopted for the FCNM from the definition put forward by UN bodies, which were elaborated in the previous paragraph.[28] As a consequence of the lack of definition, many states added a declaration to their ratification of the FCNM stressing their interpretation of the personal scope of the Convention.[29] By means of such declaration, states often excluded certain minorities for political or historical reasons[30] and followed a restrictive interpretation of the term minority; in particular they excluded non-citizens[31] or groups without long-standing or historical ties,[32] and most members of groups formed by recent immigration, explicitly from the scope of the FCNM. The ACFC generally accepts this practice and takes the definitions put forward by the states as a starting point, it adopts however a flexible approach as it does not feel bound by these definitions in its activities, for example opinions on reports of states.[33]

Furthermore, the ACFC has specified that if the definitions are of a too excluding nature, they are not seen as compatible with the FCNM.[34] Consequently, a formal recognition as a national minority from the part of the state is in principle not necessary for groups to fall under the scope of the FCNM.[35] With regards to the definition of groups formed by recent immigration as new minorities, the ACFC continuously reminds signatory states that they should also benefit from the guarantees of the FCNM, as in the case of Germany referring among other to the minority formed by immigrants originating from Turkey.[36] The Parliamentary Assembly of the CoE also took this point of view and recommended to member states to draft a specific instrument for these "special categories of minorities".[37] Yet, the ECtHR takes the approach that the definition of the term minority, "by the nature of things, [must] be left largely to the State concerned, as it will depend on particular national circumstances".[38]

28 CoE Committee of Ministers, 'Explanatory Report to the FCNM' (February 1995) H (95) 10, para 26.
29 CoE, 'Reservations and Declarations for Treaty No 157 – Framework Convention for the Protection of National Minorities' <www.coe.int/en/web/conventions/full-list/-/conventions/treaty/157/declarations?p_auth=2RpNP29s> accessed 15 December 2016.
30 Doris Angst, 'Art. 3, A. Allgemeiner Teil' in Rainer Hofmann and others (eds), *Rahmenübereinkommen zum Schutz nationaler Minderheiten* (Nomos 2015) para 13.
31 For example Armenia, Germany, Georgia, Austria, Moldavia, Czech Republic, see CoE, *Reservations and Declarations FCNM* (n 29).
32 For example Switzerland or Norway.
33 Angst (n 30) para 9.
34 See for example ACFC, '1st Opinion on Denmark' (22 September 2000) ACFC/INF/OP/I(2001)005, para 22.
35 Angst (n 30) para 12.
36 For example ACFC, 'Opinion on Germany' (1 March 2002) ACFC/INF/OP/I/008, paras 17f; ACFC, 'Opinion on Switzerland' (20 February 2003) ACFC/INF/OP/I(2003)007, para 24.
37 CoE Parliamentary Assembly (PACE), 'Rights of National Minorities' Recommendation 1492(2001), para 11.
38 *Gorzelik and Others v Poland* ECHR 2004–I 273, para 67.

When comparing the approaches at the level of the UN and the CoE, it is important to highlight that the principal instrument within the framework of the CoE, the FCNM, exclusively uses the term 'national minority' while by UN instruments, this designation is used alongside the notion 'ethnic, religious and linguistic minorities'. Yet, as the statement of the CoE Parliamentary Assembly shows, this does, in principle, not prevent an inclusion of groups formed by recent immigration. Nevertheless, there is a conflict between the approaches taken by the bodies responsible for the monitoring of minority protection instruments to the interpretation of the term minority: the UNHRC uses a wide definition, including also groups formed by recent immigration in the scope of Article 27 ICCPR and the UN Minority Declaration, thus looking at them as minorities. The ACFC and more so the ECtHR, however, leave to states wide discretion in defining the groups, which enter in the scope of the FCNM, who consequently mostly consider groups formed by recent immigration as immigrants and not minorities.

The divergent approaches in practice

Confronted with this conflict between the approaches adopted to the issue of new minorities, the question arises how these different perspectives are reflected in the interpretation of the right to freedom of religion of groups formed by recent immigration in individual cases, namely in the practice of the two bodies, which can receive individual complaints, that is the UNHRC and the ECtHR. Neither of these bodies can receive complaints solely based on a violation of the above-presented special minority instruments, but only when brought forward under a provision of the ICCPR or the ECHR respectively.[39] The examination is based on a case study of restrictions of religious practices of groups formed by recent immigration in France, which, by means of a comparison to the rest of the practice of the two bodies, shall allow the drawing of general conclusions on the practical effects of the conflicting perspectives in the debate surrounding new minorities.

Case study: restriction of new minorities' religious practices in France

The following section presents a set of cases brought by members of new minorities alleging a violation of their right to freedom of religion by France in the context of public schools. The example of France was chosen because it is possible to find cases based on very similar facts, which were decided by the UNHRC as well as by the ECtHR. One may argue that France, as a state based on the principle of secularism (*laïcité*), represents a special situation, which is not comparable to other countries. Yet, such factual particularity is the same for both bodies. It does not therefore impair the objective of this section, which is a comparison of the approaches of the ECtHR and the UNHRC to the religious freedom of members of groups formed by recent immigration.

39 Although the UNHRC could receive complaints based on Art 27 ICCPR, members of new minorities did until now not base their complaints on this provision.

The set of cases originates from a French law aiming at ensuring the secular nature of public schools (so-called 'Loi Stasi').[40] This law prohibits religious symbols or clothing by means of which students manifest their religious affiliation in an ostentatious manner. It is the expression of the concept of neutrality, the so-called principle of *laïcité*, put forward by France, which requires the ban of all religions from the public sphere.[41] Based on this law, several Muslim and Sikh students were excluded from the public school they were attending because they refused to abstain from wearing a headscarf or a turban respectively. This forced them to register in private schools or to undertake distance learning.

When analysing the respective international decisions, conflicting approaches in the responses of the ECtHR and the UNHRC can be observed:[42] the ECtHR declared all complaints manifestly ill-founded and thus inadmissible.[43] Although recognizing that the prohibition of religious symbols interferes with the students' right to freedom of religion according to Article 9 ECHR, the Court stated that the interference pursued the legitimate aim of the protection of the freedom of others and the public order by means of ensuring neutrality of public education. Furthermore, a broad margin of appreciation was left to France when it came to the necessity of the interference and the Court only examined whether the act was not disproportionate. Taking into account that the students were able to pursue their education in private schools or through distance learning, the ECtHR did not see a violation of their right to freedom of religion or belief. Restricted by the wide margin of appreciation, the ECtHR did not examine in depth whether the measure was necessary to achieve the aim of neutrality of public education. Furthermore, especially the argument concerning private schools and distance learning shows that the ECtHR does not derive a state duty of accommodation of religious practices of members of groups formed by recent immigration in this situation from Article 9 ECHR.

With regard to the prohibition of discrimination guaranteed by Article 14 ECHR, the ECtHR observed that the legal provision in question did not distinguish among different religions but applied to every ostentatious religious symbol.[44] Thereby it applied a strictly formal interpretation of the concept of

40 Loi n° 2004–228, 15 March 2004; for a short summary of the background of the law see the UN Special Rapporteur on freedom of religion or belief, 'Report on Mission to France' (8 March 2006) UN Doc E/CN.4/2006/5/Add. 4, paras 48ff.

41 Wouter de Been, 'The Quest of Neutrality and the Stench of History' in Jeroen Temperman (ed) *The Lautsi Papers: Reflections on Religious Symbols in the Public School Classroom* (Brill 2012) 184.

42 For an in-depth analysis: Emmanuelle Bribosia, Gabrielle Caceres and Isabelle Rorive, 'Les Signes Religieux au Cœur d'un Bras de Fer entre Genève et Paris: La Saga Singh' (2014) 98 *Revue Trimestrielle des Droits de l'Homme* 495.

43 *Aktas v France* App no 43563/08 (ECtHR, 30 June 2009), *Bayrak v France* App no 14308/08 (ECtHR, 30 June 2009), *Gamaleddyn v France* App no 18527/08 (ECtHR, 30 June 2009), *Ghazal v France* App no 29134/08 (ECtHR, 30 June 2009), *Jasvir Singh v France* App no 25463/08 (ECtHR, 30 June 2009) and *Ranjit Singh v France* App no 27561/08 (ECtHR, 30 June 2009).

44 For example *Aktas v France*, para 3.

equality to the case, not taking into account the adverse effects[45] of the law for Muslims, Sikhs and also other religions. Although the ECtHR seems to go beyond this formal understanding of equality in certain cases,[46] its analysis of the present case shows that this does not apply to the context of accommodation of religious beliefs of members of groups formed by recent immigration.

On the other hand, in the decision of the UNHRC with regard to the same French legislation, a totally different reasoning can be found:[47] not restricted by a wide margin of appreciation of the state, the Committee stated with regard to the necessity of the limitation of the student's freedom of religion that France had not furnished compelling evidence that, by wearing his *keski*,[48] the author would have posed a threat to the rights and freedoms of other pupils or to order at the school. Moreover, the UNHRC was also not convinced by the reasoning that the education of the student was ensured by the possibility to attend private school or distance learning. The Committee thus qualified the expulsion from school as disproportionate and found a violation of the student's right to freedom of belief according to Article 18 ICCPR. It thus clearly demonstrated that although members of groups formed by recent immigration are expected to adapt to a certain extent to majority customs, also the dominating majority needs to re-evaluate existing rules. Having adopted this decision three years after the ECtHR, the UNHRC intentionally provoked a conflict of interpretation of the right to freedom of religion.

Consequences of the divergent approaches for new minorities' right to freedom of religion

When looking for traces of their conflicting approaches to the discussion on the definition of groups formed by recent immigration as new minorities in the practice of the ECtHR and the UNHRC, it needs first to be observed that both bodies do not refer to the applicants as minorities in the respective decisions. Nevertheless, some conclusions regarding the practical reflection of the conflicting approaches can be made. A decisive factor thereby is the recognition of a state duty for accommodation of religious diversity, which underpins the system for minority protection presented above.[49]

45 Such adverse effects refer 'to ingrained habits and related systems in society, which proceed from the majority perspective, and thus do not take into account other perspectives, such as […] the adherent of a minority religion', see Kristin Henrard, 'Duties of Reasonable Accommodation in Relation to Religion and the European Court of Human Rights: A Closer Look at the Prohibition of Discrimination, the Freedom of Religion and Related Duties of State Neutrality' (2012) 5(1) *Erasmus Law Review* 59, 68.

46 See *Thlimmenos v Greece* [GC] ECHR 2000-IV 263.

47 UNHRC, *Singh v. France* (1 November 2012) UN Doc CCPR/C/106/D/1852/2008, Communication No 1852/2008.

48 A *keski* is a subtler version of a Sikh turban and was suggested by the student in question in order to comply with the 'Loi-Stasi'.

49 See section II.A.

A state duty of accommodation of minorities' religious practices

Minority instruments, for example Article 5(1) FCNM, oblige states to promote the conditions necessary for persons belonging to national minorities to maintain and develop their culture, and to preserve the essential elements of their identity, namely their religion, language, traditions and cultural heritage.[50]

A similar provision can be found with Article 4(2) of the UN Minority Declaration. The FCNM furthermore explicitly prohibits "policies or practices aimed at assimilation".[51] Yet, as the Explanatory Report to the FCNM makes clear, "this is not an endorsement or acceptance of practices which are contrary to national law or international standards"[52] as minority practices can be limited according to Article 20 FCNM or 4(2) of the UN Minority Declaration. This approach can be compared to the concept of reasonable accommodation of religious diversity developed by the Canadian Supreme Court to deal with restrictions of religious practices in the light of the human right to freedom of religion.[53] This concept requires a state "to take reasonable measures to ensure the effective enjoyment of the freedom to manifest one's religion".[54]

The underlying idea of such duties of reasonable accommodation is the achievement of substantial equality. As already elaborated in the first section, a distinction in the concept of equality is generally drawn between formal and substantive or effective equality. While a formal understanding of equality does not require the state to take special measures, but just demands that the same rules be applied to every member of society, interpreting the concept of equality in a substantive manner implies that the state needs to take action in order to guarantee that everyone has the same opportunities as well as equal access to employment, public services, education and social services in general. The adoption of such concept has as its consequence first the recognition of the construct of indirect discrimination, i.e. the interpretation of situations, in which the general application of a rule has a disparate impact on the situation of a certain group or individual as discrimination. A further consequence is the identification of corresponding state duties of reasonable accommodation, which aim at ensuring equal opportunities for members of minority religions, for example by means of exemptions from generally applicable rules, such as a prohibition of headgear, or also by the creation of a special regime, such as the introduction of a right to be released from work for prayer.[55]

50 See Ringelheim (n 9) 169.
51 Art 5 FCNM.
52 Explanatory Report to the FCNM (n 28) para 44.
53 See José Woehrling, 'L'obligation d'accommodement raisonnable et l'adaptiation de la société à la diversité religieuse' (1998) 43 *Revue de droit de McGill* 325; see also European Commission, *Reasonable accommodation beyond disability in Europe* (European Union 2013), 11ff.
54 Henrard, *Reasonable Accommodation* (n 46) 60.
55 See for this paragraph ibid, 62.

A state duty of accommodation in practice

A state duty of accommodation of minority religious practices is an essential element of the protection of religious minorities. The recognition of such duty in practice can serve as an indicator for the practical effects of the conflicting perspectives taken by the ECtHR and the UNHRC on the question of the definition of groups formed by recent immigration as new minorities.

THE EUROPEAN COURT OF HUMAN RIGHTS

The ECtHR seems to be very restrictive when it comes to claims for accommodation of religious diversity of groups formed by recent immigration; it does mostly not oblige the state to accommodate reasonable claims with regard to their religious practices,[56] but rather leaves it to the discretion of the member states of the CoE whether they adjust their policies in such a way. This could be observed already in 1981, when the European Commission of Human Rights declared the complaint of a Muslim primary school teacher in the United Kingdom, who was refused time off from work for prayer, inadmissible, because it did not find an interference with the right to freedom of religion. This was because the applicant had chosen his position out of free will and knowing that this would leave him unable to attend prayers.[57] The decision *Thlimmenos v Greece* from 2000 marked a turning point for the duty of reasonable accommodation in the jurisprudence of the ECtHR. It concerned a Jehovah's Witness excluded from the profession of a chartered accountant because he was convicted for proselytizing. Basing the argument on the prohibition of discrimination in combination with the right to freedom of religion, the ECtHR stated that the ECHR also entails an obligation to "treat differently persons whose situations are significantly different",[58] i.e. prohibiting indirect discrimination. Greece was thus in this case obliged to provide an exception from the general rule, which can be seen, although not designated as such, as an expression of the duty for reasonable accommodation. It has, however, to be noted that the applicant in this case was not a member of a new, but rather of an old minority.

In its later decisions the ECtHR turned away from this development, at least with regards to the field of religion, while for groups formed by recent immigration such a change of jurisprudence could never even be observed.[59] In practice, such approach is expressed when a broad margin of appreciation is left to the state, which has as a consequence that the ECtHR restricts its examination to a test of

56 See for example Ringelheim (n 9) 169; European Commission (n 52) 22ff.

57 *X v UK* (1981) 22 DR 27.

58 *Thlimmenos v Greece* [GC] para 44.

59 See for example *Kosteski v 'The former Yugoslav Republic of Macedonia'* App no 55170/00 (ECtHR, 13 April 2006) where the Muslim applicant missed a day of work due religious practices; *El Morsli v France* App no 15585/06 (ECtHR, 4 March 2008) where the Muslim applicant was refused entry to the French embassy due to the wearing of a veil.

unreasonableness.[60] Many times the ECtHR does not apply a strict necessity and proportionality test, which would require examining whether the measure chosen was the least restrictive and proportional for achieving the aim pursued.[61] Such hesitance to analyse alternative measures and the preference of following the arguments brought forward by the state may be due to the recently adopted Protocol No 15, which codifies the principle of subsidiarity and the margin of appreciation as explicit concepts of the ECHR.[62] Nevertheless, this line of jurisprudence confronts the applicants with the choice of abandoning their religious practice or living a life apart from majority society. Considering that the applicants in this case could be defined as members of a minority, the ECtHR's approach is thus conflicting with the basic premise of minority instruments as it expects new minorities to leave their customs and adapt to a great extent to majority society instead of protecting (religious) diversity. As such, new minorities' human rights are not effectively protected by the ECtHR against restrictions of their freedom of religion by the majority and their religious diversity is not seen as a positive contribution to society.

THE UN HUMAN RIGHTS COMMITTEE

Contrary to the ECtHR, the UNHRC seems to recognize such a state duty of reasonable accommodation for new minorities, although it does not explicitly refer to it as such. For example, in the case study above, the Committee required France to adapt its regulation and give students wearing religious headgear the possibility to attend public school. It arrived at this decision by scrutinizing the arguments brought forward by France and showing that there was no need for such prohibition in the specific case. It can therefore be observed that the UNHRC dared to interfere with domestic decisions and to scrutinize the arguments brought forward by the national instances in order to ensure their compliance with the requirements laid down in the relevant legal framework. In doing so, the Committee seems to tend more towards an interpretation of such claims of accommodation of religious beliefs from a minority perspective, although not referring to the applicants as members of minorities. Similar to Article 5 FCNM, the UNHRC obliges states to promote conditions, in which new minorities can exercise their right to freedom of religion without having to assimilate to the majority religion. Instead of forcing Muslim and Sikh students wearing 'ostentatious' religious symbols into private schools, distance learning or abstention from wearing the religious headgear, it imposes the state a duty to accommodate these religious practices as long as a restriction is not necessary and proportionate.

60 See also Keller (n 19) 53.

61 For a profound analysis of this question Olivier de Schutter, *International Human Rights Law* (CUP 2014) 378ff.

62 Protocol No 15 amending the Convention on the Protection of Human Rights and Fundamental Freedoms, 24 June 2013, Art 1, not yet in force.

The UNHRC does consequently not apply an unrestricted duty for accommodation of religious diversity, but limits such obligation with the necessity and proportionality test, as is also foreseen in minority instruments.[63] While in the above-analysed case this test led to the conclusion that the state bore a duty of reasonable accommodation of the religious difference of the applicant, the UNHRC concluded in other cases that the measure taken was necessary and proportionate to the aim pursued and a restriction of the applicant's freedom of religion thus justified. As an example the case of a Sikh who was obliged to wear a safety helmet for his work for a railway company, which made it impossible for him to follow his religious practice of wearing a turban, can be named.[64] In this way, the UNHRC tries to guarantee the best possible coordination of the different interests at stake in order to create "a climate of tolerance and dialogue [which] is necessary to enable cultural diversity to be a source and a factor, not of division, but of enrichment for each society",[65] even if this leads to a conflict with the ECtHR.

Towards a minority perspective

At the heart of international minority protection as it exists today lays the purpose to strengthen the protection of universal human rights for persons belonging to minorities.[66] The protection of minority rights today is thus closely related to general human rights law yet sees a need for additional guarantees for the safeguard of the rights of minorities due to their particular vulnerability.[67] Considering the general societal position of the groups formed by recent immigration, it can be observed that it has become increasingly socially acceptable to discriminate and stigmatize these members of our society.[68] This environment, where difference, diversity and pluralism are not perceived as positive values, makes it difficult for the groups concerned to effectively protect their religious beliefs.[69] Confronted with this situation, the question arises whether defining groups formed by recent

63 Art 19 FCNM; Art 4(2) UN Minority Declaration; see also UNHRC 'General Comment No 22 on Article 18' (30 July 1993) UN Doc CCPR/C/21/Rev.1/Add.4), para 8.

64 See for example UNHRC, *Karnel Singh Bhinder v Canada* (9 November 1989) UN Doc CCPR/C/37/D/208/1986, Communication No 208/1986 concerning the requirement to wear safety headgear during work.

65 Preamble FCNM.

66 Eide (n 7) 167.

67 Ibid, 169.

68 UN Special Rapporteur on contemporary forms of racism, racial discrimination, xenophobia and related intolerance, 'Report on the implementation of General Assembly resolution 67/154' (26 March 2013) UN Doc A/HRC/23/24, para 9.

69 For a provocative analysis of today's situation: Slavoj Zizek, 'Liberal multiculturalism masks an old barbarism with a human face' in *The Guardian* (London, 3 October 2010) <https://www.theguardian.com/commentisfree/2010/oct/03/immigration-policy-roma-rightwing-europe> accessed 22 April 2017.

immigration, as minorities would contribute to enhancing the protection of their right to freedom of religion.

The rights included in minority instruments do not apply to every minority in every case; rather, distinctions are made among different minority groups based on their need for special protection as well as on the reasonability and proportionality of the measure in question.[70] Consequently, defining groups formed by recent immigration as minorities would not entail that all their claims of accommodation of their religious beliefs should be recognized. Rather, a way would need to be found to balance the different interests in question, such as for example the need for protection of minorities within a functioning school system. This is also confirmed by the Commentary to the UN Minority Declaration, which explicitly allows for distinctions among different minorities, whose specific rights need to be determined in the application and interpretation of the respective provision.[71] Furthermore, also the ACFC advocates for such inclusion on an "article-by-article basis".[72]

Yet, as the practice of the UNHRC shows, a similar result can be achieved without referring explicitly to the concept of minority, but rather by interpreting general human rights guarantees, in this case the right to freedom of religion, in accordance with the principles of minority protection. To do so, the UNHRC uses the commonly known test of necessity and proportionality and thus requires states to accommodate religious diversity as long as the restriction of the freedom of religion is not necessary or proportionate. The ECtHR would thus have room for avoiding a conflicting approach and directing its interpretation of the ECHR within a similar minority perspective without necessarily defining members of groups formed by recent immigration as a minority or even mentioning the respective minority instruments.

The conflict between the approaches taken by minority instruments as well as the UNHRC and the ECtHR could be resolved by means of a stricter application of the necessity and proportionality test and a parallel restriction of the margin of appreciation of the member states by the ECtHR. This seems all the more warranted when taking the approach of the ACFC and the Parliamentary Assembly of the CoE into account, which both argue for a better protection of groups formed by recent immigration.[73] In doing so, the ECtHR must ensure that this determination of concrete state obligations towards these groups respects the overarching principles of the minority protection regime and also the concept of human rights, namely peace and security as well as social cohesion.[74] Furthermore, the main idea underpinning duties of accommodation, which is the full and equal participation of everyone in society, cannot be lost sight of.[75] In order to maintain social

70 Eide (n 7) 192.
71 ESC (n 23) para 7.
72 For example ACFC, *Opinion on Germany* (n 36) para 18.
73 For example ACFC, *Opinion on Switzerland* (n 36) para 24; ACFC, ACFC, *Opinion on Germany* (n 36) paras 17f; PACE (n 37) para 11.
74 ESC (n 23) para 13.
75 Henrard, *Reasonable Accommodation* (n 46) 62.

cohesion in our multi-religious society, it is thus important to ensure that all religious beliefs are accommodated in order to avoid exclusion and foster an inclusive society for all religious beliefs.[76]

Conclusion

The topic of immigration enjoys increased attention in today's public debate, not only regarding the journey of migration, but also in what concerns immigrants' integration in their host country, in particular based on their different religion. This contribution showed that the arising question of social cohesion in a multi-religious society is not a new issue, but has been treated by so-called minority instruments. By analysing the position taken by the UNHRC and the ECtHR regarding the groups included in the personal scope of these instruments, it can be shown that while the former believes groups formed by recent immigration should also benefit from such guarantees, the latter leaves the definition of the term minority to the discretion of states. This inconsistency also reflects on the practice of the two bodies, where similar claims of members of groups formed by recent immigration alleging a violation of their right to freedom of religion result in conflicting decisions. A main distinguishing element in the practice of the UNHRC and the ECtHR is the interpretation of a state duty for accommodation of religious practices, which is missing in the jurisprudence of the ECtHR about groups formed by recent immigration. Looking at the current socio-political situation, it seems however crucial that the ECtHR, rather than reinforcing the assimilationist tendencies dominating on the national level, opts for a minority perspective on claims of groups formed by recent immigration for the accommodation of their religious belief. Furthermore, such change of approach would also resolve the conflict of interpretation arisen regarding the right to freedom of religion.

Bibliography

Angst, Doris, 'Art. 3, A. Allgemeiner Teil', in Rainer Hofmann and others (eds), *Rahmenübereinkommen zum Schutz nationaler Minderheiten* (Nomos2015).

Bretscher, Fabienne, 'Diversity in Unity: Minority Protection and National Cohesion in Democracies', in Laura Marschner and Patrice Martin Zumsteg (eds), *Risiko und Verantwortlichkeit* (Dike2016) 21ff.

Bribosia, Emmanuelle, Gabrielle Caceres and Isabelle Rorive, 'Les Signes Religieux au Cœur d'un Bras de Fer entre Genève et Paris: La Saga Singh' (2014) 98*Revue Trimestrielle des Droits de l'Homme* 495.

76 Henrard, *Reasonable Accommodation* (n 46) 63; see also Fabienne Bretscher, 'Diversity in Unity: Minority Protection and National Cohesion in Democracies' in Laura Marschner and Patrice Martin Zumsteg (eds) *Risiko und Verantwortlichkeit* (Dike 2016) 21ff.

De Been, Wouter, 'The Quest of Neutrality and the Stench of History', in Jeroen Temperman (ed.), *The Lautsi Papers: Reflections on Religious Symbols in the Public School Classroom* (Brill2012).

De Schutter, Olivier, *International Human Rights Law* (CUP2014).

Eide, Asbjørn, 'The Rights of "New" Minorities: Scope and Restrictions', in Kristin Henrard (ed.), *Double Standards Pertaining to Minority Protection* (Brill2010).

Henrard, Kristin, *Devising an Adequate System of Minority Protection: Individual Human Rights, Minority Rights and the Right to Self-Determination* (Brill2000).

Henrard, Kristin, 'Duties of Reasonable Accommodation in Relation to Religion and the European Court of Human Rights: A Closer Look at the Prohibition of Discrimination, the Freedom of Religion and Related Duties of State Neutrality' (2012) 5(1) *Erasmus Law Review* 59.

Hofmann, Rainer, 'Introduction' in Marc Weller, *The Rights of Minorities in Europe* (OUP2005) 16ff.

Keller, Perry, 'Rethinking Ethnic and Cultural Rights in Europe' (1998) 18 *Oxford Journal of Legal Studies* 29.

Meijknecht, Anna, 'Minority Protection System between World War I and World War II' *Max Planck Encyclopedia of Public International Law* (MPEPIL2010).

Ringelheim, Julie, *Diversité Culturelle et Droits de l'Homme – La Protection des Minorités par la Convention Européenne des Droits de l'Homme* (Bruylant2006).

Woehrling, José, 'L'obligation d'accommodement raisonnable et l'adaptiation de la société à la diversité religieuse' (1998) 43*Revue de droit de McGill* 325.

Zizek, Slavoj, 'Liberal multiculturalism masks an old barbarism with a human face' in *The Guardian* (London, 3 October 2010) <https://www.theguardian.com/commentisfree/2010/oct/03/immigration-policy-roma-rightwing-europe> accessed 22 April 2017.

Other sources

ACFC, '1 Opinion on Denmark' (22 September 2000) ACFC/INF/OP/I(2001)005.

ACFC, 'Opinion on Germany' (1 March 2002) ACFC/INF/OP/I/008.

ACFC, 'Opinion on Switzerland' (20 February 2003) ACFC/INF/OP/I(2003)007.

ACFC, '3 Opinion on Poland' (28 November 2013) ACFC/OP/III(2013)004.

CoE, 'Reservations and Declarations for Treaty No157 – Framework Convention for the Protection of National Minorities' <www.coe.int/en/web/conventions/full-list/-/conventions/treaty/157/declarations?p_auth=2RpNP29s> accessed 15 December 2016.

CoECommittee of Ministers, 'Explanatory Report to the FCNM' (February 1995) H (95) 10.

CoEParliamentary Assembly (PACE), 'Rights of National Minorities' Recommendation 1492(2001).

Economic and Social Council, 'Commentary of the Working Group on Minorities to the United Nations Declaration on the Rights of Persons Belonging to National or Ethnic, Religious and Linguistic Minorities' (4 April 2005) UN Doc. E/CN.4/Sub.2/AC.5/2005/2.

European Commission, *Reasonable accommodation beyond disability in Europe* (European Union2013).

UNHRC, 'General Comment No 22 on Article 18' (30 July 1993) UN Doc CCPR/C/21/Rev.1/Add.4).

UNHRC, 'General Comment No 23 on Article 27 ICCPR' (8 April 1994) UN Doc CCPR/C/21/Rev.1/Add.5.

UN Special Rapporteur on contemporary forms of racism, racial discrimination, xenophobia and related intolerance, 'Report on the implementation of General Assembly resolution 67/154' (26 March 2013) UN Doc A/HRC/23/24.

UN Special Rapporteur on freedom of religion or belief, 'Report on Mission to France' (8 March 2006) UN Doc E/CN.4/2006/5/Add. 4.

UN Working Group, Universal Periodic Review, Report for the Second Cycle, Switzerland (7 December 2012) UN Doc A/HRC/22/11.

6 Conscientious objection in Swedish and Italian healthcare

Paradoxical secularizations and unbalanced pluralisms

Melisa Vazquez

Introduction

This chapter addresses contradictions in the handling of claims of conscientious objection to abortion in Sweden and Italy, arguing that both phenomena may be examples of an uncovering of "hidden rules of behavior" underlying the fabric of these two democracies, and in direct contradiction with their public declarations and conceptions. Theoretical approaches, including "intercultural translation," will be elucidated as a means of exploring possible solutions for current struggles within legal pluralism, secularism and freedom, and in defense of human rights.

Conscientious objection in Sweden: the case of Ellinor Grimmark

Sweden is among the most celebrated of European democracies, a country that has consistently stayed out of the fray of war, has invested for years in a self-proclaimed welfare democracy, and prides itself on being one of the most "modern" nations, able to function more effectively than others and skilled in taking care of all of its citizens. The concept of freedom features prominently in Swedish political and social self-conceptions. Further, Sweden has often publicly declared its ambition to provide moral leadership to other countries in light of its advanced capabilities:

> Our country must be a leading and inspirational force in the world. A country in which we close gaps and fulfill the promises of freedom we have made to our children. A country in which we invest together in people and the environment, in knowledge and competitiveness, in security in the present and hope for the future.[1]

It has been, therefore, rather startling to find the case of Ellinor Grimmark, a Swedish midwife who has unsuccessfully attempted to assert her right of conscientious objection to performing abortions. In 2013 after completing an internship, Grimmark informed the management at Highland Hospital (Höglandssjukhuset), a women's

1 Löfven (2014).

clinic in Eksjö, southern Sweden that she did not wish to perform abortions due to her personal religious convictions. She was subsequently denied an extension of her contract and informed by the head of the maternity ward that she, "was no longer welcome to work with them." She was further asked how "someone with such an attitude could at all train to become a midwife."[2] Grimmark's student funding, which was originally intended to extend for another year, was also cancelled. Grimmark then sought employment at the Ryhovs women's clinic. Once again she was informed that a refusal to perform abortions was not permissible for anyone working as a midwife in Sweden. Finally, she was offered employment at Värnamo Hospital's women's clinic, but this offer was also revoked when management discovered that Grimmark had filed a civil rights complaint against the Highland Hospital with the local Equality Ombudsman.

The Ombudsman ruled that Grimmark was not being discriminated against for her pro-life views and that the decision against her could be "regarded as a health protection" of patients requiring abortion in Sweden.[3] Grimmark, represented by Ruth Nordström, president of the organization Scandinavian Human Rights Lawyers, escalated the complaint, filing suit in the Jönköping District Court.

The controversy the case has generated extends all the way up to Swedish royalty. In October 2013, Uppsala University, Sweden's oldest, planned to host an international conference on human rights and human trafficking, organized by Scandinavian Human Rights Lawyers in cooperation with the University and the United Nations. The head speaker was to be the Council of Europe's Rapporteur on prostitution, human trafficking and modern slavery. Also slated to participate were a host of international researchers, members of the Civil Society Platform Coalition Against Trafficking in Sweden, police officials and delegates from the Parliament of Norway. HM Queen Silvia of Sweden was to receive the Scandinavian Human Dignity Award for her dedication to the cause of protecting children against abuse and exploitation.

Three days before the start of the conference, the influential daily newspaper "Aftonbladet" published an article calling attention to the involvement in the conference of Ruth Nordström, president of Scandinavian Human Rights Lawyers and counsel for midwife Ellinor Grimmark. Accusations were made that Ms. Nordström planned to use the conference, and the presence of the Queen, as an opportunity to lobby against abortion in Sweden, and that the entire event was a "pure public relations coup."[4] Following the media controversy, the conference was cancelled. Queen Silvia announced that she supported the University's cancellation and would not be accepting the award she had been offered.

As far as Grimmark's legal case is concerned, Swedish legal expert Reinhold Fahlbeck has written that Sweden's legal treatment of conscientious objection is bound by the European Convention of 1950 on the protection of Human Rights

2 Nordström (2016).
3 Diskriminerings Ombusdmannen (2014), 9.
4 Franchell (2014).

and Fundamental Freedoms (ECHR), signed by Sweden in 1993. As well known, Article 9 states:

> 1 Everyone has the right to freedom of thought, conscience and religion; this right includes freedom to change religion or belief and freedom, either alone or in community with others and in public or private, to manifest his religion or belief in worship, teaching, practice and observance.
>
> 2 Freedom to manifest one's religion or beliefs shall be subject only to such limitations as are prescribed by law and in a democratic society, are necessary with regard to the general public safety or the protection of public order, health or morals or for the protection for other rights and freedoms.

After assessing the relationship between Swedish legal provisions and the requirements of international law, Fahlbeck concludes that the ECHR is "the governing legal source regarding religious freedom in Sweden … The Convention applies in Sweden in three guises, (1) the international law binding Convention, (2) as part of EU law, and (3) Swedish domestic law. This means that it is possible 'to directly apply the Convention in Swedish court.'"[5]

Directly relevant to a legal assessment of the case is Resolution 1763 adopted in 2010 by the Parliamentary Assembly of the Council of Europe concerning conscientious objection in medical care. Paragraph 1 states:

> No person, hospital or institution shall be coerced, held liable or discriminated against in any manner because of a refusal to perform, accommodate, assist or submit to an abortion, the performance of a human miscarriage, or euthanasia or any act which could cause the death of a human fetus or embryo, for any reason.[6]

The statement is quite clear. However, there has been great resistance in Sweden on the grounds that as a resolution it should be considered to be "soft law," and that it interferes with Swedish laws guaranteeing abortion (with restrictions). The Swedish government has further argued that a midwife's participation in abortion is required per the ECHR provision that a State must guarantee, "that the interests and rights of individuals seeking legal medical services are respected, protected, and fulfilled." While the argument has been made repeatedly in the media that if conscientious objection to abortion is allowed it will threaten the material availability of abortions, this does not appear to have any factual or legal grounding in Sweden, the country with the highest rate of abortion in northern Europe.[7] Furthermore, as Fahlbeck argues, "Factors of a practical nature in the workplace fall considerably further down the hierarchical values scale with respect to the Article 9 protected right to freedom of conscience." Whereas the Convention

5 Fahlbeck (2014).
6 Resolution 1763 (2010) of the Parliamentary Assembly of the Council of Europe.
7 Makenzius (2013).

has a clearly defined right to freedom of religion, there is no parallel "right to abortion."

An additional complication in the matter is the issue of the rights, which may or may not be accorded the unborn fetus. While this issue pulls the matter into a political/moral realm, European law has not been immune to making declarations on the issue, for example in the Oviedo Convention of 1997,[8] which sets out the fundamental principles applicable in day-to-day medicine as well as those applicable to new technologies in human biology and medicine, and indeed prohibits the commoditization of the human embryo and forbids the creation of embryos for research purposes.

Though outside the field of healthcare, the ECHR case *Bayatyan v. Armenia* has been used as an example of European legal support for conscientious objection, and the role of majority consensus among European states in determining new rulings. In this case the Court held that:

> The Court has already pointed out above that almost all the Member States of the Council of Europe which ever had or still have compulsory military service have introduced alternatives to such service in order to reconcile the possible conflict between individual conscience and military obligations. Accordingly, a State which has not done so, enjoys only a limited margin of appreciation and must advance convincing and compelling reasons to justify any interference. In particular, it must demonstrate that the interference corresponds to a "pressing social need."[9]

The argument is that when there is an almost total consensus by the Council of Europe member states to accept conscientious objection regarding a certain area, a State which has not done so has minimal opportunity to justify a violation of interference with the right to freedom of conscience.

While the legal issues affecting Grimmark's case are not entirely black and white, there is a fairly strong body of evidence substantiating the validity of the claim that her right to conscientious objection under the ECHR has indeed been violated. Interestingly, there was another case in Sweden in 2004, the case of Pastor Åke Green, in which the Swedish Supreme Court voted to support the religious freedom of the defendant based on the ultimate superiority of the ECHR. Pastor Green was initially tried by the Swedish Court under a law against hate crimes for having given a sermon highly critical of homosexuals. The Supreme Court overturned the decision, stating that the rights to freedom of expression and freedom of religion provided by the ECHR, recognized to be superior to Swedish law, protected him since jurisprudence shows that a judgment

8 Convention on Human Rights and Biomedicine, Oviedo, 4.IV.1997 (ETS 164). Article 18 states: "(1) Where the law allows research on embryos in vitro, it shall ensure adequate protection of the embryo. (2) The creation of human embryos for research purposes is prohibited."

9 ©European Union, http://eur-lex.europa.eu.

would probably not be upheld by the European Court. In its judgment, the Swedish Supreme Court stated:

> The determining factor appears to be whether the restriction of Åke Green's freedom to preach is necessary in a democratic society. This means that it must be assessed whether the restriction is proportionate to the protected interest ... Considering the central role that religious conviction plays for an individual, it can be assumed a certain restraint in applying the European Convention to accept restrictions as legitimate pursuant to Article 9.[10]

The Supreme Court's final decision was principally focused on Pastor Green's right to free speech. The conclusion reached was that criminalizing Pastor Green's speech was not proportionate to his infringement of a minority group's rights to protection from "hate speech." However, in the Court's statement, references are made to the broader protection of freedom of religion by the ECHR and the need to determine whether a given restriction is "necessary in a democratic society." Specifically:

> When the European Court determines whether an alleged restriction is necessary in a democratic society, the court considers whether the restriction meets a pressing social need, whether it is proportionate to the legitimate purpose to be achieved, and whether the reasons asserted by the national authorities to justify it are relevant and sufficient.[11]

The argument against Grimmark seems to center on the notion that the availability of abortion in Sweden is a "pressing social need," and that her refusal to participate makes her unemployment in Sweden as a midwife proportionate. In order to legitimate this argument, however, the case would have to be made that her specific participation in abortions is more important than her right to manifest her religion or beliefs (as per Article 9) and that limiting this right is necessary "in the interests of public safety, for the protection of public order, health or morals, or for the protection of the rights and freedoms of others." While European states are afforded a "margin of appreciation" in their consideration of European law, as Swedish legal scholar Fahlbeck notes, this margin is closely connected with whether there is consensus among member countries regarding the issue in question; the greater the consensus, the smaller the margin of appreciation for divergence. He cites *Bayatyan v. Armenia*, in which a man eligible for military service refused on the grounds of religious belief.[12] The ECHR ruled in Bayatyan's favor, stating:

> ... pluralism, tolerance and broadmindedness are hallmarks of a 'democratic society.' Although individual interests must on occasion be subordinated to

10 Judgment of the Supreme Court of Sweden (2005).
11 *Ibid.*
12 See Fahlbeck (2014).

> those of a group, democracy does not simply mean that the views of a majority must always prevail: a balance must be achieved which ensures the fair and proper treatment of people from minorities and avoids any abuse of a dominant position … Thus, respect on the part of the State towards the beliefs of a minority religious group like the applicant's by providing them with the opportunity to serve society as dictated by their conscience might, far from creating unjust inequalities or discrimination as claimed by the Government, rather **ensure cohesive and stable pluralism and promote religious harmony and tolerance in society**.[13] [emphasis mine]

Nevertheless, on November 12, 2015, the Jönköping County District Court ruled against Ms. Grimmark, finding that the condition that a midwife perform abortions is both appropriate and necessary, and furthermore that the condition is unrelated to the alleged basis of discrimination – the violation of religious freedom. Although they are two different rights in international declarations, the Court stated that in this case it was not possible to distinguish between the right to religious freedom and the right to freedom of conscience in reference to the midwife's beliefs. Therefore, the District Court declared that there was no reason to specifically consider whether Ellinor Grimmark's conscience had been violated.[14] Her lawyer stated,

> The District Court only examined if Ellinor Grimmark was discriminated because of her religious beliefs and did not at all examine the relevant case law of the European Court. It is remarkable that the Court states that the question of freedom of conscience should only be examined if a person is not religious.[15]

The question is: why is Sweden responding in this way? And if the case is appealed to the ECHR, will a margin of appreciation be granted to Sweden for its intolerance toward Ms. Grimmark's minority views? Is this case an example of the ECHR's warning against "abuse of a dominant position"? What does it tell us about the possibilities for pluralism in Europe?

A counter case: the frenzied availing of conscientious objection in Italy

If the words "Italy," and "abortion," are put together in the same sentence, the quick mental leap to "Catholic" is likely to follow. And yet despite any generalized public conceptions that might identify Italy as a Catholic state, this is neither legally nor politically accurate. The official separation of church and state in Italy dates back to the Constitution of 1948, which specifically protects freedom of religion and articulates that the State and the Catholic Church are "independent and

13 © European Union, http://eur-lex.europa.eu.

14 *Jönköpings Tingsrätt Dom 2015-11-12*, Jönköping District Court Judgment (2015).

15 Nordström, R. (2015).

sovereign, each within its own sphere." The 1984 concordat between the State and the Holy See further solidified this separation by asserting that Roman Catholicism was not the state religion. Subsequently, Italian *laicité*[16] has been classified by the Constitutional Court among the "supreme principles of constitutional order." Italy is, by all legal and political accounts, a secular state. It should also be noted that while the material signs of a culture heavily influenced by the Catholic religion abound, as in all cultures, the reality "on the ground" is not absolute. So while the Catholic religion is taught in schools, for example, a recent study in Bologna found that 44.4% of students across eight comprehensive (elementary through middle school) schools were opting out of religion class.[17] Another recent study from the University of Bergamo and extended to the Lombardy region found that across a student population of more than 6,000, only between 20 and 40% of students can be considered to have a "good knowledge of the Catholic religion" and that their knowledge does not come from religion class at school but rather from external educational experience such as catechism classes. The religious education at school, by these accounts, would not appear to be anything like indoctrination. If we consider other Catholic "litmus test" cultural indicators we find that in 2015, after the passage of the so-called "fast divorce law," Italy saw 82,469 divorces, an increase of 57% relative to the prior year.[18] In the same year, 65% of married/in-union women between the ages of 15 and 49 reported using contraception.[19] Furthermore, even in the face of direct challenges to practices opposed by Catholic doctrine, Italians have stood firm. In 1974, the very first national referendum held in Italy—after the Italian Constitution legalized the practice—was on the topic of divorce. With an impressive 87.7% voter turnout, 59.3% of voters voted against the abolition of the divorce law. As mentioned above, the passing of the "fast divorce law" (Law n.55, May 6, 2015), has solidified divorce as a social option. In short, secularist practices in Italy have been challenged, and have held fast.

When it comes to the history of abortion in Italy, like Sweden, significant loss of life among women resulting from illegal abortions in earlier decades of the 20th century, exacerbated by cultural taboos against and lack of access to birth control methods, drove advocates to change the law pertaining to abortion.The first legal

16 Noted religion and law scholars Alessandro Ferrari and Silvio Ferrari have pointed out that the Italian version of the originally French concept of separation of church and state is not associated with "anti-religiousness" nor with the removal of religion from public space but rather, "Laicità supposes the existence of a plurality of value systems – the same dignity of all personal choices in the field of religion and conscience – it entails equal protection for religious and non-religious beliefs, and it requires State neutrality regarding both of them. As a result, this principle does not refer to state-church relations only, but it is a synthesis of the values and duties of the contemporary plural and democratic state in which religion plays a full role, like each other component of a civil society." See Ferrari (2010).

17 UAAR, (Unione degli atei e degli agnostici), primary organization of atheists and agnostics in Italy (2015).

18 ISTAT data available at: https://www.istat.it/en/archive/192521.

19 United Nations data available at: www.un.org/en/development/desa/population/publications/pdf/family/trendsContraceptiveUse2015Report.pdf.

step against the prohibition of abortion in Italy took place in 1975, when the Constitutional Court ruled that induced abortion should be permitted in the case of serious health risks for the woman. After a campaign by pro-choice feminist groups, abortion was legalized in 1978 ("Act No. 194"). Despite the condemnation of the Catholic Church, attempts to repeal the law have failed. Abortion rates are lower than Sweden's, at 203.1 interventions per 1000 live births[20] as compared to Sweden's 335.2, however some argue that these numbers should be contextualized in light of Italy's Total Fertility Rate (the lowest of 227 nations at 1.19 births per woman vs. Sweden's 1.91). Regardless, statistics show that the general trends regarding abortion rates are similar to other western European countries.[21] The two countries diverge dramatically, however, when it comes to accessibility of abortion. Whereas it does not appear to be a problem in Sweden, it is a well-documented and substantial problem in Italy.

The statistics are alarming. First, though the law is national and applies to all regions, the medical support required to uphold the law varies dramatically from one region to another. In the most extreme cases, such as Jesi hospital in Ancona, ten out of ten obstetricians have declared themselves to be conscientious objectors to abortion; 100% objection was also found in some hospitals in the cities of Brescia, Bergamo, Pavia and Varese. In the Lombardy region, 11 of 63 hospitals have no obstetricians willing to perform abortions.[22] Statistics for the south of Italy are even more stark, with cities like Bari in the Puglia region where the last remaining hospital available for abortions reached 100% objection status among the gynecological/obstetric staff.[23] The regions of Molise, Campania and Basilicata have an overall average of objectors that stands at 85%.[24] The official national average of obstetricians/gynecologists declared as conscientious objectors to abortion is 70%; however, representatives of LAIGA[25] report that their hospital-by-hospital study found the percentage to be much higher, at 91.3%.[26] The European Committee for Social Rights reports that at these rates, the worst in Europe, women's lives are overtly at risk. Indeed, cases of blatant malpractice in cases of in-progress abortions have been reported on more than one occasion.[27] Lack of care during abortion procedures has resulted from hospital staff-shift changes, as well as medical staff objecting beyond the bounds of the law.[28] While Act 194

20 Data from 2012. See *Ministro della Salute* (2014).
21 Salvini and Schifini (1996: 267–271 and 277).
22 L'Huffington Post (2014).
23 Borzacchiello (2013).
24 La Repubblica (2012).
25 *Libera Associazione Italiana Ginecologi per Applicazione legge 194*, a group of doctors lobbying for the application of Act 194 protecting abortion.
26 *Ibid.*
27 Though hospital administrators have denied the charges, the accusations of Valentina Magnanti made headlines in 2010 when she accused hospital staff of abandoning her to a hospital bathroom to deliver a five-month fetus by herself, whose induced abortion was being performed due to a severe and transmittable genetic defect.
28 In 2013, a doctor in Pordenone, Italy was sentenced to a year in prison for refusing to assist a woman who had undergone an abortion during the doctor's shift. The Court

specifically states that conscientious objection to abortion can only apply to the surgical procedure, it is widely reported that nurses, anesthesiologists, and pharmacists refuse care (and even referrals to care by others) in the name of conscientious objection. The rates of objection, in fact, appear to be on the rise,[29] and not necessarily because moral attitudes are changing. In one study it was found that while two-thirds of the medical staff would not perform abortions, only one-third claimed to be morally opposed to abortion. The cultural consensus would seem to run along the lines of, "It's ok as long as I don't have to do it." By all accounts, the situation in Italy endangers women's health rights in egregious and shocking ways.

So why is secular Italy, with a law supporting abortion on the books for decades, making it so difficult for women to have guaranteed access?[30] Why are laws protecting abortion being violated in favor of conscientious objection clauses? It might be tempting to assume that the answer is simply the prevalence of Catholicism. However, many objectors do not cite their Catholic views per se as the motivation behind their objection. Instead, they speak of the stigma attached to performing abortions, the fear of negative judgment from colleagues, the lack of quality training in the epidemiology of abortion procedures and/or the absence of the latest technical options for procedures (for example an abortive pill vs. surgical procedure), as well as the mundane/repetitive nature of a procedure that is not gratifying from a medical point of view and is considered to be ultimately the result of social failures.[31] These factors seem to be at least as important to these medical practitioners as concerns for an obligation to protect life. Though it may be expected that the Swedish argument in the Grimmark case is framed as "neutral," against the plaintiff's "religiosity," it could be less so that Italians largely do not claim Catholic beliefs as a motive for objecting. One gynecologist in Milan who is a conscientious objector stated that though she is Catholic, she is not against abortion per se; in fact, she voted in favor of Act 194. But because she finds the practice objectionable in some situations, she felt it was more coherent for her personally as a medical practitioner to object. While bombing abortion clinics and seeking to overturn abortion rulings is a regular feature of the political landscape in the US, the same cannot be said in Italy.

In support of this point is another facet of the Italian situation, a response to the crisis of mass conscientious objection, the so-called "*gettonisti*." Major state

specified that objection provisions do not apply to pre- or post- abortion care where the woman's right to health is constitutionally protected. See *Corte di Cassazione*, Section VI, Penale – Sentence n.14979, April 2e 2013.

29 According to researchers Galanti and Borzachielli, the number of objector-gynecologists went from 58.7% in 2005 to 70.5% in 2007, 70.7% in 2009, leveling off around this percentage in subsequent years with peaks, however, of 80% in southern regions. See De Leo (2012).

30 For a general philosophical/theoretical overview of conscientious objection in Italy see Saporiti (2014). For a legal analysis see Musseli and Ceffa (2014), and for a combined approach see Turchi (2009). Lalli (2011) offers a more sociological approach.

31 De Zordo (2015).

hospitals, faced with a legally prescribed need to provide abortion services find themselves without the staff to meet the need because the percentages of objectors are so high. So they have come up with a solution: hire contractors. A "*gettone*" in Italian is a coin token. "*Gettonisti*" are so-called because they offer one-off solutions to the staffing problem. Importantly, these are not privately paid doctors but rather private sector doctors paid with public funds to perform abortion services in public hospitals. And these are not rare or occasional forays into staffing solutions; the Lombardy region spends EUR 250,000 per year on these in-sourced doctors. What is interesting about this aspect of the situation is that if there were total cultural consensus against practicing abortion (as there appears to be consensus on the rejection of Grimmark's claims), we might expect that either the law would be overturned or at least that the hospitals would simply accept the high percentages of objectors and the corresponding lack of abortion services. Instead they set aside funds in an attempt to meet all of the needs presented by the situation.[32] Claims of hypocrisy would not be hard to make. But again, what's interesting is how the events in Sweden are similarly "hypocritical." On one side we have a doctor stating essentially, "It's all or none, it's too inconsistent for me to perform abortions only in some cases," and on the other side, hospital administrators stating essentially, "It's all or none, it's too inconsistent for some midwives to object while others don't."

Both Sweden and Italy are secular states with laws protecting the right to terminate pregnancy as well as laws protecting the right to object to performing the medical act of terminating a pregnancy. Nevertheless, violations of these laws are taking place. These contradictions would seem to be the result of a friction between a cultural consensus and legal statutes. In both cases, social actors are behaving according to what they believe to be the "normal way" despite the fact that they are in violation of the law. In her latest work, Saba Mahmood has argued that in conflicts requiring legal intervention at national and supranational levels, European secular majoritarian politics operate in a manner that is strikingly similar to Egyptian religious majoritarian politics.[33] She illustrates how in cases that elicit a clash of values, majoritarian interests interpret legal frameworks to their own advantage, going so far as to justify about-face decisions on the same issues (national identity cards, the veil, censorship). Discrepancies between what states say and what they do are not new. Nor are majoritarian power plays. But what if we were to go deeper than assessments of instrumentalist legal and political maneuvering to look at the taken-for-granted concepts lying dormant on the seabed of these oceans of controversy? What exigencies are being "disappeared" by an overbearing cultural consensus? What categorical assumptions are the pillars holding up this consensus? Can we excavate beneath to uncover the world of variables that have combined to produce this particular situation? Are there continuities to be found among these newly excavated realities? Can we craft new solutions that improve the balance of respect for subjects' contingencies?

32 Corica (2015).
33 Mahmood (2016), 174.

Pluralism and claims for difference: the specter of *cosification* and its shackling effect on freedom

Secular European states seem to be particularly adept at packaging righteous-sounding proclamations of neutrality and "justice." One such list of rights relevant to this chapter can be found in the "Declaration on Violence Against Women, Children and Adolescents and their Sexual and Reproductive Rights,"[34] which states that "sexual and reproductive rights are based on other fundamental rights including the right to health, the right to freedom from discrimination, the right to privacy, the right to personal integrity and freedom from torture, cruel inhuman and degrading treatment, the right of all couples and individuals to decide freely and responsibly the number, spacing and timing of having children and to have the information and means to do it, and the right to make decisions about reproduction free of discrimination, coercion and violence and thus to be free from sexual violence." And here we begin to see how the exigencies of individuals become buried in stacks of issues ranging from torture, to freedom of information, to violence. And yet, there is a crucial but unnamed entity at the heart of this giant ball of yarn: *the woman who is the subject of the conflict.*

The question of "what is man," is as old as man himself, and so too the question of woman. Even a cursory sociological glance shows that what society considers to be "grown," (the presumed difference between girl and woman) varies tremendously from place to place and from time to time. Indeed, the moment we lock down the category of woman, even in our attempts to protect women, we put a kind of cage around the very group of people we are trying to protect. When a woman's reproductive rights are being "protected," who do we mean? Is an eleven-year old female who has begun menstruating to be considered the same as a forty-year-old woman, for example? Mustn't we allow space for the possibility of *difference*? This difference includes elements such as where a particular woman is located in both time and place, how she lives and with whom, how her community defines girls and women (and sexuality and gender, for that matter), who she is in relationship with, her economic situation, and whole host of other variables that cannot be assumed to be represented in a general category called "woman." The danger in making assumptions about categories can be readily seen in cases as extreme as genocide or religious wars (where all Jews are "the same," or all Hutus, and each group is thereby targeted for annihilation). When we disregard the particulars that make up each individual's humanity whether the intentions behind this action are beneficent or harmful, the result is nevertheless problematic because we move away from what is before us, to what we have imagined or assumed a priori.

Now, if the category of "woman," is not a fixed, unchanging entity, then how could the category of "abortion," possibly be such? Abortion can be defined as a medical procedure for removing a fetus from a woman's body by means of pharmaceuticals or surgery. But again, is the abortion undertaken by an 11-year-old vs. a 40-year-old the same? The biological factors regarding future possible pregnancies

34 Organization of American States (OAS) (2014).

alone could wildly diverge. The circumstances leading to the pregnancy are also likely to be decidedly different. What about the stage of the pregnancy of each of these women? The abortive procedure, after all, regards a fetus, which also has an age (to take just one of many aspects) ranging from days to weeks to months. Each of these ages produces radical changes in the properties of the fetus. Even putting all ideology aside, disregarding the question of "when is it life," the variability of the fetus from one stage to another and the subsequent impact on definitions of abortion cannot be ignored. It is impossible to construct categories such as "abortion" or "woman" while failing to reference a whole network of relationships that have anchors in the past, in the future, in communities, in relationships with other people, and so on. These references might be somewhat explicit, as they are in this text, or they may be unnamed, as in the Declaration of Rights cited above. What they can't ever be is absent; the connotative relationships between categories exist whether we acknowledge them or not.

It is for this reason that there is a danger in treating declarations and laws regulating reproductive issues as a presumptively "objective ground" for rights and their various declinations, if they are enacted without any regard for the relatedness inherent to a woman's body and any medical procedure it undergoes, including abortion. In this regard, it should be emphasized that the form and the perceived thingness/materiality of the body and abortion have an essentializing character because they synthetize an entire web of experiential and semantic implications underlying corporeal life. What we call the womb, the 'fetus,' the perception of pain, of motherhood, etc., are not self-evident and universal truths, and above all they are not "facts" that exist independently from culture, or that can be processed regardless of our cultural schemes of categorization. The connections of sense in which both ideas about the womb, the 'fetus,' motherhood, and child-raising, as well as real-world life experiences are nestled, both foster and fill the connotative spectrum of what each woman sees, perceives, experiences, and calls "womb," "fetus," "motherhood," and so on. These connections vary according to the ecological relationship between each woman's mind and her environment, an environment that is more than simply the physical, the external, that which is presumptively placed *out there*. On the contrary, it is the synthesis of the symbolic and material elements of innumerable experiences and related categorizations of the socialized life of a woman's body, in short, of her *story*, including *all* the connotative implications it involves. Now, every connotative element calls into play rights and different aspects of semantic potentialities of rights, refashioning their reciprocal relationships. It is precisely for this reason that "de-cosifying," or de-iconizing words such as "woman" and "abortion" is an inevitable step if we want to understand the situated meaning of these words, that is, the experiences they refer to, and consequently the entire groupings of rights and their reciprocal cross-references when concretely applied to single cases, single lives with their singular stories. Without such efforts to unpack and expose the contextual and connotative landscapes living beneath words and their uses, we run the risk of aprioristically qualifying real situations lived by people – in this case, above all, women – and blindly projecting our ideological or simply personal views onto their exigencies.

In this way, women's actual needs could be completely overshadowed, and – still worse – the end result could be a superimposition of our pre-determined conceptualization schemes and values on their freedom.

Answering a question such as "what is abortion for this specific woman?" means taking into account everything that came before the moment in which she appears at the clinic, and everything that might come after an eventual abortion, that is, her future, in both its actual and imagined dimensions. This is necessary because the meaning of abortion, especially for that woman, will be a synthesis of her interpreted past and her imagined future – as it is for all symbolic beings, which is to say all humans. If we are going to discuss the "right" to abortion, this right needs precisely this terrain to germinate. Only here can the "tree of rights" grow, ramifying in its projections of sense and its inherent plurality the respect due to the rational autonomy and personal freedom of each woman. What kind of approach, then, is being implied? How can we think about a process that opens up semantic webs of meaning in comprehensive and reciprocal ways with the goal of preserving freedom and respect?

The translational path to pluralism: a method for dialoguing among differences

One approach can be defined as "trans-lation."[35] The term does not refer merely to language translation but rather to the etymology of the word, the Latin *translatus*, meaning "carried across," or, creating complex understanding across divergent life experiences. This "crossing" is both material and semantic, crossing respective spaces of existence and conceptual categories. What is the trans-lational path?[36] What does it mean to create reciprocal dialogue? While there is no single, straightforward answer to these questions, we can begin to sketch out a kind of methodology that outlines some of the steps involved.

As elucidated above, when exigencies become ossified into stiff categories empowered by identitarian viewpoints, it becomes impossible to peacefully resolve conflict. Pluralism and globalization are but two more features of modern life that rises before us, one day used as inspiration, the next as a means of fomenting conflict. And yet as the post-Hegelian dust has settled, a few interesting re-conceptualizations have emerged that seem to shine a little light in the dark. The first has already been discussed – the notion of "cosification." If the categories we use to define and constitute our world are so rigid that they refuse any interrogation, we can say that they are "frozen" in their "thingness," or cosification, like the victims of the Medusa. The identification of this pitfall allows us to understand that there is an alternative: refusing this semantic stiffness and investigating, instead, how categories not only can be, but in fact *always are*, fluid. What makes a loud noise a "disturbance" vs. a "performance" or an appreciated "warning"?

35 Ricca (2013).

36 The following section applies arguments that are original to M. Ricca, and explained in much greater detail throughout his oeuvre. See Ricca (2008, 2013, and 2014).

What makes an odor a perfume vs. a stench?[37] How do we qualify something as art vs. vandalism? Our categories make it so, and we are all endowed with significant creative abilities to shift and re-shift our categories. When conflicts arise, the trans-lational path asks that first, all parties consider the categories coming into play.

Once it is acknowledged that categories exist, have been selected (even if unconsciously), and can be changed, next there is the need to "dis-integrate" said categories by opening access to the narrative landscapes that lie beneath. This means putting on "mining helmets," (complete with head lamps) and engaging in a kind of semantic excavation. Categories that have been previously taken for granted by the exigencies of quotidian life must instead be dug out and pulled apart, viewed looking both backwards toward historical traces, and forwards toward imagined possibilities. We can think of the categories/concepts we use in quotidian life as "epitomes" or signs, that are not flat or simple but rather provide a kind of summary of relationships and experiences, and are incapable of holding still. Can the human concept of "health," for example, possibly be said to be static and unchanging across time and space? It is an existential concept, and also a representation of cultural habits. The concepts we use to create our lives are themselves both nature and nurture, they move from fixed to variable and back again. Over the course of time they are defined as objective in one moment, subjective in the next. They must be "de-composed" if they are to be understood in all their complexity. The foundation of metaphors, what unites their sources and their realizations and determines their semantic connotations in various contexts, could be made up of qualitative or emotional elements that represent "subjective" (pertaining to the subject) moments within a life story. As such they can be slippery and semantically vague. This, however, makes them flexible, able to jump across space and time to create new ideas and concepts, new ways of understanding and rendering human experience.

Categories/concepts that at first glance might seem widely divergent in their morphological representations (such as "women's biological rights") might turn out to share fundamental aspects, once they have been divested of their rigidity and opened up to reveal their connotative elements. Continuities might be found with categories that previously seemed to "live on the opposite side of the world." Newly opened categories can then engage in a process of testing the possibilities involved in using the common connotative elements between them to create an inter-categorical common space or a categorical migration.

We might say that human society is organized by the law. The law, however, is not designed exclusively for "controlling," human behavior. Instead, as an instrument "by and for the people," it provides a means for self-actualization, for the realization of desired ends. When shared semantic connotations and the continuity or ubiquity between opposing positions are uncovered, valuable legal implications can emerge. The "right to health," for example, is broad enough semantically to

37 For a deep analysis of these semantic forays and their implications, see Cancellieri and Ricca (2015).

respond to exigencies that may be engaged in ideological conflict. Furthermore, this right will undoubtedly overlap and engage with other "fundamental rights" that are typically protected by legal structures, such as the "right to freedom of conscience." A balancing of interests will need to take place to determine outcomes; specific instances of subjective exigencies will have to go through a process of intercultural translation/transaction in order to re-define and re-qualify how an individual will be protected within a particular set of circumstances.

When contesting for the protection of "rights," people are not fighting for pre-existing unequivocal protections but rather for their individual and/or community-based requisites, against what they perceive to be competing interests. Imposing one's rights "on top" of an Other's is always an erasure of the Other's subjectivity. The overlap between the projections of these subjectivities (connotative, teleological-symbolic, pragmatic) is the real battleground. Through translation and contextualization, rights claims such as the "right to conscience" emerge as connotative elements of complex phenomena that constitute only a brief moment, one angle of a larger and longer life process.

To return to our original case, as a midwife, Ms. Grimmark's voice is part of a social context that hosts the lives of every woman she encounters and the related choices regarding pregnancy and its termination. Her views on these women's lives and social conditions could contribute to empower knowledge of the social conditions engaged in the healthcare process that includes abortion. This would be true no matter what her final position regarding abortion might be. The events occurring before and after her claims, that is, the implications and relations of sense underlying her declared conviction must also be unearthed from their morphological surface appearance, enclosed by the term "conscientious objection." If we can accept that Ms. Grimmark's position belongs inside the complex web of meanings and options that make up the reproductive context, we may even begin to find continuities of sense between her exigencies and those of women seeking an abortion or other midwives who wish to provide this service. In fact, the argument has been made that providing abortions is also considered by some to be an expression of conscience:

> The conclusion that abortion provision is indeed "conscientious" by this standard is best supported by sociologist Carole Joffe, who showed in *Doctors of Conscience* that skilled "mainstream" doctors offered safe, compassionate abortion care before *Roe.*[38] They did so with little to gain and much to lose, facing fines, imprisonment, and loss of medical license. They did so because the beliefs that mattered most to them compelled them to. They saw women die from self-induced abortions and abortions performed by unskilled providers. They understood safe abortion to be lifesaving. They believed their abortion provision honored "the dignity of humanity" and was the right –

38 Refers to the landmark legal case "Roe v. Wade," which effectively legalized abortion in the United States.

> even righteous – thing to do. They performed abortions "for reasons of conscience."[39]

It could be that in efforts to preserve "the dignity of humanity," healthcare workers with ostensibly opposing points of view could find a common ground. Ms. Grimmark herself, by comparing her underlying reasons and argumentative connotations for conscientious objection with those within other women's claims might discover some continuity between the opposed positions, precisely beyond their morphological appearance. If abortion – as is being argued here – is a social process and its meaning is only an outcome of its unfolding, then every social voice can contribute to a cognitive and democratic understanding of what it is, no matter who does what in the end. The primary goal is to understand the meaning of the "what."

There are no cultural categories that contain "the objective truth," the final say on what is to be supported and what is to be "overruled." Concepts retained to be "universal" only acquire their universality in an interlocutory way, as the result of dialogue that seeks to trans-late, transact, through a process of reciprocal exchange, with a bottom-up approach that pulls into its realm of considerations all the complexities of human experience. Indeed, along these traces of human experience, as the mute parts[40] of experience are given voice through the destabilization of only apparently solid (culturally inscribed) morphological categories, concepts such as human rights can work as a kind of magnet that attracts intercultural translation. Thanks to their vagueness, they are able to provide the very plasticity needed for the reimagining of categories created to support human needs. In this way, they have a potential for inclusiveness that resonates with universal aspirations, providing semantic platforms that can sustain ever-evolving human needs, rather than turning into clubs with which to crush the "losing" party. This is not to say that concepts like human rights are capable of waving a magic wand and making conflict disappear. There will ever be opposing ideas and values struggling for recognition by legal and state institutions. But creating the possibility of cross-categorical migration and "inter-contextual resonance"[41] between things means leaving space for reinterpretations, re-imaginings, re-configurations. Just as human exigencies are in a constant state of flux, so too must the legal systems that support them be open and ready for change.

Differences and their emergence are relational processes. Identity/citizenship/subjectivity are not frozen in time and space but rather ever evolving, ever changing in response to others and to their environments. When they are pre-defined according to categories established by majorities in power, the exchanges that can give rise to genuine differences are instead in danger of being locked out, their development stunted. This is why intercultural translation, along with a previously willed separation from our "certainties," our iconized concepts, may be the only

39 Harris (2012).
40 Ricca (2013: 94).
41 Ricca (2014: 153).

way to realize genuinely free, democratic acts, responsive to the exigencies of citizens. If contrasting positions are expelled, shut out, denied any voice, dialogue and understanding become impossible. The tyranny of the majority ensues. What is at issue is greater than one midwife or even one group. The cost of failing to engage with and translate diverse (cultural) identities is an inadvertent step toward the betrayal of democracy itself.

Bibliography

Aléx, L. and Hammarström, A. (2004) Women's experiences in connection with induced abortion – a feminist perspective, in "*Scandinavian Journal of Caring Sciences*," 18/2, 60–168.

Borzacchiello, E. and Galanti, V. (2013) Aborto e obiezione di coscienza, due diritti da riequilibrare, in "*La ventisettesima ora, Corriere della Sera*," available at http://27esima ora.corriere.it/articolo/aborto-e-obiezione-di-coscienza-due-diritti-da-riequilibrare/.

Cancellieri, A. and Ricca, M. (2015) Ubiquità planetaria nei condomini. Microspazi di convivenza, corologia interculturale e diritti umani, in "*Calumet, intercultural humanities and law review*," available at http://win.calumet-review.it.

Cassel, P. G. (2009) Induced legal abortion in Sweden during 1939–1974: Change in practice and legal reform, in "*Stockholm Research Report in Demography*," 2, 4.

Castegnaro, A. (2010) Rilevare i dati nazionali sugli avvalentesi dell'Irc: criteri scientifici di riferimento e ricaduta sull'operato delle singole Diocesi, in "*Osservatorio Socio-Religioso Triveneto*," available at www.chiesacattolica.it/cci_new_v3/allegati/8946/CAS TEGNARO.pdf Retrieved January 8, 2016.

ConferenzaEpiscopaleItaliana (2012) *Indicazioni per la concessione del nulla osta ai libri di testo per l'insegnamento della religione cattolica nella scuola pubblica*, in "*Notiziario della Conferenza Episcopale Italiana*" 46/4, available at www.chiesacattolica.it/irc/ siti_di_uffici_e_serviziservizio_nazionale_per_l_insegnamento_della_religione_cattolica/ 00055438_Libri_di_testo.html.

Convention on Human Rights and Biomedicine, Oviedo, 4.IV. (1997) (ETS 164), available at http://conventions.coe.int/Treaty/en/Treaties/Html/164.htm.

Corica, A. (2015) Maria Luisa Muggiasca: 'Io obiettore perché non credo che l'aborto sia da praticare in tutti i casi', in "*la Repubblica*," available at http://milano.repubblica.it/ cronaca/2015/11/09/news/intervista_obiettore-126982781/?refresh_ce.

De Leo, C. (2012) Meno aborti in Italia rispetto all'Europa ma aumentano i medici obiettori, in "*La Repubblica*," March 7, available at www.repubblica.it/cronaca/2012/ 10/09/news/meno_aborti_in_italia_rispetto_all_europa_ma_aumentano_i_medici_ obiettori-44200039.

De Zordo, S. (2015) I veri motivi dell'obiezione di coscienza sull'abortop, in "Un'inchiesta sull'aborto," available at https://abortoinchiesta.wordpress.com/2015/05/23/obiezio ne-coscienza-aborto-ricerca-antropologica.

Diskriminerings Ombudsmannen (2014)Decision of the Discrimination Ombudsman of Sweden, April 10, 2014, available at www.do.se/globalassets/stallningstaganden/sta llningstagande-beslut-avsluta-anmalan-jonkopings-lans-landsting-anm-2014122.pdf.

Ekstrand, M. et al. (2009) Abortion decision making among teenage women in Sweden, in "*Perspectives on Sexual and Reproductive Health*," 41/3.

European Committee of Social Rights, Case Document No. 8 Federation of Catholic Family Associations in Europe (FAFCE) v. Sweden, Complaint No. 99/2013.

European Union Member States (2012) Charter of Fundamental Rights of the European Union, available at http://eur-lex.europa.eu/legal-content/EN/TXT/?uri=CELEX:12012P/TXT.

Fahlbeck, R. (2014) "Religionsfrihet och mänskliga rättigheter", in "*Juridisk tidskrift*,"1/3, 17–27, English translation author's own.

Ferrari, A. and Ferrari, S. (2010) Religion and the secular state: the Italian case, in "*Italian National Reports, Law and religion*," 16, available at www.iclrs.org/content/blurb/files/Italy.pdf.

Franchell, E. (2014) *Bra att drottningen vägrar ta emot priset*, in "*Aftonbladet*," September 10, available at www.aftonbladet.se/ledare/ledarkronika/evafranchell/article19677893.ab.

Halldén, B., Christensson, K. and Olsson, P. (2005) Meanings of being pregnant and having decided on abortion: young Swedish women's experiences, in "*Healthcare for Women International*," 26/9, 788–806.

Harris, L. (2012) Recognizing Conscience in Abortion Provision, in *The N Engl J Med*.

L'Huffington Post (2014) Aborto, l'obiezione di coscienza in Italia tra le più alte al mondo. In alcune regioni arriva al 100%, March 12, available at www.huffingtonpost.it/2014/03/12/aborto-obiezione-coscienza_n_4948926.html.

La Repubblica (2012) Sempre meno aborti in Italia aumentano i medici obiettori, available at www.repubblica.it/cronaca/2012/10/09/news/meno_aborti_in_italia_rispetto_all_europa_ma_aumentano_i_medici_obiettori-44200039/.

Lalli, C. (2011) C'é chi dice di no: dalla leva all'aborto, come cambia l'obiezione di coscienza, Milano: il Saggiatore.

Löfven, S. (2014) The Statement of Government Policy presented by Swedish Prime Minister, MrStefanLöfven, at the Swedish Riksdag October 3, 2014.

Lundgren, J. (2014) Inställd konferens visar på trång åsiktskorridor, in "*Dagen*," October 14, available at www.dagen.se/inställd-konferens-visar-på-trång-åsiktskorridor-1.274915.

McIntyre, M., Anderson, B., and McDonald, C. (2001) The intersection of relational and cultural narratives: women's abortion experiences, in "*Canadian Journal of Nursing Research*," 33/3, 47–62.

Mahmood, S. (2016) *Religious Difference in a Secular Age: A Minority Report*, Princeton: Princeton University Press.

Makenzius, M.*et al*. (2013) Sverige har Nordens högsta aborttal: Oönskade graviditeter bör ses i helhetsperspektiv – individer, vård, samhälle, in "*Läkartidningen*" 110. www.lakartidningen.se/EditorialFiles/DC/%5BCEDC%5D/CEDC.pdf.

Ministrodella Salute (2014) Relazione del Ministro della Salute sulla attuazione della legge contenente norme per la tutela sociale della maternità e per l'interruzione volontaria di gravidanza (*Legge* 194/78), available at www.salute.gov.it/imgs/C_17_pubblicazioni_2226_allegato.pdf.

Mukkavaara, I., Öhrling, K. K., Lindberg, I. (2012) Women's experiences after an induced second trimester abortion, in "*Midwifery*," 28/5, 720–725.

Musselli L., Ceffa, C. B. (2014) Libertà religiosa, obiezione di coscienza e giurisprudenza costituzionale, Torino: Giappichelli.

NOMESCO (2012) Number of induced abortions by reporting country, age and time, in "*Norden Statistics*," available at https://www.norden.org/en/theme/tidligere-temaer/theme-2012/nordisk-statistik-i-50-aar-1/statistics-from-1962-2012/abortions-pdf.

Nordström, R. (2016) The Right to Conscience in Sweden – two Swedish Midwife cases, Scandinavian Human Rights Lawyers. Available at www.livochratt.se/the-right-to-conscience-in-sweden-two-swedish-midwife-cases-part-5/.

Nordström, R. (2015) Swedish Court Ignores International Law Protecting Freedom of Conscience, media release, November 12, Scandinavian Human Rights Lawyers, available at: http://humanrightslawyers.eu/press-release-12-nov-2015/.

Organization of American States (OAS)2014. Follow-Up Mechanism to the Convention of Belém Do Pará (Mesecvi) Committee of Experts (Cevi), September 18–19, available at www.oas.org/en/mesecvi/docs/CEVI11-Declaration-EN.pdf.

Peirce, C. S. (1932) *Collected Papers of Charles Sanders Peirce, Vols. 1 & 2: Principles of Philosophy and Elements of Logic*, ed. Charles Hartshorne and Paul Weiss, Cambridge, MA: Harvard University Press.

Ricca, M. (2008) *Oltre Babele: Codici per una democrazia interculturale*, Bari: Dedalo.

Ricca, M. (2013) *Culture interdette: Modernità, migrazioni, diritto interculturale*, Torino: Bollati Boringhieri.

Ricca, M. (2014) Intercultural Law, Interdisciplinary Outlines, Lawyering and Anthropological Expertise in Migration Cases: Before the Courts, in www.ec-aiss.it EC. "*Rivista dell'Associazione italiana di Studi semiotici*," 3/3, 1–53.

Salvini Bettarini, S. and Schifini, S. (1996) Induced Abortion in Italy: Levels, Trends and Characteristics, in "*Family Planning Perspectives*," 28/6, 267–271 and 277.

Saporiti, M. (2014) *La coscienza disubbidiente. Ragioni, tutele e limiti dell'obiezione di coscienza*, Milano: Giuffrè.

Supreme Court of Sweden (2005) Judgment issued in Stockholm on November 29, 2005, available at https://web.archive.org/web/20120218220008/www.domstol.se/Domstolar/hogstadomstolen/Avgoranden/2005/Dom_pa_engelska_B_1050-05.pdf.

Turchi, V. (2009) *I nuovi volti di Antigone. Le obiezioni di coscienza nell'esperienza giuridica contemporanea*, Napoli: ESI.

Zuckerman, P. (2008) *Society without God: What the Least Religious Nations Can Tell us about Contentment*,New York: New York University Press.

7 The unfinished education

Religion, education and power struggles in multicultural Israel

Kyriaki Topidi

Introduction

Franz von Benda-Beckmann's frame on human rights in legally plural settings suggests that the study of the struggles between laws and cultures can be enlightening in order to understand better the dialogical analysis of human rights in their socio-legal dimension.[1] 'Empirical variations' of such rights are observed within Israel. While there is an obvious level of constitutional analysis, this inquiry, focusing on the right to education and religious freedom also carries the more ambitious (and nuanced) aim of offering a different perspective on how human rights may be understood, interpreted and applied by different categories of social actors, more particularly religious communities. The 'voice' of freedom of education and religion certainly belongs to governments, political parties and courts but it should also be heard from religious communities, especially within divided social contexts.

Accounts of how religious diversity challenges public education, in Israel as well as elsewhere, involve scenarios of conflict. These conflicts appear to be multilateral, non-linear and often unpredictable in their components. They arise within a single state-centred constitutional system, between a national and a supra-national entity, among the various layers of normative ordering within a state or they even arise within one and the same cultural 'enclave'.

The analysis that follows is nevertheless not an anthropological one insofar as it attempts to move beyond observing the workings of legal pluralism. The 'iron cage'[2] imprisoning lawyers, caught in the process of legitimizing the diffusion of human rights as one self-sufficient 'culture' is clearly a matter of perspective: if we accept that the door to the cage is open, the process of observation may occur both from within but also from a greater distance, in the quest for better laws.

1 Franz von Benda-Beckmann, 'Human Rights Cultural Relativism and Legal Pluralism: Towards a Two-Dimensional Debate', in F. von Benda-Beckmann, K. von Benda-Beckmann and A. Griffiths, *The Power of Law in a Transnational World: Anthropological Enquiries*, Berghahn Books, 2012, pp. 115–134, at 117.
2 Ibid at 128.

Religion within education in Israel

Most modern education systems account for and have been shaped by the interaction between religion and the state.[3] Israel is defined as a 'Jewish and democratic State'[4] which signifies that a separation of state and religion does not exist. In the field of education, the role of religion in state affairs and the state's establishment of religion find an expression in the religious tracks of the public education system.[5] In practice, this ambiguous legal framework allows the state funding of religious institutions, particularly Orthodox Jewish ones, which quite often enjoy equivalent and parallel political power from ultra-Orthodox parties in the Knesset. The combined efforts of the Ministry of Education with the Ministry of Religious Affairs actively support a wide network of ultra-Orthodox (*Haredi*) educational activities.[6] Religious educational institutions (*Yeshivas*) enjoy thus a consistently high level of financial backing, despite a duty of equal allowance. The examples of the 'Shkenazi' and the 'Sephardi Center of Fountain of Religious Education in Israel' are two ultra-Orthodox educational networks that have grown with the help of state funds.[7] These institutions offer education for lower or no fees yet of a lower quality.

One of the clearest projections of Israeli national ideology in this respect is that of a 'nation by right of religion'.[8] The aim of public education continues to be that of deepening Jewish consciousness yet within a clear religious dimension,[9] but also with an eye for closing the social gap between Jews inside Israel.[10] The 'religious primordiality',[11] however, of the state and its education system predict an imbalance in favour of the right to religious freedom, against those of equality and the right to education.

3 Corene de Wet, 'Religion in Education: An International Perspective', in Carl Wolhuter and Corene de Wet (eds), *International Comparative Perspectives on Religion and Education*, SunPress, 2014, pp. 1–3.

4 Basic Law: Human Dignity and Freedom, §1(a), 1391 L.S.I. 150 (1992), 'to protect human dignity and freedom in order to affix in a basic law the values of the state of Israel as a Jewish and democratic State …'.

5 *State Education Law*, 131 L.S.I. 137 (1953).

6 For more on this point, see Shimon Shetreet, 'State and religion: Funding of religious institutions – the case of Israel in comparative perspective', *Notre Dame Journal of Law, Ethics and Public Policy*, Vol. 13, No. 2, (1999), 421–453, at 443.

7 Shetreet (1999) at 443.

8 Julia Resnik, 'Particularistic vs. universalistic content in the Israeli education system', *Curriculum Inquiry*, Vol. 29, No. 4 (Winter 1999), 485–511 at 488.

9 Ibid at 492–3. The Jewish Consciousness Program (1958) stressed the new attitude towards religion: '… the new generation will acknowledge the Jewish-religious way of life and will respect it', Director General's Circular 36/8, 20 March 1977, sec.273. For a comprehensive account of the historical development of religious education in Isreal, see Shmuel Shamal, '"Cultural shift": The case of religion education in Israel', *British Journal of Sociology of Education*, Vol. 21, No. 3 (2000), 401–417.

10 Resnik (1999) at 494.

11 Ibid.

The design of educational pluralism in Israel: general features

Since 1975, the Israeli education system relies on a basic structure requiring six years of primary school (ages 6–12),[12] three years of junior high (ages 12–15) and three years of senior high (ages 15–17), following which students take the *bagrut*[13] and then join the Israeli Defense Forces (IDF) for a compulsory military service.[14]

The basis for Israel's education system relies on a model of cultural pluralism, promoting the creation and preservation of religious/cultural pluralism, which is based on cultural enclaves. The fundamental distinction within the Hebrew school systems foresees three sub-systems: (a) the secular state schools (*mamlachti*), (b) the religious state schools (*mamlachti dati*), and (c) the ultra-Orthodox schools, classified as independent schools and serving an approximate 8–10 per cent of the total Israeli population.[15] These latter schools are also benefiting from state funds. A fourth segment of the system counts Arab schools (Christian, Druze or Islamic).[16]

Both state and state religious schools are under the supervision of the Ministry of Education, Culture and Sport. The language of instruction in Jewish schools is Hebrew, while in Arab schools it is Arabic. A separate educational system is maintained for Arab students, although the possibility for Arab students joining the Jewish track exists.

In primary education, religious studies are part of the curriculum for all types of schools and although teaching methods are determined by the schools themselves (teachers and principals) and local authorities, the content of the curriculum is laid down by the Ministry of Education. For secondary schools, there is more flexibility in the design and organization of the content of education than at the primary school level.[17] Within Israel's occupied territories (the Gaza Strip, the Golan Heights, the Sinai Peninsula and the West Bank), education is provided by

12 Compulsory education in Israel begins at the age of 5.

13 Academic Secondary School Leaving Examination, resulting in a credit-system required for higher education.

14 Military service is compulsory for all Jews and Druzes but voluntary for Christians, Circassians and Muslims. It has a three-year duration for men and a two-year duration for women.

15 Mirjam Künkler and Hanna Lerner, 'A private matter? Religious education and democracy in Indonesia and Israel', *British Journal of Religious Education* (2016), 1–29 at p. 11 provide the following statistical breakdown of students based on 2012 figures: among 595,000 Jewish students in elementary schools, 55% attended secular schools, 19% religious state schools and 25% ultra-Orthodox schools (Central Bureau of Statistics, 2012).

16 Article 1, 1953 State Education Act. According to the Act, public education has three streams: the national education track, serving the Jewish, Arab and Druze populations; the national religious education track, serving religious Jews and the national-incorporating education track, serving secular Jews who opt for programmes enhanced with intensive Jewish studies and emphasize Jewish identity.

17 There is a basic distinction between academic and vocational tracks at secondary level. Grades 10–12 are not compulsory.

combined public and private sponsorship.[18] The educational system in these areas is heavily influenced by the Egyptian and Jordanian systems. Only the Golan Heights follow the same curriculum as Arab schools in Israel. Finally, serving the ultra-Orthodox community,[19] ultra-Orthodox schools are non-public schools.

The Arab school system, catering for the educational needs of approximately 25 per cent of all school students in Israel,[20] is also supervised by the Ministry of Education. The curriculum in these schools is adapted to the religion of the student body (Muslim or Christian) and similarly schools in Druze or Circassian villages adapt the curriculum to the cultural needs of their respective student populations.[21] The 1953 State Education Law provides specifically for non-Jewish schools to follow a differentiated curriculum that corresponds to 'their special conditions'.[22] The 1996 National Education Regulations established an advisory council on Arabic education (Advisory Council on Arabic Education) with the aim to promote equality in recognition of cultural specific needs.[23]

In terms of curricular content related to religion, in secular state schools the curriculum does not include religion classes, although Bible lessons (*Tanach*) are mandatory but organized from a literary perspective. Religious state schools include religious studies together with general studies in their programmes.[24] These schools are governed by an autonomous division within the Ministry of Education, under the direction of the Council of Religious Education. Unlike the students of the ultra-Orthodox schools, graduates of religious schools may take the *bagrut* allowing them to apply to academic institutions for higher education.[25] The religious nature of the religious state schools is particularly pronounced as it

18 Following the 1994 Oslo Accords, Palestinians took over responsibility for their education system. Based on a centralized model, the curriculum, textbooks and regulations are sourced from the government. Education is provided in three types of schools: boys', girls' and co-educational ones, each representing roughly a third of the total number of schools. United Nations Relief and Work Agency serves children in refugee camps, an estimated 23% of the total Palestinian student population. For more on these points, see Nadir Altinok, 'The hidden crisis: Armed conflict and education', Paper commissioned for the Education for All Global Monitoring Report 2011, 2011/ED/EFA/MRT/PI/11, at pp. 15–16.

19 Shulamit Almog and Lotem Perry-Hazan, 'Contesting religious authoriality: The Immanuel "Beis Yaakov" School segregation case', *The International Journal for the Semiotics of Law*, Vol. 26, No. 1 (2012), 211–225, at 212. There are three main subgroups in the ultra-Orthodox Community: The Lithuanians, the Hasidim and the Sephardi. See also Gila Stopler, 'The right to an exclusively religious education – The ultra Orthodox community in Israel in comparative perspective', *G.A.J. Int'l & Comp. L.*, Vol. 42 (2014), 743–796, at 748.Overall, 40% of the Jewish population defines themselves as secular, 20% as religious and 40% as traditional (Shetreet, 1999, at 452).

20 Künkler and Lerner (2016) at 10.

21 Künkler and Lerner (2016) at p. 10.

22 State Education Law, 5713–1953, 7 LSI 113 §4 (1952–1953).

23 National Education Regulation (Advisory Council on Arabic Education) 1996, Art. 5(1).

24 This category of schools is the only one defined by law (State Education Law, 5713–1953, (1952–2003)).

25 Künkler and Lerner (2016) at 10.

has a pervasive orthodox religious character in the provision of all educational services.[26]

The final category of ultra-Orthodox or *Agudat* schools enjoy state recognition but are considered 'non-official'.[27] The main networks running these schools are the Independent Education Network and the Sephardic Centre of Religious Education in Israel (also known as 'The Fountain of Religious Education' – *Mayan Ha'hinuch Ha'torani*).[28] The level of supervision of the Ministry of Education on these schools is considerably lower, although the state supplies up to 75 per cent of their budget. It is relevant to stress, however, that schools associated with *Agudat* (Israel's Independent Education Network and Shas' Fountain of Religious Education) enjoy full curricular autonomy as well as state funding.[29] Overall, ultra-Orthodox schools are exempt from a number of secular studies such as maths, science, history, geography, English, etc. As an indication of the type of education provided, after the age of 13, ultra-Orthodox (male) pupils have to focus on religious studies alone, to the exemption of all other topics.

The way the ultra-Orthodox sub-system of public education is organized in Israel raises the obvious question of the quality of education provided within it. The 1953 State Education Act provided for a 'core curriculum' requirement but one has to wait until 2003 for a detailed programme of the mandatory 'core curriculum' for primary education and until 2007 for one for the secondary education system.[30]

The suggested practice emerging from the provision on the 'core curriculum'[31] requires fully funded schools (i.e. Hebrew secular schools, Hebrew religious state schools and Arab schools) to teach the entire 'core curriculum'. The transfer of government funds to these schools is clearly conditioned on the implementation of this requirement. Additionally, in order to achieve recognition, a school must teach at least 75 per cent of the core curriculum as set by the Ministry of Education. A school that teaches that curriculum is consequently also eligible for 75 per cent of state funding given to public schools.[32]

26 The 1953 State Education Law, in paragraph 18, allows the Council for Religious Education to ensure, for example, that all teachers and staff in religious state schools are religious themselves.

27 The legal basis for this ambiguous legal status is to be found in the Compulsory Education Act, 5709–1949, 3 LSI §1 (1948–1949) and is defined as the educational institutions 'which the Minister by declaration published in *Reshumot* (Official Gazette), has declared to be a recognized educational institution'. The decision for Agudat to opt out of the official education stream and obtain the status of 'recognized' schools was based on a willingness for autonomy, prioritizing cultural advancement on the basis of religion. (Cf. Shamal (2000) at p. 407.)

28 Founded by the Sephardic political party 'Sephardi Keepers of Torah', also known as *Shas*. (*Itahdut Sephardim Shomrei Torah*).

29 In this respect, Künkler and Lerner (2016) at 12 note the difficulty to determine the level of state funding hinting at an intentional lack of transparency (see in particular their footnote 35).

30 Basic (Core) Curriculum 1995 and Basic (Core) Curriculum 2007 respectively.

31 The 'core curriculum' includes the subjects of the Bible, social studies, Hebrew, English, maths, science, art and sports.

32 Mandatory Study Act 5510–1949, SH No.26, p. 287.

The actual practice related to the implementation of the 'core curriculum' is diverging nevertheless from the initial intention of the lawmakers. There is evidence that ultra-Orthodox schools violate this condition, although comprehensive data is still lacking.[33] Case law such as *High Schools Teachers Union v. Minister of Education (2004)* or *Centre of Jewish Pluralism v. Ministry of Education (2007)* demonstrate that the scope of the 'core curriculum' is limited in these schools. The content of education provided in these establishments merits therefore a closer look: the actual content of lessons, the textbooks used and the selection and training of educators are left to the autonomous control of these schools. There is also a discrepancy between the educational content in the programme designed for ultra-Orthodox girls and that for ultra-Orthodox boys: in the former case, greater weight is placed on general studies, considered inferior in the ultra-Orthodox society,[34] while in the latter, the weight of education revolves around religious texts alone. The political leverage exercised by ultra-Orthodox communities seeking to maintain (and expand) educational autonomy was sealed with the 2008 Unique Cultural Institutions Law, exempting state-funded secondary ultra-Orthodox schools for boys (grades 9–12) from 'core curriculum' entirely.

Normative justification of close entanglement between religion and the state in education in Israel

The privileged position of religion in public life in Israel in combination with the strong standing of the Jewish Orthodox community are sourced from the 'status quo agreement' between religious leaders and the secular Mapai party that formed a government after independence.[35] The content of the 'status quo agreement' remains fuzzy, although it did initially translate into formal and informal regulations.[36]

The agreement and its implementation transformed the exchange between religion and state in Israel to a 'conversation about synagogue and state.'[37] The partial establishment of Orthodox Judaism relies heavily on the privilege of all Jews in Israel being subjected to Orthodox Jewish religious personal laws. Correspondingly, other recognized religious communities are also subject to personal religious laws of their respective religions.

33 Cf. Künkler and Lerner (2016) at 13. See also the case law discussed below, in particular footnote 76.
34 Ibid at 14.
35 Künkler and Lerner (2016) at p. 7.
36 For example, Kosher dietary observance in governmental institutions, exclusive Orthodox jurisdiction of marriage and divorce, exemptions of ultra-Orthodox students from the military service and an autonomous Orthodox education system.
37 Michael Karayanni, The 'Other' Religion and State Conflict in Israel: On the Nature of the Religious Accommodations for the Palestinian-Arab Minority', in W. Brugger and M. Karayanni (eds), *Religion in the Public Sphere: A Comparative Analysis of German, Israeli, American and International Law*, Springer and Max Planck Institute for Comparative Public Law and International Law, 2007, pp. 333–377, at 336.

At the difference of religious accommodations conceded to the Palestinian-Arab minority, which reflected a continuation of the Ottoman *millet* system, Jewish religious accommodation became integral part of the public sphere.[38] The main argument supporting the discrepancy in the treatment of the two communities, according to Maoz, claims that '(d)ivest Jewish culture and heritage from religious elements and one is left rather empty handed.'[39] Inequalities in the educational content between the two ethnic tracks could be observed early on: Arabs were educated in Judaism and Israeli Jewish history, while not exposed to Palestinian history and culture. Hebrew is required in Arab schools while Arabic is optional in some Jewish schools. Efforts to include elements of Arab history, literature and culture were nevertheless made later on.[40]

Insistence on uniformity within the Israeli education system, especially in the early post-independence years, was indeed presented as a project aiming at the 'general good' of the people, yet not all voices were provided with equal opportunities to be heard.[41]

One of the main targets of the Israeli education system has been the closing of the gap of achievement observed among various communities within the country. To support this goal, the first two legislative acts on education, following the birth of the State of Israel, protected the right to education without discrimination on the basis of race, religion or gender (Compulsory Education Act 1949) and equal opportunities in accessing education regardless of political or other affiliation (State Education Act 1953). This legislative framework was heavily reliant on the principle of equity and included the intention to distribute the same curriculum, under the same conditions to all (e.g. same teacher-student ratio, same number of teaching days per school year, etc).[42] The practical discrepancies between schools results in Hebrew as opposed to Arab schools led to subsequent five-year affirmative action plans in the 1990s with the aim to improve conditions mainly in the Arab school sector.[43]

38 Karayanni (2007), at 338.

39 A. Maoz, 'State and Religion in Israel', in M. Mor (ed.), *International Perspectives on Church and State*, Fordham University Press, 1993, pp. 239 et seq. at p. 243.

40 Muhammed Amaraa, Faisal Azaiza, Rachel Hertz-Lazarowitz and Aura Mor-Sommerfeld, 'A new bilingual education in the conflict ridden Israeli reality: Language practices', *Language and Education*, Vol. 23, No. 1 (2009), at 18.

41 Cf. Ami Pedahzur, 'The paradox of civic education in non-liberal democracies: The case of Israel', *Journal of Education Policy*, Vol. 16, No. 5 (2001), 413–430 at 416. Pedahzur, in fact, classifies Israel as a 'non-liberal democracy', particularly inspired by Sammy Smooha's concept of *ethnic democracy*, defined as a democratic system of government wherein rights are granted to all citizens although favoured status is only given to the majority (Ibid, at 417).

42 Altinok (2011) at p. 28.

43 Among positive changes between 1999 and 2001, the increase of enrolment rates of children between the ages of 14 and 17 was noticeable in the Arab sector by 26% (compared to 6% in the Hebrew sector). Cf Altinok (2011) at 28 for more on this point.

The 1953 State Education Act projected a centralized education system based on achievement, the principle of equality and liberty. Constitutionally, it resonated well the inception of the rights to equality and to education, by organizing public education through the uniform distribution of financial resources and by guaranteeing the choice for students and their parents of the stream of education best suited to their needs and beliefs. In practice, however, the law accentuated disparities between ethnic and social classes, with the affluent communities consistently securing enhanced access to resources for their schools.[44] Paragraph 2 of the Act is explicit in that respect:

> The goal of State Education is to establish a basic education in this State upon the values of Israeli culture and scientific achievements, on the love of the homeland and loyalty to the State and Nation of Israel

Reforms in 1968 targeting social integration and the closing of gaps failed due to slow implementation and lack of political will.[45] Academic achievement remained correlated to ethnic background.

Constitutional plurality and religious diversity

The ambiguous principle of equality

The canvas of public education in Israel has been increasingly painted with colours of aggressiveness and violence: between the secular and the religious, the older generations and the new immigrants, the Ashkenazi and the Mizrahi, the Jewish and the Arabs.[46] Social fragmentation takes the form of discontent arising from Israel's mixed secular-cum-religious legal system. The level of this discontent is particularly visible in the ambiguous position accorded to the principle of equality.

For historical reasons and pre-state experiences of discrimination and persecution, Israel's Declaration of Independence placed emphasis on the principle of equality. While the Declaration states that Israel would be a 'Jewish State', it was declared to 'ensure complete equality of social and political rights to all its inhabitants irrespective of religion, race or sex; it will guarantee freedom of religion, conscience, language, education and culture'.[47]

The principle at stake failed, nevertheless, to be endorsed within a formal constitutional text, due to resistance from religious political parties in the Knesset to confront the freedom of conscience with equality. Such a constitutional confrontation would involve the reconsideration (and reconfiguration) of the religious

44 Alexandra F. Leavy, 'The failure of education policy in Israel: Politics vs bureaucracy', *CUREJ Electronic Journal*, 2010, at p. 26, http://repository.upenn.edu/curej/115, visited on 21.06.2016.

45 Ibid at pp. 29–30.

46 Ami Pedahzur (2001), at 427.

47 The Declaration of the Establishment of the State of Israel, Iyar 5, 5708 – May 14, 1948, Official Gazette No.1, p. 1.

monopoly in family matters,[48] a privilege that the religious actors and pious citizens were not prepared to let go.

Without a formal constitution or a bill of rights, the Israeli constitutional system relies on the 1992 Basic Law: Freedom of occupation and the 1992 Basic Law: Human Dignity and Liberty to regulate and address civil liberties. Together with decisions of the Israeli High Court, they form the sources of constitutional law. Judicial review is unclear within this framework: after 1992, and the passage of the two Basic Laws, the Court may, under circumstances, strike down laws violating individual rights.

A partial constitutional bill of rights, the Basic Law: Human Dignity and Liberty, introduced a projected remedy to the absence of constitutional force for the principle of equality through the recognition of the principle of human dignity. Human dignity (*kevod haadam*) was understood in the text as the superiority of human rights listed, not to be violated except by a law in accordance with the values of the State of Israel as a Jewish and democratic state.[49]

Specifically for education, there is no explicit right to education in the *Basic Laws*, yet the 1949 Compulsory Education Act, the 1953 State Education Act and the 2000 Pupils' Rights Law cover the right.[50] Both the 1949 and the 2000 Acts contain explicit non-discrimination provisions on the basis of ethnicity in the registration, admission or creation of separate classrooms within a school. Yet these prohibitions apply only to local authorities or the schools, but not the central government.

The effect of the two major Basic Laws on Freedom of Occupation and on Human Dignity and Liberty intensified the debate on the relationship between religion and state. The 'Jewish' and 'democratic' character of the State of Israel provoked the questioning of the compatibility between these two characteristics.[51] Indicatively, the constitutional marginalization of the Palestinian-Arab community inevitably re-surfaced in both legal and public policy debates:[52] it was further intensified upon the observation of the gaps in the public accommodation and

48 Frances Raday, 'Equality, Religion and Gender in Israel', *Jewish Women: A Comprehensive Historical Encyclopedia*, 1.03.2009, http://jwa.org/encycopedia/article/equality-religion-and-gender-in-israel at p. 1.

49 See indicatively the content of the 1951 Women's Equal Rights Law guaranteeing gender equality before the law, elevating it to a principle for interpretation for ambivalent legislation while subordinating it to Halakhic rules on marriage and divorce on 'prohibition and permission to marry and divorce' (cf. Raday, 2009, at 2). The rationale for the opposition in the Knesset was simply that the principle of equality (particularly for women) must be subjected to the principles and practice of Judaism.

50 The latter stipulates that: 'every child and youth in the State of Israel has the right to an education according to all instructions of the law'.

51 For an analysis on this point cf. M. Karayanni (2007?) at pp. 345–6, in particular his footnotes 49 and 51.

52 The Palestinian-Arab community in Israel has been described as 'the most remote excluded community from the state's meta-narratives' in Gad Barzilai, *Communities and the Law: Politics and Cultures of Legal Identitites*, University of Michigan Press, 2003, pp. 10–11, at pp. 7, 42.

state funding of religious institutions between Jewish and Arab communities,[53] not exclusively attributed to the demographic preponderance of (Orthodox) Jews in Israel.[54]

In this respect, the issue of religious accommodations appears to operate on the basis of a variable geometry, to the extent that is creates a reversed type of multiculturalism, where autonomy becomes synonymous with the imposition of a patriarchal minority culture on the liberal majority.[55] As the more detailed outline of the patterns of discrimination will illustrate below, the right to education, while having been recognized in an idiosyncratic constitutional form, nevertheless is implemented at the expense of the right to equality. The result is an asymmetric education in its contents and in its effects: it promotes a one-sided multicultural project 'where Arab students are educated for control and Jewish students for ethnocentric rule.'[56]

Before judicial *fora*, there seems to be an essential(-ized) distinction made between the balancing of equality and religion in the private sphere as opposed to the public one. In the former, the highest jurisdictions of the country have traditionally refused to consider equality in the context of divorce proceedings.[57] In the latter, a sophisticated web of balancing tools has been devised by the Supreme Court to decide on these clashes. In the *Poraz* case,[58] involving a challenge to the decision not to appoint women to the electoral board for the Tel Aviv municipal rabbi, the Court held that while 'equality is an important principle but ... a relative principle' (at 336), it was determinative in this case because there was no real barrier, in the form of a *halakhic* prohibition, to the functioning of a municipal rabbi, if women sat on the electoral board (at 337).

In the *Nevo* case,[59] on the issue of equal retirement age for women, the Supreme Court, per Justice Cheshin, described equality as

> The king of principles – the most elevated of principles above all others ... So it is in public law and so it is in each and every aspect of our lives in society. The principle of equality infiltrates every plant of the legal garden and

53 See indicatively cases HCJ, 240/98 *Adalah – The Legal Center for the Rights of the Arab Minority in Israel v. The Minister for Religious Affairs*, 52(5) P.D. 167, 178 (1999); HCJ, 1113/99 *Adalah – The Legal Center for the Rights of the Arab minority in Israel v. The Minister for Religious Affairs*, 54(ii)P.D. 164 (2000); HCJ, 2422/98 *Adalah – The Legal Center for the Rights of the Arab Minority in Israel v. The Minister of Labor and Welfare* (not published). Cf. *The State of Israel, Implementation of the ICCPR: Combined Initial and First Periodic Report of the State of Israel* (1998) at 228.

54 Karayanni (2007?) at 362.

55 Ibid, at 355.

56 HRW 2001 Report, at 92.

57 See indicatively *Plonit v. Plonit* 51(1) PD 198 (1997) where the High Court unanimously dismissed a case based on a ruling of the Grand Rabbinical Court refusing to oblige a husband, separated from his wife for more than six years, to give her a divorce.

58 Bagaz 953/87 *Poraz v. Lahat, Mayor of Tel Aviv et al.* 42(2) P.D. 309 (1988).

59 Bagaz 104/87 *Nevo v. the National Labour Court et al.* (22.10.90).

> constitutes an unseverable part of the genetic make-up of all the legal rules, each and every one … The principle of equality is, in theory and practice, a father-principle or should we say a mother-principle …

Further to that and breaking away with the limits of formal equality, the Court has incorporated the notion of affirmative action and accommodation in order to build the concept of *equal opportunity*, obviously aiming at a 'socio-dynamic' type of equality.[60] For affirmative action, the Court recognized the need to give preference to weaker groups in an attempt to correct past injustice and to promote equality of ability.[61]

The Supreme Court's approach towards the principle of accommodation requires a conciliation between the need for individuals to realize their potential, irrespective of their special characteristics, and the general goals of the continuation of society's existence.[62] In other words, a construct that rejects special treatment but also complete blindness to discriminatory practices.

The role of the state in Israel in the provision of religious services

On a global scale, in both constitutional and governance terms, the state-centred mode of education is in decline. New actors and organizations are increasingly taking more active parts and discretion over educational processes on a global scale. Local schools, parents associations, municipalities and regional councils are devising and shaping, together with the state, educational agendas. In Israel, this diversification of educational services becomes important for the purposes of this study in assessing the content of education from the angle of religious diversity,[63] particularly within ultra-Orthodox communities.

The essential question that arises with respect to state funding of religious schools in Israel is a recurring one. There is little disagreement that the public financing of religious/denominational schools is controversial. Given that the right to education affords the possibility for parents' (and to some extent the communities to which these families belong) to educate their children according to their beliefs, the question becomes what kind of state-funded education should be

60 Term borrowed from Raday (2009) at 6.

61 See indicatively the case IWN II (*IWN v. Minister of Labor*, 52(3) P.D. (1998) 630), where the Supreme Court accepted that affirmative action was an integral part of the principle of equality.

62 Cf. *Miller v. Minister of Defense* 49(4) P.D. (1995) on the refusal of a female to enter the pilots' course of the Israel Air Force on grounds of her sex.

63 Furthermore, the translation of curricular policies to classroom practice has to account for gaps in implementation. For more on this, see Aaron Benavot and Nura Resh, 'Educational governance, school autonomy, and curriculum implementation: A comparative study of Arab and Jewish schools in Israel', *Journal of Curriculum Studies*, Vol. 35, No. 2 (2003), 171–196, at 172. According to Benavot and Resh, current tools for overseeing implementation of educational policies include on-site inspection, mandatory achievement examinations, regulated teacher-training programmes and authorized lists of school textbooks. (Ibid, at 173.)

available to them.[64] Assuming that in a liberal democracy the state must fund compulsory education, that public institutions and policies should not promote a particular conception of the 'good life', and that public aid of such schools is constitutionally permissible, to what degree does it require state intervention in religious practices within such schools? Also, connected to this first question, does this intervention enhance or reduce religious freedom?[65]

Medina argues that in the Israeli context, the major concern behind state intervention should be the facilitation of religious freedom by securing access to religious services.[66] He also rejects the common argument that the extent of government support dictates also the extent and legitimacy of intervention. Further to that state intervention, in his view, may also be mandated in circumstances where there is a risk that a certain religious practice may cause harm on other interests (e.g. gender equality). The underlying threat present in state intervention remains, however, that government regulation may be perceived or interpreted as 'biased, sectarian or aimed at secularization and promoting values of liberalism' and labelled as an act against the protection of religion.[67]

In education, affording the possibility for education according to one's beliefs and world vision, prima facie serves the purpose of the wider access to religious freedom. A more careful consideration of the effects of Haredi education may nevertheless demonstrate a more nuanced conclusion that is likely to result to a conflict leading to an infringement of either religious freedom or the right to education.

Educational diversification according to religious belonging: the example of Ultra-Orthodox education

In the early days of Israeli statehood, educational affairs were tightly controlled by political authorities. The initial aims of state education in Israel were threefold: first, to ensure between-school equality, as there were a variety of streams of education available; second, to strengthen the state's influence over the socialization of future citizens, through the medium of a unified national curriculum; and third, to contribute to the assimilation of new immigrants.[68] The official curriculum approach, in that respect, followed the 'melting pot' ideology combined with the goal of building a 'bottom-up' new Israeli Jewish identity.[69] For the Arab

64 Johan de Jong and Ger Snik, 'Why should states fund denominational schools?', *Journal of Philosophy of Education*, Vol. 36, No. 4 (2002), 573–587.
65 Both questions have been pertinently analysed and discussed, outside the context of education, in Barak Medina, 'Enhancing freedom of religion through public provision of religious services: The Israeli experience', *Israeli Law Review*, Vol. 39, No. 2 2 (006), 127–157.
66 Ibid, at 130. Medina's primary field of application in this context is sourced from the case law surrounding the regulation of religious sites of worship.
67 Ibid, at 137.
68 Benavot and Resh (2003) at 176.
69 Ibid, at 178.

component of the population, there was less clarity in educational goals, with more emphasis on controls over school practices and educational content. More recently, however, in the light of the decentralization of diffusion of educational policies, more school autonomy is allowed for in that sector too.

The four sub-sectors of Israeli education, i.e. Jewish state-secular, Jewish state–religious, Jewish independent ('ultra-Orthodox') and Arab, have developed parallel educational narratives, reflecting the religious identities of the communities that they have been serving. For the purposes of the present analysis, the case of the ultra-Orthodox publicly funded education will be considered, as an illustration of the normative clash between education and religion.

Haredi society has been identified as a 'society of scholars' but one that relies on the state in order to pursue its mission.[70] The socio-economic structure of ultra-Orthodox communities is directly related to the educational model prevalent in the schools dedicated to these communities. High fertility rates with low workforce participation are economically suffocating the ultra-Orthodox families that count among the poorest communities in Israel.[71] Due to the specificity of family structure among them, whereby men study the Torah and women have children, these families have grown heavily dependent on state benefits.[72] Interestingly, the employment dynamics within the same group were quite different at the time of the establishment of the Jewish state: women's fertility rates were comparable to those of other Jewish women while men quitted religious studies to get jobs upon marriage.[73]

The category of ultra-Orthodox schools draws particular attention because it has increasingly developed a level of resistance to the mandatory school curriculum.[74] In 2012, the ultra-Orthodox education system spread to 25 per cent of primary and 23.3 per cent of secondary school students, within a broad background of a rapidly growing student population turning to these schools.[75] These schools reject the teaching of core subjects such as history, English or science. This

70 See the work of Menachem Friedman, *The Haredi* (1991) as quoted in Cohn (2012) at p. 4.

71 According to 2010 figures of the National Insurance Institute, 65 per cent of the Haredi population suffered from poverty in comparison to 23.7% of the entire Jewish population (as quoted in Margit Cohn (2012), 'Taking a Bus from Immanuel to Mea Shearim: The Role of Israel's High Court of Justice in Regulating Ethnic and Gender Discrimination in the *Haredi* Ultra-Orthodox Sector', http://ssrn.com/abstract=2176401 at p. 17).

72 Stopler (2014) at 749.

73 Ibid.

74 Künkler and Lerner (2016) at p. 3.

75 Ibid, at p. 3. The authors claim that the percentage of students in religious state-funded schools has tripled in the last 20 years. Today, one in every four students in the Jewish educational system attends an ultra-Orthodox school. This is not surprising given that the average fertility rate of ultra-Orthodox women is at 7.7 children per woman, as opposed to 2.6 children per woman among the general Jewish population. (Data is from 2001 and is included in Hagai Levin, The National Economic Council – 'The Haredi Sector in Israel: Empowerment through workforce integration', 10 (2009), as quoted in Stopler (2014) at 748.

rejection has led to Supreme Court decisions regarding the enforcement of Core Curriculum standards in state-funded ultra-Orthodox schools.[76]

Educational philosophy

Education for girls in Haredi establishments is organized in a loaded social environment.[77] Clearly the right to education is not denied to these students yet it comes in a context of gendered religious and cultural expectations emanating from their communities. Education and schooling for these girls represents a necessary stop prior to their final 'destination': marriage to a man who devotes his life to the study of the Torah, having as many children as possible and the responsibility for managing her household.[78] In the light of the growing necessity for these students to become the main breadwinners within their households, education is necessary in order to get employment. But not any education. Their education is not the product of free choice: 'a girl's education is meant, first and foremost, to serve the family rather than the girl's personal needs, or their wishes for self-fulfillment.'[79]

Ultra-Orthodox education of boys is heavily sourced from religious studies, with few (if at all) secular subjects taught. Contemporary ultra-Orthodox communities have idealized the goal of continuous study of the Torah, which has become the sole aim of their education.

From a formal legal standpoint, the requirements of both the right to freedom of religion and of education appear satisfied. In essence, nevertheless, the principle of equality is strikingly missing, as the aim of such education is primarily to serve the patriarchal order prevalent within the ultra-Orthodox community.

76 See e.g. *High Schools Teachers Union v. Minister of Education (2004); Amnon Rubinstein v. the Knesset (2012).*

77 Increasingly, studies claim that, in the Israeli case, student performance is influenced by the family's cultural environment. Within religious families, the prevailing reading environment affects students' reading habits (Yariv Feniger, Yossi Shavit and Hanna Ayalon, 'Religiosity, reading and educational achievement among Jewish students in Israel', *International Journal of Jewish Education Research*, Vol. 7 (2014), 29–67, at 31). De Graaf, De Graaf and Kraaykamp already in 2000 suggested that parental reading habits best predict students' school success. (N.D. De Graaf, P.M. De Graaf and G. Kraaykamp, 'Parental cultural capital and educational attainment in the Netherlands: A refinement of the cultural capital perspective', *Sociology of Education*, Vol. 73, No. 2 (2000), 92–111). As Judaism places cultural emphasis on books and reading, observant families provide an environment more conducive to studying, leading children from such families to better school results (Feniger et al. (2014) at 35). Indicatively, students in the state religious sector were found to read more than students in the state sector. The percentages are 69% against 43% respectively. Cultural capital, thus, seems to be linked with Jewish religiosity, although scholarship cannot as of yet quantify the causal effects of school type and cultural/religious background on academic outcome (Ibid, at 47).

78 Shulamit Almog and Lotem Perry-Hazan, 'The ability to claim and the opportunity to imagine: Rights consciousness and the education of ultra-Orthodox Girls', *Journal of Law and Education*, Vol. 40, No.2 (2011), 1–31, at 2.

79 Ibid, at p. 3.

In terms of rights-consciousness, understood as 'the process that enables people to define their aims, wishes, and difficulties in terms of rights', Almog and Perry-Hazan, in their work, identify two essential shortcomings particularly for female members of these communities: first, these girls are not apt to reflect on and plan their personal growth and second, they are unaware of their human rights entitlements and because of that fail to identify the constant violation of these rights.[80]

Content of education

The curriculum for ultra-Orthodox girls contains both religious and secular subjects.[81] Within religious studies, female students are not taught the Talmud.[82] Among secular subjects, they are taught linguistic skills, grammar, literature, history, geography, mathematics, English, science, music and art.[83] Following graduation from high school, and after two years of continuing studies, a common career path followed by ultra-Orthodox girls has been teaching.[84] Yet given the saturation of the job market of ultra-Orthodox teachers, other career perspectives have begun to be considered by these girls.[85] The difference in content of school education between ultra-Orthodox girls and boys is striking: the latter only focus on religious texts after the end of their primary school education.[86]

Within a cultural setting of gender inequality, sourced from the ultra-Orthodox interpretation of the *halacha* (Jewish Religious Law), the rights to freedom of religion and freedom of education produce adverse effects of subordination and legal dis-empowerment. Ultra-orthodox girls and young women are not able to exercise the full span of their legal entitlements despite receiving a (basic) education.[87] Both gender and religious/cultural conventions operate as factors preventing the development of human rights education within these schools.

The paradox, within this segment of the ultra-Orthodox community, is characterized on one hand by the central position and recognition of the right to educate these girls according to their religious faith but at the same time by its outcome, which is 'education for ignorance'.[88] Utilizing the concept of 'honour', the ultra-Orthodox communities require that the individual demonstrates

80 Ibid, at p. 4.
81 'Beis Ya'akov' Schools area usually the schools for ultra-Orthodox girls.
82 The Talmud is instead the most significant subject-matter for the education of ultra-Orthodox boys.
83 Almog and Perry-Hazan (2011) at p. 6.
84 Ibid.
85 Professional studies leading to computing careers, accounting, graphics, architecture and even fashion are being also considered (cf. Almog and Perry-Hazan (2011), at p. 6).
86 This is legally validated by the 2008 Culturally Unique Educational Institutions Act, discussed elsewhere in this chapter.
87 For more on agency and legal (dis)-empowerment within religion, cf. Topidi et al. (eds), *Religion as Empowerment: Global Legal Perspectives*, Routledge, 2016.
88 Tamar El-Or has described ultra-Orthodox female school graduates as 'educated and ignorant' depicting well the prevalent paradox. (Cf. Tamar El-Or, *Educated and*

honourable behaviour by blocking any notion of personal autonomy and free choice.[89] The gender factor within public education in Haredi schools for girls is elevated to a guiding principle, relying on the undisputed and undisputable status of Halakhic interpretation, in order to deconstruct the essence of education for girls.

Some authors categorize the phenomenon as an expression of extreme multiculturalism that neglects the state's responsibility to maintain and promote human rights education.[90] Indeed, it is open to debate whether relevant education is afforded to these female students, in an environment where collective religious rights take precedence over individual ones.

Case law

Case law sheds light on the judicial and to some degree the societal perceptions on what is the normative consensus for the issues at stake. Frances Raday points out that: 'case law, whether constitutional or not, represents an amalgam of the priorities of petitioners … and the perceptions of judges based on their professional training and their individual perspectives.'[91] In this sense, by carefully observing cases that reached courts in Israel pertaining to the balancing of religious rights and the right to education, one may be able to locate the points of tension, while getting a sense of the implications of the clashes between the fundamental rights concerned. In both cases mentioned below, Court decisions mark the beginning of a process unique for each case. Post-decision dynamics indicate the weakness of the intervention of the judiciary as an agent for social change.[92] Cases become, in many ways, more than the sum of their parts, supporting the view that '[f]or the most part, Court decisions are tentative and reversible like other political events.'[93]

The Immanuel 'Beis Yaakov' School segregation case[94]

In educational terms, many ultra-Orthodox *Sephardic* families (originating from North African or Arabic countries) seem to prefer sending their children to ultra-

Ignorant: Ultra-Orthodox Jewish Women and their World, Lynne Rienner Publishers, 1994, p. 200.)

89 Almog and Perry-Hazan (2011) at p. 20.

90 'The prevailing international human rights standard guarantees four features of the right to education: (a) Availability of functioning educational institutions and programmes … (b) Accessibility of educational institutions and progamme to everyone, without discrimination … (c) Acceptability of the form and substance of education … (d) Adaptability of education … to the needs of changing societies and communities and to … the needs of students within their diverse social and cultural settings'.

91 Frances Raday, 'Equality, Religion and Gender in Israel', Jewish Women's Archive, http://jwa.org/encyclopedia/article/equality-religion-and-gender-in-israel, at p. 1 (last accessed 19.04.2016).

92 A similar point is made by Cohn (2012) at 26 in relation to the same and additional cases.

93 Louis Fischer, 'The curious belief in judicial supremacy', 25 Suffolk U.L. Rev. 85, 87 (1991).

94 HCJ 1067/08 *Noar Kahalacha Association v. The Ministry of Education* (06.08.2009).

Orthodox *Ashkenazi* (originating from Europe) schools, despite the existence of ultra-Orthodox *Sephardic* schools, established by *Shas*, the party representing the latter in Israeli Parliament (Knesset).[95] *Ashkenazi* schools are considered more prestigious by reference not to academic considerations but to the degree of piety and adherence to strict ultra-orthodoxy.[96] In these schools, there is an established precedent of discrimination.[97] But while ultra-Orthodox schools may select students according to religious affiliation, they many not apply selection criteria on the basis of ethnic origin and/or social status.

The *Beis Yaakov* ultra-Orthodox school for girls in Immanuel has practised since 2007 a policy of segregation between Ashkenazi Jews and Sephardic Jews in favour of the former.[98] When assessing the policy of segregation, Justice Arbel's concurring opinion balanced equality and the right to denominational education as follows:

> A different treatment of equals, discrimination and segregation mean the adoption of an arbitrary double standard that has no justification. The segregation completely undermines interpersonal relations. The feeling of discrimination leads to the destruction of the fabric of human relationships …
>
> It is important to emphasize that the right of a community to denominational education on the basis of religious differences does not release it from the obligation of equality … Although as a rule a certain sector of the population may impose demands on religious issues in order to realize purposes relating to religious education of the kind that it espouses, these requirements should not be confused with requirements that are based on ethnic backgrounds, nor should we be misled by the religious-ideological cloak which it is disguised.[99]

Ultimately, the Israeli Supreme Court considering in 2009 this policy, declared it illegal.[100] The refusal of ultra-Orthodox parents to follow the judgment led the Court to order their imprisonment. The fathers were indeed imprisoned for ten

95 The social division between Ashkenazi and Sephardi communities has been of great concern in the process of creation and maintenance of the State of Israel. It has acquired a central role and remains maintained in Haredi society, with a clear preponderance of the Ashkenazi (cf. Cohn (2012) at p. 5).

96 Cohn (2012) at p. 11.

97 See for example AP (Jerusalem) 241/06 *Association for Civil Rights in Israel v. Ministry of Israel* (51 Report 2010, pp. 931–986), the State Controller and Ombudsmen. There are quotas established for Sephardi girls to obtain admission that raise to a maximum of 30 per cent. The quota is the result of Rabbinical decree (cf. Cohn (2012) at p. 11).

98 Ultra-Orthodox Sephardic Jews have a socio-historical background of systematic marginalization (cf. Almog and Perry-Hazan (2012), 211–225, at 213).

99 At para. 117 of the judgment.

100 The facts of the case relied on the de facto division of the school into a 'Hasidic Track' and a 'General Track' resulting in the creation of two segregated schools, with a wall separating them in the school itself and a class timetable that prevented contact between the girls attending the two sections. The Israeli Supreme Court found the 'Hassidic Track' to be discriminatory.

days, following which their release was announced after an agreement to perform a joint seminar the last three months of the school year was reached.[101] In the meanwhile, in late August 2010, the Ministry of Education accepted the request of some parents of students attending the 'Hasidic Track' of the school to establish a new school that would not receive state funds but would uphold the essence of the discriminatory admission policy. The Israeli Supreme Court, closing the case, noted the danger in the Ministry's decision in upholding the segregationist approach of the school concerned.

The Immanuel 'Beis Yaakov' case demonstrates and contains a set of constitutional trends with wider implications: First, in the Israeli context, it seems that fundamental rights and constitutional law have a limited role to play as a 'generator of social change' within the ultra-Orthodox community.[102] Any changes in this setting concerning this group seem to require internal agency, leaving a marginal role for state constitutional law to play.

Second, the assumption or acceptance of the 'secondary' or ancillary role of law leads us to reflect on the configuration between the right to religious freedom and other fundamental rights such as equality (and non-discrimination) or education. The clear and unambiguous precedence of the right to religious freedom came at the cost of the observance of the right to equality. This is neither a unique nor an isolated feature of the Israeli context. Further to that, it appears that religious freedom also comes at the expense of the right to education.

The Core Curriculum case law

The conflict between religious educational autonomy and the perception of the role of the (liberal) democratic state is well illustrated in the series of the *Core Curriculum* cases.[103] The cases elucidated how ultra-Orthodox boys' education in publicly funded schools is missing essential elements of core education by not teaching comprehensively basic subjects such as maths and English, citizenship lessons and the core democratic values of tolerance and equality and focusing instead on Torah studies. The cases relied on an argumentation whereby the aim of the Core Curriculum is to enable students to acquire basic knowledge and skills, as well as values allowing them to function independently in a pluralistic society. It has been also designed to allow all students equal opportunities to develop their personality.[104]

The Court, in assessing the clash between parental autonomy to decide on the education of their children and the importance of a core curriculum in a divided country, such as Israel, found for a violation of the children's right to education.[105]

101 Almog and Perry-Hazan (2012) at 215.
102 Ibid at 223.
103 HCL 4805/07 *The Center for Jewish Pluralism – The Movement for Progressive Judaism in Israel v. Ministry of Education et al.* (unreported), http://elyon1.court.gov.il/files_eng/07/050/048/r28/07048050.r28.htm.
104 See in particular §31 of the judgment as per Procaccia J.
105 Ibid, at §55, 58

Despite the projected finding by the Supreme Court on the issue declaring that the state should not continue to fund these schools on the basis of the arguments mentioned, the Israeli lawmakers passed a law labelled as Unique Cultural Educational Institutions Act,[106] allowing high schools for ultra-Orthodox boys (*Yeshivot Ketanot*) to continue receiving the equivalent of 60 per cent of the funding awarded to public schools irrespective of the content taught. The rationale of the Act ironically relied on liberal multicultural theory and democratic principles to justify it.

It is difficult to ignore in this particular instance the political power play behind the Act from the perspective of the blatant inequality and challenge that it creates for many categories of right-holders: the ultra-Orthodox students that will get an education without connection to the work-market, perpetuating the circle of poverty for many families, the non-Orthodox students that will have to 'share' state funding with schools that do not fulfil the same requirements as theirs, and finally, their parents as taxpayers that have to contribute towards a school system that applies double standards, often allowing for the violation of fundamental rights and principles.

Educational pluralism, autonomy and accommodation of religious identity

Further to the four features of the right to education, as defined by the UN Committee on Economic, Social and Cultural Rights framed as *available, accessible, acceptable* and *adaptable*, the Convention on the Rights of the Child (CRC) provides that education should promote 'the development of respect for the child's parents, his or her own cultural identity, language and values, for the national values of the country in which the child is living, the country from which he or she may originate, and for civilizations different from his or her own.'[107] By extension, Article 30 of the CRC ensures the same rights to children belonging to ethnic, religious or linguistic minorities 'to enjoy his or her own culture, to profess and practice her or her own religion, or to use his or her own language'.[108]

The implications of the right to *adaptable* education are wide and revolve around many layers of public policy. From schools admission and allocation of funds to religious schools to cultural exemptions from schools or the content of curricula, there are many parameters that legislators and policy makers need to plan and account for in execution of the right. At the ground level, educators

106 The Unique Cultural Educational Institutions Act, 5769–2008, §1. A 'unique cultural educational institution' is defined in the Act as an educational institution which gives systemic education that originates from the way of life of the unique cultural group and is in accordance with the unique characteristics of the group. The only group to which the Act applies is the ultra-Orthodox communities.

107 Art.29(1)(c) of the Convention on the Rights of the Child (G.A. Res. 25 XLIV, 44 U. N. GAOR, Supp.No.49, UN Doc. A/RES/44/25 (1989), also in 28 I.L.M. 1448 (1989).

108 Article 30 CRC.

ultimately shape, however, the final meaning and scope of the right to education.[109] This competition of agents to claim authority on what the right to education involves and how it secures (or not) religious identity accentuates the centripetal tendencies of education, particularly in Israel.[110] The limitations of state law as a normative rule become hence particularly obvious: If we accept that 'legal responsiveness depends on people with different identities, who narrate law differently, and differ as to what expectations it should fulfill',[111] any legal assessment of the religious diversity in public Israeli education must take note of the re-framing of legal provisions as they travel from the Knesset to individual classrooms.

The observation of the interaction of law with socio-cultural norms appears, therefore, essential to study education law in a context of established plurality. Constitutional provisions and international human rights may guarantee through their wording a standard of legal protection (e.g. freedom of educational choice or equal opportunities) yet the different aspects of the right to education when confronted with religious values (sourced from religious freedom and human dignity in the case of Israel) may become alienated. The study of the process of (mutual) alienation makes the search for 'good' law meaningful. Such a process would explain, for example, the resistance within ultra-Orthodox schools to apply government standards on education.

While the state, according to the liberal point of view, should remain neutral on its citizens' religious beliefs and ways of life, open neutrality raises the standard of state intervention to assist and protect religious minorities, especially at times where illiberal practices are involved. For Israel, the special relationship of ultra-Orthodox communities with the state secures the state's support for a religion that is essentially illiberal but the same state does not extend the same level of involvement through support of other religious communities. Whether the accommodation towards the ultra-Orthodox communities' group-based entitlements is therefore normatively acceptable remains a hotly contested matter.[112]

Within ultra-Orthodox Jewish communities, tradition embodies the cultural standard applicable as it reflects the 'ways … imperatives have been interpreted throughout the generations by Halakhic sages.'[113] At the same time, tradition, as

109 The content of policy thus depends on the methods, ideas and expertise of the implementing agents, i.e. the teachers (Lotem Perry-Hazan, 'From the constitution to the classroom: Educational freedom in Antwerp's ultra-Orthodox Jewish schools, *Journal of School Choice*, Vol. 8 (2014), 475–502, at 3).

110 Cf. Perry-Hazan (2014).

111 Gad Barzilai, 'Beyond relativism: Where is political power in legal pluralism?', *Theoretical Inquiries in Law*, Vol. 9, No. 2 (2008), 395–416, at p. 404.

112 See the seminal work of Will Kymlicka, *Mutlicultural Citizenship: A Liberal Theory of Minority Rights*, Clarendon Press, 1995, at p. 37 where the author claims that 'liberals can and should endorse certain external protections, where they promote fairness between groups, but should reject internal restrictions which limit the right of group members to question and revise authorities and practices'.

113 Menachem Mautner, 'A Dialogue between a Liberal and an Ultra-Orthodox on the Exclusion of Women from Torah Study' (2013), available at https://papers.ssrn.com/sol3/papers.cfm?abstract_id=2169400 , at p. 30.

a binding force, implies a single concept of 'good life', against the plurality of the good within liberal societies.[114] The right to education, as implemented within these communities, provokes inquiries as to whether there is sufficient 'harm' to dictate state intervention within illiberal religious groups.[115] Connected to this question stands also the question of whether the duty of the (multicultural) state is to hold diversity at its core, providing thus the framework for the peaceful co-existence of groups with diverse conceptions of the 'good life'.[116]

There is therefore a considerable degree of hermeneutic and physical 'violence' that is generated by the desire of the Orthodox Jewish establishment's wish to preserve religious patriarchal hegemony within religious schools.[117] This level of 'violence' is maintained and framed as a perpetual conflict for cultural, religious and to some extent also political hegemony between secularist-libertarian elites and the ultra-Orthodox community, who represent a genuine type of *enclave* communities.[118] The expressions of this clash have shaped an independent political agenda for the ultra-Orthodox groups that has led, among others, to demonstrations against the driving of cars and public buses on the Sabbath, to opposition to proposals to draft ultra-Orthodox youth to army service or against the right of women to sit in religious councils or enjoy an equal share of matrimonial property in divorce proceedings.

The Israeli state over its short constitutional history has not hesitated to endorse this type of religious hegemony although it may be claimed that this choice was guided by concerns rooted in political pragmatism, rather than ideology.[119] Group

114 Ibid, at p. 32.

115 Joseph Raz in *The Morality of Freedom* (Clarendon Press, 1986), on the question as to whether cultures of such communities should be tolerated, ultimately concedes: '(W) renching them out of their communities may well make it impossible for them to have any kind of normal rewarding life whatsoever because they have not built up any capacity for autonomy. Toleration is therefore the conclusion one must often reach' (at p. 424).

116 This discourse is linked to *diversity liberals*, opposed to *imperial liberals* (such as early Raz himself) and was coined by Richard Shweder (Find reference FN 11 Mautner, at p. 235–236).

117 For a similar view, see Frances Raday, 'Claiming Equal Religious Personhood: Women of the Wall's Constitutional Saga', in Winfried Brugger and Michael Karayanni (eds), *Religion in the Public Sphere in the Public Sphere: A Comparative Analysis of German, Israeli, American and International Law*, Vol. 190, Springer, 2007, pp. 256–298, at p. 267.

118 An *enclave* is defined as 'the typical structure of a community that chooses to disengage from mainstream society'. For more on this point, see Yohai Hakak and Tamar Rapoport, 'Excellence or equality in the name of God? The case of ultra-Orthodox enclave education in Israel', *The Journal of Religion*, Vol. 92 (2012), 251–276, at 256. The authors explain also how Haredi education serves also the purpose to protect the community against possible defections of its members (at p. 257), in the light of instances of evasion of Haredi men into other areas of activity such as occupational training programmes and the labour market (at 261).

119 Raday at 269–70.

discrimination permitted by the Israeli legal system remains, persistently present in the religious jurisdiction over personal status.[120]

Apart from the commonly debated question as to how cultural dissent may be protected within ultra-Orthodox communities,[121] the right to autonomy that religious communities are awarded within the Israeli legal system seems to take precedence over universalistic values (and rights). Whether out of deep multiculturalist conviction, or political pragmatism, as already stated, individuals belonging to these communities are assumed to have provided their tacit consent to a set of normative commitments, including their right to be discriminated in some cases.

So while cultural and religious ways of life carry an essential source of social cohesion, or 'the glue that holds society together', constitutionally the case of religious diversity in public education in Israel highlights the continuing struggle between the right to equality and that of freedom of religion.

Several questions in this complex web of connections deserve clarification. First, with regards to education, what is the level of regulation and control of schools that provide religious as well as educational services, especially when funded partially or wholly by the state? In a famous passage from *Everson v. Board of Education*, Justice Jackson declared: '[i]f the state may aid … religious schools, it may therefore regulate them. Many groups have sought aid from tax funds to find that it carried political control with it.'[122] In Israel, the extent of public involvement is not proportional to the level of regulation in ultra-Orthodox schools. One normative explanation for this may be that the Israeli state is not aiming for enforcing compliance with liberal norms but rather with facilitating the collective and individual exercise of freedom of religion.[123]

Critical voices of the intensive involvement of the state, such as that of Izhak Englard, argue nevertheless that:

> [the] integration [of the established Orthodox Rabbinate into the State's organization], viewed by the Zionist religious parties as a positive

120 The maintenance of personal status law is a direct historical offshoot of the millet system practised under the British Mandate, prior to the genesis of the State of Israel. The pluralistic character of the system allowed the various communities (Jewish, Muslim and Christian) to have their own religious courts with exclusive jurisdiction over questions of personal status of members of their communities (in particular marriage and divorce.)

121 See in that respect the very interesting series of Israeli Supreme Court judgments on the Women of the Wall case law (Hoffman I-III) where the right of women to religious prayer was de-constructed without discussing the women's right to equality: HCJ 257/89 *Anat Hoffman v. Western Wall Commissioner* 48(2) PD 265 (1994); HCJ 3358/95 *Anat Hoffman v. the Prime Minister Office*, Tak-Al 2000 (2) 846; HCJ 4128/00 *Prime Minister Office v. Anat Hoffman*, P.D. 57(3), 289 (2003).

122 330 U.S. 1, 27 (1947) (Jackson J., dissenting).

123 For a similar point, see Barak Medina, 'Does the Establishment of Religion Justify Regulating Religious Activities? – The Israeli Experience', in Winifred Brugger and Michael Karayanni (eds), *Religion in the Public Sphere: A Comparative Analysis of German Israeli, American and International Law*, Max Planck Institut für auslandisches öffentliches Recht und Völkerrecht, Springer 2007, pp. 299–332 at p. 317.

> manifestation of the State's identification with Judaism, has exacted a rather high price of lost independence vis-à-vis the government and a corresponding loss of moral stature.[124]

Seen from a distance, one may argue that despite the obvious religious diversity provided for in public education in Israel, the role and scope of education in the public space is and remains primarily to 'provide an educational means to convert ideology into social objectives, and to facilitate individuals' needs …'.[125] Clearly these goals are sustaining societal fragmentation, rather than a qualitative enhancement of the exercise of religious freedom in consonance with equality and tolerance.

Religious diversity in the form of curricular diversity, otherwise, very explicit in the structure of the schools, remains incomplete. The various tracks available within the school system, based on religious identity, secure the exercise of the right to religious freedom as well as the right of parents to have their children educated according to their beliefs. Any reform, however, towards the introduction of more diverse-friendly content is hindered by this same school-diversity: the decentralization of the administration of public education, combined with the variation in the curricular interpretation produce content asymmetries and pillarization.[126] Variable curricular interpretations are particularly visible in Jewish studies, which in certain cases receive a disproportionate degree of emphasis at the expense of other core subjects.

Legislation in 2008 has furthered this asymmetric trend as it has loosened the Ministry of Education's control over curricular content in ultra-Orthodox schools. The latter may still receive funds without having the corresponding duty to implement proportionally the 'core curriculum', as already explained.[127] The law was challenged in *Amnon Rubinstein v. The Knesset (2012)* on the basis of the violation of the students' right to human dignity and liberty because of the limiting of education to religious studies at secondary ultra-Orthodox boys-schools. The Supreme Court rejected the claim. The privileges of the ultra-Orthodox community in education, while a clear application of the right to religious freedom, come at the cost of a weaker enforcement of the right to education and connected to that, a growing socio-economic isolation of the groups concerned.

The balancing between a state's own universal principles with the reality of a multicultural population is therefore awkward in the Israeli context: the

124 As quoted in Medina (2007) at p. 330.

125 Yaacov Iram and Mirjam Schmida, *The Educational System of Israel*, Greenwood Press, 1988, at pp. 113–114.

126 These factors are highlighted in greater detail in Nura Resh and Aaron Benavot, 'Educational governance, school autonomy, and curriculum implementation: Diversity and uniformity in knowledge offerings to Israeli pupils', *Journal of Curriculum Studies*, Vol. 41, No.1 (2009), 67–92.

127 The level of funding raised to 60% of the regular funds given to other schools implementing the Ministry's 'core curriculum' (cf. Neta Sela, 'Yeshivas to receive State funds without teaching basic subjects', Y Net News, 24 July 2008, at http://ynetnews.com/articles/0,7340,L-3572383,00.html.

educational system is the product of ideology combined with religion, whether one refers to the national conflict between Arabs and Jews or to the divide between religious and secular segments of society.[128] Education policies shift in opposing directions at times depending on the political parties, members of the Knesset, cabinet ministers and interests involved, in defiance of constitutional guarantees and the paramount principle of human dignity as understood in Israeli law.[129] The growth of sectoral polarization of Israeli society from the 1980s onwards is also responsible for the current shape of the educational landscape.[130]

Education and democratic governance

The implications of this constitutional choice are far from clear: the dilemma between state-supported religious education, founded on an established religion model, and a clear separation between religion and state may be answered in different modes. The Israeli constitutional scenario of state entanglement in religion has produced arguments claiming the excessive (mis)-use of state funds in religious educational institutions.[131] Due to the low cost of Haredi education, these institutions enjoy a comparative advantage over other educational institutions within Israel drawing students at a fast speed towards a Haredi way of learning. Socially, this preference shapes students by limiting their choices in their later professional life.

There is also an observed antithesis in the position that branches of government take when balancing the right to religion as opposed to other fundamental rights particularly equality and education. The judiciary tends to support a balanced protection of human and civil rights when conflicting with freedom to and from religion, while the legislative and the executive lower the guards of constitutional protection under pressure most likely emanating from political considerations and the radicalization over time of the groups concerned.[132] The growing disapproval of the choices of Israeli political leadership (and of secular society) indeed push a segment of the traditional Jews towards the adoption of a 'pseudo-haredi' style of life, with increased submission to rabbis that take on additional roles.[133]

At the same time, there is a steady stream of ultra-Orthodox non-Zionist groups claiming political and societal agendas that go against the pluralist nature

128 H.A. Alexander, 'Education in the Jewish State', in Ilan Gur-Ze'ev (ed.), *Conflicting Philosophies of Education in Israel/Palestine*, Kluwer Academic Publishers, 2000, at p. 129.

129 Cf. Leavy (2010).

130 Leavy (2010) at p. 22 cites two examples demonstrating the wider trend: In the early 1980s, the Ministry of Education was controlled by the National Religious Party and gave preferential treatment to state religious schools in budget allocations and staffing decisions. In 1996, the same party controlled the Ministry of Education and withheld funding for the implementation of the Shenhar and Kremnitzer Commission Reports that were seeking to reform Judaic and civic studies.

131 Shetreet (1999) at 422.

132 Ibid at 439.

133 Adam S. Hofri-Winogradow, 'A plurality of discontent: Legal pluralism, religious adjudication and the state', *Journal of Law and Religion*, Vol. 26, (2010), 101–133, at 122.

of Jews, democratic values or tolerance. The question of how 'traditional' Jews, defined as 'middle of the road, moderate in matters of tradition ... and supporting democracy'[134] position themselves within this clash remains an open issue worthy of further analysis.

In the meantime, the ultra-Orthodox community has developed steady access to political power with the aim of obtaining important budgets destined to finance community-related activities.[135] More than that, the political representatives of the community have served in key political positions, shaping thus a multitude of issues affecting the broader Israeli society.[136] In that context, the process of introduction of the ultra-Orthodox agenda items in the public sphere is clearly not restricted to education.[137]

This process does not cease to provoke vigorous reactions whenever connected to the concepts of citizenship and the duties connected to it. Stopler suggests that members of ultra-Orthodox communities may indeed be acting as 'partial citizens', when exempting their schools from teaching their children basic skills or critical thinking.[138] The elements that render, however, the balance untenable, even within a multi-pluralist frame, are the degree of involvement of the ultra-Orthodox in political (and municipal) affairs and the heavy subsidization that they receive by the state in return.

The transformation of the members of these communities to a 'community of religious scholars' for its male members, combined with its isolation from the rest of the society has led in parallel to their ideological radicalization.[139] It is hard to dispute that educational autonomy has had an impact in this process that will only continue to grow.[140] In terms of empowerment, it is also clearly showcased how ultra-Orthodox groups, and their leaders, far from powerless, have and maintain direct access to state power,[141] enforcing fully their ideology in the public space, favouring an education 'of ignorance'. The contrast with Arab Palestinian students is not so great in the effects of public education: it differs in that they are the recipients of an education to which they have not played any meaningful role in shaping.

134 Ibid, at 449.On the disproportionate influence of Haredi political parties in the Israeli Parliament, cf. indicatively the results of the 2009 general elections: Central Elections Committee for the 18th Knesset, www.knesset.gov.il/elections18/heb/results/main_Results.aspx.

135 Stopler (2014), at p. 788.

136 Stopler (2014) at 788 states the positions of Minister of Interior, Minister of Housing, Deputy Minister of Health, Minister of Religious Services, President of the Parliamentary Committee on Finance and Mayor of Jerusalem.

137 Stopler (2014) mentions at 789 several examples of incidents demonstrating the clash between ultra-Orthodox religious ideology and liberal democratic values of the state.

138 Ibid, at 790. The term 'partial citizens' is sourced from Jeff Spinner-Halev's work.

139 Ibid, at 793.

140 See indicatively Yarden Skop, 'Forecast: Only 40% of Israeli students will attend non-religious schools by 2019', *Ha'aretz Daily*, 7 August 2013, www.haaretz.com/news/national/premium-1.540130.

141 In the 18th Knesset, four of 34 ministers were Shas members, the party was also represented by a Deputy Minister in the Education Ministry. (Cf. Cohn (2012), at p. 6.)

Part III

Processing conflict

8 Feminist dilemmas

The challenges in accommodating women's rights within religion-based family law in India

Tanja Herklotz

Introduction

Speaking about religion and gender equality often means speaking about conflict, regardless of which religion is concerned or which part of the world one looks at. In this conflict, one side stresses culture, tradition and religious freedom, whereas the other side stresses a right to equality between men and women. The Indian "personal law" system, according to which the individual is governed by the family law of her or his religious community, is one field in which this conflict is particularly visible. India's personal laws are a contested terrain, in which not only religious freedom is played out against gender equality, but in which these aspects are also intertwined with arguments around identity, nationality, modernity and secularism. While "the gender aspect" of the personal laws is often mentioned in a way that suggests a coherent viewpoint on the issue from a women's rights perspective, *a* feminist position vis-à-vis the personal laws does not actually exist. Thus – to make the story even more complicated – looking at the personal laws through a gendered lens provides us with a rather fragmented picture and another set of conflicts and challenges.

When positioning themselves on the issue of personal laws, many feminists and women's rights activists in India face a dilemma. On the one hand, the fact that personal laws often discriminate against women has led feminists to criticise these laws as patriarchal and in need of reform. On the other hand, many Indian feminists do not want to mimic the secular agenda of their Western counterparts when thinking about the reform of personal laws, but seek to accommodate cultural and religious identity. Against the background of broader debates on Third Wold feminism,[1] intersectionality, legal universality and cultural relativism, this chapter will outline the manifold feminist engagements with personal laws. Drawing on feminist scholarship and publications by Indian activists and women's rights groups, I will differentiate between two main positions. The first one is the call for a Uniform Civil Code (UCC) and other major *state-led* reforms. This approach draws on specific ideas of

1 The terminology refers to Mohanty's (1991) work. Her concept of Third World Women as an "imagined community" will be elaborated below.

modernity and secularism, constitutional provisions and international human rights law. Its focus on a "perfect law", however, bears the risk that the provisions on paper will not be implemented on the ground. The second approach calls for *community-led* reforms. This position accepts legal pluralism as a fact and acknowledges the intersection of gender and religion. While this approach is more embedded in the "real world" of Indian women, the downside of it is that it compromises the aim of gender equality.

The two approaches that I juxtapose here can be related to Amartya Sen's (2009) distinction between "arrangement-focused" and "realisation-focused" views of justice. With this distinction, Sen not only draws on European Enlightenment philosophy where one approach[2] concentrates on "perfect justice" through certain institutional arrangements whereas another approach[3] is concerned with the social realisation of justice through the removal of the world's "manifest injustice" (A. Sen, 2009, pp. 5–7). He further makes out a similar distinction in Sanskrit literature: that of *niti* and *nyaya* (A. Sen, 2009, p. 20). While both words stand for justice, *niti* denotes an arrangement-focused concern, suggesting that the active presence of some institutions, regulations and behavioural rules would indicate that justice is being done, while *nyaya* is a concept of realised justice based on evaluating people's actual lives and the situations that they experience (A. Sen, 2009, pp. 20 et seq.). In the context of the Indian personal law system, the aspiration of a Uniform Civil Code could be seen as an arrangement-focused (*niti*) approach, aspiring to "perfect justice", while the attempt to bring about small step community-led reforms could be seen as a realisation-focused (*nyaya*) approach, focusing on the actual life of the people.

In what follows I will first outline the controversies around the personal laws in India (I). I will then embed the positions of Indian feminist scholars and women's rights activists vis-à-vis the personal laws in broader debates on Third Wold feminism, intersectionality, legal universality and cultural relativism (II). Against this background, I will present the two main feminist positions with regard to the personal laws: the call for state-led reforms (III) and the call for community-led reforms (IV). The conclusion will indicate a possible way forward (V).

I. Contesting India's personal law system

Like many other post-colonial states, India maintains a personal law system, according to which certain family and property matters (marriage, divorce,

2 The concept that Sen calls "transcendental institutionalism" is related to a contractarian mode of thinking put forward by philosophers like Thomas Hobbes, John Locke, Jean-Jacque Rousseau and Immanuel Kant.

3 Different versions of "comparative" approaches have been put forward, for instance, by Adam Smith, Marquis de Condorcet, Mary Wollstonecraft, Jeremy Bentham, Karl Marx and John Stuart Mill.

maintenance, guardianship, adoption, succession and inheritance) of Hindus, Muslims, Parsis and Christians as well as Jews are governed by their respective religious laws.[4] While personal laws per se are an ancient phenomenon, the Indian system of personal laws in its present form dates back to the late 18th century when the administrators of the East India Company exempted parts of "religious" law from the purview of their regulatory action (Bajpai, 2011, p. 183; Menski, 2003, p. 161; Parashar, 1992, p. 62). Although the area of family law was not completely excluded from intervention,[5] the British colonisers refrained from a unification process comparable to the reforms in penal law with the enactment of the Indian Penal Code in 1862.

Demands for a secular Uniform Civil Code to replace the personal laws were articulated during the Indian independence movement (Austin, 2001, p. 17) and continued after independence and during constitution-making (Mansfield, 2005). The main features of this discourse were nationalism, secularism and modernity on the one hand vs. religious and cultural freedom, community identity and minority protection on the other (Agnes, 2011, p. 150; Baird, 2005, pp. 19–20; Parashar, 1992, pp. 230–231). The issues of gender justice and equality were not very prominent at this time. The "intricate compromise" (Menski, 2008, p. 221), which advocates and opponents of the UCC agreed upon eventually, was to make the introduction of the Code a non-enforceable Directive Principle. Article 44 of India's constitution states: "The State shall endeavour to secure for the citizens a uniform civil code throughout the territory of India". Other than Fundamental Rights, Directive Principles function as "instruments of instruction to the Government" (Das Basu, 2013, p. 158) but do not directly create any justiciable rights in favour of individuals, nor can a law be declared unconstitutional on the sole ground that it contravenes a Directive Principle. As of the present day, a Uniform Civil Code has not been enacted.

From a gendered point of view, the personal laws are problematic as they contain inherent inequalities. Not only do these laws treat women of different religious communities differently – Hindu, Muslim, Christian, Parsi and Jewish women have different rights and obligations – but also the personal laws treat men and women within the same religious community differently – women (in all religious communities) have different rights and obligations than men. This usually equates to discrimination against women, for instance with regard to inheritance rights, polygamy, divorce grounds, child adoption or guardianship rights.[6] Due to this

4 Buddhists, Jains and Sikhs are counted in the "Hindu" category; see for instance Section 2(1)(b) of the Hindu Marriage Act of 1955.

5 Legislative reforms occurred with regard to specific topics. In addition, the colonisers also modified the personal laws through the interpretation by British judges, making the personal laws a "curious amalgam of religious rules and English legal concepts" (Parashar, 1992, p. 307).

6 For a more in-depth analysis of the problematic aspects see for instance Parashar (2005), Jenkins (2009) or Agnes (2011) or the publications of women's rights organisations like Saheli and the Working Group on Women's Rights.

inherent discrimination, the personal laws already featured among feminist discourses in pre-independence times (Menon, 2012, p. 151), and they became a central issue of debate with the so-called "third" women's movement beginning in the 1970s.[7]

But while it might be assumed that feminist scholarship and women's rights activism have disapproved of the personal laws per se and have favoured their replacement through secular law, this is not actually the case. Rather, the Indian scenario shows us that there are manifold conflicting feminist positions vis-à-vis the personal laws, ranging from a call for large-scale state intervention to small step reforms through community work. It is consequently not possible to speak about *the* feminist position on the personal laws; one can only make out different strands of positions and argumentations. By contextualising the gendered notion of personal laws, we understand that this is not merely a conflict between women's rights and tradition, religion and culture in which one side or the other prevails. Rather, the topic of personal laws and gender is a multi-dimensional and highly complex issue in which various aspects are intertwined and Indian feminists and women's rights activists are confronted with difficult challenges and dilemmas. Understanding and untangling the different arguments and viewpoints (to ultimately suggest ways of solving the conflicts) renders it necessary to first locate Indian feminism in a broader context.

II. Contesting Western feminism: contextualising gender discrimination

Although allied in its fight for gender equality and its critique of patriarchal structures, feminism in India (and more broadly in the global South) not only differs[8]

7 This movement is regarded as the "third" women's movement because it follows firstly the social reform movement of the 19th century and secondly the engagement of women during India's independence struggle. Its beginning is usually located in the 1975–76 Emergency, although numerous formal and informal women's groups had already formed in the early 1970s (Agnihotri, 2001). The 1970s also mark the emergence of women's studies centres at Indian universities. For a more detailed analysis of the women's movement's engagement with the topic of personal laws and the UCC see Herklotz (2016).

8 Firstly, Indian feminist topics to a certain degree differ from Western feminist topics, when thinking, for instance, about dowry related or caste related crimes. Secondly, the organisation of the Indian women's movement and to a certain degree its means of agitation are also distinct. In particular, the early Indian women's movement was based on a concept of "autonomous" organisations (R. Sen, 2014, p. 335); it drew on voluntary members rather than paid staff and was sceptical towards (Western funded) NGOs. These features still shape Indian women's rights activism today. In terms of means of agitation, activists often drew on posters, songs and street theatre (Kumar, 1993, p. 143; R. Sen, 2014, p. 434) – means that could easily be assessed by illiterate women too. While Epp's (1998, p. 107) assessment of the Indian women's movement as institutionally "weak" seems one-sided and inappropriate, it is of course correct that Indian women's rights activism is located in and adapts to specific cultural, social and

from but has also explicitly distanced itself[9] from "Western" feminism. While it is surely difficult (if not impossible) to make general statements about "Third World" or "global South" feminism on the one hand and "Western" or "global North" feminism on the other, without essentialising, some general aspects nevertheless illuminate the following engagement with the Indian feminist discourse on personal laws. Of course neither of these feminisms constitutes one coherent bloc; they are heterogeneous in themselves.

Third World feminism emerged in opposition to mainstream second-wave Western feminism. It criticised the latter for defining the meaning of gender primarily in terms of "middle-class, white experiences" (Mohanty, 1991, p. 7) and largely subscribing to an oversimplified idea that women everywhere face the same oppression merely by virtue of their gender (Seodu Herr, 2014, p. 2).[10] It accuses Western feminism of drawing on cultural imperialist concepts of global South cultures as "backward and patriarchal", and of regarding the oppression of women from the global South as "simply *worse* than that of white women in the West" (Seodu Herr, 2014, p. 5). Mohanty understands Third World women as an "imagined community" – a concept that allows for an analytical exploration of "the links among the histories and struggles of third world women against racism, sexism, colonialism, imperialism, and monopoly capital" (Mohanty, 1991, p. 4). The community of Third World women is "imagined" not in the sense that it is not "real", but "because it suggests potential alliances and collaborations across divisive boundaries" (Mohanty, 1991, p. 4). Third World feminism addresses the multiple and complex forms of women's oppression in specific social, historical and political contexts. In their attempt to provide an adequate picture of women in the global South, Third World feminists have stressed, in particular, the "intersection" of gender, race, class, religion and ethnicity (Mohanty, 1991; Seodu

political contexts. For a more elaborate analysis of Indian women's rights activism see Kumar (1993), Agnihotri (2001), and Sen (2014).

9 Some Indian women's rights activists and scholars have gone as far as dropping the term "feminism" altogether, due to its association with Western feminism. A prominent example of those who "disclaim the label and yet support the cause" (Desai, 2006, p. 14) is the activist, scholar and journal editor Madhu Kishwar. In her essay entitled "Why I Do Not Call Myself a Feminist", she states that though standing "committed to pro-women politics" she resists "the label of feminism because of its over close association with the western women's movement" (Kishwar, 1990, p. 3). While this position is not necessarily representative and "most active spokespersons" among the Indian women's movement would indeed "claim a feminist identity for themselves" (John, 2004: 54), it nevertheless exemplifies the difficulties in positioning themselves that many feminists and women's rights activists in India and the global South face.

10 Another branch of feminism related to women in the global South is transnational feminism. The two concepts are, however, distinct from each other: Third World feminism "aims at generating descriptively reliable feminist analyses by Third World women themselves of Third World women's diverse forms of oppression and different modes of resistance" while transnational feminism is "primarily interested in feminist organizations, networks, and movements occurring outside and beyond individual nation-states at the *transnational* level" (Seodu Herr, 2014, p. 2).

Herr, 2014, p. 5). This "intersectionality" has different consequences. For instance, women who belong to two disadvantaged groups are "multiply burdened" and often marginalised to the advantage of more privileged group members (Crenshaw, 1989). In addition, these women often have to choose between the conflicting political agendas pursued by the different groups to which they belong (Crenshaw, 1991, pp. 1251–1252).

For the Indian context, two aspects thus need to be kept in mind. The specific post-colonial and socio-cultural context in which Indian women live brings its own issues and struggles with it. Western feminist arguments and concepts, which merely focus on the gender aspect and leave aside more complex forms of discrimination, cannot be transferred to this different locale, without adapting them to the different context. Second, women in India may belong to more and less privileged communities and consequently their lives, concerns and their priorities may differ. The early Indian women's movement largely ignored such differences. It was primarily led by and focused on urban middle- or upper-class Hindu women (Agnes, 1995, p. 138; Kumar, 1993, p. 106)[11] while minority women (like Muslim women or Dalit women) fell out of the visual range and were marginalised.[12] Only more recently, Indian feminists and women's rights activists recognized "that 'women' do not exist as a single homogeneous category" (Menon, 2012, p. 157) and that an intersectional approach requires a "double commitment" from Indian women's rights activists who "cannot confine their struggles to women's interests alone" but must "be sensitive" to minority claims as well (Sunder Rajan, 2008, p. 80). This might in practice render it more complicated to pursue a feminist agenda as it means finding a balance between combining "respect for the local" and the aim of gender equality (Jeffery, 1999, p. 231).

The challenge of balancing broader (feminist) aims and values with the particularities of local culture and tradition plays out in a specific way when it comes to the law. Here, the issue is often framed in terms of the universality of human rights vs. cultural relativism (when thinking in broader terms of international law) or legal universalism vs. legal pluralism (when thinking in smaller dimensions of national or local law). This discourse is central for Indian feminists' positions vis-à-vis the personal laws. Indian feminists need to balance between those approaches that regard a "universal" set of (human) rights – including gender equality – as a panacea against women's oppression, and those approaches that stress the importance of their societies' intrinsic values and warn of cultural imperialism.

The dilemma for Indian feminists (as for other feminists in the global South) is the following: on the one hand, as "assertions of cultural difference could be

11 Agnes (1995, p. 139) further stresses that initially the women's movement drew largely on Hindu symbols like Shakti and Kali.

12 To be sure, today the dual discrimination is addressed by a number of very specific women's groups, for example Muslim women's organisations such as Bharatiya Muslim Mahila Andolan or Aawaaz-e-Niswan or Dalit women's groups such as the National Federation of Dalit Women or the All India Dalit Mahila Adhikar Manch.

used to legitimate patriarchal practices" (Brenner, 2003, p. 27), they seek to prevent this. On the other hand, they also repudiate a hegemony that "treats Western practices as the measure of progress for women and for society" (ibid). With regard to family law in India, this means that Indian feminists must navigate between a universalistic approach calling for a uniform set of secular laws to replace personal laws on the one hand, and a cultural relativist approach that advocates for the maintenance of the religion-based laws as markers of religious community identity on the other. The next two sections will discuss in detail how far Indian feminists and women's rights activists manoeuvre between these two different standpoints and what arguments they use. In order to structure the manifold different positions, I differentiate between two main standpoints: state-led reforms and community-led reforms. Both approaches are further diversified by different lines of argumentation.

III. State-led reforms

Some feminists and women's rights activists call for major state-led reforms in the ambit of personal laws. They follow what Sen (2009) calls a *niti* approach, attempting to establish a "just institutional arrangement". Most prominently, such reforms refer to the introduction of a Uniform Civil Code to replace or complement the personal laws. But other than an all-encompassing UCC, other major interventions through secular state law – similar to the enactment of the Special Marriage Act (SMA) in 1954 – are imaginable too. While feminists and women's rights activists who favour state-led reforms always draw on gender equality, they often employ additional reasons for their argumentation and phrase their arguments in different ways. Slightly outdated in the context of the demand for a UCC is the argumentation that draws on secularism and modernity, which used to be dominant during the late 1970s and early 1980s (see III 1). Today's argumentations mainly draw on the Indian constitution and international human rights law (III 2). Furthermore, some authors explicitly repudiate the perception of religious personal laws as sacrosanct and unamendable (III 3).

1. Secularism and modernity

As elaborated above (in section II), grounding the call for a UCC on ideas of secularism and modernity was commonplace in the decades that followed India's independence. The Indian women's movement – which in its early phase largely supported the introduction of a UCC – took up these arguments and linked them to gender equality. The 1974 report of the Committee on the Status on Women in India[13] is representative of this line of argumentation. It

13 "Towards Equality: Report of the Committee on the Status of Women in India", 1974. Available at: http://pldindia.org/wp-content/uploads/2013/04/Towards-Equality-1974-Part-1.pdf, last accessed 27.4.2016.

bases its call for the "expeditious implementation" of a UCC on gender equality, but also holds that the absence of such a Code is "an incongruity that cannot be justified with all emphasis that is placed on secularism, science and modernisation". Similar lines of argumentation can be in found in Dhagamwar's work (1989, p. 53 et seq.), early newsletters of the Delhi-based women's organisation Saheli (1986) and publications of the Working Group on Women's Rights (WGWR) (1996). In Saheli's view (1986), "most religions are products of a less developed society, and to implement religious codes of conduct which might have been appropriate at some point of time would be to negate all growth and development and would be regressive". Family law should thus undergo the same unification and secularisation process that criminal law underwent long ago. Just as nobody would demand that a criminal be punished according to religion-based customs – "[n]obody promotes chopping off of limbs" – it would be unreasonable to ask for different standards when it comes to family law (Saheli, 1986; similarly Dhagamwar, 1989, p. 54). The argument here follows a concept of a linear development from less developed to modern societies in which modernity includes the unification and secularisation of laws and the banning of religion-based customs.

Today, the concept of modernity (or rather "modernities", see Eisenstadt, 2000) has changed. Among other aspects, it is less tied to the idea of uniform law. Instead (as I will show below), the concept of legal pluralism has taken hold. But till today, scholars still bemoan that personal laws, which were developed during the British colonial rule, are outdated and remain "frozen in time": "While the English law has moved on, Indian personal laws are fossilized in the name of religious inviolability" (Parashar, 2005, p. 307).

2. *Constitutional and international human rights law*

Feminist scholars and women's rights activists today draw less on the idea of modernity and more on legal provisions – first and foremost the Indian constitution and besides that international human rights law. According to article 14 of the Indian constitution "[t]he State shall not deny to any person equality before the law or the equal protection of the laws". According to article 15, "[t]he State shall not discriminate against any citizen on grounds only of religion, race, caste, sex, place of birth or any of them". With regard to these equality provisions the personal laws are not only problematic because they treat the different religious communities differently, but also because they treat men and women within the same religious community differently (Dhagamwar, 1989; MacKinnon, 2006; Parashar, 2005; Pradhan Saxena, 2008).[14] Feminist scholarship also draws on article 44, which

14 Indeed, a famous Mumbai High Court ruling (*The State of Bombay v. Narasu Appa Mali*, AIR 1952 Bom 84) did not see a conflict here. It held that personal laws were not "laws in force" within the purview of article 13 of the constitution and were therefore not void even when they came into conflict with the provision of equality

explicitly envisions the introduction of a Uniform Civil Code (MacKinnon, 2006) and stresses that as long as India maintains different personal laws, it cannot fulfil the preamble's promise of secularism (Jaising, 2011, p. 9). Scholars further employ the provisions of the Convention on the Elimination of All Forms of Discrimination against Women (CEDAW)[15] and the Universal Declaration on Human Rights (Jaising, 2011).

Small-scale reforms carried out in collaboration with the people of the religious communities and the community leaders and spokespersons, it is argued, would not do justice to either the constitutional provisions or international human rights law. It is "naive to believe that the religious community leaders of Muslims, or any other community for that matter, will work for attaining gender equality" (Parashar, 2005). One suggestion is that of an *optional* Code, according to which "a sex-equal family law would be available to all religious communities at the initiative and with the consent of the women of those communities" (MacKinnon, 2006, p. 201).[16] Women would "decide for themselves which legal regime to elect" (MacKinnon, 2006, p. 200). Others regard an optional Code as insufficient unless at the same time the discriminatory provisions within the personal laws were also amended (Jaising, 2005, p. 16). Indira Jaising, a feminist scholar and executive director of the Lawyer's Collective, writes: "if the choice is to be meaningful at all, it must be between gender-just secular law and personal laws that comply with the requirements of equality. Unequal laws ought not to be enforced by the State" (Jaising, 2005, p. 16).

3. Disenchanting personal laws

Lastly, scholars who favour major state-led reforms argue that there is no reason why personal laws should *not* be amended, abolished or replaced. This line of reasoning repudiates the objection that personal laws – often referred to as "religious personal laws" – are somewhat sacrosanct and unamendable. This argumentation acknowledges the importance of religion in a society but separates religion-based personal laws from religion itself. Along the lines of Voltaire's opinion that the Holy Roman Empire was neither holy, nor Roman, nor an empire, I bring the

under the constitution. This argumentation was – indirectly – dismissed in an *obiter dictum* of the Supreme Court (*C. Masilamani Mudaliar & Ors v. The Idol of Sri Swaminathaswami Thirukoil*, 1996 AIR, 1697), where the court stated that personal laws must be consistent with the constitution's fundamental rights provisions.

15 India signed and ratified CEDAW in 1980 and 1993 respectively, but made reservations to specific provisions. Most importantly, with regard to articles 5 (a) and 16 (1) of CEDAW, the Indian Government declared that it ensures "these provisions in conformity with its policy of non-interference in the personal affairs of any Community without its initiative and consent".

16 To a certain degree such an optional Code is already in place with the Special Marriage Act (SMA) of 1954. Here it has been suggested to further enlarge the scope of the SMA. A model for such an optional Code was drafted by the Forum against the Oppression of Women in the 1990s (see Menon, 1998, p. 258).

feminist argument in this regard down to the phrase that "religious personal laws" are neither "religious", nor "personal", nor even "laws".

1 Religious personal laws are not "religious". Legislative interference in the personal laws is often rejected with the argumentation that "the religious rules are sacrosanct and eternal or that no one else but the religious experts may introduce change" (Parashar, 2005: 295). It is also argued that for the members of a religious community these laws are important "markers of identity" and that they must be protected by the constitutionally guaranteed freedom of religion.[17] For instance, in a recent newsletter, the All India Muslim Personal Law Board (AIMPLB), along with other Muslim organisations, argues that personal laws "are derived from religious texts or scriptures"; they are of "unique relevance" for "cultural identity" and consequently "any kind of interference … is not only a violation of religious freedom in the constitution but will put an end to [the community's] unique cultural identity", which makes the introduction of a UCC "unacceptable".[18] Contesting these arguments, feminists stress that personal laws are human-made "constructs" and therefore are anything but sacrosanct (Parashar, 2005, p. 307). The debates during colonial times on reforms regarding sati, Hindu widows' remarriage or the removal of caste disabilities as well as respective legislative interventions and the re-interpretation of personal laws through jurisprudence expose the personal laws' "immunity to change" as "fictitious" (Parashar, 2005, pp. 293–294). Furthermore, women's rights groups have stressed that the constitutional protection of religious freedom will not override the right to gender equality, which is equally protected by the constitution (Saheli, 1986).
2 Religious personal laws are not "personal". The labelling of religion-based customs as "personal" laws is related to a dichotomy between the public and private spheres. Family law is supposed to fall into the private sphere, in which the state is reluctant to interfere (Jaising, 2013; MacKinnon, 2006, p. 194 et seq.).[19] Feminists and women's rights activists have long tried to disrupt this notion by arguing that "the personal is political" (a slogan of the women's movement, not only in India, but in many parts of the world) and that the state has an obligation to protect women's rights in the "private" realm too (Parashar, 2005, p. 297). They argue that

17 Art. 25 of the Indian constitution guarantees the right to free profession, practice and propagation of religion. Art. 26 grants religious denominations among others the right to manage their own affairs in matters of religion.

18 http://aimplboard.in/images/media/Press13-10-2016%20ENGLISH.pdf, last accessed 3. March 2017.

19 In 1983, for instance, the Delhi High Court in *Harvinder Kaur vs. Harmander Singh Choudhry* (AIR 1984, Delhi 66) held that in the "sensitive" private sphere of marriage "the cold principles of Constitutional Law" could not be applied, as this was like pushing "a bull in a china shop".

family and religion must not be beyond the control of external values (Parashar, 2005, p. 297) and that by calling personal laws "personal", women would be denied their legal right to equality (MacKinnon, 2006, pp. 196–197).

3 Religious personal laws are not "laws". Lastly, it is argued that the various religion-based customs and social practices should not even be termed "law", as this labelling would achieve an "implied immunity" from questioning them (Parashar, 2013, p. 17). Parashar (2013, p. 13) stresses that the "fact that people organize their lives by reference to various systems of rules" does not mean that such systems must be termed legal systems. On the contrary, the "appending of the label 'law' carries a message of the authoritative nature" (ibid, p. 17). The reliance on the discourse of legal pluralism and the invocation of the status of law for all kinds of practices may legitimize gender discriminatory regimes (ibid, pp. 10–11) and thereby enable "institutional discrimination" (ibid, p. 17). Law, in her opinion, must not simply reflect what is being practised in society, but must "construct social reality" (Parashar, 2005, p. 309).

4. Summary and critical thoughts

With references to modernity, secularism, constitutional provisions and international law, a number of feminist scholars and women's rights activists have called for major state-led reforms in the area of personal laws. They also – rightfully – have unmasked the argument of the immutability of the personal laws put forward by religious community spokespersons as hypocritical. But are these – more theoretical – feminist suggestions and lofty plans for a UCC feasible for application in the real world? Or is the idea of "perfect justice" (A. Sen, 2009) just that: an idea, not suitable to be practised in reality?

To be sure, there is some concrete engagement with the possible content of a UCC too. Scholars and women's groups have elaborated draft codes,[20] none of which have, however, come close to be debated in parliament. The reform proposals often remain vague and refrain from detailed explications of how and by whom these reform processes should be brought about. Recently it has been suggested that the enactment of a Uniform Civil Code be supplemented by a well-regulated state-recognised regime of religious alternative dispute resolution (Ahmed, 2016) to accommodate both women's rights and religious identities. According to this proposal, uniform laws would apply to statuses such as marriage, divorce or adoption, while other family law matters – like the financial terms of a divorce or disputes related to maintenance or the division of marital property – could be resolved using alternative dispute resolution (Ahmed, 2016). This suggestion, to a certain degree, maintains the current "mix and match" system where state and non-state law coexist, but likewise

20 See an overview of the different projects and draft codes in Agnes (2011, p. 177).

seems to try to bring more clarity into this system. But whether the introduction of a UCC or other secular laws could in practice "tidy up" the messy system – the dense web of different laws, actors and dispute resolution forums – and do away with the fact that many people do not access state law and state institutions is indeed highly questionable.

IV. Community-led reforms

Opponents to state-led legislative approaches would like to see reforms from within the religious communities – even if this means slowing down the reform process and watering down feminist goals. This approach – arguably initiated by Flavia Agnes and her Mumbai-based organisation *Majlis* – seems to be the dominant position among Indian women's rights groups today.[21] In Agnes' view, "small and significant reforms within the personal laws governing minority communities have greater relevance to minority women than the rhetoric of an all encompassing and overarching Uniform Civil Code" (Agnes, 2001, p. 3973; similarly Rahman, 1990, p. 498). This position fits with studies showing that "Third World women's resistance often does not involve an explicit demand for gender equality or radical social restructuring in order to achieve feminist goals. Instead, Third World women tend to opt for gradual changes that result from their collaboration with their male counterparts to enhance their communal influence vis-à-vis other members and improve living standards of their families and of the community itself" (Seodu Herr, 2014, p. 5). Concurring with Sen (2009), they follow a *nyaya* approach that is concerned with the "social realisation" of justice.

The pitfalls of this approach are indeed its "slow and gradual" transformation (Agnes, 2001, p. 3976) and the danger that in the process of bargaining for reforms with religious communities feminist goals might be watered down (Parashar, 1992, p. 229). Nevertheless, for the advocates of this position, the advantages – its actual effect on the ground due to the autochthonous character of the laws – seem to outweigh the disadvantages. The argument for community-led reforms is often based on the acceptance of legal pluralism as a

21 Throughout time, a number of organisations have followed the path that Majlis struck early on. The left-leaning All India Democratic Women's Association (AIDWA), which initially promoted a UCC, now favours a gradual change from within the communities (Hasan, 2014, p. 268; Murthy & Dasgupta, 2011, p. 129). The Muslim women's organisation Bharatiya Muslim Mahila Andolan pushes for reforms within Muslim personal laws and has drafted a gender-just *Muslim Family Act.* Organisations like Awaaz-e-Niswan and the Women's Research and Action Group in Mumbai, the Confederation of Voluntary Associations (COVA) in Hyderabad, the Muslim Women's Forum in Delhi and the Tamil Nadu Muslim Women's Jamaat have constantly pushed for reforms in Muslim personal law (Murthy & Dasgupta, 2011, p. 124). Other groups like the Joint Women's Programme have been working with some success to reform the Christian personal laws since the 1980s (Murthy & Dasgupta, 2011, p. 129).

fact (see IV 1). As indicated above, many people do not recur to state law in the first place. In the Indian context, the issue is also related to politics and the feminist positioning vis-à-vis the BJP (IV 2). Lastly, scholars claim that only through community-led reforms can intersectionality truly be practised, as this approach does not focus exclusively on gender, but also takes into account that religion plays a crucial role for many women (IV 3).

1. Accepting legal pluralism

One strand of argumentation draws on the discourse of legal pluralism and the limited power of state law in impacting on people's behaviour. Legal pluralism refers to the presence of multiple legal orders within one social field (Griffith, 1986), such as state law or customary law based on culture or religion or other value systems. The phenomenon of legal pluralism is certainly not confined to the global South, but plays out here in a particularly visible way. Not only among academics, but also among international organisations and NGOs there seems to be a trend towards accepting legal pluralism as a fact and dealing with it rather than holding on to an idea of modernity through state centred legal unification processes (Sezgin, 2010). For the Indian context, legal anthropologists have depicted the huge diversity of non-state legal systems. In Basu's (2015, p. 97) words, the contemporary Indian legal system "exhibits thriving legal pluralism through a variety of formal and informal, rural and urban, large and intimate options." Solanki (2011) speaks of a model of "shared adjudication" according to which the Indian state enjoys only restrained autonomy and willingly splits its adjudicative authority with (informal) societal sites such as sect councils, mosques, "doorstep courts", women's organisations and lawyers' offices.[22]

These depictions represent the wide gap between the law in the books and the law as practised on the ground (Menski, 2000, p. 143). As the limited number of people getting married under the secular Special Marriage Act exemplifies, even if secular laws are in place, people tend to make little use of them. Indian feminists and activists who favour small-scale community-led reforms tend to dismiss the one-size-fits-all approach promised by "universal" human rights and favour "a more nuanced and culture specific theory of women's rights" and "a position which is rooted within Third world realities" (Agnes, 2011, p. xxviii). With their approaches they take into account the reality of people "on the ground" and work at this level to bring about change.

22 The impact of this plurilegal system on gender equality is of course debated. While some authors stress that multilocational justice systems allow for "forum shopping", which can actually facilitate gender equality (Solanki, 2011), others stress that the coexistence of different possibilities for pursuing grievances is not necessarily an advantage because people must navigate between difficult choices and sometimes contradictory directives (Basu, 2015, p. 183).

2. *"Strange bedfellows":[23] the political angle of the personal law debate*

Other standpoints favouring community-led reforms face the political realities in India and the fact that the Hindu right wing party BJP has also articulated calls for a UCC.[24] While it is debatable whether this call is seen as a serious political agenda or as mere lip service to the perceived expectations of their voters, the BJP's pro UCC articulations have certainly had an impact on feminist positioning. Already in the 1980s and 1990s, feminist scholars complained that the BJP used the UCC rhetoric as a "political weapon" (Kishwar, 1993, p. 3) to silence religious minorities (Mullally, 2004, p. 673). Some scholars speak of a "hijacking of the secular agenda" (Mullally, 2004, p. 673). In a climate marked by inter-community tensions – fuelled by the Supreme Court's ruling in the *Shah Bano* case[25] in 1985 and the demolition of the *Babri Masjid* in Ayodhya in 1992 – many feminist scholars and women's rights activists realised that their call for a UCC would support the "wrong" side. They found it difficult to pronounce again and again how far "their" UCC was different from the one that the BJP aspired to and in large parts drew back from the "uneasy alliance with Hindu right-wing groups" (Agnes, 2012, p. 35).[26] There has been a visible shift among feminist scholars and women's rights groups *away* from the call for a UCC. Notably, though, there was not immediately a common position to be taken up instead and it took a while to fill this vacuum.[27]

3. *The intersection of gender and religion*

In their call for small-scale reforms, many feminist scholars and women's rights activists draw on the importance of intersectionality (Agnes, 2011, p. xxvii; Menon, 2012, p. 157). This topic became especially relevant with the *Shah Bano* case, which exemplified the identity conflicts for religious women. While Mrs. Shah Bano won her case, the Supreme Court judgment created such

23 Murthy and Dasgupta (2011, p. 154).
24 See footnote 18.
25 *Mohd. Ahmed Khan v. Shah Bano Begum and Ors*, AIR 1985 SC 945. The case was an appeal by a Muslim man against a High Court judgment that (following earlier Supreme Court decisions) had granted maintenance to a divorced Muslim woman. The Supreme Court rejected the ex-husband's claim that under Muslim personal law he was not required to pay maintenance after the *iddat* period (roughly three months) and after having paid her an amount as *mehr* (a form of dower). Instead, the judges held that the secular provision of Section 125 Code of Criminal Procedure applies to all citizens irrespective of their religion and hence overrides the personal laws. The judgment led to severe agitation among the Muslim population, stirred further by the Muslim Personal Law Board, which regarded the judgment as an interference in Muslim personal law.
26 Some women's groups maintained their position but changed their terminology, dropping the term "uniform", and now speaking of a "common", a "gender-just" or an "egalitarian" civil Code, see for instance Saheli (1995). Most groups, however, gave up their call for a UCC completely.
27 For a more elaborate description see also Herklotz (2016).

strong repercussions among the Muslim community and Shah Bano came under so much pressure that she eventually gave up the maintenance the court had approved for her (Gangoli, 2007, p. 41; Menon, 2012, p. 153).[28] The intersection of gender and religion, argue some scholars and activists, can only be adequately accommodated by giving up the idea of a uniform Code and instead working towards small-scale reforms in a step-by-step approach and in collaboration with the religious communities.

In the view of Flavia Agnes (2011, p. 73), one positive example of such small step reforms was the reform of Christian personal laws – brought about in a long and difficult process through the initiatives of individual Christian women, women's rights activists and other actors, including Agnes herself. Various discriminatory provisions among the Christian personal law such as the "stringent and near impossible" grounds under which Christian women could obtain divorce[29] (Agnes, 2011: 69) or the discriminatory law of succession[30] have been challenged during the last decades. It took a series of High Court judgments,[31] interventions from the side of the Indian Law Commission, joint meetings of the leaders of various Christian religious denominations, legal experts, and community representatives and the submission of bills to the Indian Government (Agnes, 2011, pp. 71–72) to finally bring about the desired change in 2001 when the Indian parliament passed a bill amending the Christian personal law.[32] Due to its autochthonous character – grown out of (perceived) consent among the community – the law is claimed to enjoy a large degree of acceptance among the people.

4. Summary and critical thoughts

The second feminist approach favours small-scale community-led reforms over large-scale state-led reforms. The proponents of this position draw on the fact that India's legal landscape is pluralistic, that the topic of the UCC is highly politicised and that community-led reforms best accommodate

28 This is not to undermine the fact that many Muslim women were also emboldened by the *Shah Bano* decision, as subsequent cases show.

29 Section 10 of the Indian Divorce Act stipulated that while a husband could get divorced only on the grounds of adultery, the wife had to prove additional grounds such as cruelty or desertion complementing the man's adultery (Agnes, 2011, p. 69).

30 Under the Tranvancore Christian Succession Act of 1910 the daughter's right to inherit was limited to one-fourth of the share of the son or 5000 Rupees, whichever was less.

31 On the right to divorce see *Swapna Ghosh v. Sadananda Ghosh*, AIR 1989 Cal 1 SB; *Mary Sonia Zachariah v. Union of India*, 1990 (1) KLT 130 and *Ammini v. Union of India*, AIR 1995 Ker 252 FB. On the right to succession see *Solomon v. Muthiah (1974) 1 MLJ 53* and *Mary Roy v. State of Kerala, AIR 1986 SC 1011* as well as *Ammini v. Union of India, AIR 1995 Ker 252* and *Pragati Varghese v. Cyri George Verghese, AIR 1997 Bom 349.*

32 The most significant aspect of the amendment was that it made cruelty, adultery, and desertion independent grounds of divorce. It further introduced the remedy of divorce by mutual consent and a change in the regulation on maintenance (Agnes, 2011, p. 72).

intersectionality. The disadvantages of this approach are exemplified in the reforms of Christian personal laws: it took several decades and was extremely cumbersome to bring about the legal and societal changes and many women were not able to make use of the new laws, because these came too late. The example of the reform of Christian personal law also shows that it is often impossible to draw a crystal clear distinction between state-led and community-led reforms. This specific reform process also involved state courts and other state actors. And lastly, it is of course difficult to tell how far the process in which "Christian women … shed the century-old shackles under which they had been burdened for well over a century" (Agnes, 2011, p. 73) really changed women's situation on the ground. "Perfect justice" is certainly not brought about with this approach, but then that is also not the aim this *nyaya* approach. Rather, the aim is the "removal of manifest injustice" (A. Sen, 2009, p. 7), or in our context, a step towards equality.

V. Conclusion

The chapter has distinguished between two main feminist positions on religion-based personal laws. The first position – the *niti* or "arrangement-focused" approach – is a more theoretical or academic approach that draws on constitutional values and international human rights law. Its proponents suggest the introduction of a UCC as a "just institutional arrangement". At the same time, they refrain from providing concrete explanations of how such a Code should look, who should be involved in the drafting process, how the concerns of different societal groups would be taken into account and how far the introduction of such a Code would change the world in which Indian women live. The second position – the *nyaya* approach – seems to be one that is favoured by women's rights organisations that are familiar with the situation "on the ground". It accepts legal pluralism as a fact and stresses the intersection of gender and religious identities. Its advocates tolerating the imperfection of community-led reforms, because they believe in the effectiveness of such reforms in making a change to the lives of many women.

Can either of these two approaches be considered better than the other? Sen (2009, p. 9) stresses that the *niti* approach – the search for "perfect justice" – has problems: firstly, there may be no reasoned agreement on the nature of the "just society" (problem of feasibility), and secondly, the idea of an (unavailable) perfect situation does not help us in choosing between the feasible alternatives at hand (problem of redundancy). Thus, the *nyaya* approach, concerned with the *advancement* of justice, seems preferable to him (A. Sen, 2009, pp. 8–9). "If a theory of justice is to guide reasoned choice of policies, strategies or institutions, then the identification of fully just social arrangements is neither necessary nor sufficient" (ibid, p. 15). Applying this argument to the context of personal laws in India means putting aside the idea of perfect justice through the introduction of a UCC; or at least, the clinging on to the idea of a UCC – a dream that might or might not be realised at some point in the future – must not get in the way of actual community-led reforms that advance justice here and now.

Sen gives us some guidelines for the advancement of justice. Most importantly, he stresses that we must focus on "the choices that are actually on offer" "rather than speculating on what a perfectly just society ... would look like" (A. Sen, 2009, p. 106). Scholars and women's rights organisations have pointed out that in the Indian pluri-legal scenario gender justice can be advanced on different levels, through different means and with the help of different actors. It happens through the (inter)action of activist judges, skilful lawyers, women's organisations and social workers (Solanki, 2011). Scholars like Agnes (2011), Subramanian (2014) and Serajuddin (2011, 2015) have depicted how in the area of personal laws courts slowly bring about gender justice in a step-by-step approach. And Menski (2008) points out how these court decisions work in concert with parliamentary interventions. Also, reality shows us that many reform approaches cannot actually be clearly categorised as either "community-led" or "state-led", and that the different approaches often go hand in hand. Feminists and women's rights activists should thus not oppose each other, but rather see where they can work together. To be successful, the various reform approaches must also incorporate the gendered dimension of personal laws into a larger discourse on socioeconomic discrimination against women (Hasan, 2014). Thus, when considering the "options that are actually on offer" (A. Sen, 2009, p. 106), these different levels of law, actors involved and connected topics should be taken into consideration. Only through an effort on many levels, and through constant reassessment, dialogue and negotiations can the advancement of justice for women in personal law systems be brought about.

Bibliography

Agnes, F. (1995). Redefining the Agenda of the Women's Movement within a Secular Framework. In T. Sarkar & U. Butalia (Eds.), *Women and Right-Wing Movements: Indian Experiences* (pp. 136–157). London: Zed Books.

Agnes, F. (2001). Minority Identity and Gender Concerns. *Economic and Political Weekly*, 36(42), 3973–3976.

Agnes, F. (2011). *Family Law*, Volume I: *Family Laws and Constitutional Claims*. New Delhi: Oxford University Press.

Agnes, F. (2012). From Shah Bano to Kausar Bano: Contextualizing the "Muslim Woman" within a Communalized Polity. In A. Loomba & R. A. Lukose (Eds.), *South Asian Feminisms* (pp. 33–53). Durham, NC: Duke University Press.

Agnihotri, I. (2001). Re-reading Histories. *Seminar*, 505.

Ahmed, F. (2016). Remedying Personal Law Systems. *International Journal of Law, Policy and the Family*, 30(3), 248–273.

Austin, G. (2001). Religion, Personal Law, and Identity in India. In G. J. Larson (Ed.), *Religion and Personal Law in Secular India: A Call to Judgment* (pp. 15–23). Bloomington: Indiana University Press.

Baird, R. D. (2005). Religion and Law in India: Adjusting to the Sacred as Secular. In R. D. Baird (Ed.), *Religion and Law in Independent India* (2nd ed., pp. 8–34). New Delhi: Manohar.

Bajpai, R. (2011). *Debating Difference: Group Rights and Liberal Democracy in India*. New Delhi: Oxford University Press.

Basu, S. (2015). *The Trouble with Marriage: Feminists Confront Law and Violence in India*. Oakland, CA: University of California Press.

Brenner, J. (2003). Transnational Feminism and the Struggle for Global Justice. In J. Sen, A. Anand, A. Escobar & P. Waterman (Eds.), *The World Social Forum: Challenging Empires* (pp. 25–34). New Delhi: Viveka.

Crenshaw, K. W. (1989). Demarginalizing the Intersection of Race and Sex: A Black Feminist Critique of Antidiscrimination Doctrine, Feminist Theory and Antiracist Politics. *The University of Chicago Legal Forum*, 1998, 139–167.

Crenshaw, K. W. (1991). Mapping the Margins: Intersectionality, Identity Politics, and Violence against Women of Color. *Stanford Law Review*, 43, 1241–1299.

Das Basu, D. (2013). *Introduction to the Constitution of India* (21 ed.). Gurgaon: Lexis Nexis.

Desai, N. (2006). *Feminism as Experience: Thoughts and Narratives*. Mumbai: Sparrow.

Dhagamwar, V. (1989). *Towards the Uniform Civil Code*. Bombay: Tripathi.

Eisenstadt, S. N. (2000). Multiple Modernities. *Daedalus*, 129, 1–29.

Epp, C. R. (1998). *The Rights Revolution: Lawyers, Activists, and Supreme Courts in Comparative Perspective*. London: The University of Chicago Press.

Gangoli, G. (2007). *Indian Feminisms: Law, Patriarchies and Violence in India*. Aldershot: Ashgate.

Griffith, J. (1986). What is Legal Pluralism? *Journal of Legal Pluralism*, 24.

Hasan, Z. (2014). Religion, Feminist Politics and Muslim Women's Rights in India. In K. Kannabiran (Ed.), *Women and Law: Critical Feminist Perspectives* (pp. 264–273). New Delhi: SAGE.

Herklotz, T. (2016). Dead Letters? The Uniform Civil Code through the Eyes of the Indian Women's Movement and the Indian Supreme Court. *Verfassung und Recht in Übersee*, 49(2), 148–174.

Jaising, I. (2005). Gender Justice: A Constitutional Perspective. In I. Jaising (Ed.), *Men's Laws, Women's Lives: A Constitutional Perspective on Religion, Common Law and Culture in South Asia* (pp. 1–22). New Delhi: Women Unlimited.

Jaising, I. (2011). Introduction. In I. Jaising (Ed.), *Elusive Equality: Constitutional Guarantees and Legal Regimes in South Asia, Malaysia and China* (pp. 1–13). New Delhi: Women Unlimited.

Jaising, I. (2013). Gender Justice and the Indian Supreme Court: The Post-Colonial Project. In O. Vilhena, U. Baxi & F. Viljoen (Eds.), *Transformative Constitutionalism: Comparing the Apex Courts of Brazil, India and South Africa* (pp. 230–243). Pretoria: Pretoria University Law Press.

Jeffery, P. (1999). Agency, Activism, and Agendas. In P. Jeffery & A. Basu (Eds.), *Resisting the Sacred and the Secular: Women's Activism and Politicized Religion in South Asia* (pp. 221–243). New Delhi: Kali for Women.

Jenkins, L. D. (2009). Diversity and the Constitution in India: What is Religious Freedom? *Drake Law Review*, 57(4), 913–947.

John, Mary E. (2004). Feminism in India and the West: Recasting a Relationship. In M. Chaudhuri (Ed.), *Feminism in India* (pp. 52–68). New Delhi: Kali for Women.

Kishwar, M. (1990). Why I do not Call Myself a Feminist. *Manushi*, 61, 2–8.

Kishwar, M. (1993). Breaking the Stalemate: Uniform Civil Code vs. Personal Law. *Manushi*, 77, 2–5.

Kumar, R. (1993). *The History of Doing: An Illustrated Account of Movements for Women's Rights and Feminism in India 1800–1990*. New Delhi: Kali for Women.

MacKinnon, C. A. (2006). Sex Equality under the Constitution of India: Problems, Prospects and "Personal Laws". *International Journal of Constitutional Law*, 4(2), 181–202.

Mansfield, J. H. (2005). The Personal Laws or a Uniform Civil Code? In R. D. Baird (Ed.), *Religion and Law in Independent India* (pp. 207–245). New Delhi: Manohar Publishers

Menon, N. (1998). Women and Citizenship. In P. Chatterjee (Ed.), *Wages of Freedom: Fifty Years of the Indian Nation-State* (pp. 241–266). Delhi: Oxford University Press.

Menon, N. (2012). *Seeing Like a Feminist.* New Delhi: Zubaan, Penguin.

Menski, W. (2000). *Comparative Law in a Global Context: The Legal Systems of Asia and Africa.* London: Cambridge University Press.

Menski, W. (2003). *Hindu Law: Beyond Tradition and Modernity*New Delhi: Oxford University Press.

Menski, W. (2008). The Uniform Civil Code Debate in Indian Law: New Developments and Changing Agenda. *German Law Journal*, 9(3), 211–250.

Mohanty, C. T. (1991). Introduction: Cartographies of Struggle: Third World Women and the Politics of Feminism. In C. T. Mohanty, A. Russo & L. Torres (Eds.), *Third World Women and the Politics of Feminism. Bloomington*: Indiana University Press.

Mullally, S. (2004). Feminism and Multicultural Dilemmas in India: Revisiting the Shah Bano Case. *Oxford Journal of Legal Studies*, 24(4), 671–692.

Murthy, L., & Dasgupta, R. (2011). *Our Pictures, our Words: A Visual Journey through the Women's Movement.* New Delhi: Zubaan.

Parashar, A. (1992). *Women and Family Law Reform in India: Uniform Civil Code and Gender Equality.* New Delhi: SAGE.

Parashar, A. (2005). Just Family Law: Basic to all Indian Women. In I. Jaising (Ed.), *Men's Laws, Women's Lives: A Constitutional Perspective on Religion, Common Law and Culture in South Asia* (pp. 286–322). New Delhi: Women Unlimited.

Parashar, A. (2013). Religious Personal Laws as Non-State Laws: Implications for Gender Justice. *The Journal of Legal Pluralism and Unofficial Law*, 45(1), 5–23.

Pradhan Saxena, P. (2008). Succession Laws and Gender justice. In A. Parashar & A. Dhanda (Eds.), *Redefining Family Law in India: Essays in Honour of B. Sivaramayya* (pp. 282–305). New Delhi: Routledge.

Rahman, A. (1990). Religious Rights versus Women's Rights in India: A Test Case for International Human Rights Law. *Columbia Journal for Transnational Law*, 28, 473–498.

Saheli. (1986). Towards a Uniform Civil Code. Retrieved from https://sites.google.com/site/saheliorgsite/.

Saheli. (1995). Egalitarian Civil Code: An Issue of Gender Justice. Retrieved from https://sites.google.com/site/saheliorgsite/.

Sen, A. (2009). *The Idea of Justice.* Cambridge, MA: Harvard University Press.

Sen, R. (2014). Mapping Women's Activism in India: Resistances, Reforms and (Re)-Creation. In L. Fernandes (Ed.), *Routledge Handbook of Gender in South Asia* (pp. 333–346). Abingdon: Routledge.

Seodu Herr, R. (2014). Reclaiming Third World Feminism: Or Why Transnational Feminism Needs Third World Feminism. *Meridians: Feminism, Race, Transnationalism*, 12(1), 1–30.

Serajuddin, A. M. (2011). *Muslim Family Law, Secular Courts and Muslim Women of South Asia: A Study in Judicial Activism.* Karachi: Oxford University Press.

Serajuddin, A. M. (2015). *Cases on Muslim Law of India, Pakistan and Bangladesh.* New Delhi: Oxford University Press.

Sezgin, Y. (2010). Introduction to the Special Issue. *The Journal of Legal Pluralism and Unofficial Law*, 42(60), 1–4.

Solanki, G. (2011). *Adjudication in Religious Family Laws: Cultural Accommodation, Legal Pluralism, and Gender Equality in India*. Cambridge: Cambridge University Press.

Subramanian, N. (2014). *Nation and Family: Personal Law, Cultural Pluralism, and Gendered Citizenship*. Stanford: Stanford University Press.

Sunder Rajan, R. (2008). Women between Community and State: Some Implications of the Uniform Civil Code Debates. In J. R. Jakobsen & A. Pellegrini (Eds.), *Secularisms* (pp. 76–107). Durham, NC: Duke University Press.

WGWR. (1996). Reversing the Option: Civil Codes and Personal Laws. *Economic and Political Weekly*, 31(20), 1180–1183.

9 *Tamāshā*

The theatrics of disputing and non-state dispute processing

Kalindi Kokal

Dispute processing is a social phenomenon. The mechanisms that a community and its members resort to for dispute processing are derived from the community's sense of order which amongst other things is also embedded in its social structure, religio-cultural background and everyday life practices. In this chapter, dispute processing is observed as a space of resistance, emancipation and performance where the resilience of norms is tested. Based on fieldwork carried out over fourteen months between 2014 and 2016 as part of my doctoral research, this chapter engages in a discussion of the significance of performance in dispute processing through a description and analysis of the element of *tamāshā*. A *tamāshā* conceives an exaggerated response to a situation which, with regard to disputes, often takes it beyond being only a matter between the disputing parties. With the help of case studies from Gonjhé, a fisherman's village (Koḷīwādā) in Maharashtra, and the agrarian village communities in the Dharamgarh valley of the Kumaon Himalayas in the State of Uttarakhand,[1] I adopt an interdisciplinary approach drawing from law and anthropology to develop an ethnographic account of dispute processing to elucidate the role of *tamāshā* in the processing of disputes.

Disputes as memories and reflections

Felstiner, Abel and Sarat (1981, 639) note that, 'people never fully relegate disputes to the past, never completely let bygones be bygones: there is always a residuum of attitudes, learned techniques, and sensitivities …'. Disputes often involve traumatic, shocking and or emotional situations. What interestingly follows is that disputes leave impressions, which many times remain like vivid memories (Nadel and Sinnott-Armstrong 2012, 7–28) recollected on many occasions as part of reflections of interpersonal relationships or in order to emphasise those relationships that were either undermined or fortified in the process.

An aspect that plays a key role in the formation of such impressions is the performance of the dispute and its processing. The performance of a dispute is also crucial in determining whether a dispute will become the focus of community gossip and attention. Like all performances, those concerned with disputing and

1 Names of all villages and respondents have been changed to maintain confidentiality.

dispute processing could also have a theatrical element, one that is exaggerated, either in form or content or both, to the extent of being almost unreal in reference to what may be perceived as 'realistic' or 'reasonable' in the context in which it arises. In the Hindi or Marathi language such theatrics are referred to as a '*tamāshā*'. The term *tamāshā* does not find a direct translation in English, but could be generally understood as an act or series of acts that result in the creation of a spectacle or a dramatic scene. The act may become a spectacle because of the actual physical performance the actors might undertake or because of the content and style of dispute processing that sets it apart from the 'ordinary'.[2] As a result, whether the performance is considered a *tamāshā*, depends greatly on the social structure of the community, its responses to disputes generally and the normative orders that guide their processing.

Often the public face of a dispute, a *tamāshā* could be characterised as a 'ritual aspect' (Gennep 2004) of dispute processing. A *tamāshā* could have several different implications for the disputing parties themselves as well as for the broader community at large. The case studies in this chapter show how the element of *tamāshā* despite its various forms – from vociferous to more subtle – remained important in communities like those studied for its ability to facilitate the creation of 'liminal spaces' (Turner 1979). Liminality, as we shall see in the next sections, provided the aggrieved or disputing parties scope for challenging established behavioural protocols for processing their disputes without disturbing the overall demeanour of their social relationships and thereby the experience of interconnectedness that underscored their sense of order. This analysis proposes that understanding the element of performance in dispute processing may be crucial to conflict studies as it reveals the significance of 'disputes' – as a type of social process – in a particular community which may ultimately shed light on the choice of dispute processing mechanisms people may select for the 'resolution' of disputes.[3]

Tamāshā: The creation of liminal spaces

Fieldwork revealed that the village communities in Gonjhé and the Dharamgarh valley shared an experience of interconnectedness that originated partly on

2 The author is a PhD candidate at the Max Planck Institute for Social Anthropology, department of Law and Anthropology. Her research interests include a focus on non-state dispute processing, legal pluralism and state law and religion from an interdisciplinary perspective. The author would like to thank Dr. Bertram Turner and Dr. Dominik Müller for their insightful comments that encouraged her to delve further into making this topic a substantive interdisciplinary engagement. The term ordinary here is placed in quotes because what comprises the 'ordinary' may differ in every community and context.

3 A fair share of literature in anthropology (Ramsbotham, Woodhouse, and Miall 2011) discusses the usage of terminology pertaining to 'dispute' and 'conflict'. This chapter understands 'disputes' as a type of conflict (see Nader 1978, 15, for disputes as a stage of conflict); conflict being the 'widest set of circumstances in which parties perceive that they have mutually incompatible goals' (Ramsbotham, Woodhouse, and Miall 2011, 9).

account of their religious and cultural backgrounds and partly as a result of everyday life practices. The element of *tamāshā* was vital to understand in the context of dispute processing in these communities, because of its capacity to enable disputing parties an exercise of agency that helped them protect their individual interests without disturbing their position within the community's circle of solidarity. I use the description of 'ritual processes' developed by Arnold Van Gennep and the concept of 'liminal spaces' from Victor Turner's work, which takes off from Gennep's theory to explain how the element of *tamāshā* works within dispute processing.

Gennep identified three aspects of the ritual process: separation, transition and incorporation.

> The separation phase marks … departure from the normal social world and its attendant values, norms and habituated patterns of behaviour. The transition represents what scholars term as the 'liminal state', a space in which the usual customs and conventions do not apply, creating an atmosphere of ambiguity. Turner describes the liminal state as 'anti-structure' connoting the relaxation of mores and rules of everyday structure … Finally, the incorporation stage consists of what Turner calls 'reintegration,' the activities that facilitate re-entry into the everyday social milieu … (Davidheiser 2006, 1–2)

The element of *tamāshā* is characterised by these three aspects. The exaggerated nature of a *tamāshā* separated it from habituated patterns of behaviour and placed the performer in a 'liminal-like' or 'liminoid phenomenon' (Turner 1979, 491) which was often 'experimental in character' (Turner 1979, 492) and within which usual conventions and social behavioural expectations became suspended. Explaining liminality, Turner (1979) describes that it places an individual:

> … literally 'being-on-a-threshold,' … a state or process which is betwixt-and-between the normal, day-to-day cultural and social states and processes of getting and spending, preserving law and order, and registering structural status. Since liminal time is not controlled by the clock it is a time of enchantment when anything might, even should, happen. (1979, 465)

The discussion that follows will show that *tamāshā*, as an intervening event, acted as a pause in the course of a disputing situation and became significant for its capacity to enable, and sometimes also include, reintegration of the protagonist into the everyday patterns of community life, a fact that may have been or was threatened to be disturbed because of the dispute.

Tamāshā: the theatrics of dispute processing

The term *tamāshā* is native to both Hindi and Marathi language and therefore was understood in the same sense in both the locations of fieldwork. For its emphasis on dramatics, a folk dramatic form of which the *lāvaṇi* performance, a traditional dance form in rural Maharashtra, is a component, is also referred to as a *tamāshā*. The traditional *lāvaṇi* is characterised by verve and vigour and consists usually, though not always, of an erotic song presented mostly by women (Ranade 2000, 197–99). Interestingly, the *tamāshā* involving a dance performance or as a ritual aspect of disputes actuates several similar sentiments between its spectators. An example would be the fact that while both types *tamāshās* undoubtedly become a source of entertainment for the spectators, the people engaging in them – the dancers in a local *lāvaṇi* performance and parties to dispute processing *tamāshā* – are rarely looked upon favourably in a community.

Like street theatre, a *tamāshā* creates a space that is full of potency and potentiality, experiment and play. As Turner (1979, 466) describes: 'There may be a play of ideas, a play of words, a play of symbols, a play of metaphors. In it, play's the thing'. One of the very reasons the performance of a dispute could become a *tamāshā* is because this performance is public, spontaneous and dramatic, almost becoming a form of street theatre. *Tamāshā* is comparable to street theatre not just because of its style of display, but also for reasons of what is enables the performer to achieve. When fully imagined, felt and skilfully presented, street theatre is known to widen perception and consciousness, enabling the audience to participate more fully in the lives of their fellow human being. Street theatre encompasses a 'direct reflection of values' (Singh 2016, 4) and the style enables the audience to develop empathy with the performers, understand their motivation and comprehend the realities of social and personal existence. Street theatre is not a work of fiction, but arises fully out of real life experiences. Similar to how Mathur (1964) describes drama in rural India, *tamāshā* too 'does not face the dilemma that confronts the modern sophisticated drama – keen to be treated as a social institution but pulled towards the introspective realm of the abnormal individual' (1964, 83). Like rural drama, in the element of *tamāshā* the performer is 'not torn between these opposing desires' (1964, 83). S/he can entertain without inhibition and preach without reservation.

As the case studies that follow will reveal, the form of *tamāshā* is not homogeneous. Some *tamāshās*, as in the second case study, may be 'prescribed and predetermined by custom; for example, religious performances that occur at fixed points in the annual cycle …'. In other instances, a *tamāshā* may have a 'contingent, ad hoc character, sometimes developing out of the dispute itself, sometimes representing a response or adjustment to [the] events …' (Turner 1966, 239). On the whole, for its expatiated form of expression and fairly flagrant style of communication, *tamāshās* arising from disputes are perceived to bring dishonour (*beizzati*) or damage social standing, and are often equated to 'washing one's dirty linen in public'. Therefore, the more respectable a person or household was, the more cautious they were of being associated with a dispute-related *tamāshā*.

A stage in dispute processing was usually perceived as a *tamāshā* if it involved an exaggerated reaction as opposed to what the community perceived as reasonable in the situation at hand. Depending on the context, therefore, a public exchange of verbal abuse and insults or some physical assaults or approaching the police station or a local leader could all constitute acts of *tamāshā* in specific circumstances.

From the protagonist's perspective, a *tamāshā* could be perceived to serve several purposes; sometimes to bring the issue into 'public' space, or because it was the intention of one of the parties to the dispute, to 'make a statement or a point' or merely to test boundaries and see how far one could go. The next part will consider each of these elements in more detail to describe and analyse how a *tamāshā* plays out in the context of performing disputes.

Case study 1: Tamāshā *as an act of drawing boundaries*

In a Koḷīwādā *tamāshā*-s as a form or part of dispute processing were described to be quite commonplace,[4] particularly among the fisherwomen. Shouting matches in shrill tones, the hurling of obscene verbal abuse and sometimes a threatening with the knife used to cut a fish (*koytā*) were recounted as 'typical' features of such *tamāshā*-s in Gonjhé. Fisherwomen more than men, as was commonly narrated to me and concurrently witnessed, were popular for creating such *tamāshās*, the term used even locally to refer to such scenes. Such *tamāshās* were often visible during early morning interactions for collection of water at the public water tap, in the late evenings when women were busy sorting the fish for the next day's sale and sometimes between neighbours who were known not to get along. Interestingly during such *tamāshās* women took the forefront, even if the dispute may have actually been between their men. Additionally, once a dispute became a *tamāshā*, it would typically attract a lot of onlookers, but no one would usually intervene to halt it. The *tamāshā*, as instinctively as it started, would also come to an end similarly; more often than not because of practical constraints. Such local *tamāshās* in the Koḷīwādā were perceived to have a lot of implications, but most crucial among which was that a dispute escalating into a *tamāshā* worked to set the boundaries of interaction, be it between neighbours, kin, couples or strangers. Women taking the lead in such *tamāshās* also indicated the crucial position of women in setting the boundaries for themselves and their household. For instance, one morning, at the common water tap providing water from the local Gram Panchayat,[5] which was then shared by three households, a fight broke out at 5 a.m.[6] Every day one woman, Neela Chogle, would get up ahead of the others to line her vessels in front of the tap. This way she would get the maximum amount of the drinking water that was supplied only for two hours every morning. From my informants and my stay in this neighbourhood, I had known that this had been an issue that the other two women – Dinisha and Kala – had been complaining about within their respective households for a long time. On the day a *tamāshā* occured, Dinisha ensured to reach the tap and lined her pots in front of it before Neela

4 For Koḷīwādā see page 1 above.

5 The Gram Panchayat is a state body of local self-government constituted under the U. P. Panchayat Raj Act 1947 (Uttaranchal Amendment) Act, 2002 in Uttarakhand and Bombay Village Panchayats Act, 1958 in Maharashtra.

6 This case study is based on observation of the actual event, notes from fieldwork and conversations with the different parties involved in the dispute. Village Gonjhé, Maharashtra, March 2015.

arrived. Kala had followed suit and by the time Neela arrived, she realised her pots were last in order that day. This infuriated her and an argument broke out. The high-pitched shouting brought people from the neighbouring homes into their *verāndāhs*. Hema, another neighbour, freed an enraged Dinisha off her sleepy 2-year-old daughter, who clung to Dinisha's waist, as the mother and the aunts fought ferociously. The husbands of all three women remained discreetly in the backgrounds and so did men from other households. The *tamāshā* lasted all of about 30 minutes after which it stopped as abruptly as it had started, with the women returning to their homes. Dinisha's pots were filled and Kala had already begun to fill hers. A few things resulted from this *tamāshā*. Dinisha and Kala publicly displayed their disagreement with Neela's behaviour. This allowed all the women to gauge how appropriate their own stand was and the nature of support they had in this regard. The *tamāshā* had already elicited some responses from the neighbours, as many sympathised with Dinisha and Kala and agreed that Neela's lining her pots first at the tap every day was unfair. Some even suggested a practical compromise. 'Why don't each of you place your pots at position one, two and three in rotation?' Hema had said to Kala and Dinisha later in the day. Simultaneously, Neela had got the hint that her arbitrary behaviour would not be tolerated anymore. The *tamāshā* had in other words set the tone of the interactions between all three women, particularly with respect to the sharing of the water tap. When I asked why the husbands had not intervened to calm their wives, Vishnu Bhatle, one of the neighbours said to me: 'Who will fall into a fight between the women (*bāykanchyā bhāngaḍit koṇ paḍnār*). It is a matter that concerns them, let them sort it out. Plus this way they will vent out their anger and bicker less at home.' Clearly, the non-intervention by men was strategic. In the Koḷīwādā, women dominated the domestic sphere and community relationship networks. If some fisherwomen did not get along, it was also rare to see their husbands interacting. Water collection, as much as, determination of the relationship with their neighbours, fell within the women's sphere of control and men knew better than to intervene in it. A reputation of engaging in *tamāshās* and keeping such a reputation alive was advantageous to the fisherwomen also as a defence mechanism for their own selves. One prominent consequence of these *tamāshās* was that the men in the community always remained wary about getting into an argument with these women, and even if they did, accusations or the show of power was often retracted at the slightest hint of a *tamāshā*. The nature of their professions often saw fisherwomen travelling to remote interior villages to sell their fish; they interacted with a wide variety of people and travelled in crowded public transport buses and walked many miles on their own sometimes late into the evening. When in the village, many of these women had to manage the household single-handedly as the husbands used to be away at sea for weeks together. In such a situation, the element of *tamāshā* that was perceived to be characteristic of their interactions worked perfectly to secure the fisherwomen from being taken advantage of – emotionally, financially or physically – and with men, particularly, it acted to counter-balance the power equations within and outside their homes.

Case study 2: Tamāshā *as an act of testing limits*

In the villages of the Dharamgarh valley, *tamāshā* was a prominent element of the dispute processing mechanism involving spirits and deities. Spirits and deities were believed to inhabit the same universe as humans and their interventions in everyday life were seen in the form of people being caught in their spell, being impacted by their wrath or being impersonated or possessed by them. Malik (2016, 196) explains this phenomenon to be the result of an idea of selfhood which is 'mutable, fluid or hybrid' which makes the distinction between the deity or divine being and human being not a 'firmly bounded one', but one that is 'permeable'. *Tamāshās*, such as the one discussed in this section, are an integral part of the manner in which the community sustains its belief in spirits and deities impacting on the course of people's lives. There are various categories and types of performances that belief in the supernatural world enables. For instance, at the community level in the Dharamgarh valley there were complex and extended ritualistic ceremonies such as *jāgars* (Fanger 1990) to 'awaken' family deities or other deities so that they may tackle the ghosts (*bhūt* and *bhūtiyān*) possessing a family member and *ghaṇiyālis* to show gratitude to and appease deities for fulfilment of wishes. Usually, this was followed by sacrifice of a goat, chicken or wild pig, or all three, to appease the awakened spirit or deity. During these religious performances, there was the narration of a mythological story at some point of which the deity communicated with the audience or tackled a ghost possessing an individual through an impersonator. Healing of the aggrieved party was usually contingent upon the intervention of divine power that was made present during these rituals. Healing, in this context, can been defined 'as a matter of returning the individual to a real (or imagined) state of well-being, wholeness or completeness' (Malik 2016, 205–6).

Awakening spirits and deities entailed one type of performance,[7] but the intervention of a spirit or deity was realised most often through misfortunes expressing themselves in the form of ill health or financial trouble in the concerned person's life, compelling an altogether different kind of performance by aggrieved parties. Since the entire community shared such a belief (Dusche 2016), performances allowed the performer leeway of expression and behaviour that were in fact part of such person's effort to tackle the said grievance. This case study will use the example of women claiming to be being caught in the spell of a *mashiāṇ* as a type of the *tamāshā* and the significance such a performance might hold for the new bride and her connection with the family.

Mashiāṇ was the term used to refer to spirits that cast their spells on unmarried girls. *Mashiāṇ* is a form of possession-trance involving the perceived takeover of

7 See Fanger (1990) for a detailed description of the performance a *jāgar* entails. Fanger does not make a distinction between a *jāgar* and a *ghaṇiyāli* and seems to encompass both types of rituals under the concept of *jāgar*. This varies from the data I conducted during fieldwork, where a *jāgar* was conducted to awaken a deity to exorcise the aggrieved party from possession by a *bhūt*, where as a *ghaṇiyāli* was conducted to awaken a deity to seek solutions to any other problems. *Ghaṇiyālis* were often conducted also to just please a family deity or in fulfilment of a vow.

the body and person of the actor by another entity – a spirit, an ancestor, another living person, or even an animal. As Bourguignon (2004, 559) explains: 'the self of the actor is then in abeyance and the behaviour presented is that of the other, so that major transformations are accepted'. In the village communities of the Dharamgarh valley it was believed that a *mashiāṇ* was the spirit of an individual who had died an unnatural death who cast its spell on women. More often than not, therefore, such spirits were discerned to be those of a male individual. From my sessions of participant observation in consultations by various *puchiāri*-s, I gathered that the *mashiāṇ* was usually perceived to get hold of unmarried girls most likely when they were crossing streams of water in the forests. They were believed to come alive after the girl was married, usually causing health- or behaviour-related disturbances (see also Fanger 1990, 175).

In the village of Jamkuda, Draupadidevi practised as a *puchiāri*. A *puchiāri* was one of the many actors involved in facilitating access to the world of spirits and deities. Typically, she was consulted to understand the cause of one's troubles, misfortunes or grievances whether health-related or otherwise. Bhanwardevi was one such lady who visited the *puchiāri* because her daughter-in-law, she alleged, was behaving strangely.[8] 'She doesn't work. If there are two glasses lying on the table, she will wash one glass and leave the other,' complained Bhanwardevi, who had travelled with her daughter-in-law and some other relatives to this *puchiāri* from very far. Bhanwardevi's son had been married for a few months at the time of the visit and the daughter-in-law apparently was not living up to her role very well. Draupadidevi, calmly looked at the daughter-in-law and took her wrist to feel her pulse, in the way of an ā*yurvedic* doctor. 'She is easily angered. She cannot focus on anything for long. She doesn't seem interested in anything. She does not feel hungry and she is restless. She is possessed by the *mashiāṇ*, a gift in dowry from her maiden home,' revealed Draupadidevi,[9] as Bhanwardevi nodded in agreement to all of what Draupadidevi had analysed about the daughter-in-law. Clearly all these activities had been part of Bhanwardevi's daughter-in-law's *tamāshā*.

In another instance, Kailash Pant from the village of Kheti narrated, how the *mashiāṇ* that had caught his wife, had given his family so much trouble ('*paréshān kar diyā thā*') for the first six months after his marriage. 'My wife behaved extremely strangely in the first months after marriage. She would not talk to anybody, would remain very silent and lost in her own thoughts; disinterested in work and falling ill very often,' recollected Pant, who had completed the rituals to get his wife released from the spell of the *mashiāṇ*, a few weeks before I met him.[10]

8 This case study is based on interviews with Bhanwardevi and her daughter-in-law, and participant observation of their session with Draupadidevi, Uttarakhand, 15 March 2016.

9 Dowry is a gift that is given by the bride's family to the groom and his family at the time of marriage. While in origin dowry is deemed to be a feature of Hindu marriage, it is prevalent as a custom in several different communities, including those of Muslims and Christians, in South Asia (See also Menski 1998).

10 Notes from various conversations with Kailash Pant, Uttarakhand, January 2016.

From my sessions of participant observation in Draupadidevi's attic where she held her consultations, I realised that being caught in the spell of a *mashiāṇ* was a very common feature interspersing the lives of many daughters-in-law in their matrimonial homes in the villages in these mountains. Marriages in the hill villages took place between villages that were located fairly far away from one another. The work of a girl tended to double once she became a daughter-in-law and in the initial months she may have been expected to handle both household and farm-related chores along with adjusting into the new environment of her matrimonial household and village, where she rarely knew anyone except maybe the contact person through whom the marriage proposal came. Husbands with employment in cities returned to their jobs within days of the marriage and the new bride had to cope with all these new changes on her very own. Being caught in the spell of a *mashiāṇ* therefore enabled perfect scope for a *tamāshā*, that gave a woman enough leverage to behave as she felt, sometimes in order to slow down the pace of adjustment in the new environment, sometimes to determine the boundaries of interaction with new family members and sometimes merely to make her point within the flow of expectations that became incidental to her position in the household.[11] At the same time, she could also test the tolerance levels of her matrimonial family. The *tamāshā* of being cast in the spell of a *mashiāṇ* thus gave a daughter-in-law a lot of scope to test the tolerance levels of her matrimonial family with regard to expectations from her. Bhanwardevi's daughter-in-law, for instance, was probably getting away with doing the household work in a manner that she pleased and at the same time could also make out the extent to which she could stretch the boundaries of what was expected from her. Similarly, Pant's wife by not interacting too much with her new family members expressed her reluctance towards being socially correct all the time. And both women could manage this without such behaviour getting in the way of their long-term relationships with the matrimonial family. The *tamāshā* enabled them to surpass a disputing situation, which could otherwise have arisen because of conflicting interests and the expectations incidental to the nature of the relationship between a daughter-in-law and her matrimonial home not being met. The fact that a new bride would take time to adjust to the practices and environment in the new household was probably understandable, but not always acceptable to those around her. And therefore engaging in the *tamāshā* of being possessed by a *mashiāṇ*, in some ways, became more or less a necessary part for the new daughter-in-law's self-preservation efforts (Bourguignon 2004, 571). It allowed her space through a safe distance created by acting in odd ways that raised suspicions of her being possessed.

Visiting several *puchiāri*-s was also part of this entire *tamāshā*. Moore, during her fieldwork in the Meo community in Rajasthan, found in the case of the 'maulavis' whom 'villagers shopped from … to the next' (1993, 533) families in the Dharamgarh valley also did not remain content with the analysis of one

11 One could draw parallels with Erin Moore's (1993) observation in a Rajasthani village where women used to get 'sick' 'as a mode to seek justice. Moore described this phenomenon as 'somatization of conflict'. (1993, 524).

puchiāri alone. They are bound to visit others too, either to confirm to what extent the analysis of the first *puchiāri* was accurate (if the analysis of the second *puchiāri* is similar to that of the first, the first one is considered reliable) or until the desired result with respect to their grievance was achieved. In fact in many instances it was with the beginning of such visits that the performance of the daughter-in-law became public. Since *mashiāṇ* experiences were routine in every household and had been experienced over generations, once in public knowledge, the family in question was able to cope better with the situation. The excuse of the *mashiāṇ* allowed family members to legitimately vent their disappointment about the new daughter-in-law's behaviour to neighbours and kin, without it becoming a focus of gossip (see also Opler 1958). At the same time, the efforts of the matrimonial family to help their daughter-in-law 'heal' were evidence of their intentions to ensure the well-being of a family member – a fact always advantageous for the social reputation of the said family. The rituals for releasing the woman from the hold of the *mashiāṇ* would only commence once the analysis of three or more *puchiāris* coincided. During this period, the daughters-in-law's performance continued and was tolerated. The rituals usually lasted anywhere between six months to a year and were interspersed with visits to the *puchiāri*, who guided the family as to how to best awaken the family deity who would exorcise the daughter-in-law of the ghost. Crucial to releasing the woman from the hold of the *mashiāṇ* and all the rituals involved, was the location where the *mashiāṇ* cast its spell on the girl. Since the *mashiāṇ* casted its spells on unmarried girls, the location of where the girl was caught by the mashiāṇ was usually deemed to be a stream in the vicinity of her natal home and therefore,[12] many of the rituals allowed the woman recurrent visits to her natal home, sometimes including extended stays. Grover (2009) highlights in a different context, '… parental support is a highly-valued attribute of the arranged marriage system, especially when it enables a period of refuge or prolonged shelter and stay in the natal home during marital difficulties' (2009, 9). Grover (2009, 16) observed that parental shelter as a form short-term intermittent refuge offered vital security to married women. In the context I describe, visits to the natal home, probably worked to help strike the balance and reduce the impact of the initial matrimonial shock. It also gave the woman regular breaks from work in her matrimonial home, as she slowly got accustomed to her new life which was perceived within the community as her regaining composure or 're-aggregation', where she assumed a 'relatively stable state once more and by virtue of this, has rights and obligations vis-à-vis other' (Turner 2008, 327). Within the community, this re-aggregation was explained as healing that followed from accurate interpretation and advice by the *puchiāri* resulting in successful appeasement of the *mashiāṇ*.

12 In earlier years, cremation of a deceased individual was carried out in the vicinity of streams if the nearest river was too far. However, nowadays with the expansion of the road network, people prefer (also because it is easier) to visit an electric crematorium or the closest river bank to carry out the cremations. However, the belief that spirits linger near streams is connected to the funeral rituals that used to be carried out there.

Case study 3: a Tamāshā *to curtail a* Tamāshā

This case study is a fairly complex one and entails the performance of one *tamāshā* to curtail the extension of another. In the village of Phwāri – an army officer (now former) – Bhupalsingh Meher – was alleged by Deepa Meher's father to have sexually abused Deepa.[13] Both boy and girl belonged to and resided in the same village and thereby were part of the same *birāderi*, an 'exogamous segment of caste in India, in which boys and girls are considered brothers and sisters and hence cannot be marriage partners' (Blunt 1931, 104–31). Deepa's father proceeded to make a police complaint against Bhupalsingh for having 'raped' his daughter. The incident, as I was told, also appeared as a news item in one of the local vernacular newspapers. When Mohansingh, the *Grām Pradhān* heard about this incident – in part from the police and in part from village gossip – he along with some other respected persons from the village suggested to Bhupalsingh that,[14] if what was being alleged was true, the matter was best sorted out within the *birāderi* itself. 'I went to the boy's house and asked him whether a sexual assault of the kind that had been complained about had actually transpired. I told him not to take the matter lightly and broach the subject of settlement if such an act had actually transpired. But his brother was a senior army officer and said he would handle the matter independently,' said Mohansingh. Following this, the police report led to a criminal case being filed against Bhupalsingh and when he received the summons, he heeded Mohansingh's advice and requested that a *birāderi pancāyat* be convened to negotiate the issue.[15] 'The father of the girl [Deepa's father] said he would agree to withdraw the case for three lakh rupees [300,000]. A bond for two lakh rupees was made and it was agreed that Deepa's father would receive the two lakh rupees after he withdrew the case. A further bond of one lakh rupees would be made thereafter and this would be settled immediately. But we don't know what happened; probably his lawyers told him that he would be better off pursuing the case in court, and so he never withdrew the case and we destroyed the bond,' said Mohansingh. The case continued in court, which Bhupalsingh along with his family and Deepa along with hers had to pursue independently. 'No one [from the village] went as witness. The boy had his immediate family members supporting him and the girl had hers. No one from the village stood by either party,' said Mohansingh, who felt that this entire '*tamāshā*' had been absolutely unnecessary and had brought much *beizzati* to the

13 This case study is based on various interviews conducted between January and June 2016 and specifically on 29 January 2016 and 27 February 2016 with the residents of village Phwāri and the neighbouring villages of Khasi and Binjal in Uttarakhand during my stay there.

14 The *Grām Pradhān* is the elected head of the village and its representative in the state-supported Zillā Parishad, the body that oversees the working of the Grām Pancāyat. The villages of Phwāri are part of the Gram Panchayat that consists of two more villages.

15 A simple explanation of the *pancāyats* is a council engaged in regulation of caste and/ or village affairs. For more details see Cohn (1959), Bose (1960), Ishwaran (1964), Lemons (2010) and Headley (2015).

entire *birāderi*. Bhupalsingh was eventually convicted and he received a jail term of ten years . He also ended up losing his job in the army. Some years ago, the girl was married off to a boy from a far-off village.

There were several interpretations of this *tamāshā* – which entailed visits to the police station, expenditure of court processes and difficult negotiations in the *birāderi pancāyat* – and of why Deepa's father processed the dispute in the manner he did. I will describe here two of the most common narratives. The two fairly different narratives came from two different sections of the village and much of this is also based on how I was positioned with relation to the narrators. The younger generation in Phwāri and the neighbouring village of Khasi, youths who had been Deepa's and Bhupalsingh's friends, said that Bhupalsingh and Deepa were romantically involved and the act alleged to be 'rape' was actually consensual sexual activity that may have transpired in the course of this affair. Such a liaison would have been totally unacceptable in the village community. It was a social taboo and both families could have been ostracised for this behaviour, if it were admitted to. Therefore, a *tamāshā* of this sort was in order and was in fact required to save face and prevent the truth caming out publicly. By filing a police complaint and pursuing even the court case, Deepa's family wanted to establish their predisposition to community values and norms, and anything less than this extreme performance would have probably been perceived as conceding to contributory negligence. Another explanation of this *tamāshā* came from the more elderly in the community. Without making any reference to the alleged liaison between Deepa and Bhupalsingh, the community elders stated that Deepa's father only wanted to extort some money out of Bhupalsingh and he used the opportunity of the *birāderi pancāyat* to see how much he could extort. The police complaint was more in revenge of some history of disputes between the two families. However, in the way things turned out eventually, it was that Deepa's father did not withdraw the case and Bhupalsingh ended up with a ten-year term in prison and loss of his secure army job. So had it been a matter of money as the village elders claimed, then Deepa's father probably would have agreed to Bhupalsingh's offer and withdrawn the case, since a settlement in the *birāderi* would have certainly been more lucrative than pursuing a court case. But clearly, from the way things proceeded, it did not seem that this was the case. And therefore, that the *tamāshā* might have occurred in order to escape social ostracism and *beizzati* on account of a socially unacceptable liaison was far more likely than for reasons of extortion. Here it is important to note, also, my position as a researcher within the community. To the village elders who were mostly men, I was a 'woman' and 'a lawyer' – still more an outsider than to the youngsters in the village, who were closer in age and treated me more like a 'colleague' and 'friend', and often shared stories of their own experiences in college and otherwise were quite open with me. The village elders also held the notion of '*birāderi izzat*' (honour), more dearly than the younger generation. And therefore, there was enough reason for the village elders to hesitate in disclosing to me the fact of such a liaison and what they made of it. At the time of the incident, Deepa was still unmarried and being ostracised from the village community or even a hint of acquiescence to such a liaison could put at stake her chances of ever finding an appropriate match. A court case was an extreme step, but was probably thought necessary by her family in order to properly victimise Deepa's position and in turn establish her innocence in relation to this entire situation. At the same time, a court case was a fairly unusual mechanism of dispute processing in the village communities in the Dharamgarh valley and particularly so if the dispute was between members of the same *birāderi*. However, this exaggerated response to a dispute situation that the community was willing to help the parties negotiate was rather unexpected by the community. As we saw, Deepa's father initially engaged in negotiations in the *birāderi pancāyat*, but nevertheless went ahead with pursuing the matter in court. This element of spontaneity and unpredictability, in addition to the extremity in the form of dispute processing contributed towards making Deepa and her family 'liminal entities', to whom the habituated norms of behaviour automatically stopped applying so long at this phase lasted. The advantage for them was that the court case rather than the cause of it became the focus of the community's attention. Consequently, Deepa and her family escaped being ostracised from the village community and were able to reincorporate themselves into the community's circle of solidarity once the case was disposed of by the court.

This *tamāshā* was vigorously pursued by both parties, as it involved the sanction of legal norms in different legal orders – spiritual, social and practical. In the social background of these village communities, remaining unmarried was practically not feasible for men of this community and unacceptable or challenging for the women. Socially, a match of two people from the same village was not acceptable for fear of the spiritual sanctions this may invoke on the community that accepts it and also because of the power equation that it caused to collapse. As a result, to avoid *tamāshā* of a different sort, the performance that this type of dispute processing entailed was probably perceived as necessary.

Understanding the significance of *tamāshā* in the context of dispute processing

Extremity, as can be gathered from these case studies, is a characteristic of *tamāshā* and it is the extreme nature of all these actions that facilitates a distance between the audience and the performance, creating a state of 'liminality' that causes a momentary deflection of what is ordinarily expected from the role of such a person. Liminality causes the creation of a social space where the conventions and scripts of everyday life are loosened, thus enabling a transformation at the level of self as well as one at the level of the community (Davidheiser 2006). The element of *tamāshā* in dispute processing creates this liminal space enabling a departure from the normal social world and its habituated patterns of behaviour.

The case studies in this chapter establish that the purpose of a *tamāshā* is manifold, but it yielded in the context of these communities two specific advantages for the performers – one at the level of expression and the other at the level of the experience of interconnectedness. As part of this conclusion, I deal with each of these advantages separately.

a. Tamāshā, *a tool of communication*

The performative element in dispute processing as we see from the above case studies can be extremely liberating. In all three instances, the element of *tamāshā* contributed to the performer becoming a 'liminal entity' and opened up channels of communication between the performer and the audience and among the audience themselves that would otherwise have not been possible in the given social circumstances. Liminal entities, as we saw at the beginning of the chapter, as a result of the space are 'neither here nor there; they are betwixt and between the positions assigned and arrayed by law, custom, convention and ceremonial' (Turner 2008, 327). In every situation, whether it be the dispute over shared water resources between Neela Chogle, Dinisha and Kala, or the looming threat of a situation of dispute arising out of the feelings of distress that overcome a new bride in her matrimonial home, or tackling the consequences of a socially completely unacceptable liaison, the element of *tamāshā* therefore enabled each of the performers to challenge a certain behavioural protocol and to open up spaces for continued co-existence.

Of course, in addition to opening up channels of communication, what cannot be ignored is the indirect influence of such communication on the course of behaviour that follows between the parties and subsequently on the processing of the dispute in question. Society, as a process is punctuated by situations that have intervals between them. Turner (1966) explains that 'political situations' are interposed by different types of 'intervening situations'. 'Intervening situations will have left their imprint on the subsequent patterns of behaviour' (1966, 240). A *tamāshā* could be understood as an intervening situation played out in the course of a dispute in order to influence consequent patterns of behaviour between the disputing parties and the community at large. As much as the element of *tamāshā* creates a liminal space for the performer where norms, customs and ordinary expectations are suspended, we cannot possibly overlook the impact that a *tamāshā* will have on the tone of the relationship such performer(s) may have with the other disputing parties and the community at large. The scope of the chapter would not allow me to go into detail about the nature of dispute processing that follows an intervening *tamāshā*, but it nevertheless remains significant to the processing of the dispute generally.

b. Tamāshā *to navigate self-preservation*

A *tamāshā* encompasses a certain degree of intensity and concentration, where what the performer wants to communicate becomes the centre of focus; but the dramatic streak that underscores such a communication blurs the appropriateness of such communication and ensures that the performers remain connected to the audience despite how controversial or provocative the content communication is. Therefore, it becomes a perfect medium just like a play or an actual *tamāshā* performance, where a person can express his or her feelings and intentions in the moment of being a performer, but at the same time continues to remain a part of the audience or the community in his individual self.

Felstiner (1974, 63) explains that '[t]he dispute processing practices prevailing in any particular society are a product of its values, its psychological imperatives, its history and its economic, political and social organisation'. In societies such as Gonjhé and villages in the Dharamgarh valley, remaining interconnected to one's community and continuing to be part of its circle of solidarity was essential for a variety of reasons cutting across religious, social and practical planes. Within the social normative of the community, therefore, preservation of the self was not perceived to be disconnected from preservation of the community and vice-versa. As a result, disputes and their processing in village communities such as Gonjhé and those in the Dharamgarh valley must be understood in the context of the dynamics of the kinship networks and caste ties. In addition to common customs and traditions in the social and religious sphere, both in Gonjhé and the villages of Dharamagarh valley, the people in the villages shared the same source of livelihood. For the Koḷī community of Gonjhé it was fishing and for the people in the mountains it was agriculture. As a result, in these villages collective action was required by people for several activities which were beyond the means of their own household, for example, in any type of constructions, agricultural activities, for ritual performances, during marriages and funerals, etc. Disputes in their very nature bring about a discord in relations, albeit oftentimes one which is only temporary. Navigating such situations of conflict can be tricky in such societies as the parties to the dispute must ensure that they can achieve what they want in regard to the dispute while remaining sensitive to the fact that they have to continue to live together with one another and the community after such a situation has passed. The element of *tamāshā* in dispute processing, as we have seen from the above case studies, became useful and productive in such a context.

'Understanding social behaviour requires an interpretive perspective that examines how behaviour is changing, unpredictable, and unique to each and every social encounter' (Carter and Fuller 2015, 2). Individuals identify themselves and others in the context of social structure and accordingly take on certain roles. Stryker (1980, 57) defines roles as 'expectations which are attached to [social] positions'; or 'symbolic categories [that] serve to cue behavior'. Therefore, to every role, there is attached a set of expectations. In the case of Neela, Dinisha and Kala these expectations were attached to their roles as neighbours. In the case of Bhanwardevi's daughter-in-law and also Pant's wife they were attached to her role as daughter-in-law and in the case of Deepa and Bhupalsingh, the expectations were attached to their roles as junior and unmarried members of a *birāderi*. However, there is always a gap between what one is as an individual and what is expected of oneself in the role s/he takes on. Drama encompasses role-play that creates a liminal space enabling the performer to bridge this gap and in that strike a balance for his or her own preservation which includes securing his or her interests as an individual, but also as a member of the community. Being cast in the spell of a *mashiāṇ*, as we saw, allowed the daughter-in-law to express a part of herself which was not in consonance with her role as daughter-in-law. Similarly, the shouting matches that Koḷī women were known to engage in, allowed them to reveal a part of their identities which are not in conformity with their socially legitimated roles as 'women' generally and 'mothers', 'wives', 'daughters', 'sisters' and so forth. On account of the *tamāshā* their dispute processing involved, these women could address their grievance in a manner of their choice and yet secure themselves against the risk straining their overall relationship with the community. Likewise, pursuing a court case rigorously was probably not in line with the expectations attached to being members of the same kinship network, but it enabled Deepa and her family to save face on another front and escape social ostracism.

Conclusion

Tamāshā as an element of dispute processing somehow has always been over-simplified by legal scholars. The state legal order tends to dismiss emotions and life details, often perceiving them as inefficient and treating them with impatience.[16] Engendering a liminal space for the varied exercise of agency as is established in this chapter is only one of the reasons why the analysis of *tamāshā* becomes significant in the context dispute processing. Along with the creation of informal and non-structured spaces that enable 'different' voices to be heard, these case studies also indicate the possible connection the nature of a *tamāshā* might have with the choice of dispute processing mechanism. In the first case study, for instance, the *tamāshā* arose in the course of a dispute between individual parties and the nature of this *tamāshā* would in fact decide the pattern of interaction that would follow between the disputing parties, which was ultimately the goal. The second case study presented a situation in the form of daughter-in-law's grievance which, on escalation, could have resulted in an intra-family dispute with an individual on the one hand and the family on the other. The social unit of a family being a very important one in the context of the said community, care was taken so as to ensure that the grievance redress was of a nature that prevented the situation from intensifying into a full-blown dispute that could adversely impact long-term relationships. Though exaggerated, the *tamāshā* in this situation played on sentiments and beliefs familiar to the community. In the third case study, however, we see that the *tamāshā* involved mobilizing the state machinery. The dispute involved not just individuals but social units – the families and the *birāderi*. The conflicting situation was likely to disturb two sets of relations – between a family and the community at one level and between two families at another level. And the *tamāshā* was used to sort of put the situation into a mode of 'shock' (and thereby alienating it from the community) by the disputing party exploiting territories unfamiliar to the community. This establishes that there is a definite cue for scope to further research and explore whether, in what way and to what extent the type of *tamāshā* that intervenes a disputing situation is likely to give us an idea of the course that the processing of the said dispute is likely to follow.

16 See Basu (2015), in particular chapter 3 for an ethnography of performances in courtrooms.

Bibliography

Basu, Srimati. 2015. *The Trouble with Marriage: Feminists Confront Law and Violence in India*. Oakland, CA: University of California Press.

Blunt, E.A.H. 1931. *The Caste System of Northern India*. London: Oxford University Press.

Bose, Nirmal Kumar. 1960. 'Conflict and Its Resolution in Hindu Civilisation'. *Journal of the Department of Letters, University of Calcutta* 3: 1–49.

Bourguignon, Erika. 2004. 'Suffering and Healing, Subordination and Power: Women and Possession Trance'. *Ethos* 32(4): 557–574.

Carter, Michael J., and Celene Fuller. 2015. 'Symbolic Interactionism'. *Sociopedia.isa*. www.sagepub.net/isa/resources/pdf/Symbolic%20interactionism.pdf.

Cohn, Bernard S. 1959. 'Some Notes on Law and Change in North India'. *Economic Development and Cultural Change* 8(1): 79–93.

Davidheiser, Mark. 2006. 'Rituals and Conflict Transformation: An Anthropological Analysis of the Ceremonial Dimensions of Dispute Processing'. In *Beyond Intractability*, edited by Guy Burgess and Heidi Burgess, Conflict Information Consortium, University of Colorado. www.beyondintractability.org/essay/rituals-and-ceremonials.

Dusche, Michael. 2016. 'Būtas and Daivas as Justices in Tuḷu Nāḍu: Implications for the Philosophy of Law'. *South Asia Chronicle* 6: 11–36.

Fanger, Allen C. 1990. 'The Jāgar: Spirit Possession Séance among the Rajputs and Silpakars of Kumaon'. In *Himalaya: Past and Present*, edited by M.P. Joshi, Allen C. Fanger, and C.W. Brown, 173–191. Almora: Sri Almora Book Depot.

Felstiner, William L.F. 1974. 'Influences of Social Organization on Dispute Processing'. *Law & Society Review* 9(1): 63–94.

Felstiner, William L.F., Richard L. Abel, and Austin Sarat. 1981. 'The Emergence and Transformation of Disputes: Naming, Blaming, Claiming'. *Law & Society Review* 15(3/4): 631–654.

Gennep, van. 2004. 'The Rites of Passage'. In *Death, Mourning, and Burial: A Cross-Cultural Reader*, edited by A.C. Robben, 213–223. Oxford: Blackwell.

Grover, Shalini. 2009. 'Lived Experiences Marriage, Notions of Love, and Kinship Support amongst Poor Women in Delhi'. *Contributions to Indian Sociology* 43(1): 1–33.

Headley, Zoé E. 2015. "The Devil's Court!". In *Regimes of Legality*, edited by Daniela Berti and Devika Bordia, 227–257. New Delhi: Oxford University Press.

Ishwaran, K. 1964. 'Customary Law in Village India'. *International Journal of Comparative Sociology* 5(2): 228–243.

Lemons, Katherine. 2010. '*At the Margins of Law: Adjudicating Muslim Families in Contemporary Delhi*'. PhD dissertation, Berkeley, University of California. http://escholarship.org/uc/item/6f66n4dn.

Malik, Aditya. 2016. 'The Darbar of Goludev'. In *The Law of Possession*, edited by William S. Sax and Helene Basu, 193–225. New Delhi: Oxford University Press.

Mathur, C.J. 1964. *Drama in Rural India*. Bombay: Asia Publishing House.

Menski, Werner, ed. 1998. *South Asians and the Dowry Problem*. Stoke-on-Trent: Trentham Books.

Moore, Erin. 1993. 'Gender, Power, and Legal Pluralism: Rajasthan, India'. *American Ethnologist* 20(3): 522–542.

Nadel, Lynn, and Walter Sinnott-Armstrong, eds. 2012. *Memory and Law*. Oxford Series in Neurosceince, Law, and Philosophy. New York: Oxford University Press.

Nader, Laura. 1978. *The Disputing Process: Law in Ten Societies*. New York: Columbia University Press.

Opler, Morris E. 1958. 'Spirit Possession in a Rural Area of Northern India'. In *Reader in Comparative Religion*, by W.A. Lessa and E.Z. Vogt, 553–566. Evanston, IL: Row, Peterson, and Co.

Ramsbotham, Oliver, Tom Woodhouse, and Hugh Miall. 2011. *Contemporary Conflict Resolution: The Prevention, Management and Transformation of Deadly Conflicts*. Cambridge: Polity Press.

Ranade, Ashok D. 2000. 'Thoughts, Values and Culture: The Performing Arts'. In *Intersections: Socio-Cultural Trends in Maharashtra*, edited by Meera Kosambi, 194–209. London: Sangam Book.

Singh, Nikita. 2016. 'Social Movement in India: Street Theatre as a Voice of on Marginalized Group'. Unpublished manuscript (with author).

Stryker, Sheldon. 1980. *Symbolic Interactionism: A Social Structural Version*. Menlo Park, CA: Benjamin/Cummings.

Turner, Victor. 1966. 'Ritual Aspects of Conflict Control in African Micropolitics'. In *Political Anthropology*, edited by Marc J. Swatz, Victor Turner, and Arthur Tuden, 239–246. Chicago, IL: Aldine Publishing.

Turner, Victor. 1979. 'Frame, Flow and Reflection: Ritual and Drama as Public Liminality'. *Japanese Journal of Religious Studies* 6(4): 465–499.

Turner, Victor. 2008. 'Liminality and Communitas'. In *A Reader in the Anthropology of Religion*, edited by Michael Lanbek, 2nd ed, 326–339. Oxford: Wiley-Blackwell.

10 Can law 'sustain' cultural diversity?

The inheritance laws of Indian minority communities and the Italian legal system

Chiara Lapi

Introduction

Our contemporary globalized scenario is characterized by the encounter of many different people who belong to different cultures, religions, customs, habits and speak different languages, and for that reason, draw from different systems of values. Reasoning about "difference" implies clarifying the term. The concept of difference builds itself in relationship with the concept of identity. "Differing from the others constitutes the identity of everybody" (Ruggenini 2007). It happens that the two concepts are often in conflict. Indeed, the fear of losing one's own identity induces the rejection of difference (Ruggiu 2013). Undoubtedly, recent migratory waves, of concern to Europe, cause a stronger perception of the sense of "difference", particularly on behalf of the autochthones, who would often like to avoid relations with migrants, considering them different in a negative sense (Bauman 2006).

Nowadays, even the law has to cope with the concept of "difference". A state legal system, which is uniform, positivist, and an expression of institutional power (Consorti 2013), has indeed to handle claims which, although often only apparently, are not compliant with its juridical principles. Law has, however, always been influenced by culture (Mezey 2001): both the activity of the legislator and of the jurists who interpret the law are strongly linked to the social context, and therefore, to the culture of the state where they occur (Parolari 2016).

Therefore, the link between law and culture is not new: it has always existed. However, it could be said that nowadays law has to deal with a new challenge: "sustaining" cultural diversity. I use this expression intentionally since it evokes the title of H. Patrick Glenn's book, *Legal Traditions of the World: Sustainable Diversity in Law*. According to Glenn, the legal traditions of the world[1] tend – because of globalization (Glenn 2011) – to go beyond the borders of the context where they were born and developed. Therefore, they blend together: in this way, the identity of each population, which originally was linked to a specific cultural and legal tradition, becomes less clear, rigid and uniform. Moreover, religions have a big influence on these legal traditions (Glenn 2011; Ricca 2002).

1 These traditions – according to Glenn – are at least seven: the Hindu tradition, the Islamic tradition, the Common law tradition, the Civil law tradition, the Talmudic tradition, the Confucian tradition and the chthonic tradition.

Given that culture influences legal traditions, reflecting on the possibility and on the way that law can sustain culture diversity is crucial in our contemporary globalized society. Law should be a tool to manage social conflicts (Lapi 2015) but it is not often able to do this since it neglects to recognize the role of culture. This chapter aims to understand if and how law can sustain cultural diversity through the analysis of a case study: a number of Indian communities, settled in Italy, apply inheritance rules based on their values, which are often different from or even in contrast with Italian values. The Italian legal system is called to cope with these different rules.

The Indian family presents features that are not present in the Western family, or more precisely, in the common conception of a Western family. Men exercise a notable role in the management of family patrimony and in the protection of women. These features have significant consequences on the juridical ground, such as in inheritance, which follows – though only apparently – unthinkable criteria for a Western state. For instance, many Indians, indeed, consider it normal that a woman, when the head of the family dies, renounces to her share of inheritance in favour of her brothers, simply by signing a paper which attests her waiver. This rule has overcome the boundaries of the Indian sub-continent. Indeed, some interviews realized during my fieldwork within Indian communities settled in Italy show that Indians continue to feel the compulsory nature of this rule even if they live very far away from India.

On the other hand, this rule is seemingly not compliant with the laws of the Italian legal system, which provide for full equality between men and women on the ground of inheritance. However, an analysis based on the knowledge of "cultural codes" of Indian minorities reveals that the waiver of the inheritance is a rule, which is compliant with the principle of solidarity characterizing the Indian family. Indeed, a woman chooses to renounce to her share of inheritance in favour of her brothers in order to thank them for the economic help that they usually offer her during her life. For instance, brothers help their sisters get married.

This rule challenges the Italian legal system, which admits the waiver of the inheritance only in specific hypotheses sanctioned by Article 519 of the Italian civil code. Moreover, the fact that the Indian waiver of inheritance is done by sisters in favour of brothers could be contrary to the principle of equality between men and women provided by Article 3 of the Italian Constitution.

This chapter claims that in some cases the Italian legal system should be able to allow Indian minorities to apply their own rules by creating juridical solutions, despite the differences between these rules and the Italian ones. In order to reach this result, one of the useful methods is to take into account the "cultural codes" of minorities. Since discussion on Indian people residing in Italy implies also reasoning on the rights of minorities, this chapter focuses on how the Italian legal system protects minorities. Through the case study of a minority group who lives in Italy, the Ladina minority in Alto Adige, this analysis will show that Italy, despite the presence of immigrants, has always managed the claims of minorities which were not compliant with the principles of the state. In short, I assume that state legal systems – such as the Italian legal system – already have the tools to manage cultural diversity. The most important thing is therefore to bring to the surface how state legal systems can manage the aforementioned diversity. Law could certainly take more advantage of the sociological method. Indeed, my case study shows that the knowledge of rules (and, particularly, of the roots of these rules), which immigrant people follow, would ease the resolution of normative clashes.

Method and data collection

The analysis in this chapter is based in part on fieldwork and in part on theoretical research. The fieldwork has been realized, so far, in two Indian communities who live in Italy: one is in Novellara, a small town in the province of Reggio Emilia, and the other is in Sabaudia, a town in the province of Latina (Bertolani, Ferraris and Perocco 2011).

These communities are identified on the basis of religion. People who belong to these communities are Sikh. Novellara boasts the biggest temple in Europe (after that of London). Sabaudia has a Sikh temple too, though smaller than that of Novellara. However, both temples are important since they are places of worship where the Sikh people meet. The principal tool of my fieldwork was interviews. Even though it was possible to speak with some Sikh people who were very kind and helpful, it was not easy to ask questions about their ways of dividing family property when the head of family dies. People are quite wary and sceptical about questions concerning such delicate issues. For this reason, I was able to ask people more questions in Sabaudia than in Novellara, since, in the first case, I was assisted by Marco Omizzolo, a scholar who knows the Sikh community of this town very well. He acted as professional mediator between the Sikh community of Sabaudia and myself (Omizzolo 2013; Omizzolo 2014).

Hindu inheritance laws between judicial system and customary rules

In order to understand why people coming from India and settled in Italy feel the compulsory nature of the rule to renounce their inheritance, it is necessary to analyse the history of inheritance laws in India. This analysis focuses on Hindu inheritance laws, that is on the laws which are contained in the Hindu personal law. Indeed, in India family matters – marriage, divorce, maintenance, adoption and inheritance – are ruled by religious laws, such as Hindu law, Muslim law, Parsi law, Jewish Law or Christian Law (Herklotz 2015). These laws are applied on the basis of religious belonging of people so that – for instance – when a Hindu man dies, his property will be divided according to the Hindu personal law. The relevance of analysing Hindu inheritance laws is linked to the fact that, nowadays, these laws are applied not only to Hindu people, but also to Sikhs (Menski 1989).

Although nowadays in India, women and men, according to the Hindu Succession Amendment Act 2005, have equal rights of inheritance (Agrawal 2010), for many years women have been title holders of limited rights of succession. For many years, Hindu laws of succession have followed the rules contained in two texts dating around the 12th century AD: the commentary of *Mitākshāra* and the digest of *Dayabagha*. Both texts established very strong limits to the inheritance rights of women.

According to the *Mitākshāra* system, two types of property existed: the joint family property and the separate property. The former was held jointly by four generations of male members – a man, his sons, his grandchildren and his great-grandchildren – who became co-parceners on birth. Women could not be co-parceners. In the joint family property, the women had only the right of maintenance as incoming wives, as widows, and as unmarried daughters. If the daughter married, she was entitled to marriage expenses and associated gifts.

On the other hand, the separate property regime included property which was self-acquired and any property inherited from persons other than a man's father, paternal grandfather or paternal great-grandfather. In a man's separate property, his widow could inherit a limited estate, but only if there were other conditions, such as the absence of sons, agnatic-grandsons, agnatic great-grandsons and she remained chaste. The expression "limited estate" or "limited interest" means that the woman could enjoy the property for her lifetime, but she could not normally alienate it. Only in specific and restricted cases, the woman could alienate her property, as in the case of performing pious and religious acts (Agarwal 2015). Many inscriptions, found within temples dating back to the period between the 10th and 15th centuries, prove lands' endowments by women. Nevertheless, these endowments were aimed to obtain protection from men, as husbands, sons, or brothers. Therefore, once again, the woman was not free to use her property as she wanted.

Under the *Dayabagha* system,[2] the probability of a widow or a daughter inheriting some property was somewhat greater than under the *Mitākshāra* system. Since there was no difference between ancestral and separate property, the widow, and after her, the daughters were recognized as heirs even when the man's share in the joint family estate had not been divided before his death. Hence, unlike under Mitākshāra, the women inherited an interest in all property, irrespective of whether it was ancestral or separate. Both systems recognized some female property rights by the term of "stridhan", which literally means "property of a woman". There are many interpretations on what "stridhan" exactly included. On the one hand, some think that it included only movables, given to a woman by her parents, brothers, or relatives before or at the time of her marriage, and by her husband after marriage. On the other hand, some think that it included also immovable

2 It differs from the *Mitakshara* system essentially for the fact that the man can ask his share of property only at the death of the head of family, whereas, in the *Mitākshāra* system the man can ask his share also during the life of the head of family (Das 2007). In the *Mitākshāra* system, the bequest happened on the basis of the survivorship: therefore, the birth of a son caused the decrease of the share of other living man within the family, while the death caused the increase of the share. In contrast, in the *Dayabahaga* system, the share, which every male member of the family can ask only at the death of the family's head, was definite and did not change if the males of family increased or decreased.

property, such as land, which women, in few cases, inherited. However, beyond the specific rules about women's inheritance contained in the *Mitākshāra* and *Dayabagha* systems and beyond the exact meaning of "stridhan", it is important to highlight the fact that women were considered a "special category" in the field of the right of property. They did not have the same rights as men who were considered the absolute managers of all family property. This way of conceiving the role of women and men within the family was also the result of the Hindu concept, according to which women played a specific role within the family. While the man managed family property, the woman had to generate sons. If she did not give birth to a son, she could not attend sacrifices to propitiate gods (Jamison 1996; Anderson 2004). After all, Hinduism – as many other religions – perpetuates the idea that everyone has specific roles within the society and within the family. This idea is compliant with the maintenance of a specific structure of power, directed to the control of goods and wealth.

During British colonization, *Mitākshāra* and *Dayabagha* became the official rules, which regulated litigation on inheritance among Hindu people. Indeed, Warren Hastings, the governor of Bengal, in 1772, decided that, Hindu people had to apply Hindu law in all litigation which concerned family issues, such as marriage, divorce, maintenance, adoption, inheritance (the so called "listed subjects"), while Muslim people had to apply, in all litigation on the same subjects, Islamic law (Francavilla 2008). Therefore, the rules contained in the *Mitākshāra* and *Dayabagha* went out from the limbo of the religious and legal Hinduist tradition and became – to some extent – official laws. It is possible to argue that, if British colonization had not happened in India, inheritance rules would have developed differently.

From these two systems, all the ensuing Hindu inheritance legislation – which counts the Hindu Women's Rights to Property Act, the Hindu Succession Act 1956 and the Hindu Succession Amendment Act 2005 – developed. These were attempts to create some significant steps on the ground of gender equality.

Nevertheless, while on the juridical ground the regime moved toward greater gender equality, especially with the help of many feminist organizations, in India women who inherited were considered "share-snatchers" (Saxena 2008). This idea was deeply rooted and therefore, difficult to eliminate. Even nowadays, although the Hindu Succession Amendment Act 2005 recognizes the equality of the sexes in successions, in some cases, in India, the fact that women have rights of property and are able to inherit – as men – is perceived in a negative way. In order not to be socially stigmatized, the woman often prefers to renounce the inheritance in favour of her brothers through the signature of a paper in which she declares this intention. This practice can be interpreted, however, in two ways. On the one hand, it is in contrast with the law codified in the Hindu Succession Amendment Act 2005 and for this reason, it discriminates against women, favouring men. On the other hand, it is a practice which deserves to be studied in depth since it is linked to the concept of the *joint family*. In this type of family, the duties toward the wealth of family prevail over the rights of individuals. Although there is not a single definition – among scholars – of *joint family*, some elements identify it: a group of people, who are related to one another by kindred (usually three generations, that is the man, his wife, his sons, their wives and children), hold property in common, generally live under one roof and participate in common family worship (Ramu 2006). The *joint jamily* has been and – to some extent – is even nowadays a fundamental part of the Hindu social organization (Sinha 1993). The ancient Hindu scriptures, such as the Veda, recognize the value of the *joint family* as a place where husband and wife fulfil the *dharma*, participating together in religious ceremonies (Sharma 2004). Therefore, from the origins of Hinduism, the *joint family* is linked to the *dharma* which, as "the duty to do the right thing at the right time, at any point of one's life" (Menski 2006), attributes specific roles to individuals within the family and society. Also among the Sikhs of the Punjab (Grewal 1998), the model of the joint family is widespread and perfectly compliant with the values of Sikhism, such as mutual duties within the kindred system (Angelo 1997). Therefore, it is possible – once again – to consider the *joint family* as the best social structure to fulfil *dharma*. Moreover, as some scholars observed, *dharma* is central not only for Hinduism, but affects other indigenous religious traditions of India, such as Buddhism, Jains and Sikhism (Howard and Sherma forthcoming).

As a consequence, the practice of the surrender of inheritance – if read in the context of the *joint family* – could be interpreted as the fulfilment of a duty on behalf of sisters toward brothers, and not as an example of gender inequality. For these reasons, qualifying and judging this custom as a discrimination against women would signify ignoring the complex framework which concerns the way to understand the family in India.

Customary rules within Indian communities in Italy

From the interviews realized both in the Sikh communities of Sabaudia and Novellara, it emerges that the waiver of inheritance rights of sisters in favour of brothers is still typically common. It seems that Indian people whom I interviewed do not feel that this practice could discriminate against women. When I asked them why women sometimes prefer to leave their share of inheritance to their brothers, despite the Hindu Succession Amendment Act 2005 (which – as previously said – is applied also to the Sikh), they answered that sisters often feel the duty to renounce their inheritance. Indeed, in India it usually happens that, when sisters get married, brothers help them pay for the marriage expenses.

What happens to the inheritance when the head of family dies within the Indian communities in diaspora? Do Sikh people apply the rule of renunciation of inheritance also in Italy? Obviously, many of these people will apply the rules of the Italian civil code which provides for full equality between men and women in inheritance rights. The Italian legal system has, however, to take into account the fact that there are people who live within its borders and who claim the application of their customary rules. Moreover, it may happen that immigrants apply their own customary rules without the official legal system knowledge. In this second event, the risk of conflicts between official laws and unofficial customary rules is more important than in the first one. So, how should the Italian legal system behave when people belonging to minority groups would like to apply their own customary rules?

It is not possible to offer one only answer to these questions. Many different values are involved. On the one hand, the unity of families of Sikh immigrants could be impaired if communities in diaspora were obliged to apply the rules of inheritance of the Italian legal system. On the other hand, the Italian legal system cannot automatically allow minorities to apply their own rules since it would lose its authority and reason for being.

Minorities within the Italian legal system

According to data of the National Institute of Statistics (ISTAT), the Indian population living in Italy in January 2016 is 150,456.[3] Among them, Hindus are 72,000, while Sikh are 17,000.[4] Thus, the Hindus and the Sikhs who live in Italy represent minority groups.

The Italian legal system protects minorities. Particularly, Article 6 of the Italian Constitution stipulates that "The Republic protects linguistic minorities by specific laws". Even though it concerns only linguistic minorities, the provision has to be interpreted in the sense that the Italian constitution (and therefore, the Italian legal system) protects all kinds of minorities. The principle of equality which bans discrimination on the basis of race, language, religion, (Art. 3 Constitution) and the guarantee of inviolable rights to the human being both as an individual and as a member of social communities in which he/she lives (Art. 2 Constitution), represent protection available to all minorities and not only to linguistic ones (Lattanzi 2013). Article 6 of the Constitution was implemented through Law 482/1999 containing "rules for the protection of linguistic historic minorities".

Minority is a concept which can be defined in relation to the concept of majority since it presents some peculiar characteristics which are different from those of the majority. Sikh minorities, who are within the Italian territory, are characterized by the fact that they are composed of immigrants who belong to a specific religion (Sikhism) and speak a different language. Also the way to conceive the family, the patrimonial relationships among its members, and the way to devolve property among the heirs at the death of the head of family, represents other features which distinguish the Sikh from the majority of Italian people.

Since the concept of minority is "broad and naturally endless (Lattanzi 2013)", even immigrants can be considered a "minority". All minorities are bearers of cultural codes which are usually different from those of the majority.

Some particular examples of inheritance "laws" in Italy

Among the linguistic historic minorities taken into account by Law 482/1999, some present features in the managing of family relations and of family property

3 See www.tuttitalia.it/statistiche/cittadini-stranieri/india.

4 See "Immigrati e religioni in Italia: gli ortodossi sono più numerosi dei musulmani". Available at www.ismu.org/2016/07/in-italia-ortodossi-piu-numerosi-dei-musulmani.

which are similar to those of Indian minorities. So, it is not the first time that the Italian legal system has had to cope with juridical diversity, which is the mirror of cultural diversity.

Particularly, among people who speak the German language and the Ladino dialect and who live in Alto Adige, a specific kind of property has spread which is called, in German, "Geschlossener Hof", translated into Italian by the expression "maso chiuso" (Mori and Hintner 2013). "Maso" signifies a rural dwelling which consists of agricultural lands, pastures, a cattleshed and a barn. "Chiuso" means "closed": it indicates the fact that the complex of goods of which the "maso" consists of, cannot be divided either by *inter vivos* acts, such as a sale, or by *mortis causa* acts, such as in succession (Barba 2011). As a consequence, for many years, the laws concerning "maso chiuso" stated that the entire property – at the death of the head of family – was assigned to the eldest male. Only in 2001 (Gruber 2012), by the enactment of "provincial law 17/2001",[5] was discrimination between men and women on the ground of the inheritance of "maso chiuso" abolished. Indeed, Article 11, concerning the indivisibility of the "maso", requires that "within the context of the division of the inheritance property, *maso chiuso* has to be considered as an indivisible unit and can be assigned to only one male heir or to only one female heir".

From my research, it also emerged that in another part of Italy, until a few years ago, inheritance rules which favoured men over women were in force. It is the village of Comelico Superiore (in the province of Belluno in the Veneto region) where the Ladino dialect is used (Casanova Fuga 1997), and for this reason, people living there are protected as a linguistic and historic minority on the basis of Italian Law 482/1999. In this village, there is an ancient institution, called "Regola",[6] consisting of collective family property of woods and pastures which, till a few years ago, was handed down to the male descendants (Trebeschi 2008; Fant 2012). Women were excluded from the possibility to become heirs of the patrimony of the Regola. Some years ago a man who was one of the administrators of the Regola filed an appeal against these unfair rules at the competent tribunals of the Italian state. Both the "Corte d'Appello of Venice" (17 May 2012) and the "Corte di Cassazione" (7 July 2015) gave reason to the request of the administrator and decided that the rules of the statute of the Regola were against the principle of gender equality as contained in the Italian constitution (Dal Mas 2015).

Both in the "maso chiuso" and in the "Regola", it was considered normal for many years that women did not inherit. In both institutes, the rules have changed only recently and survived for many years after the adoption of the Italian constitution in 1948, which provides for the principle of full equality between men and women. This means that for a long period the Italian legal system has

5 "Provincial law" means that it is applied on the territory of the autonomous province of Bolzano, in Alto Adige.

6 The entire name is "Regola di Casamazzagno". Casamazzagno is the name of a hamlet of the municipality of Comelico Superiore in the province of Belluno.

tolerated rules which discriminated against women. These rules changed when the times were ripe, and not before. Both in the "maso chiuso" and in the "Regola", the management of the family property was entrusted to men considered, as a matter of common consent, the only people able to administer it for the prevalent interest of the family.

We can see a sort of lowest common denominator which links the concepts of the "maso chiuso", "regola" and "joint family". The three concepts are characterized by the application of customary rules which – to some extent – differ from the official laws of the state. The rule of renunciation of inheritance, linked to the concept of the *joint family*, often applied even nowadays in India, and which could be applied also by Indian people living in Italy, is compliant to a specific conception of family and property. This way of conceiving family privileges the family interest over the individual interest and sees property as an entity to be managed in a collective way. For this reason, it considers that is has to remain undivided.

Some customary rules establish roots because of historic, social and environmental circumstances. For instance, in the mountain areas – such as in the case of Alto Adige and Belluno (Veneto) – the agricultural land and the pastures have been fundamental sources of income, but also in some parts of India, as in Punjab, agricultural land is considered very important. Therefore, maintaining the unity of this kind of property was considered a safe method to avoid the dispersion of wealth. To this need, patriarchal mentality, typical of many societies, is added, which considered the male as the only holder of property.

Conclusions

The inheritance rules of the "maso chiuso" and "regola" show that the Italian legal system has already known rules which are different from those of the state. On the whole, people do not realize that – as D. J. Anton said – "uniformity is death", while "diversity is life".[7] How many different systems of managing property can we discover studying other systems of laws, as customary laws? Through the comparison among different systems of managing property, we can find some similarities which concern the Italian minorities and the minority of immigrants.

Since rules are created to respond to a concrete need, we have to see if this concrete need is not in contrast with the principles of the legal system where this norm is to be applied. For instance, the Italian constitution recognizes the value of solidarity which is surely a basic value of a lot of systems for managing property within the family, such as renouncing inheritance, or maso chiuso, and Regola, for the interest of the protection of the family.

Minorities have characteristics which distinguish them from the majority. I think that the legal order has the duty to observe these differences, value, analyse and respect them to the extent that they are compatible with the founding

7 D. J. Anton also observes: "diversity is the main resource of life, diversity provides flexibility," and "the future of living systems is a result of multiple current options".

principles of the legal system. That implies seeing if it is possible to find accommodating solutions for their diversities, being well aware that diversity is richness. In the case of the Indian communities, the Italian legal system does not demand that Indian immigrants, who feel the compulsory nature of the rule of the surrender the inheritance, automatically apply Italian law. Rather, it has to verify if the woman wants to effectively renounce the inheritance in favour of her brother (or brothers). If it appears that this will is real and not coerced, the Italian legal system would have to allow Indian women to renounce to their share of inheritance. Indeed, Article 519 of the Italian civil code concerns the "statement of the renunciation of inheritance" which is admitted also in the Italian legal system, as long as it has been made according to the rules provided by the code itself.

The need to accommodate diversity on juridical grounds, moreover, derives from the fact that every issue which concerns human interests is based on the concept of diversity. The discoveries of biology – and above all that of the structure of the human DNA thanks to James Watson and Francis Crick in the 1950s – as applied to anthropology show that "human diversity is much more than skin deep and much variation exists between people and populations in blood types, enzymes, disease susceptibility, and other biochemical and genetic traits" (Anemone 2011). Likewise, the challenge of law is to sustain cultural diversity as an added value following human nature.

Bibliography

Agarwal, B. (1995) "Gender and Legal Rights in Agricultural Land in India", *Economic and Political Weekly*, 30(12): A 39–A 56.

Agrawal, K. B. (2010) *Family Law in India*, Alphen aan den Rijn (the Netherlands): Kluwer Law International.

Anderson, L. M. (2004) "Women in Hindu Traditions", in L. M. Anderson and P. Dickey Young (eds.), *Women and Religious Traditions*, Toronto: Oxford University Press, 1–42.

Anemone, R. L. (2011) *Race and Human Diversity: A Biocultural Approach*, London and New York: Routledge.

Angelo, M. (1997) *The Sikh Diaspora: Tradition and Change in an Immigrant Community*, New York and London: Garland Publishing.

Anton, D. J. (1995) *Diversity, Globalization and the Ways of Nature*, Ottawa: International Development Research Center.

Barba, V. (2011) "La successione nel maso chiuso", in G. Petrelli (ed.), *Formulario notarile commentato*, edited by Giovanni Bonolini, Volume Settimo, Tomo Primo. *Successioni e donazioni. Le successioni per causa di morte*, Milano: Giuffré, 1746–1815.

Bauman, Z. (2006) *Liquid Fear*, Cambridge: Polity Press.

Bertolani, B., Ferraris, F. and Perocco, F. (2011) "Mirror Games: A Fresco of Sikh Settlements among Italian Local Societies", in K. A. Jacobsen and K. Myrvold (eds.), *Sikhs in Europe: Migration, Identities and Representations*, Farnham and Burlington, VT: Ashgate, 133–162.

Casanova Fuga, F. (1997) *Il dialetto ladino a Costalta di Comelico*, Costalta di Cadore (Belluno): Edizioni del "Gruppo Musicale di Costalta".

Chase, O. G. (2009) *Gestire i conflitti. Diritto, cultura, rituale*, Roma-Bari: Laterza.

Consorti, P. (2013) *Conflitti, mediazione e diritto interculturale*, Pisa: Pisa University Press.

Dal Mas, F. (2015) "La Regola di Casamazzagno ha torto. La Cassazione chiude una vertenza lunga 15 anni in particolare contro la discriminazione femminile", http://corrierealpi.gelocal.it/belluno/cronaca/2015/07/08.

Das, P. K. (2007) *Universal's Handbook on Hindu Succession: Property Rights of Women and Daughters*, New Delhi: Universal Law Publishing.

Fant, F. (2012) "In Comelico. Regole, le donne ammesse alla successione. La Corte d'Appello di Venezia elimina le discriminazioni a favore degli eredi maschi", http://corrieredelveneto.corriere.it/belluno/notizie/cronaca/2012/4-ottobre-2012.

Francavilla, D. (2008) "Il diritto indù", in S. Ferrari (ed.), *Introduzione al diritto comparato delle religioni. Ebraismo, islam e induismo*, Bologna: Il Mulino, 71–72.

Glenn, H. P. (2011) *Tradizioni giuridiche nel mondo. La sostenibilità della differenza*, Bologna: Il Mulino. Italian translation and edition edited by Sergio Ferlito. [Original edition: Glenn, H. P. (2010) *Legal Traditions of the World: Sustainable Diversity in Law*, fourth edition, Oxford: Oxford University Press.]

Grewal, J. S. (1998) *The New Cambridge History of India*, II.3: *The Sikhs of the Punjab*, revised edition, Cambridge: Cambridge University Press.

Grossi, P. (2006) *Società, Diritto, Stato. Un recupero per il diritto*, Milano: Giuffré.

Gruber, L. (2012) *Eredità. Una storia della mia famiglia tra l'Impero e il fascismo*, Milano: Rizzoli.

Herklotz, T. (2015) "Religion-Based Personal Laws in India from a Women'sRights Perspective: Context and Some Recent Publications", http://dann.rewi.hu-berlin.de/doc/Herklotz_Personal_laws_Suedasienchronik.pdf, 1–30.

Howard, V. R. and Sherma, R. D. (eds.) (forthcoming) *Dharma: The Hindu, Buddhist, Jain and Sikh Traditions of India*, London: I.B.Tauris.

Jamison, S. W. (1996) *Sacrificed Wife/Sacrificer's Wife: Women, Ritual and Hospitality in Ancient India*, New York: Oxford University Press.

Lapi, C. (2015) "The Role of Law within Religiously Divided Societies: A Conflict Creator or a Conflict Solver?", in M. Mollica (ed.), *Bridging Religiously Divided Societies in the Contemporary World*, Pisa: Pisa University Press, 175–187.

Lattanzi, G. (2013) "La tutela dei diritti delle minoranze in Italia", www.cortecostituzionale.it/documenti/relazioni_internazionali/RI_20130606_LATTANZI.pdf., 1–17.

Menski, W. (1989) "Diritto dell'India", in *Enciclopedia giuridica*, 11, Roma: Istituto della Enciclopedia Italiana, 16–18.

Menski, W. (2006) *Comparative Law in a Global Context: The Legal System of Asia and Africa*, second edition, Cambridge: Cambridge University Press.

Mezey, N. (2001) "Law as Culture", *Yale Journal of Law & the Humanities*, 13(35): 35–67.

Mori, E. and Hintner, W. (2013) *Il maso chiuso. La sua storia e la normativa vigente*, Bolzano: Fondazione UPAD (Università Popolare delle Alpi Dolomitiche).

Omizzolo, M. (2013) "Le migrazioni tra terra, capitale e lavoro nell'epoca della globalizzazione. Migranti, caporalato e sfruttamento in provincia di Latina, Caserta, Nardò e Rosarno", *La Rivista di servizio sociale. Studi di scienze sociali applicate e di pianificazione sociale*, 4: 60–79.

Omizzolo, M. (2015) "Il movimento bracciantile in Italia e il caso dei braccianti indiani in provincia di Latina dopati per lavorare come schiavi", in M. Omizzolo and P. Sodano (eds.), *Migranti e territori. Lavoro, diritti, accoglienza*, Roma:Ediesse, 60–80.

Parolari, P. (2016) *Culture, diritto, diritti. Diversità culturali e diritti fondamentali negli stati costituzionali di diritto*, Torino: Giappichelli.

Ramu, G. N. (2006) *Brothers and Sisters in India: A Study of Urban Adult Siblings*, Toronto: University of Toronto Press.

Ricca, M. (2002) *Diritto e religione. Per una pistemica giuridica*, Padova: Cedam.

Ruggenini, M. (2007) "La verità in questione. Identità, differenze, conflitti", in L. Ruggiu and F. Mora (eds.), *Identità, differenze, conflitti*, Milano: Mimesis, 23–48.

Ruggiu, L. (2007) "Introduzione", in L. Ruggiu and F. Mora (eds.), *Identità, differenze, conflitti*, Milano: Mimesis, 9–20.

Ruggiu, L. (2013) *Il giudice antropologo. Costituzione e tecniche di composizione dei conflitti multiculturali*, Milano: Franco Angeli.

Saxena, P. P. (2008) "Succession Laws and Gender Justice", in A. Parashar and A. Dhanda (eds.), *Redifining Family Law in India: Essays in Honour of B. Sivaramayya*, New Delhi: Routledge.

Sharma, R. K. (2004) *Indian Society: Institutions and Changes*, New Delhi: Atlantic Publishers and Distributors.

Sinha, R. (1993) *Dynamics of Chance in the Modern Hindu Family*, New Delhi: Concept Publishing Company.

Trebeschi, A. (2008) "Atteggiamenti da evitarsi nell'amministrazione di una Regola. Scuola di diritto regoliero", www.regole.it/DocAppr/atteggiamenti.pdf., 1–11.

Part IV

Resolving conflict

11 Multiculturalist conflicts and intercultural law

Pierluigi Consorti

Introduction

In this chapter, I move from a standpoint arguing that multicultural and pluralist societies produce social conflicts because diversities seem to be unavoidable contradictions. When faced with conflicts, we almost instinctively go on the defensive; we tend to avoid conflicts rather than deal with them. The law is ontologically a social structure conceived as a set of practices to prevent conflicts. It prescribes several judicial models to manage conflicts deciding who is right and who is wrong in accordance with its prescriptions. In this way, the law has become, over time, almost a self-referential institution, which appears self-sufficient and often even distant from the mechanisms that work in everyday life. Since the law is prevalently an instrument of power, conflicts arising from and feeding off the coexistence of plural societies often appear impervious to legal dynamics.

As a preliminary statement, I assume that the law is a social and cultural phenomenon that involves different kinds of rules and not only the State law (Prakash 2005). The coexistence of plural diversities in the same multicultural public space is undoubtedly an opportunity, but it is also a very problematic issue. The "Huntington prophecy" (Huntington 1996) is always around the corner: social and legal pluralism appears as a turned-off fuse.

To rescue themselves from this danger scholars and politicians have proposed multiculturalist solutions. It is now a fact that the ideology of multiculturalism has generated more negative effects than positive ones creating social fragmentation, minority separateness and cultural relativism in the public sphere (Caravantes 2010; Lennon 2016). We are therefore at a crossroads. As Patrick Glenn stated, the public discourse on social relations "consist(s) of a dichotomy between separation and isolation on the one hand and a form of social absorption or integration on the other" (Glenn, 2006, p. 222). That is the consequence of a typical multiculturalist approach. In this frame, the law is more a reason for a conflict than a tool for conflict management (Lapi 2015a).

In the first part of this chapter I will focus on a theoretical approach to conflict and social conflict management. As separation is supposed to be the result of a multiculturalist legal approach to multicultural diversity, I argue that there is a difference between the multiculturalist and the interculturalist approach.

Then I will focus on intercultural law. I will define it as an initial research path, which is functional to the construction of a legal lexicon, helping in structuring political dialogue in cosmopolitan and/or multicultural democracies. Furthermore, intercultural law will be described as a practical tool to manage social multicultural conflicts.

Conflict and social conflict management

It is not necessary to demonstrate that cultural, ethical, religious and legal pluralism point out elements of diversity that frequently conflict when next to each other. The question is how to face those multicultural conflicts since multiculturalist recipes failed. I think that the first step is to consolidate the shift of paradigm by which conflict, that was once considered (almost exclusively) as an evil to foil, could now be looked at as an opportunity. I am not so ambitious to attempt to define the concept "*conflict.*" That is a "titanic" challenge engaged in throughout the social sciences where experts have espoused a range of differently nuanced positions. The idea of conflict expressed by different scholars should be viewed in connection with their original context, but this type of excursus goes beyond the scope of this chapter that, more modestly, aims at providing a descriptive interpretation of social conflict, which increasingly reveals itself as the motor of social and political evolution (Tilly and Tarrow 2007).

I adopt a pragmatic point of view related to Peace Studies, based on the work of Johan Galtung (Galtung 1972 and 2004). I assume that the common root to every conflict is the *contradiction*. Then, since it is impossible to prevent contradictions, I argue that conflict prevention is not a rational goal. Nevertheless, we can change paradigm remaining in the frame of *preventing violence*, as this is possible if we manage conflicts approaching them in a very complex and holistic way (Patfoort 2004). To better understand this point I give the metaphoric image of conflict as an iceberg. The ice that everyone sees is only the final and most noticeable part of an enormous predominant mass submerged under the water surface. Acting on the surfaced portion of the iceberg does not make sense if we are not aware of what is "below it." Analyzing conflict means looking below the surface (Miall 2004). This frogman's work highlights the extent of the progressive development of the ethnic, cultural or religious conflicts within society largely centered on issues of identity.

New borders run across the states, which no longer represent homogeneous social identities, but reflect cultural, religious and ethical pluralism. Cultural boundaries replace State borders (Lapi 2015b), so we have to face a new dimension of social conflict, characterized by several demands for identity recognition. "Be yourself" is the call in environmental battles and in gender as well as LGBT rights movements: the rights of a single group or of a local community often seem in opposition to "everybody's rights." Some scholars have hypothesized the ontological impossibility of reconciling conflicts marked by a "conflict of values" (Angstrom 2001). Since the basis of individual and collective identity consists of values, which are seen as untouchable and non-negotiable, these "conflicts of values" appear unsolvable. Nevertheless, a more careful investigation of the iceberg would permit us to detect the area of conflict that often does not surface. Interests, needs, feelings, passions will emerge as fundaments for the claim of rights that groups are entitled to in order to maintain their identity and have access to the decision-making power that other groups enjoy (Miall, 2007). In other words, it is not so much the existence of absolute identity values that is at stake here, but rather the recognition of rights and the satisfaction of interests that can be reached managing conflicts by nonviolent approaches.

Cultural and legal shock

We can now draw attention to the cultural dimension of conflict. Identity takes on a specific role in conflict between parties, as it is characterized by differences that seemingly cause conflicts. This setting would lead to the assumption that the parties in conflict are inevitably opposed and definitely destined to clash. As stated above, the greatest reason for conflict itself, lies in the *contradiction*, that depends on the will of the parties in conflict.

As first forewarning, we shall acknowledge the existence of plural presences, better understood through the method that anthropologists have called "decentralization." This consists in becoming aware of one's own reference values, customs and behaviors and sharing these perspectives with the values, customs and rules which define others' identity. This process has been described as cultural shock: a reaction of displacement or anxiety which seizes "those who are involved with strangers either by chance or for professional reasons, outside their socio-cultural context" (Tilly and Tarrow 2007). The expression "cultural shock" underscores the lack of both communication and understanding, which leads to the risk of a conflict. This occurs if one reacts to certain behaviors without realizing the underlying values producing them, which may be considered scandalous or even alarming because perceived as too far removed from one's "guiding principles."

Two examples may be helpful. A Canadian social worker could not understand why a large North African family had reserved a special room of their small house as "the prayer room," even making it off limits to the children. The Western employee's value system was such that she could not fathom sacrificing the children's well-being for reasons she deemed trifling. In her opinion, the Muslim family was an authoritarian institution, more interested in meeting religious requirements than ensuring the children's welfare (Cohen-Emerique 1984). This way of thinking did not take into account the North African family's perception of space, or the fact that they did not feel crowded in their house. They really valued the symbolic-religious dimension, instead. The family's choice of reserving a space for prayer was not as such a sacrifice, as the social worker perceived it. Furthermore, there were no mosques in their city and so the room took on a public role, unimaginable to a Western observer who does not try to "decentralize" himself.

Another "cultural incident" refers to food taboos and the different importance assigned to them in various cultural settings. The director of a dormitory for immigrants, prevalently populated by young Arab-Muslims, accepted a young

Portuguese man suffering from alcoholism. The Portuguese man kept alcoholic beverage and pork in the community refrigerator, causing conflict with the North Africans, who found this behavior unacceptable.

The instances recounted above describe situations that may not necessarily be conflictual. Cultural shock can resemble a misunderstanding or the need to deepen understanding. However, when there is a conflictual situation, it is normal to refer to a system of rules that can solve it. At this point, the law comes, inevitably, into play. When the parties either share the same legal system as citizens of the same State, or are members of the same religious confession or belong to the same ethnic group, the legal parameter of reference is easier to recognize. Things can get really complicated when the conflicting parties refer to different legal systems, or expect recognition for behaviors acceptable in their own culture but forbidden by the law in the of country residence. For example, the problem can occur in the case of a Muslim husband who expects to educate his daughter in accordance to his faith while his wife – the girl's mother – does not agree; or a man who wants to marry while being still married to his first wife. In both cases, State law offers solutions that can define the legal terms of the issue. In the first example, the judge would order the parents to find an agreement in the interest of the minor, whereas in the second case, no civil registrar would celebrate the wedding. Nevertheless, in both cases, the legal solution, albeit correct, would not have the merit of intervening in the matter of the conflict. In the first situation, the parents will continue to argue each claiming only one religious education; in the second situation, the man can go to Morocco, marry his second wife and return in Europe (Sona 2016).

As we can see, the judicial solution is not effective here because it does not explore the hidden portion of the iceberg. The law, as exemplified above, appears mainly as an institutional phenomenon. The world of rules seems far removed from social life. At the same time, it reveals a degree of adaptability that would allow it to find answers suitable to the demands of multicultural societies. Yet, the law, especially in this field, seems only to be concerned with expressing its power.

Having to be "equal for everyone" – and having to differentiate between formal and substantial equality too – the law is usually incapable of safeguarding diversity and, sometimes, it even creates legal monstrosities, for example when legal subjectivity subdivides "citizens" from "foreigners," and the latter in "EU citizens" and "non-EU citizens." These legal qualifications assume a big power to differ in the extent of the protection granted first to human beings, and not to citizens only. The degree of tutelage is gradually reduced to the level of having no rights at all, in the case of "Others," especially if "different," who, in fact, have no rights to claim. So, it happens that "EU foreigners" have the same rights as "EU citizens," while "non-EU foreigners" have rights only if they have a legal residence permit. If the foreigner is an "illegal immigrant" he simply does not "exist." These kinds of legal edifices contribute to the construction of barriers, which prevent or simply hinder encounters among people. From a legal perspective, we cannot avoid wondering: "what about *human* rights?"

That is what I define as a "legal shock": Rules, concepts, meanings that once appeared clear and unequivocal, lose their value when placed in a plural and multicultural society, peopled by men and women who have trouble finding their common traits, thus preferring to relate to each other using the conflictual term "we" in opposition to "you." In this way, the perception of "the other" as something (and not *someone*) different, far, strange, unknown and therefore dangerous, is strengthened (Ricca 2013, pp. 10 ff.). State law is therefore called upon to assure rights and duties. The guarantee of an orderly and safe coexistence depends firstly on the imposition of State law, before any exploration of shared and consensual solution among the parties in conflict. However, State law does not just happen. It is the result of political choices and partly derives from long past legal *habits*, which are resistant to innovations entailed in social evolution. In the course of time, the repetition of reinforced patterns is no longer suitable for the needs of present day society; it rather exhibits a kind of resistance on the part of the legal system to reach the heart of the mechanisms occurring inside multicultural societies. Persisting globalization coupled with present day migrations has changed our frame of reference. For instance, we can notice that the connection to the territory tends to become increasingly less significant, even if the difference between those imposing globalization and those suffering from it is notable.

In legal terms, these plural presences, which are difficult to pinpoint, pose the problem of recovering a balance between individuals and community. Cultural affiliation is increasingly becoming the hallmark of personal identity in demand of recognition rights, particularly those of minorities. Legal shock prevents the effective application of the law in cultural conflicts because jurists lack the necessary tools to investigate the submerged part of the iceberg. They see the tip of it; looking at the conflict in act, probably they have abstract and general rules to apply. Yet, the conflict remains.

Law and identity

Legal shock is overloaded by cultural issues, produced by the difficulty to face with the supposed vagueness of concepts such as "culture" and "identity" (Cotterell 2013). Multiculturalism contributed to reify and separate cultures and identities also through law, while anthropologists have reached the conclusion that there is no such thing as "cultural identity." More specifically, the social sciences view the concept of "cultural identity" as highly unstable, as demonstrated by research completed during the last century by American socio-psychologists who were searching for patterns to describe immigrant integration problems. The construction of such identity patterns soon collided with reality, making it impossible to conceive identity as something unchangeable and repeatable independently from its relational context (Mead 1934). This is why the naturalistic metaphor of roots is often abused to represent cultural identity, seen as immanent to individuals, stable and permanently defining them. Changing identity would mean becoming "uprooted."

The idea of a single and unchanging identity causes violence (Sen 2006). Social psychologists have nevertheless noticed the existence of a "social identity" allowing individuals to connect their psychological features to the social environment in which they are immersed (Tajfel and Turner 1986). If cultural identity is basically stable, social identity is in itself plural, as it is characterized by multiple affiliations regarding gender, age, social level, religion, nationality and so on.

Viewing public space, as if it were populated by mushrooms (which have no roots), would be a mistake. Human beings are structurally absorbed in networks of emotional dependence. These roots could be ambiguous and, in any case, even tree branches grow in different directions and never produce fruits or flowers equal to themselves. What is more, a tree cannot choose its neighbors, while, on the contrary, human beings can. Barbara Henry has pointed out the importance of "rewriting the grammar of justice" with the ability to distinguish between "the relationships one would like to defuse or break off and those which are essential, depending on the different priorities alternating in our lives" (Henry 2011, p. 21).

Identities are built through individual processes of inclusion and exclusion, through choices of symbols, beliefs and common values, which are neither innate nor casual. The construction of identity is neither mythical nor illusive, but real and linked to social context. Identity may be, at the same time, the result of self-affirmation (identitarian self-qualification) and external attribution (hetero- or exo-identity (P.J. Simon 1999, p. 49)). The latter is often based on negative factors through which the majority describes the minority.

We must highlight that, in the case of cultural conflicts, the main point is not their solution but rather the ability to manage these conflicts through practices of decentralization, which allow the understanding of each parties' reason. In the case of cultural or religious conflicts, this approach can be misleading and even damaging. Aiming at the *management*, instead of the *solution* of the conflict, would be preferable (Consorti 2013).

I have already pointed out that what is common to all conflicts which is the contradiction between two points of view, which, in a sense, are both true. The point is not to fight against someone who holds a different position, but the ability of bridging points of view, and promoting communication among the parties. In this way, it is possible to find satisfactory solutions for everyone; it is just enough to "bypass the criteria of either being right or wrong to access the criteria of communication" (Cozzo 2004, p. 78).

If conflict can never be erased, it is possible to activate those communicative procedures allowing the exploration of the submerged part of the iceberg, connecting it with the tip. Thus, conflict is transformed in a meeting place, which promotes the dialogue necessary to restore differences within the common horizon of comprehensibility. It is necessary to listen and to identify with the reasons of our counterpart, who is not necessarily the enemy (Goss-Mayr 1996), and with whom it is possible to build a truthful relationship transcending the conflict itself. To achieve this goal we need to fill the ignorance gap separating the two sides by putting ourselves in situations that can generate conflicts so complicated as to suggest that the only way "to win" would be to use violence against our opponents.

The idea of such a "clash of ignorance" was used by Edward Saïd (Saïd 2001) in contrast with that of "clash of civilizations" (Huntington 1996). These conflicts can be managed by a "secular dialogue" (Consorti 2011): a dialogue that Raimon Panikkar has called "dialogal dialogue," "in which the other is *alter* (the other) and not *alius* (an-other), a neighbor and not a stranger," someone who, through dialogue, helps us discover "the *altera pars* (the other side) of ourselves" (Panikkar 2002, p. 72).

Multiculturalist law

I mentioned the legal shock that strikes jurists confronting cultural conflict. The principles and the legal institutions which have made Western civilization great – i.e. the human dignity of each person as basis for the recognition of individual and communitarian human rights and the development of democracy (Urbinati 2008) – appear trapped in social processes and political transformations caused by the multiculturalist approach. The latter reified identities (Benhabib 2002) and stunt to understand the hybridization process that involves all identities.

In this context, the law plays a particularly significant role, which sometimes receives little attention. Apparently, the legislator assumes that the public opinion in multicultural societies views the presence of foreigners as dangerous and is particularly obsessed with the threat of multiracialism. The "Others" almost lose their human form, since they are perceived as outposts of dangerous cultural infiltrations, aimed at disrupting the very society that has received them. They are in fact expected either to remain as guests or to become integrated, which means acquiring the customs and the mentality common to the majority's presumed cultural identity. In other words, the fact that others no longer remain within the boundaries of "their home" but move "to our home," greatly concerns those who, as part of the majority, see the founding principles of their cultural and religious identity as being at risk.

It is not necessary to recall how multiculturalist scholars developed this issue. Their theses are not a whole without *nuances* (Dusche 2004). Nevertheless, we can find a common key that connects all multiculturalists: they stand for the right to diversity, under the limit of the law. That is not new. Imagining the law as a prescriptive limit is a very classical perception. Furthermore, their theses grow from a common ground: cultural identities are fixed in a well-defined cultural and geographic space. They want to protect cultural diversities, but to achieve this goal they face culture as unchangeable. Multiculturalist theses have built several "aviaries" where each cultural group has to live. If everybody remains in his/her own "birdcage," the society will be safe and able to prevent social conflicts. Those who want to fly out must accept the conditions decided by the State: that is the first multiculturalist dilemma, accepting diversity on condition. Over all they have to accept to be integrated: that is the second multiculturalist dilemma, overcoming separation by a compulsory change of identity. It means accepting diversity without contradictions in order to prevent conflicts. That is impossible.

As a result, multicultural coexistence is perceived as a problematic issue, especially in terms of social safety. Although a "reasonable accommodation" schema sometimes approaches this issue, the multiculturalist integration model prevails. That is a problem: it remains in the frame "we-you." Nevertheless, European states follow this path. The idea underlying the process of integration is "not just (or, no longer) the voluntary progression leading to rootedness in the hosting territory, but is strictly a legal obligation" (Biondi Dal Monte and Vrenna 2013, p. 254). The rejection of relations that may trigger cultural change or hybridization processes is justified, although paradoxically, through rhetoric and practices that purport to "protect" and enhance the "value of diversity" of different cultures, by the above-mentioned "bird-cages." The risk here is retracing the path of "old fashioned" biological racism, which – notwithstanding its scientific inconsistency – has produced contagious outcomes (Balibar and Wallerstein 1988).

The intercultural law: culture and interculture

I argue that it is possible to follow an alternative model, that some Italian scholars define as "intercultural law" (Ricca 2008a, b; Consorti 2013; Fuccillo 2014). When speaking of intercultural law, I have frequently been asked a simple as well devastating question: "What has interculture to do with the law?". If my interlocutors are jurists, they suppose that they are able to define "the law," but, at the same time, they do not feel comfortable with interculture, although the latter is a very used (probably, sometimes misunderstood and abused) word.

To be honest, defining "the law" is not a simple task. A jurist, however, presumes to know what the law is (Hart 1994). Actually, I do not want to highlight this point; nonetheless I guess that it is something really not yet well defined, especially when related to religious and cultural issues. I agree with Glenn that "state law, as fact, is normatively dumb, autistic, incapable of dialogue or exchange with other forms of normativity. Its separation from them would be insurmountable" (Glenn 2006, p. 226). However, to better understand how the law intertwines with cultural diversities, we need first to define "cultural diversity" as well as "culture."

To identify culture we can use several definitions. I choose the classical one given from Edward Tylor. In 1871, he stated that "culture, or civilization, taken in its broad, ethnographic sense, is that complex whole which includes knowledge, belief, art, morals, law, custom, and any other capabilities and habits acquired by man as a member of society" (Tylor 1871, p. 1). In this definition we can find three seeds that sprout in the future. The first is the similitude between "culture" and "civilization." The second is the special broad ethnographic (and not general) point of view adopted by Tylor. The third is the attention given to the "complex whole" composed by different elements that are unified by one's social membership ("as a member of society") and then the openness list ("and any other capabilities and habits acquired …").

Denys Cuche has already well described the evolution and the actual significance of culture in social sciences (Cuche 2010). On the basis of his work, it is enough to underline for our purposes only how the notion of culture adopted during the last century points to the new question about identity, moving from the original religious diversity – adopted for example by Tylor – to the actual cultural diversity.

As I cannot fully address these issues here, I will instead surf on their waves coming back to my initial conclusion; it is appropriate to indicate "interculturalism" as an alternative to "multiculturalism." In real terms, this standpoint has been reached by Ted Cantle (Cantle 2014; Girishkumar 2015), especially in a European perspective (Barrett 2015), that is quite different from the North American one (Bouchard 2012), or the Latin American one (Heise, Tubino and Ram Del Pozo 1992).

Since European literature uses English as a hub language, let me spend a few words to distinguish interculturalism from cross-culture, an expression more frequently used in the Anglo-Saxon social scientific literature (Loth 2006). Big conceptual differences probably do not exist between "interculture" and "cross-culture": both denote their distance from "multiculturalism," and from this point of view they could be interchangeable. But since EU English-written documents always use the word "interculture" as well as it is used in other languages, such as Italian, French, Spanish, German, I assume the prefix *inter* is quite different from *cross*. *Cross* means "go through": if you stab someone, your dagger crosses his or her body. *Inter* means connect. It creates relations, as a bridge that links the banks of a river. Therefore, interculture shows better than cross-culture a relational approach and gives the idea of bridging – and not only crossing – that characterizes intercultural studies.

In this wider context, interculture is itself a work in progress, open to contributions from several disciplines, which, despite diversities and specific characteristics, can share the construction of dynamic relationships based on dialogue and on the encounter with others. Thus, interculture has a value-driven nature marked by more or less explicit connections to other spheres, such as peace education, non-violence and anti-racism. Interculture embraces a more general cognitive displacement inherent to the encounter with diversity. As a result, although we must admit that there is no unambiguous definition of interculture, I suggest using this expression to designate *a relational approach that implies a kind of dialogical method as its main feature.*

I am aware that such a general definition may mean something to the social sciences, but in legal terms it appears too vague, making it appropriate to ask ourselves what relation may there be between law and interculture. The fact is that the former appears fairly defined, while the latter seems to hide behind a sort of *burqa*, concealing interculture. The viewpoint adopted by jurists complicates the matter, as we undertake the agonizing search for typifying definitions, possibly prescriptive on the one hand, while on the other, focusing on legal acts and papers that simply do not contain any useful reference concerning this matter. Sometimes we find references to "intercultural dialogue": this can be useful in political and institutional terms, but seemingly distant from the routinely legal practice.

The possibilities of intercultural law

To explore the legal implications of cultural diversity, the Association of Legal Philosophy organized in June 2006 a conference entitled "The possibility of Intercultural Law." The matters were faced in a very theoretical way, the conclusion was that intercultural law "is not a recent invention but part of (most) legal traditions, also within contemporary Western societies" (Drosterij, Hildebrandt and Huppes-Cluysenaer 2006, p. 220). The balance between a practical and an epistemological approach was discussed, without giving a definitive answer (Drosterij 2006). Dieter Höffe focused on criminal law and gave an important contribution straddling the two axes (Höffe 2008). However, I agree with Mario Ricca who designates intercultural law as an initial research path, which is functional to "the construction of a legal lexicon, helpful in structuring political dialogue in cosmopolitan and/or multicultural democracies" (Ricca 2008). That is to say that the law can also be a tool to manage multicultural conflict in an interculturalist and not a multiculturalist way. In the 2006 conference, Patrick Glenn stated that "the concept of intercultural law" is "a 'possibility' and nothing more" because of three obstacles: the concept of culture in itself, its "unquestionably western character" and "the question of the role of the national legal system as an instrument of separation" (Glenn 2006, pp. 231–234). Nevertheless, he admitted that within states several forms of application of non-State law already exist, such as the so-called "Islamic Courts" in the United Kingdom – that play an active role in personal and family law disputes, although not formally recognized by civil authority – and the arbitration of family law matters provided in Ontario by the 1991 Arbitration Act (Glenn 2006, p. 238), although revised in 2006.

In my opinion, if State law does not resist the interferences developed by non-State law, there could be considerable scope to manage these multiculturalist conflicts using intercultural law, since the law is a social and cultural phenomenon. This would mean that using the existing law with the help of intercultural resources. This work should be developed both in a theoretical and practical level.

On a first level, experts of law have to deepen the potential intersections with other disciplines, especially with psychology and anthropology. They will help us better understand how to manage cultural diversity (Bruner 1979), by considering that actually cultural diversity is a European value (Arts and Hagenaars 2003), though its significance according to European law is not yet completely clear (Bellucci 2016). Anthropologists can provide important suggestions, for instance towards building an inclusive legal definition of citizenship (Pinxten 2006). In this way, future interculturalist lawyers would be able to bridge diversities suggesting "legal path" that will support both other scientists in their intercultural research and politicians (that are ultimately the law makers) in changing their current multiculturalist approach.

Within this frame, intercultural law should sustain the European Union's cosmo-political democracy in order to enrich the internal democratic dimension of single states, which are intersected by inner communitarian boundaries. With the loss of the nineteenth-century representation of a sole national conscience, the rule of law is forced to choose between "broadening inclusion and renewing closure" (Habermas 1998, p. 143). Intercultural law can foster in this way the institutional dynamic proposed for example by the Council of Europe in 2008 (Council of Europe, 2008) – run through annual meetings concerning the religious dimension of intercultural dialogue (Bellati Ceccoli 2014) – as well as by the procedures indicated by the art. 17 TFEU. The latter states that the EU shall maintain an open, transparent and regular dialogue with churches, religious associations, communities as well as philosophical and non-confessional organizations, hence with the institutional representative of cultural (and religious) diversities. Thus, it seems that there is an already defined choice: removing the multiculturalist direction of closure to be oriented towards interculturalism. That in itself suggests an inclusive broadening of democratic forms of participation extending the rights of citizenship even to rhetoric and self-narration. Encounter and dialogue are the best tools against fundamentalism and prejudices. Hence, the law is set in the framework of contemporary institutional experience, which, by overcoming multiculturalist difficulties, offers conflict management procedures, which are based, above all, on the profound understanding of differences.

From this point of view, cosmopolitanism and interculture are the two sides of the same political-institutional-coin. While the former is carried out in legal contexts (which are constitutional in nature) the latter focuses more on the legal cores of practical day-to-day life.

This consideration introduces the second, more practical, frame. In anthropological terms, we can say that intercultural law relies on the decentralization process: understanding differences leads to self-understanding, helps to analyze conflictual drives and transforms them into positive energy, eliminating the recourse to violence. The mere fact that intercultural law is set within the path of transformative mediation is, in itself, a positive result. Since intercultural law is concerned with the legal relationships that are marked by identitarian differences, its purpose is to place these differences in narrative correlation, thus ensuring the protection of rights connected with identitarian assertions, within the precincts of State law. In order to come to terms with such a predicament, it is essential to achieve first-rate knowledge of "other" cultural expressions but, above all, excellent legal knowledge is indispensable. Knowledge of "other" cultures or "other" religions is very useful, as long as this is not limited to folklore (i.e. the obvious traits) and includes the silent features as well.

If we settle for a mere linguistic translation of specific different laws, confusion may occur. For instance, we can look at the form of contracts. For a Western jurist it is clear that contractual freedom must harmonize with the principle of contractual justice: *bona fide* and *equity* integrate (and correct) the contract with which the judge can modify an agreement between parties. On the other hand, according to Asian values, *bona fide* and *equity* develop through different cultural canons, overturning their interpretation. In the frame of globalized *lex mercatoria, Gross Disparity* and *Hardship* are the result of this cultural exchange, as accepted within the Unidroit principles (Galgano 2006). This is enough for the traditional jurist, who finds in a code what he is looking for. Nevertheless, for the intercultural jurist this is only the first step, as he needs to understand how these cultural diversities affect the willingness to negotiate, referring them to "our" conceptual categories.

The intercultural jurist will need to go further to provide cultural translations, which will enable parties to "really" understand each other, beyond form. His contribution will have to act like the bridge connecting the shores of a river, allowing inhabitants of both sides to meet. The need to find corresponding meanings moves the parties to the bridge, which, at last, facilitates the dialogue between them. Unlike the interpreter, who allows speakers of different languages to communicate, the intercultural jurist is the meeting point. He creates the third space in which parties can directly manage a legal dialogue. Since the intercultural jurist is aware of the underlying conflicting dimensions, he acts while considering relational transformations.

Intercultural law and the narrative approach

Intercultural translations transfer not only words but concepts as well, which also take on meaning from the wider context in which they are set. Removed from its original environment, the same word acquires different meanings. Nevertheless, the intercultural perspective is enriched by the above-mentioned narrative approach, which enhances the relational factor, "de-essentialising the need to speak the same language" (van Brakel 2006). As highlighted by Jerome S. Bruner, self-narrations express, in a simple manner, the "mutual interdependence" among emotions, cultural traditions and social life (Bruner 1992, p. 45). In particular, self-narratives such as autobiographies, are structured according to established "identity indicators" (Bruner 1997), which simultaneously appear as literary stories, combining elements of truth with falsehood. Every story is thus true and false at the same time. More precisely, self-narratives are a kind of personal re-interpretation of one's identity, set in a wider context, which the narrator can recreate through the dialogue with the listener. Bruner reaches the conclusion that "narrative talent characterizes humanity in the same way the standing position or the opposable thumb do" (Bruner 2002, p. 97). If narrating is an inescapable necessity for human beings who need to establish their role in the world, as well as their identity and alterity, the intercultural jurist will certainly be able to lend his creative contribution to the conflict management in multicultural societies by learning the art of listening and the ability to transform conflict.

Here is an example, which will allow us to reconnect to the main theme. The term "marriage" activates specific cultural indicators common to the Christian matrix. It is a legal act initiating a legal relationship producing a number of patrimonial, as well as subjective consequences. On this matter, law and culture are significantly beginning to undergo variance, as well as reconciliation. "De facto couples" or "homosexual couples" are examples, which some legal systems equate to traditional marriage, which remains the reference point. So we use expressions such as Jewish or Islamic or Hindu marriage, even if the adjective here is more important than the substantive, because those relationships are not at all the marriage we suppose, but we can suppose they are a marriage, albeit in "their style."

The intercultural lawyer is aware that there are many marriage significations and he will interpret that relationship according to the couple narration, without prejudicial point of reference. From this starting point, he will be able to correctly transpose that bond into legal framework, legitimizing its legal consequences, as they relate to the State law and eventually to non-State law.

Intercultural law beyond formal law

It is time to dwell on the practical prospects offered by intercultural law. To manage multiculturalist conflicts we have to begin a process of reaching beyond the jurist's traditional tools. Beyond laws and verdicts, contracts and acts, it is necessary learning to grasp the significance of these symbolic legal acts, placing them within the kaleidoscope of multicultural society. We can thus retrace their correct meanings by reconstructing the intercultural lexicon that allows everyone to feel at ease.

This need of comfort and ease is well explained by Mario Ricca (Ricca 2008b, pp. 220ff.), who reminds us of the difficulties confronting the jurist, who has to unravel a circumstance marked by the legal recognition of cultural difference. He focuses his analysis on the importance of understanding signs within the context in which they are carried out: we raise a finger when we want to speak or ask a question during an assembly, call for attention or make a higher bid at an auction. The same physical gesture takes a different meaning depending upon the context, which is in turn subjected to symbolic interpretation. I realize I am at an auction only if I know what it is; if I have never been to one, I may think I am attending a lecture, taking the auctioneer for an art historian. Therefore, the interpretation of context and individual signs depends on our understanding of the situation in which we are immersed. Raising a finger during an auction produces definite legal effects; declaring to have asked for a turn in the discussion will be to no avail. If the auctioneer announces the winner and he is the person who last raised his hand, this person is required to purchase the auctioned item at the set price. Saying "I did not know" will not change the situation, as "everybody knows" that if one raises a finger during an auction, he automatically expresses his wish to purchase that item at the negotiated price.

In this line of reasoning the problem lies in "everybody knows." For well-known reasons, herein taken for granted, the law directs us towards the pretension that "everyone knows," which in some cases lies on common cultural features supporting the argument that "it is impossible not to know that …." Nonetheless, we have seen that in multicultural societies these references are no longer common and homogeneous and the day-to-day life is ruled by several different laws. The intercultural jurist has to bridge all those laws in a practical and lawful unity. Increasing awareness that laws are culturally influenced, hence they change and evolve. For this reason Werner Menski settles for the existence of a Hindu legal code in Great Britain that is different from the Indian code, while at the same time resolves for an English *shariat*, which is different from the traditional one. There is an *angrezi dharma* as well as *angrezi shariat* (Menski, 2003).

The already mentioned "sustainable accommodations," also called "cultural accommodations," are other legal tool borrowed from the social sciences that can support the intercultural law (Consorti 2013, pp. 215 ff.). The proposal made in 2008 by the Archbishop of Canterbury Rowan Williams (Williams 2008) indicates an interesting direction towards an intercultural law. Through these instances, I assume that the laws can also change dialoging in an intercultural way.

Intercultural law will thus support the process of hybridization that cultural diversities are already living within multicultural societies (Vieira 2014).

References

Angstrom, Jan. "The International Dimension of Ethnic Conflict." *Studies in Conflict &Terrorism* 24, no. 1(2001): 59–69.

Arts, Wil, and Jacques Hagenaars. *The Cultural Diversity of European Unity: Findings, Explanations and Reflections from the European Values Study*. Leiden, Boston: Brill, 2003.

Balibar, Etienne, and Immanuel Wallerstein. *Race, Nation, Classe, les identités ambiguës*. Paris: La decouverte, 1988.

Barrett, Martyn, ed. *Interculturalism and Multiculturalism: Similarities and Differences*. Strasbourg Cedex: Council of Europe Publishing, 2015.

Bellati Ceccoli, Guido. "Aspetti giuridici degli 'Incontri annuali del Consiglio d'Europa sulla dimensione religiosa del dialogo interculturale'." *Quaderni di diritto e politica ecclesiastica* 22, no. 2(2014): 563–573.

Bellucci, Lucia. "The Notion of 'Cultural Diversity' in the EU Trade Agreements and Negotiations: New Challenges and Perspectives." *The Italian Law Journal* 2, no. 2 (2016): 433–444.

Benhabib, Seyla. *The Claims of Culture: Equality and Diversity in the Global Era*. Princeton: Princeton University Press, 2002.

Biondi Dal Monte, Francesca, and Massimiliano Vrenna. "L'accordo di integrazione ovvero l'integrazione per legge." In *La governance dell'immigrazione. Diritti, politiche e competenze*, edited by Emanuele Rossi, Francesca Biondi Dal Monte and Massimiliano Vrenna. Bologna: Il Mulino, 2013.

Bouchard, Gérard. *L'Interculturalisme. Une point de vue québécoise*. Montreal: Édition du Boréal, 2012.

Bruner, Jerome S. *On Knowing: Essays for the Left Hand*. Cambridge, MA: Harvard University Press, 1979.

Bruner, Jerome S. *La ricerca del significato*. Torino: Bollati Boringhieri, 1992.

Bruner, Jerome S. "A Narrative Model of Self-construction." In *The Self across Psychology: Self-Recognition, Self-Awareness, and Self-Concept*, edited by J.G. Snodgrass and R.L. Thompson, 145–161. New York: New York Academy of Sciences, 1997.

Bruner, Jerome S. *La fabbrica delle storie. Diritto, letteratura, vita*. Roma-Bari: Laterza, 2002.

Cantle, Ted. "National Identity, Plurality, Interculturalism." *The Political Quarterly* 85, no. 3(2014): 312–319.

Caravantes, Ernesto. *From Melting Pot to Witch's Cauldron: How Multiculturalism Failed America*. Lanham: Hamilton Book, 2010.

Cohen-Emerique, Margalit. "Choc culturel et relations interculturelles dans la pratique des travaileurs sociaux. Formation par la méthode des incidents critiques." *Cahiers de sociologie économique et culturelle (Ethnopsychologie)* 2 (1984): 183–218.

Cohen-Emerique, Margalit. "Le choc culturel, methode de formation et outil de recherche." In *Guide de l'interculturel en formation*, by E.M. Lipiansky, edited by J. Demorgon and E.M. Lipiansky. Paris: Retz, 1999.

Consorti, Pierluigi. "Interreligious Dialogue: A Secular Challenge." *Stato, Chiese e pluralismo confessionale*, 2011: 1–6.

Consorti, Pierluigi. *Conflitti, mediazione e diritto interculturale*. Pisa: Pisa University Press, 2013.

Cotterell, Roger. *Law, Culture and Society: Legal Ideas in the Mirror of Social Theory*. Farnham: Ashgate, 2013.

Council of Europe. White Paper on Intercultural Dialogue: "Living together as equal in dignity". Strasbourg: Council of Europe, 2008.

Cozzo, Andrea. *Conflittualità nonviolenta. Filosofia e pratiche di lotta comunicativa*. Milano: Mimesis, 2004.

Cuche, Denys. *La notion de culture dans les sciences sociales*. IV ed. Paris: La Découverte, 2010.

Dal Lago, Alessandro, and Salvatore Palidda. *Conflict, Security and the Reshaping of Society*. London and New York: Routledge, 2010.

Drosterij, Gerard. "Editorial Afterthoughts: The Liberal-Fundamentalist Cookbook." *Netherlands Journal of Legal Philosophy* 35, no. 3(2006): 361–366.

Drosterij, Gerard, Mirelle Hildebrandt, and Liesebeth Huppes-Cluysenaer. "Introduction: The Possibility of Intercultural Law." *Nederlands Tijdschrift voor Rechtsfilosofie en Rechtstheorie* 35, no. 3(2006): 215–221.

Dusche, Michael. "Radical Multiculturalism versus Liberal Pluralism." *Ethical Perspectives* 11, no. 4(2004): 238–249.

Fuccillo, Antonio, ed. *Esercizi di laicità interculturale e pluralismo religioso*. Torino: Giappichelli, 2014.

Galgano, Francesco. *La globalizzazione nello specchio del diritto*. Bologna: Il Mulino, 2006.

Galtung, Johan. "Theories of Conflict. Definitions, Dimensions, Negation, Formation." *Transcend International*. 1972. https://www.transcend.org/files/Galtung_Book_Theories_Of_Conflict_single.pdf (accessed December 20, 2016).

Galtung, Johan. *Transcend and Transform: An Introduction to Conflict Work*. London: Pluto, 2004.

Girishkumar, Divya. "Multiculturalism or Interculturalism?" *Journal of Intercultural Studies* 36, no. 6(2015): 729–735.

Glenn, H. Patrick. "Legal Traditions and the Separation Thesis." *Netherlands Journal of Legal Philosophy* 35, no. 3(2006): 222–240.

Goss-Mayr, Hildegard. *Wie Feinde Freunde werden. Mein Leben mit Jean Goss für Gewaltlosigkeit, Gerechtigkeit und Versöhnung*. Freiburg: Herder, 1996.

Habermas, Jurgen. *L'inclusione dell'altro. Studi di teoria politica*. Milano: Feltrinelli, 1998.

Hart, H.L.A. *The Concept of Law*. Oxford: Clarendon Press, 1994.

Heise, Maria, Fidel Tubino, and O. Odin Ram Del Pozo. *El desafío de la interculturalidad*. Lima: Centro Amazónico de Antropología y Aplicación Práctica, 1992.

Henry, Barbara. "Coesistenza interculturale e mediazione dei conflitti identitari." In *Esperimenti interculturali. Prove d'autore*, edited by Serena Gianfaldoni, 13–22. Pisa: Plus, 2011.

Höffe, Otfried. *Derecho Intercultural*. Barcellona: Gedisa, 2008.

Huntington, Samuel. *The Clash of Civilizations and the Remaking of World Order*. New York: Simon & Schuster, 1996.

Lapi, Chiara. "The Role of Law within Religiously Divided Societies: A Conflict Creator or a Conflict Solver?" In *Bridging Religiously Divided Societies in the Contemporary World*, edited by Marcello Mollica, 175–187. Pisa: Pisa University Press, 2015a.

Lapi, Chiara. "Europe: From National-State Borders to Cultural and Religious Identitaries Borders." *Scienza e pace* (June 2015b): 1–15.

Lennon, Simon. *The Failure of Multiculturalism*. Pine Hill Books, 2016.

Loth, Marc. "Crosscultural Communication in Language and Law: Reply to van Brakel." *Netherlands Journal of Legal Philosophy* 35, no. 3(2006): 285–294.

Mead, George. *Mind, Self and Society*. Edited by Charles W. Morris. Chicago: University of Chicago Press, 1934.

Menski, Werner F. *Ethnic Minorities in English Law*. London: Trentham Books, 2000.

Menski, Werner F. *Hindu Law: Beyond Tradition and Modernity*. New Delhi: Oxford University Press, 2003.

Miall, Hughes. "Conflict Transformation: A multidimensional Task." In *Transforming Ethnopolitical Conflict: The Berghof Handbook*, edited by Alex Austin, MartinaFischer and Norbert Ropers, 67–90. Wiesbaden: Springer Fachmedien, 2004.

Miall, Hughes. *Emergent Conflict and Peaceful Change*. Basingstoke: Palgrave Macmillan, 2007.

Panikkar, Raimon. *Pace e interculturalità. Una riflessione filosofica*. Milano: Jaca Book, 2002.

Patfoort, Pat. *Sé defendre sans attaquer. La puissance de la nonviolence*. Mechelen: Jeugd & Vrede, 2004.

Pinxten, Rik. "Separation, Integration and Citizenship." *Netherlands Journal of Legal Philosophy* 35, no. 3(2006): 241–251.

Prakash, Shah. *Legal Pluralism in Conflict: Coping with Cultural Diversity in Law*. London: Glass House, 2005.

Ricca, Mario. *Dike meticcia. Rotte di diritto interculturale*. Soveria Mannelli (Cs): Rubbettino, 2008a.

Ricca, Mario. *Oltre Babele. Codici per una democrazia interculturale*. Bari: Dedalo, 2008b.

Ricca, Mario. *Culture interdette. Modernità, migrazioni, diritto interculturale*. Torino: Bollati Boringhieri, 2013.

Saïd, Edward. "The Clash of Ignorance." *The Nation*, October 22, 2001: 11–13.

Sen, Amartya. *Identity and Violence: The Illusion of Destiny*. London: Allen Lane, 2006.

Simon, Herbert A. *The Sciences of the Artificial*. Cambridge, MA: MIT Press, 1996.

Simon, Pierre J. *Le bretonnité. Une ethnicité problématique*. Rennes: Terre de Brume Editions, 1999.

Sona, Federica. "Defending the Family Treasure Chest: Navigating Muslims Families and Secured Positivistic Islands of European Legal System." In *Family, Religion and Law: Cultural Encounters in Europe*, edited by Prakash Shah, Marie-Claire Foblets and Mathias Rohe, 115–142. London and New York: Routledge, 2016.

Tajfel, Henry, and John C. Turner. "The Social Identity Theory of Intergroup Behaviour." In *Psichology of Intergroup Relations*, edited by S. Worchel and W.G. Austin, 7–24. Chicago: Nelson Hall, 1986.

Tilly, Charles, and Sidney Tarrow. *Contentious Politics*. Boulder, CO: Paradigm Publishers, 2007.

Tylor, Edward B. *Primitive Culture: Researches into the Development of Mythology, Philosophy, Religion, Art and Custom*, 2 vols. Vol. 1. London: John Murray, 1871.

Urbinati, Nadia. *Representative Democracy: Principles and Genealogy*. Chicago: The University of Chicago Press, 2008.

van Brakel, Jaap. "De-essentialising across the Board: No Need to Speak the Same Language." *Netherlands Journal of Legal Philosophy* 35, no. 3(2006): 263–284.

Vieira, Ricardo. "Life Stories, Cultural Métissage, and Personal Identities." *SAGE Open*, (January–March 2014): 1–12.

Williams, Rowan D. "Civil and Religious Law in England: A Religious Perspective." *Ecclesiastical Law Journal* (2008): 262–282.

12 Addressing the possibility of normative conflicts around human rights

The concept of adaptation

Peter G. Kirchschlaeger

Introduction

Religious faith is considered as one of the essential elements of human existence protected by human rights, which enable every human being to survive and to live as human (Kirchschlaeger, 2013d, pp. 194–195). Human rights protect the freedom of the individual to religion and belief and to participation in the cultural life of the community (articles 18 and 27 of the Universal Declaration of Human Rights of 1948) and therefore enhance indirectly religious practice. Religious and world-view-based communities enjoy indirect protection by human rights because the latter are individual rights. Human rights represent the perspective of the individual, not of the community: human rights do not protect religion as such but the freedom of the individual to share the beliefs, thoughts and worldviews of a community, to be part of a community, and to practice their way of life – or not.

At the same time, while their main focus is of religious, theological, transcendent, or metaphysical character, religious and worldview-based communities assume a moral and legal role as well. In this dimension they can be perceived as societal actors contributing to the public discourse, to political opinion-forming and decision-making processes, and to a peaceful coexistence in society. They can be categorized as non-state actors.

While they share common elements with other non-state actors (e.g., corporations, NGOs) (Kirchschlaeger, 2016, pp. 59–60), they differentiate themselves from them in the following aspects (Kirchschlaeger, 2017a, pp. 133–157): Firstly, religious and worldview-based communities live morality as they strive for the moral good. This embraces to figure as an example for others, e.g., religious and worldview-based communities can take a stand for the oppressed, for humans suffering injustice, and they can act as advocates for human rights. (Of course this does not mean that religious and worldview-based communities always succeed in meeting these moral and legal expectations.) Secondly, they form morality. On the basis of their horizon of belief and of understanding, they define ethical principles, and they set moral norms (e.g. different religious and worldview-based communities have contributed and continue to contribute to the genesis and the development of human rights). Thirdly, they contribute moral convictions to the public and political discourse. They support states, the international community (e.g., the UN), and other non-state actors with a moral foundation (Boeckenfoerde, 2006, p. 112; Habermas, 2004, pp. 43–56). Fourthly, religious and worldview-based communities justify moral and legal norm-systems of the society. They are able to position humans within a broader horizon of meaning by introducing a religious, theological, and respectively transcendent perspective. This provides members of these communities with access to moral and legal norms of society and allows them to link them with their own faith, religion, and worldview (e.g., religious justifications of human rights build a non-exclusive (Bielefeldt, 2006, pp. 253–260) bridge between religious and worldview-based traditions and human rights showing members of the specific communities that their own beliefs and human rights in their multidimensionality (Kirchschlaeger, 2013a, pp. 77–95) can go hand in hand. Fifthly, religious and worldview-based communities are protected indirectly by human rights in this unique role (Kirchschlaeger, 2013b, pp. 353–374), which differentiates them from other societal actors.

The status of human rights as individual rights can represent a source of normative conflicts. From the perspective of a collective – e.g. religious and worldview-based communities – human rights can seem to be an individualistic approach undermining the values of a community. In addition, there is a possibility that a community claims collective rights overruling individual rights. This can create realities where normative conflicts between the collective and the individual occur: groups in religious and worldview-based communities interpret human rights in ways that seriously limit their scope, understand the tradition and teaching of their community in a way that does not respect human rights in general or the human rights of some humans, and act as bystanders when human rights violations occur within or outside their communities; they can even be part of movements or actions opposing human rights, or they can actually assume the role of perpetrators of human rights violations.

Another source of normative conflicts builds on the claim of universality of human rights. This claim means that "everybody matters" (Appiah, 2007, p. 174) – within or outside a religious or a worldview-based community. Differing from "not everybody matters", it emerges clearly that without their universality, human rights, some specific human rights, or some humans as holders of human rights would not be respected – within and outside of religious and worldview-based communities.

Obviously the universality of human rights impacts on religious and worldview-based communities, and the question arises if this is legitimate or not. The controversial potential of the claim of universality of human rights is enhanced on the one hand by some positions within the moral discourse about the groundings of human rights calling for an end of the search for a justification of human rights by defining human rights "un hecho del mundo" (Rabossi, 1990, p. 161) – as a "fact of the world" – and by neglecting the need for their justification. On the other hand, the idea of a "universal culture of human rights" promoted by the international community and human rights organizations can sound like the striving for a uniform culture. In this case, normative conflicts between particular norms and universal norms or respectively between normative pluralism and universal norms can occur.

In order to understand better these possibilities of normative conflicts and how to address and maybe resolve them, this chapter discusses, in a first step, the legitimacy of human rights as individual rights of all humans; and the justification of the universality of human rights. With this first step the necessity of a justification of human rights is emphasized (Kirchschlaeger, 2007, pp. 55–64) – in order to pay respect to the autonomy of all humans embracing the right to know the reasons why their freedom is restricted by human rights. Human rights find themselves at the centre of the discussion of normative conflicts in this chapter because they represent a catalogue of norms with a strong claim of universality implying a corresponding controversial potential while enjoying at the same time more global acceptance than any other system of moral or legal norms.

In a second step, the legitimacy of the impact of the universality of human rights within religious and worldview-based communities is elaborated. In a third step, the patterns of argumentation of different religious and worldview-based communities, or some groups within these communities, against human rights, will be assessed from an ethical perspective. In a fourth step, the model of "adaptation" will be examined as the way forward in understanding the correlation between religious and worldview-based communities and human rights dialogically in order to address the possibility of normative conflicts in a way which could contribute to the resolving of such conflicts.

Justifying human rights as individual and universal rights

Any attempt to justify human rights must satisfy the requirements of a rational and critical moral framework. "A rational or critical morality is one that claims for itself rational justifiability for its principles. Moral principles are rationally justified if they are generally endorsed by, that is to say acceptable to, all affected persons, given their full equality and effective self-determination" (Koller, 1990, p. 75). A response to the question as to why every human is a holder of human rights – which embraces human rights as individual and universal rights – is given by the principle of vulnerability. This explicative justification-model consists of several elements that are grouped into a first, second, and third step of filtering.

First step of filtering

Firstly, the principle of vulnerability starts with a human's self-awareness of his/her own vulnerability (Kirchschlaeger 2013d, pp. 231–267). For example, a healthy human knows that she/he could fall ill in the future. This can be a frightening process for humans because it forces them to accept their vulnerability and finite nature.

Secondly, during this awareness-building process a human recognizes ex negativo the "first-person-perspective" (Runggaldier, 2003, pp. 143–221). This means that humans recognize that they are subjects of this awareness-building process. Humans understand that they make and interpret this basic anthropological situation of vulnerability as a subject (meaning as the first person singular) who is acting, deciding, and living as a human (Honnefelder, 2012, pp. 171–172).

Nobody else than a human as a subject of her life lives and experiences her individual life. During the awareness-building process of one's own vulnerability and of one's own "first-person-perspective", humans put themselves in a relationship with the self. This opens access to the "self-relation". The latter embraces the embedment of the "first-person-perspective" and the interaction between an individual and her or his own self.

Thirdly, even the "first-person-perspective" and the "self-relation" prove to be vulnerable because – in order to remain with the above-mentioned example – if an illness threatens the survival of an individual, this danger encompasses the "first-person-perspective" and the "self-relation" as well.

Fourthly, during the awareness-building-process of one's own vulnerability and of one's own "first-person-perspective", humans put themselves in relation with all other humans, recognizing the vulnerability of all other humans. Humans become equal in terms of vulnerability; they share this vulnerability.

Fifthly, during the awareness-building-process of their own vulnerability and of their own "first-person-perspective", humans understand that they share not only the vulnerability with other humans but also the individual "first-person-perspective" on the individual vulnerability, and the individual "self-relation". They recognize the equality of all humans in their vulnerability, the "first-person-perspective", and "self-relation". They realize that the "first-person-perspective" and "self-relation" are prerequisites for human life because every human is subject of her respectively his own life. Nobody else can live her or his life in her or his stead. While humans can be different in all aspects of their existence (including, e.g., reason, needs), every human lives his/her own life with a "first-person-perspective" and a "self-relation" which enable humans to be aware of their existence and to reflect on it.

Sixthly, on the basis that humans perceive the vulnerability of their own "first-person-perspective" and their own "self-relation", they understand the same vulnerability for the "first-person-perspective" and the "self-relation" of others. Facing this vulnerability, humans primarily want just to survive as well as to live a life with dignity. Survival and life with dignity should not be taken away from humans. The guarantee of both should be enforceable in order to be sure of the protection by human rights. It should be valid in a different dimension because vulnerability can embrace the legal, the political, the historical, and the moral dimensions. Survival and life with dignity should be guaranteed without any preconditions because of their highest significance for humans. All humans share the same concern for survival and for a life as a human. It is an individual concern because it is accessible by the "first-person-perspective" and the "self-relation" but it is at the same time universal. Based on this entire multi-layer awareness-building process leading to recognition of the vulnerability of the "first-person-perspective" and the "self-relation" shared with all humans, humans are prepared to entitle all humans and himself / herself to human rights in order to actively balance and compensate in the case of a transition from vulnerability to violations. It is reasonable for a human to find consensus with all humans on human rights-protection for everyone – although there are responsibilities corresponding to human rights – because of the openness and uncertainty of the transformation from vulnerability to violation. Alternative forms to protect oneself from vulnerability, including violence or oppression, are less attractive than human rights from a pragmatic perspective, as one does not know on which side one will end up because of the openness and uncertainty of transition from vulnerability to a violation. Therefore human rights, consisting of universality and equality, protect everyone in the same way in his or her survival and life with dignity.

Following on from the six points discussed above, the seventh is the principle of vulnerability. It corresponds to vulnerability, to the "first-person-perspective", and to the "self-relation". It possesses moral quality and is of normative nature unlike vulnerability itself. Based on the principle of vulnerability, humans entitle each other to human rights. Therefore humans are not right-holders because they are vulnerable. Humans are right-holders because they deliberate on their own vulnerability and its relevance, because they become aware of the "first-person-perspective" and of the "self-relation" of themselves as well as of all humans; because they get to know the former as a prerequisite for human life; because they recognize the vulnerability of the "first-person-perspective" and the "self-relation" shared with all humans. In other words, because of the principle of vulnerability, they assign each other human rights. The principle of vulnerability is therefore a starting point for justifying human rights per se as well as specific human rights.

Eighthly, the principle of vulnerability can be the basis for confronting new experiences of suffering, violations, and injustices. This correlates with a dynamic understanding of human rights: if such new threats – e.g., in the process of digital transformation of society (Kirchschlaeger, 2017b, pp. 240–248) – make the protection of essential elements of human existence necessary, a further development of human rights is possible in order to ensure that such rights meet these new challenges.

The eight points above can be summarized as the first step of the filtering of a justification-model based on the principle of vulnerability. Not all elements and spheres of human existence are protected by human rights but only those where protection is required by the principle of vulnerability.

Second step of filtering

The second step of filtering builds on the considerations above and goes into more detail regarding the elements and spheres of protection to which all humans are entitled as holders of human rights. Naturally the consensus about protection against the possible consequences of vulnerability does not include all elements and spheres of human existence. Which elements and spheres of human existence should be placed under the protection of human rights? Which criteria should inform the selection of these elements and spheres of human existence?

As a starting point, historical experiences of injustice must be considered under which humans are suffering or could suffer because of the principle of vulnerability. These experiences of injustice and the principle of vulnerability make humans take action against those injustices and make them do something to prevent such violations from happening again.

Should all historical experiences of injustice under which humans are suffering – or could suffer because of the principle of vulnerability – be protected by human rights? Not every experience of a violation can be avoided by human rights. There is a need for a selection of experiences of injustice that warrant protection through human rights. The call for a selection leads to the question of which criteria should be used in this selection pursuing the identification of specific human rights.

This selection can be based on the description above and the above-mentioned prioritization because it indicates which protection humans first of all want. They allow the understanding of which characteristics make a historical injustice require human rights-protection. Primarily, humans want to survive and to live as human (fundamentality). Humans become aware that vulnerability concerns their survival and their life as a human and the survival and life as humans of all humans (universality). They get to know the vulnerability of the "first-person-perspective" and the "self-relation" – the prerequisite for human life shared with all humans. Survival and life as a human should not be taken away from any human (inalienability). Facing the openness and uncertainty of the transformation from a vulnerability to a violation, this protection should be guaranteed to all humans without conditions (categorical character). This protection must be legally enforceable (enforceability) in different dimensions (multidimensionality) in order to ensure that every human is able to survive and to live a life as a human in the same way (equality) because all humans – every individual with his or her "first-person-perspective" and "self-relation" (individual validity) – share this concern. Therefore the selection of the specific human rights is based on the following eight criteria:

1 Fundamentality (human rights protect a minimum standard of essential elements and spheres of human existence which a human needs in order to survive and in order to live a life as a human (preserving his/her humanity and dignity);
2 Universality (Kirchschlaeger, 2011, pp. 301–312) (all humans have human rights – always, everywhere, and in every case);
3 Inalienability (human rights cannot be lost or acquired);
4 Categorical nature (all humans have human rights without any conditions, namely they do not have to pay taxes or respect the law in order to enjoy human rights);
5 Enforceability (human rights must be legally enforceable);
6 Multidimensionality (human rights must be implementable in the legal, political, historical, and moral dimension);
7 Egalitarian nature (all humans have human rights; this means all humans in the same way, to the same extent, and with the same access);
8 Individual validity (every human has human rights as an individual, not as part of a collective).

These eight criteria inform selection of the specific human rights as criteria to decide whether a historical experience of injustice should be placed under the protection of human rights with a specific human right.

Third step of filtering

The third step of filtering involves application of the eight criteria mentioned above in order to identify the elements and spheres of human existence, which need to be protected by human rights.

At this point, it can be stated on a meta-level that this model of justification aims to respect the requirements of a rational and critical moral framework (Koller, 1990, p. 75). This justification-model based on the principle of vulnerability meets the requirement of applicability to all specific human rights as it was shown indicatively on another occasion (Kirchschlaeger, 2013d, pp. 290–335; 2015b: 121–141).

The legitimacy of the impact of the universality of human rights within religious and worldview-based communities

The legitimacy of the impact of human rights as individual and universal rights within religious and worldview-based communities could be questioned by individuals or groups within the communities or by the communities, if human rights violations occur and if their particular norms or practice are in opposition to universal human rights. In addition, religious and worldview-based communities could doubt the validity of human rights for themselves by emphasizing the alleged secular origin of human rights (Ruteere, 2014, p. 8) and could understand themselves as presumed "human rights-free zones".

In both cases, the following argumentation could be applied in order to underline the legitimacy of the impact of human rights within religious and worldview-based communities and in order to delegitimize human rights violations and particular norms and practices violating human rights. Since human rights can be justified morally based on the principle of vulnerability as individual and universal rights, all humans are holders of human rights – everywhere and at any time. This entitlement of all humans with human rights has an impact on religious and worldview-based communities because in the interaction between religious and worldview-based communities and humans, the communities must respect humans as right-holders – inside and outside religious and worldview-based communities. In other words, humans do not give up their human rights by entering a community or by being a member of a community.

Given the necessity of human rights, given the significance of this minimum standard for survival needed to preserve the humanity and dignity of individuals, human rights must be addressed as challenges for the whole of society and all societal actors – including religious and worldview-based communities – especially the ones with more power, influence, and ability to make a difference. In the preamble of the Universal Declaration of Human Rights of 1948, duties of states and "every individual and every organ of society" correspond to human rights. Article 5 of the International Covenant on Civil and Political Rights of 1966, Article 5 of the International Covenant on Economic, Social and Cultural Rights of 1966, and Articles 28 and 29 of the African Charter on Human and Peoples'

Rights of 1981 go in the same direction. This reflects that in many contexts and situations non-state actors possess power and influence, which should lead to the understanding of human rights as legal obligations on religious and worldview-based communities. Human rights ask religious and worldview-based communities to contribute towards their realization – be it in their own context or in other contexts. These contributions by religious and worldview-based communities are expected from them as is the case with other non-state actors. Within and outside their communities, religious and worldview-based communities can enhance the respect for human rights; they can call their members to respect and support the realization of human rights indicating to them the consensus between their own traditions, their own values and principles, and human rights. Religious and worldview-based communities can take a stand and raise their voice for victims of human rights violations if the voice of the marginalized is not heard or if the marginalized do not have a voice in the democratic opinion-forming and decision-making processes of a society. This role of advocacy is often played by religious and worldview-based communities, also because, maybe in another context, they can find themselves in a position of a discriminated minority and therefore possess an understanding of this marginalized situation.

This argumentation is reinforced from the perspective of a right-holder or a possible real victim of a human rights violation: it is not of primary significance who is the protector or the violator but the realization of his/her human rights.

Finally it must be acknowledged, as mentioned above, that different religious and worldview-based communities contributed to the genesis and the development of human rights (Hersch, 1990). Human rights stand not just on a secular but also on a religious leg (Joas, 2011).

Beyond that, it is possible that religious and worldview-based communities position themselves against human rights based on their focus on the collective, while perceiving human rights as individualistic and therefore as a threat for their own community. The basis of this perception of human rights represents a fundamental misunderstanding of human rights. The holders of human rights are individuals, not collectives, although this does not make them "individualistic". In distinction from "individualistic" which gives the individual the absolute priority, human rights are individual rights, which embrace corresponding duties as they are not exclusive rights but human rights. As one shares them with all other humans, these rights come with the corresponding duties to contribute to the realization of human rights of all other humans. "Rights are grounds of duties in others" (Raz, 1986, p. 167). In addition, one must consider Article 29 of the Universal Declaration of Human Rights of 1948 as well where the individual as holder of human rights is embedded in a collective which he or she needs for his or her own development and for which he or she should take care as well.

The encounter of human rights as universal norms and particular norms can provoke the use of patterns of argumentation by religious and worldview-based communities on their correlation to human rights which will be discussed below.

Patterns of argumentation by religious and worldview-based Communities on their correlation to human rights

While particular contexts apply to the use of human rights, their universality, and their validity, it is plausible (and sometimes one could even observe) that religious and worldview-based communities apply the following patterns of argumentation.

A schematic representation of these indicative patterns of argument is attempted. Of course due to its schematic, indicative, and summarizing character, this representation will be limited and will not pay full respect to the entire spectrum of individual lines of argumentation. At the same time, this representation enables the discovery of some common problems and challenges in the ways of reasoning and allows some clarification about them.

If one looks, for example, at the discourse on the right to vote for women in Switzerland at the end of the last century, some patterns of argumentation for excluding a group of humans from human rights in general or from some human rights by a collective entity – led to a normative conflict between particular norms in a region in Switzerland excluding women from the right to vote and universal norms embracing equal rights for women and men. The right to vote for women has existed in Switzerland only since 1990. Although it was introduced at federal level on 7 February 1971 with a two-thirds majority vote, only on 25 March 1990 could women vote in the entire country. This resulted from a judgment by the Swiss Federal Court on a case brought forward by women from the canton Appenzell Innerrhoden pointing out that it was against the constitution to exclude women from political decision-making-processes (*Neue Zuercher Zeitung*, 2011).

In the discussion about the right to vote for women in the canton Appenzell Innerrhoden, the following patterns of argumentation against this right for women could be identified:

1 The role which was foreseen for women as individuals by the collective – namely as mothers – was not compatible with political participation.
2 The contribution of women without a right to vote as individuals to the collective was essential for the functioning, for the progress, and for the survival of the society.
3 A change of the voting-rights would open the doors to something which a majority of the society did not support or considered as "evil": in the case of the discussion about the right to vote for women it was argued that voting-rights for women would bring bolshevism to Switzerland (Gariup, 2011).
4 The presumed self-understanding of women argued in the sense of: "if you asked women, they wouldn't want to participate in political opinion-forming and decision-making processes".
5 The lack of the necessary competences of women to exercise this human right.
6 One's own tradition and culture, in the sense of: "this is part of our tradition and culture", and "we are different and a special case – and this is good as it is, and it should remain like this".

7 One's own history, in the sense of: "looking back, in the past we have always done it this way".
8 One's own history as a success-model, in the sense of "we have been very successful this way".
9 One's sovereignty, in the sense of "this is our decision".
10 The internal cohesion against external influences: "we don't let others interfere with our internal matters".

In different combinations and order, these ten patterns of argumentation dominated the democratic opinion-forming and decision-making process at that time in Switzerland. They are of indicative nature because one can encounter them in situations and contexts where particular actors, e.g., religious and worldview-based communities, try to oppose the universality of human rights and their validity by finding arguments for the exclusion of an individual or a group from human rights-protection in general or from some particular human rights. These patterns of argumentation of exclusion can be found in all religious and worldview-based communities and are independent of a specific context in the defence of a particular human rights-violating position against the universality of human rights.

Counter-arguments against these patterns of argumentation of exclusion embrace:

1 The reversal of the burden of proof. This means asking for "good reasons" as mentioned above, when enforcing patterns of argumentation for exclusion. This also means that they are based on arguments which are plausible and acceptable for all humans in a sense of a model of thought and not a real referendum. It will be probably difficult to present "good reasons" for these patterns of argumentation of exclusion.
2 The following observation also weakens the argumentative force of these patterns of argumentation for exclusion: they are presented as independent of the specific context, crossing boundaries of religious and worldview-based communities of the subject taking these positions, and of the subject using them, although they pretend to be part of the individual and particular context, history, tradition, culture, religion, state, etc. These patterns of argumentation of exclusion are presented as particularly typical and unique for a specific context, history, tradition, culture, religion, or worldview-based community, although they are brought forward in the exact same way as "particularly typical" and "unique" in other contexts, traditions, cultures, religions, and worldview-based communities as well. This means that the alleged particularity and uniqueness of one's own claim for the exclusion is shared by other contexts, traditions, cultures, religious and worldview-based communities as well, in order to exclude a human or some humans from human rights in general or from a specific human right. This implies that actual arguments for exclusion do not depend on the perspective of the particular position but are shared across boundaries among religious and worldview-based communities and

must therefore have another ground than one's own unique context, history, tradition, culture, religion, or worldview which does not consist for example of something "typically Swiss", in the case of the right to vote in Switzerland, but of something defended by some individuals, groups, and circles which try to exclude some humans from human rights.

3 On this basis, it needs to be examined if these patterns of exclusion do not depend on particular interests of some humans or some groups rather than on the alleged context, history, tradition, culture, religion, and worldview as pretended. Maybe it could be more adequate to characterize them as illiberal because of their opposition against the respect for human dignity and against the universality of human rights, and because of their readiness to neglect a human or some humans, their human rights or a specific human right. Maybe it could be more adequate to identify their origin in the claim of sovereignty and power by some individuals and groups, instead of relying presumably on particularity or on uniqueness.

4 If the alleged particularity or uniqueness falls as basis of the patterns of argumentation for exclusion, the alleged divergence of human rights as universal norms with one's own context, history, tradition, culture, religion, or worldview, and the undermining of human rights on the basis of the "own", loses its argumentative force.

5 On the basis of the analysis so far, if some individuals, some decision-makers, circles, or groups use these patterns of argumentation of exclusion, this could result in a loss of their credibility and acceptance due to a lack of coherence and argumentative force.

6 Based on this critical examination of the patterns of argumentation of exclusion, an assessment of a religious or worldview-based community acknowledges the opposition and the protest against such exclusion within their own collective and distances itself from the perception of religious or worldview-based communities or states as homogeneous, monolithic, precisely definable, eternally constant, infinitely existing, and never-changing entities. Rather, it embraces the complexity of the consistence of the collective, its heterogeneous character (including, e.g. conservative or liberal positions), its changes and transformation-processes, its progresses and backlashes, its growth, its decline, its contributions to and against the human rights tradition. Where human rights affect religious and worldview-based communities, they strengthen those forces within the communities that are already committed to upholding human rights on the basis of, or respectively in accordance with their own religion and worldview.

7 A tendency to claim bigger differences between the different religious and worldview-based communities than they are in reality can be recognized because communities change faster than one would think from the outside (Griffin, 2015, p. 562).

8 Individuals, representatives, decision-makers, collectives of particular contexts should remember that human rights protect them indirectly in maintaining their uniqueness, as mentioned above – something which cannot be assumed

as guaranteed naturally due to the potential of one particular context to deny another particular context its right to exist. The protection of the autonomy of the individual by human rights enables therefore diversity and pluralism (An-Na'im, 2000, p. 95). Universal human rights protect the particular standpoint by protecting humans as different and unique individuals rather than as members of a collective. In this way, human rights guarantee to everyone – and not just to the ones with power, with influence, or with a strong socio-economic background – the right to be unique, particular, and different. Human rights ensure all humans the respect of all others for their uniqueness and particularity (Gozdecka, 2016, p. 177). It is the protection of all humans in their autonomy that allows all humans to be particular, unique, and different. This implies a constitutive role of human rights for religious and worldview-based diversity and plurality by protecting the autonomy of all humans as a condition for pluralism and diversity (Raz, 1986, pp. 395–399). At the same time, particularity and uniqueness have their limits in human rights (Marie, 2003, p. 225) in order to enable everyone – and not just some humans – to be particular, unique, and different. "People should have available to them many forms and styles of life incorporating incompatible virtues, which not only cannot all be realized in one life but also tend to generate mutual intolerance. Such an autonomy-valuing pluralistic morality generates a doctrine of freedom. It protects people pursuing different styles of life from the intolerance which competitive pluralism has the inherent tendency to encourage, and it calls for the provision of the conditions of autonomy without which autonomous life is impossible" (Raz, 1986, p. 425). Human rights serve as preconditions and framework for religious and worldview-based diversity because they ensure that plurality can become reality and – also against opposition – legitimate diversity (Hoeffe, 1990, pp. 135–150).

9 Enjoying this indirect protection by human rights implies respect for the entire catalogue of human rights on the basis of the principle of indivisibility of human rights. This means that the entire catalogue of human rights needs to be respected. All human rights must go hand in hand. Therefore, every human right must be implemented optimally and in a way that accords with all other human rights being implemented optimally at the same time. This approach has also a fundamental influence on situations where it seems that one right needs to be curtailed in order to respect another right. Instead of assuming a conflict of rights, every right is already from the beginning understood as being embedded in the catalogue of all the other rights and the rights of all humans.)

10 The next question that must be raised relates to how helpful and how precise categories which are used on a regular basis in such lines of argumentation like "West" and "East" are, and which epistemological discovery one gains with their application in a normative discourse, as the relevance of a geographical position for normative discourse can be doubted. Of course it cannot be denied that the historic background, the context, the location, the time, etc., influence insights, ways of thinking, and positions. In the normative discourse, a justification based solely on place of origin and the time of genesis and

development cannot live up to the criterion of universalization introduced above for critical morality and ethics and remains limited in its validity and argumentative force. This can also be shown if the universality of human rights is connected with their contingent and historical genesis and development.

While the historical examination of the genesis and development proves that human rights "did not fall from heaven" but were agreed upon by humans and can explain the "how" of the human rights tradition, it cannot provide neither a moral justification of human rights nor a justification which is adequate for the claim of universality of human rights, as a historical justification remains always particular and therefore not universalizable.

Besides that, the geographical position as a normative argument turns out not to be helpful because the categorization based on a geographical position always depends as well on the standpoint. If one argues, for instance, from Lucerne, Vienna is located in the geographical "East" although in the general human rights discourse it belongs usually to the "West".

Moreover, such categories cannot hide a tendency toward a racist basis as they suggest that humans in one geographically defined context differ from humans in another geographically defined context in essential elements and areas of human existence, which are necessary for survival and for a life as a human.

In addition, both categories are dominated internally by heterogeneity and pluralism whose internal streams (e.g. liberal, conservative, and traditionalist voices) are often more similar to their equivalents in the other category than to their neighbours within their own category. In other words, the use of categories like "East" and "West" must fail because it is overlooked that liberal voices in all categories are often more similar than liberal and conservative voices of the same category.

Furthermore, the use of such categories embraces the assumption and the construction of allegedly definable and comprehensible, monolithic and homogeneous, eternal, static, and contradicting "worlds" (e.g., "East" – "West"). This construction of such "counter-worlds" is an expression of an oversimplification which does not take into account global interaction and exchange, and which does not respect the diversity of and within traditions, religions, cultures, civilizations, value-systems, and worldviews. It is part of the assumption and the construction of such "counter-worlds" to pretend to know exactly what the so-called "West" and "East" respectively is and on which values they are based. The reality is much more complex, and the values of the so-called "West" and respectively "East" are hardly accessible because their existence as such is doubtable due to the dominating heterogeneity within the "East" and the "West". An attempt of a comprehensive definition of the so-called "East" and "West" must fail in face of the pluralistic composition of the two constructed poles. It must fail, as well, because it disregards the internal diversity and heterogeneity of such categories.

Because of the previous ten arguments, the concept of "adaptation" allows the understanding of the correlation between religious and worldview-based communities and human rights dialogically in order to address the processing of normative conflicts in a way which could contribute to their resolution.

Adaptation: a model for bringing human rights and religious and worldview-based communities together

An adaptation process makes it possible to link one's own religious and worldview-based foundations with human rights. As opposed to "interpretation" which does not exclude the possibility that the content of human rights can change,[1] "adaptation" preserves the identity of human rights but translates them into a language of one's own religion. Adaptation gives access to human rights from the perspective of one's own religion by identifying and indicating key concepts, main principles, and core values of one's own religion and worldview overlapping with human rights. In addition, adaptation follows also the proposals of substance for key concepts of human rights (e.g. human dignity, freedom).

Beyond that, adaptation embraces the discourse on the reasons justifying human rights, which can lead to justification-models relevant for religions and worldviews. Such justifications may be limited in their immediate relevance with regard to the world outside a specific community, since they are based on ideas that are difficult to grasp or follow for those outside the community, and the ideas lack directly convincing rationality. Thus, they may fail because they do not comply with the pluralistic addressees and the claim to universality of human rights. At the same time, they have an internal function, since they grant access to human rights of a particular quality, and achieve a significant motivational impact. A justification-model based for example on a religious belief might possess extraordinary intensity and touch a believer in a manner a rational approach could not. A religious justification-model of human rights increases the probability that concrete engagement will follow the recognition of human rights and the individual responsibility for the realization of human rights.

Furthermore, such models can strengthen the validity of human rights within a specific community. Without an additional internal justification of human rights, it might be assumed by some, as mentioned above, that human rights are something purely secular, i.e. that they have no relevance for the traditions, cultures, religions, or worldviews in question. This conclusion, however, clearly contradicts the universality of human rights, and shows the necessity for attempts of justifying human rights from the point of view of religious and worldview-based

1 E.g., the Cairo Declaration on Human Rights in Islam of 1990 is an "interpretation" of human rights because it changes their content, among others with its article 24: "All the rights and freedoms stipulated in this Declaration are subject to the Islamic Sharia."; or its article 19: "There shall be no crime or punishment except as provided for in the Sharia."; e.g. the Bangkok Declaration of Human Rights of 1993 represents an "interpretation" of human rights because it changes their content, among others with its article 6: "Reiterate that all countries, large and small, have the right to determine their political systems, control and freely utilize their resources, and freely pursue their economic, social and cultural development."

communities. These attempts at justifying human rights based on a religious and worldview-based foundation as part of adaptation prove to be bridge-building between religious and worldview-based communities and human rights.

The concept of adaptation also embraces the potential that religious and worldview-based communities cannot only provide this access to human rights by giving a justification for them but that they can also contribute to a "culture of human rights" by fostering awareness-building for human rights within their own communities and with respect to the public in general. Religions can be an advocate for human rights. The concept of a "universal culture of human rights" is introduced by several human rights instruments (e.g., the UN Declaration on Human Rights Education and Training of 2011).[2] A "culture of human rights" has nothing to do with a "globalized culture" which intends to replace other cultures. The idea behind "universal culture of human rights" is not to create a uniform culture, which excludes any form of contextualization. "Culture of human rights" means that the structure, the actions, and responses of an entire society are informed by and based upon human rights (Article 4 of the UN Declaration on Human Rights Education and Training [Kirchschlaeger, 2012, pp. 150–165]). A "culture of human rights" depends on contributions from different actors, including religious and worldview-based communities by demonstrating to their members the commonly shared elements of their own tradition and human rights.

Finally the concept of "adaptation" embraces also a dialogue of reciprocal critique of adaptation. While human rights have a legitimate impact on religious and worldview-based communities as elaborated above, human rights can at the same time be criticized by religious and worldview-based communities, for example when the international human rights discourse emphasizes some specific human rights while neglecting others, not respecting the principle of indivisibility of human rights (for example by focusing on the political rights while neglecting the social, economic and cultural rights). Furthermore, religious and worldview-based communities contribute to the human rights discourse with their criticism of misbalances, their identification of illegitimate emphases, their perception of abuses of human rights (e.g., by states) for other political purposes (Kirchschlaeger, 2013c, pp. 255–260) or poor performance by state or non-state actors playing the role of advocates of marginalized humans whose voice is not heard enough. The criticism by religious and worldview-based communities stays always within the limits human rights themselves define as it is foreseen by the concept of "adaptation". Beyond that, religious and worldview-based communities can offer a critical reading of human rights from their perspective of a wider horizon of meaning, which can show the human rights discourse's possible blind spots or new challenges. For example, the Jewish-Christian understanding of human dignity which derived from the biblically grounded teaching (Genesis 1:26–27) of the creation of humans in God's image as man and woman – that is to say in their difference and not

2 The author has contributed as a consultative expert to the development of the UN Declaration on Human Rights Education and Training during the entire preparation process of the Declaration.

genderlessly (Vogels, 1994, pp. 200–202; Greenhalgh, 1992, pp. 9–14) – could help to overcome the "gender-blindness" (Heimbach-Steins, 2009, p. 232) of the discourse on human dignity and human rights.

> Most women's experiences of human rights violations are gendered, and many forms of discrimination or abuse occur because the victim is female. Women whose rights are being violated for reasons other than gender (as political prisoners or members of persecuted ethnic groups) often also experience a particular form of abuse based on gender, such as sexual assault. (Bunch, 1995, pp. 12–13)

In this *dialogical correlation of reciprocal critique*, religious and worldview-based communities can on the one hand be the object of critique, when communities are expected to respect human rights and to contribute to their realization. On the other hand, religious and worldview-based communities contribute to the human rights discourse with proposals and their own criticism.

Adaptation gives the chance to address the possibility of normative conflicts in a promising way. It embraces human rights and religious and worldview-based communities as partners of a critical discourse and of concrete and practical efforts about essential elements and spheres of human existence necessary for survival and for a life with human dignity for all humans. Adaptation emphasizes the necessity of contributions by religious and worldview-based communities to the respect, protection, implementation, and realization of human rights as well as to the human rights discourse enabling the human rights discourse and -practice to remain coherent with their own idea. At the same time, adaptation will lead to a stronger identification of religious and worldview-based communities with human rights and more "ownership" for them. Human rights need religious and worldview-based communities as allies because of their uniqueness, their power and influence, and their ability to make a difference for the cause of human rights.

References

An-Na'im, A.A. 2000. Islam and Human Rights: Beyond the Universality Debate, ed. L. Henkin, *Proceedings of the Annual Meeting of the American Society of International Law: American Society of International Law* 94, pp. 95–103.

Appiah, K.A. 2007. *Der Kosmopolit. Philosophie des Weltbürgertums.* Muenchen: C. H. Beck.

Bielefeldt, H. 2006. Universal Rights and Religious Traditions. In: Kirchschlaeger, P.G. and Kirchschlaeger, T. eds., *Human Rights and Religions: International Human Rights Forum Lucerne (IHRF) VI.* Berne: Staempfli Verlag, pp. 253–260.

Boeckenfoerde, E.-W. 2006. Die Entstehung des Staates als Vorgang der Säkularisation. In: BoeckenfoerdeE-W., *Recht, Staat, Freiheit. Studien zur Rechtsphilosophie, Staatstheorie und Verfassungsgeschichte.* Frankfurt a. M.: Suhrkamp, pp. 92–114.

Bunch, C. 1995. Transforming Human Rights from a Feminist Perspective. In: Peters, J. and Wolper, A. eds., *Women's Rights, Human Rights: International Feminist Perspectives.* New York: Routledge, pp. 11–17.

Gariup, D. 2011. Der harzige Weg zum Frauenstimmrecht. Politthink.ch. [Online]. 7 February [Accessed 7 April 2017]. Available from: http://polithink.ch/2011/02/07/der-harzige-weg-zum-frauenstimmrecht/.

Gozdecka, D.A. 2016. *Rights, Religious Pluralism and the Recognition of Difference: Off the Scales of Justice*. New York: Routledge.

Greenhalgh, S. 1992. Creative Partnership in Genesis. *Scripture Bulletin* 21, pp. 9–14.

Griffin, J. 2015. The Relativity and Ethnocentricity of Human Rights. In: Cruft, R., Liao, S.M. and Renzo, M. eds., *Philosophical Foundations of Human Rights*. Oxford: Oxford University Press, pp. 555–569.

Habermas, J. 2004. Intoleranz und Diskriminierung. In: Mattioli, A., Ries, M. and Rudolph, E. eds., *Intoleranz im Zeitalter der Revolutionen. Europa 1770–1848*. Zuerich: Orell Fuessli, pp. 43–56.

Heimbach-Steins, M. 2009. Human Rights – Whose Benefits? Critical Reflections on the Androcentric Structure of Human Rights and its Consequences on the Social Participation of Women. In: Sitter-Liver, B. ed., *Universality: From Theory to Practice. An Intercultural and Interdisciplinary Debate about Facts, Possibilities, Lies and Myths. 25th Colloquium of the Swiss Academy of Humanities and Social Sciences*. Freiburg i. Ü.: Academic Press Fribourg, pp. 229–257.

Hersch, J. 1990. *Das Recht, ein Mensch zu sein. Leseproben aus aller Welt zum Thema Freiheit und Menschenrechte*. Basel: Helbing und Lichtenhahn.

Hoeffe, O. 1990. *Kategorische Rechtsprinzipien*. Frankfurt a. M.: Suhrkamp.

Honnefelder, L. 2012. Theologische und metaphysische Menschenrechtsbegründungen. In: Pollmann, A. and Lohmann, G. eds., *Menschenrechte: Ein interdisziplinäres Handbuch*. Stuttgart: J. B. Metzler, pp. 171–178.

Joas, H. 2011. *Die Sakralität der Person. Eine neue Genealogie der Menschenrechte*. Berlin: Suhrkamp.

Kirchschlaeger, P.G. 2007. Brauchen die Menschenrechte eine (moralische) Begruendung? In: Kirchschlaeger, P.G., Kirchschlaeger, T., Belliger, A. and Krieger, D. eds., *Human Rights and Children, International Human Rights Forum Lucerne (IHRF) IV*. Berne: Staempfli Verlag, pp. 55–64.

Kirchschlaeger, P.G. 2011. Das ethische Charakteristikum der Universalisierung im Zusammenhang des Universalitätsanspruchs der Menschenrechte. In: Ast, S., Mathis, K., Haenni, J. and Zabel, B., eds., *Gleichheit und Universalität. Archiv für Rechts- und Sozialphilosophie 128*. Stuttgart: Franz Steiner Verlag, pp. 301–312.

Kirchschlaeger, P.G. 2012. Die neue UN-Erklärung zu Menschenrechtsbildung und -training. *Zeitschrift für Menschenrechte* 6(2), pp. 150–165.

Kirchschlaeger, P.G. 2013a. Die Multidimensionalität der Menschenrechte – Chance oder Gefahr für den universellen Menschenrechtsschutz? *MenschenRechtsMagazin* 18(2), pp. 77–95.

Kirchschlaeger, P.G. 2013b. Religionsfreiheit – ein Menschenrecht im Konflikt. *Freiburger Zeitschrift für Philosophie und Theologie* 60(2), pp. 353–374.

Kirchschlaeger, P.G. 2013c. Menschenrechte und Politik. In: Yousefi, H.R. ed., *Menschenrechte im Weltkontext. Geschichten – Erscheinungsformen – Neuere Entwicklungen*. Heidelberg: Springer Verlag, pp. 255–260.

Kirchschlaeger, P.G. 2013d. *Wie können Menschenrechte begründet werden? Ein für religiöse und säkulare Menschenrechtskonzeptionen anschlussfähiger Ansatz. ReligionsRecht im Dialog 15*. Muenster: LIT-Verlag.

Kirchschlaeger, P.G. 2015a. Adaptation – A Model for Bringing Human Rights and Religions Together. *Acta Academica* 47(2), pp. 163–191.

Kirchschlaeger, P.G. 2015b. Das Prinzip der Verletzbarkeit als Begründungsweg der Menschenrechte. *Freiburger Zeitschrift für Philosophie und Theologie* 62(1), pp. 121–141.

Kirchschlaeger, P.G. 2016. *Menschenrechte und Religionen. Nichtstaatliche Akteure und ihr Verhältnis zu den Menschenrechten. Gesellschaft – Ethik – Religion 7.* Paderborn: Ferdinand Schoeningh Verlag.

Kirchschlaeger, P.G. 2017a. Religionen als moralische Akteure. In: Bergold, R., Sautermeister, J. and Schroeder, A. eds., *Dem Wandel eine menschliche Gestalt geben. Sozialethische Perspektiven für die Gesellschaft von morgen. Festschrift Katholisch-Soziales Institut KSI.* Freiburg i. B.: Herder Verlag, pp. 133–157.

Kirchschlaeger, P.G. 2017b. Roboter und Ethik. *Aktuelle Juristische Praxis,* 26(2), pp. 240–248.

Kirchschlaeger, P.G. 2017c. *Mass-Losigkeit und andere ethische Prinzipien des Neuen Testaments, Leuven.* Biblical Tools and Studies31. Leuven: Edition Peeters (in print).

Koller, P. 1990. Die Begründung von Rechten. In: Koller, P., Varga, C. and Weinberger, O. eds., *Theoretische Grundlagen der Rechtspolitik. Ungarisch-Österreichisches Symposium der internationalen Vereinigung für Rechts- und Sozialphilosophie. Archiv für Rechts- und Sozialphilosophie 54.* Stuttgart: Franz Steiner Verlag, pp. 74–84.

Luebbe, H. 1990. *Religion nach der Aufklärung.* Graz: Styria.

Marie, J.-B. 2003. De l'universalité des principes à l'universalité des pratiques des droits de l'homme. In: *Avancées et confins actuels des droits de l'homme aux niveaux international, européen et national. Mélanges offerts à Silvio Marcus Helmons.* Brussels: Bruylant, pp. 219–229.

Neue ZuercherZeitung. 2011. Der lange Weg zum Frauenstimmrecht. *Neue Zuercher Zeitung.* [Online]. 4 February. [Accessed 7 April 2017]. Available from: https://www.nzz.ch/frauenstimmrecht-1.9350588.

Rabossi, E. 1990. La teoria de los derechos umanos naturalizada. *Revista del Centro de Estudio Constitucionales* 5, pp. 159–175.

Raz, J. 1986. *The Morality of Freedom.* Oxford: Clarendon.

Runggaldier, E. 2003. Deutung menschlicher Grunderfahrungen im Hinblick auf unser Selbst. In: Quitterer, J., Runggaldier, E. and Rager, G. eds., *Unser Selbst – Identität im Wandel neuronaler Prozesse.* Paderborn: Ferdinand Schoeningh Verlag, pp. 143–221.

Ruteere, M. 2014. Bridging Valleys: Harnessing the Power of Religious Movements for and Human Rights. A Briefing Paper for the Raoul Wallenberg Institute for Human Rights and Humanitarian Law – Turkey. Unpublished.

Vogels, W. 1994. The Human Person in the Image of God (Gn 1, 26). *Science et Esprit* 46, pp. 189–202.

13 Adjudication in a pluralized legal field

Proposing communication as an analytical device

Gopika Solanki

Introduction

The body of literature on legal pluralism views the co-presence of multiple laws and orders and their interactions through the lens of conflict over sovereignty or jurisdictional boundaries; it also poses a question regarding hierarchy of laws and their enforcement (Griffiths 1986; Moore 1973; Richland 2011). Contestations over multiple laws governing the family in postcolonial societies are important sites to test these assertions, as most postcolonial states arrived at varied accommodative arrangements with religio-cultural groups in the governance of the conjugal family, and have adopted different models of legal pluralism. Concerns of gender justice animate discussions of these power-sharing arrangements between state and religio-cultural communities, as laws of marriage and divorce govern the division of property within the conjugal family, family construct, religion, and gender roles and identities, and shape the boundaries of religious groups (Mukhopadhyay 1998; Shachar 2001; Solanki 2011; Yuval-Davis 1997). Many feminists have emphasized the nature of conflict between various laws, suggesting that legal pluralism in the governance of the family subjects individuals to multiple normative orders, and that religious and customary laws – inherently patriarchal – conflict with constitutional provisions that guarantee equality and freedom in law (Nussbaum 1997; Okin 1999). Moreover, they have also pointed out that religious and customary family laws violate the principles enshrined in international conventions, such as the Convention on the Elimination of All forms of Discrimination against Women (CEDAW).

In contrast to these approaches, and focusing on diverse legal agents and orders in the adjudication of family law in India, this chapter asks the question: what dynamics shape the interactions between multiple and contradictory sources of law and authority? Drawing upon my previous work (Solanki 2011), and illustrating through case studies that map the interchanges between various legal authority centers in the governance of marriage under Muslim family law,[1] this chapter

1 In general, the term "Islamic law" covers both the *Sharia* (the divine law) and *fiqh*, which is the product of human understanding that sought to interpret and implement the *Sharia* (Esposito 1982, 105). Islamic jurisprudence has developed as the science of interpretation of both the Quran (the revelation of God) and the *sunna*, which is the

places forth an agonistic notion of communication that captures the exchange between diverse legal orders. Drawing upon Luhmann's idea of communication (Luhmann 1992, 1995), this chapter foregrounds the notion of communication as constitutive, consisting of interlinked and ongoing events involving information processing, utterances, and understanding, taking place in a field between a rich array of actors, laws, and organizations, and producing open-ended outcomes. Viewing these interactions through this typology, this chapter argues that while various normative legal orders can conflict with one another, they are often, but not always, intractable. In addition, it is also possible to conceive of these complex and multilayered interactions between laws and sources of authority as resulting in cooperation, harmonization, and action, containing within them the potential for change.

This analysis illustrates that potential for change by discussing constructions of triple *talaq* (a form of Islamic divorce) in diverse legal forums, and mapping the interactions between various legal bodies and actors. The chapter is based on ethnographic research conducted in state courts, caste councils, and other informal bodies in Mumbai that adjudicate marriage (between 2002 and 2003 and 2013 and 2014, in the summer of 2008, and during December 2015).

The chapter is divided into two sections. The first section explains the Indian model of legal pluralism and lists heterogeneous sources of laws and authority governing divorce among Muslims. The second section discusses two case studies in the context of adjudication, and maps the field of communication in the governance of divorce under Muslim family law.

The Muslim Personal Law in the Indian context

The Indian state has negotiated group-specific power-sharing arrangements with the Muslim minority and with other religious and customary groups in the governance of the family. The Indian state practices what I call a "shared adjudication model" (Solanki 2011) in the sense that the state splits its adjudicative authority in matters of marriage and divorce with societal actors and organizations among religious and customary groups. As a result, adjudication takes place in multiple sites, and each adjudicative site – formal or informal – provides a forum for interaction among state and societal laws and legal actors.

Three types of organizations govern the family among all religio-customary groups, including Muslims. The first one, formal organizations, consists of state

Prophet's statements and the tacit approval of certain deeds of which he had knowledge (Haddad and Stowasser 2004, 5). The elaboration of law depended on the Quran and the *sunna* and on the application of juridical reasoning to discover the reason behind each rule, and to apply it in a specific context (Esposito 1982; Hallaq 2001) Thus, the interpretive science relied on a methodology called *ijtihad*. The resultant bodies of law – classical *fiqh* schools (*madhabib*) – in which the details of law are stated and recorded are Hanafi, Maliki, Shafi, and Hanbali. In India, the majority of Sunni Muslims follow the Hanafi school of law.

courts and formally registered organizations (such as Muslim charitable and religious organizations, sect councils, and civil society organizations). The second typology includes informal groups, or "doorstep courts" (Solanki 2011), such as residents' associations, prayer groups, loose networks of women, and civic groups. The third typology consists of individuals (such as local fixers and politicians, lawyers, religious clergy, individual kinspersons, and members of legal or social work professions). Given that multiple organizations and actors comprising civic, religious, and customary sources of authority adjudicate in matters of Muslim laws, the following section maps the diverse laws and bodies that govern Islamic divorce.

State law and key trends in the adjudication of Muslim Personal Law in state courts

The Muslim Personal Law in India is partially uncodified, and is a mixture of local and folk law, popular perceptions, religious law, customary laws, state legislations, and judicial precedents. In general, in state courts the Muslim family law recognizes three types of divorce – *talaq ahsan, talaq hasan, and talaq-ul-biddat.* The *talaq ahsan* consists of a *single* pronouncement of divorce made during a period of menstruation followed by sexual abstinence during *iddat*, a period of three months and ten days (Mulla 1955, 267). The second type of divorce, *talaq hasan*, consists of three pronouncements made during successive *tuhrs* (menstrual cycles) with no sexual relations taking place during this time (Mulla 1955, 267). The *talaq-ul-biddat*, what is known as "triple talaq" (divorce), is one of the most controversial forms of divorce in Muslim laws. The *talaq-ul-biddat* consists of three pronouncements (of divorce) made during a single *tuhr* (menstrual cycle) in one sentence, or a single pronouncement made during a *tuhr* clearly indicating an intention to irrevocably dissolve the marriage (Mulla 1955, 267). The husband has to pronounce the divorce and the wife has to receive the divorce. During the colonial and early postcolonial periods, courts accepted both oral and written forms of triple talaq as being valid. However, this created confusion as husbands claimed to have divorced wives and, at times, wives denied divorces. In other instances, many wives claimed that their husbands had divorced them, and the husbands had opposed the divorce. As a result, courts mostly recognized the written but not oral form of divorce. Usually, the standard practice has been for the husband to send a written letter, proclaiming divorce, to the wife by registered post, and the wife's signature (in some cases) become proof of divorce. The majority of judgments in state courts accepted this view.

However, scholars have failed to highlight a countertrend during adjudication. There is no legal certainty in state law with respect to the regulation of triple talaq. In 1981, the Division Bench of Gauhati High Court prescribed two conditions for a valid "talaq," which are: "(1) Talaq must be for a reasonable cause; and (2) it must be preceded by an attempt of reconciliation between the husband and wife by two arbiters, one chosen by the wife from her family and the other by the husband from his family and if such attempts fails, 'talaq' may be effected."[2] This view was reinforced by the Supreme Court in 2002[3] and by other state high courts.[4] Indeed, the Aurangabad bench of the Bombay High Court in the Dagdu Pathan case held that if contested, the factum of talaq has to be proved by the husband; it can be valid only if it is pronounced in front of witnesses, if there have been earlier attempts at reconciliation (which have failed), and if both parties have a copy of it.

Religious laws and sources of religious authority in law

There are multiple sources of religious authority in India. The All India Muslim Personal Law Board, an organization created in 1973 to intervene in the issue of Muslim religious family law, sees triple talaq as a valid practice in Islamic law and jurisprudence. In contrast, the All India Shia Personal Law Board does not recognize triple talaq; religious seminaries differ in their interpretation. For instance, the Ahl-e Hadith, a sect that recognizes the direct interpretation of the Quran and the Hadith, does not permit triple talaq and sees the practice as un-Islamic.

Customary laws and sources of authority

The Muslim community is internally heterogeneous and divided along linguistic, cultural, sectarian, class, and caste lines. Many Muslim customary laws (which are different from religious laws) prohibit triple talaq. For instance, several Shia and Sunni sects (such as the Bohras and Khojas in Mumbai) do not recognize or practice triple talaq. Indeed, they have their own laws in which divorce is granted following a process in which the parties, the sect authority represented by their Jamaat (or sect council), and family members from both sides arrive at mutually acceptable decisions (Solanki 2011).

The triple talaq is also governed by communities, and the distinction between social and religious aspects of law is thin on the ground. Many groups self-regulate themselves; for instance, a group of Sunni Muslims (which hail from the same native place and settled in Mumbai during the early 20th century) maintain affinal and marriage ties to their native villages in one administrative unit in the neighboring province (Solanki 2011). This group, following the village's practice and custom, has banned triple talaq. The enforcement mechanism is tied to the practice of endogamy – the man who gives triple talaq does not get to marry a second wife from these villages, and his action results in a loss of social ties, prestige, and his

2 *Rukia Khatuns v. Abdul Khalique Laskar*; reported in (1981 1 GLR 375).
3 *Shamim Ara v. State of U.P.*; 2002 SC 3551.
4 If contested, the factum of talaq has to be proved by the husband; it can be valid only if it is pronounced in front of witnesses, if there have been attempts at reconciliation earlier (which have failed), and if both parties have a copy of it. See for instance *Dagdu S/O Chotu Pathan Latur v. Rahimbi Dagdu Pathan, Ashabi*; 2003 (1) BomCR 740.

family's reputation, which also affects the marriage and other social relations of his siblings and children.

Religious family laws and civic sources of authority

Civic sources of authority, such as women's groups, charitable organizations, and nongovernmental organizations (NGOs) tend to privilege state law but use a mixture of religious family laws, customary laws, and state laws in their adjudication practice. Other sources include Jamaats (councils), prayer groups, slum dwellers' associations, and other doorstep courts. Feminist groups differ in their approaches to adjudication. Some feminists want to continue to interpret Islamic laws according to feminist ideals, while others believe that secular laws that are common to all should govern the family.

As a result, the governance of the Muslim family law takes place in a socio-legal sphere with crisscrossing laws, multiple sources of authority, and narratives about law, Islam, and gender roles and rights. How do we map this field and capture interactions between various laws and centers of authority? Delineating this immensely diverse field through tracing disputes in the adjudication process of Muslim family law governing marriage, I suggest that Luhmann's notion of communication serves as a useful analytical tool to characterize the interplay between various layers of law and legal actors in this field. Nicolas Luhmann (1992, 1995) puts forth an idea of communication as a combination of information, utterance, and understanding. For Luhmann, communication "has no goal or end, no immanent entelechy" (Luhmann 1992, 255), such as consensus; though "episodic goals can be formed without making goal positing the goal of the system" (Luhmann 1992, 255). While values might underlie communication, they "lead an extra ordinarily labile psychological existence. They can be used on one occasion and not on the other without being supported by a psychological deep structure" (Luhmann 1992, 265). For Luhmann, communication is constitutive in the sense that each communication is part of a preceding and succeeding chain of communication, and each communication exists as part of a larger field of communication events in a system. Following Luhmann, while divesting his theory of some of its ontological concepts (see also Jansen 2016), I suggest that the interconnections and exchange between diverse laws and normative legal orders are best captured as communication, and not as conflicts over sovereignty. Communication in this respect refers to a connecting but agonistic space that handles incommensurability, as well as identification, similarities, and overlap between different actors; it is open to poly-narratives, a rich array of interests, ideologies, agendas, and epistemic and moral frames. This allows a range of possible outcomes. The following section will illustrate these points.

Public action, deliberation, and discussion

In an afternoon in January 2003, in a large hall of a women's organization, a public meeting is organized to discuss aspects of Muslim Personal Law that are seen as unjust and unequal by women. The public meetings have been facilitated by the secular Muslim women's group, called Awaaz-e-Niswan (henceforth AEN), which worked then in south-central Mumbai. The group was formed in the 1980s, and since then it has been a secular feminist collective run by Muslim women. The group focuses on the issues and concerns of Muslim, and offering its counselling and legal services to women across religious boundaries and focusing on Muslim women's rights within the framework of feminist political solidarity (Solanki 2011). From its inception, it combines individual intervention in the informal dispute resolution process with social action (Solanki 2011, 2017).

The meeting is attended by local groups that work on neighborhood issues, and some have links with secular parties (such as the Congress Party and Samajwadi Party). Some workers from the Communist Party of India's (CPI's) women's wings are also here. The meeting is also attended by some autonomous women's groups and NGOs that work on adjudication and arbitration in family law-related matters. Some of the local qazis and lawyers are present as well, as are qazis that are affiliated with the Jamiat Ulema e Hind.

The agenda of the meeting is to discuss women's experiences of triple talaq and the direction of reforms in Muslim Personal Law. The local groups have requested that some space be set aside to discuss a local question: two young girls aged 16 and 17 have been married by their parents to older Arab men, and the local civil society organizations want to plan a public awareness campaign to prevent such marriages in the future. The NGOs, political parties, women's groups, and some qazis are in favor. A few qazis dissent, as they earn their living solemnizing such marriages.

The public meeting begins with a welcome and story-telling. Several women who have experienced triple talaq narrate their stories. As the section below demonstrates, what we see here is the women's engagement with other stakeholders who also shape adjudication. Women's engagement in these processes enables reflexivity and self-knowledge, and evokes empathetic moments from the audience. This forum is a platform that articulates women's moral and political voice. It also publicizes the "private" domestic concerns and politics of women's status and rights in the family – it brings to light not only the legal dispute but other dimensions of gender inequality as well (the question about whether the second child's gender had prompted divorce, for instance). These women's socio-religious legal stories also invite all those present to scrutinize religious practices from a critical distance. This enables an action-oriented approach to justice, enabling localized solutions to the question.

This section narrates two such cases which take a longitudinal approach to the case study method. I interviewed and followed up on these cases over the period and new developments are shared here. This part of the chapter taps into the complexities of adjudication in Muslim Personal Law on the ground; it captures convergence, diffusion, and integration between various stakeholders. The multi-party platform for discussion on the adjudication of triple talaq initiated by the feminist organization AEN, showcases (for analytical purposes) the effective story-telling by women, the dialogue and polylogue between various stakeholders, public argumentation and deliberation, and a multi-perspective view of the complexities involved in the adjudication of triple talaq. Women litigants use effective and richly detailed accounts that are also supported by evidence, and are structured with the clear intent to deliver the pitfalls of triple talaq, the issues in navigating diverse legal systems, and voice their expectations. Parties both agree and disagree with one another, mobilize around common goals, and set up concrete agendas for further dialogue and change.

Story-telling, deliberation, and follow-up

Tahira's story

Tahira, a young woman in her late 20s gets up to speak. She has studied up to high school, and at the moment she is trying to learn tailoring in order to support herself and her two daughters. She has been burned by triple talaq, she said (mein triple talaq se jali hun). Tahira was married to her husband, Majid, for five years and has a daughter. She described her life with her husband as an ordinary one. She said that her mother- and sisters-in-law often harassed and taunted her, but she never had any serious conflicts with Majid. When she was pregnant with their second child, she went to her parents' house in the last days of her pregnancy. She gave birth to her second daughter there, but no one from her husband's family came to visit the newborn. She and her family grew apprehensive, believing that the reason for this neglect might be because of the second child's gender. A month after the delivery, her husband called and told her that he didn't want her back. "I have given you talaq," he said. She was stunned. She had not received any letter of talaq as of yet. Her family members then took two arbitrators with them to her husband's house to talk over the matter and see if there could be reconciliation, but Majid's family refused to meet them and reiterated that her husband had divorced her.

Tahira and her family approached the AEN for help. The feminist activists associated with the AEN advised her to file a case to receive maintenance for her and her two daughters in the Family Court under Section 125, CrPC,[5] as under this section, married Muslim women can ask for maintenance. Majid argued in court that he had divorced her; therefore, he was not liable to provide maintenance to Tahira under this law. He produced a signed copy of a registered letter. The letter was a fatwa (legal opinion), written by a qazi, pronouncing talaq. Tahira maintained that she had never signed this letter and the signature was forged. She accused her husband of having bribed the postman and obtained her false signature on the registered letter.

5 Section 125 of the Code of Criminal Procedure, 1973, pertains to orders for the maintenance of wives, children, and parents. Married women of any religion can file for maintenance under Section 125 CrPC without filing for any matrimonial remedies under any personal laws. This section is popular among poorer members of society, because the recovery of arrears is easier: the law enables the Family Court to attach the property of the defaulter in case of non-payment of maintenance.

Tahira and her family went to another qazi to explain this case, and the second qazi's legal opinion differed regarding the validity of the talaq. He stated that Tahira had not received the talaq, and opined that it was not valid as it had not been communicated to the wife. The second qazi upheld the status of the marriage in his fatwa. She presented this fatwa in court, but the court refused the second qazi's fatwa and accepted the husband's version. The standard of proof required in Family Court is not stringent and the court stated that evidence regarding factual causation offered by Majid was stronger than Tahira's evidence of forgery. The sole evidence was the signature of Tahira, which she disputed; no handwriting experts were called on to testify. The technicality of Islamic jurisprudence was not considered at all as being important in court, also showing a high degree of judicial discretion in lower courts in India (Solanki 2011).

Tahira ended her story at the public meeting with questions to ponder: "I want to ask my brothers and sisters gathered here – what did I do wrong? Is it right to desert a wife without giving any reason? Where do we go for justice? The court doesn't listen to us, it listens only to men. If we come to the community, some support us and others don't. Where do we go for justice?"

Tahira's narration brings to the fore the dispute between her and her husband, Majid, over whether talaq was granted. This is not merely a question of conscience; this is equally a social and gendered dispute. The dissolution of marriage has enormous consequences for Tahira – she loses economic support, social and legal status as a wife, and has the sole responsibility of providing for two daughters without any formal training. The maintenance amount that she receives is too low to support her and her two children. Her legal status is also questionable – she has not received any communication of talaq as she states, and as a result, she believes she is still married. This hampers her ability to marry again until she obtains a divorce. On the other hand, Majid's legal status does not affect his ability to marry again, as polygyny is allowed under Muslim Personal Law in India.

It would be too simplistic to recast this case as a dispute between religious law and the state law; there are differences between different clergy over what consists triple talaq and what evidence is acceptable. The judicial precedent allows the court the privilege to read either way (as precedent exists in both directions), but the court chooses to privilege the husband's version over the wife's. This also brings up the feminists questioning the binary divide between religious law and state law, and the feminist arguments (especially in the Indian context) about the state law protecting the woman as opposed to religious law (Parashar and Dhanda 2008).

Tahira completed her story in the meeting, and the discussion began surrounding this issue. Scholars have suggested that story-telling can bridge the gap between dialogue and discussion, as it contains empathetic moments in which persons can transcend the tension between self and other as they craft and listen to stories (Black 2008). We find here that story-telling allows an opportunity for reflection upon the lived experiences of the other; it also promotes further deliberation, generates solutions, and plans for public action around issues. For instance, during the meeting discussion, one of the qazis opined that this talaq was not valid even if

Tahira had signed it, because the husband had not returned the *mehar* (a dowry) amount to the wife. A Muslim marriage (*nikah*) is composed of an offer (made by a woman or her guardians), an acceptance of the offer (by the groom), and a mehar payment. The mehar is payable on demand (payable upon the dissolution of marriage by death or divorce) (Section 290, Mulla 1955, 251). In this case, there was no proof that the amount of mehar, which was 25,000 rupees, had been paid to the wife. Taking on this thread of the conversation, the AEN workers who were coordinating the event stated that these cases were common, and that such legal uncertainty and corruption among the clergy needed to be tackled. They stated that greater public awareness needed to be created so that women were not cheated.

The meeting also debated the question of state law and judges, and the legal uncertainty in state courts. Judges and lawyers are trained in civil law in India and do not receive training in Islamic jurisprudence. The qazi and others asked the lawyers and the AEN and other women's groups of the necessity to educate the judges and lawyers practicing in the Family Court on the intricacies of Muslim Personal Law.

I followed up on this case later, in 2008. Two years after this meeting, Tahira heard that Majid was getting married again. Although polygamy is allowed in the Muslim Personal Law, it was not commonly practiced among their kingroups. On the day of his marriage, Tahira and her parents and family members along with local social workers went to Majid's fiancée's house and appraised them of the ongoing dispute. "This can also happen to you," they told Majid's fiancée, whose family members immediately called for Tahira's husband. Majid, his family, and some relatives rushed to the husband's fiancée's house. Their neighbors called up Tahira's family and told them there was a threat of violence. Fearing that the situation would spiral out of control, Tahira's family called the AEN, and the workers rushed over. The group (consisting of the social workers, the AEN workers, Tahira's family, Majid's family, and Majid's fiancée's family) then went to the police station to resolve the dispute. At the station, in the presence of the police officer on duty they held a joint meeting to discuss what might be done. A local qazi was called; her husband then officially divorced Tahira, paid the mehar (returned her dowry), and made a formal promise to provide maintenance for his two daughters from the first marriage with Tahira.

The role of the police here is more of a social one; the idea of the state's coercive role (Abrams 1988) is invoked by litigants to ensure that there is no private violence during these negotiations. The involvement of the police is part of a carefully crafted and scripted routine to give legitimacy to the outcome of this process of negotiation, and is frequently used by disputing parties in India. The trappings of the idealized state are invoked through conducting this negotiation in a police station, though this work finds no mention in any police manual, and there would be no state record of this role. There is immense rule flexibility in these negotiations, though locally acceptable precepts form the background structure of comprehension of legal rules – voluntary obedience of the parties to the process and the solution are usually presumed and there are no formal enforcement mechanisms.

Scholars suggest that women tend to approach informal forums, and if they are unsuccessful there, they turn to state courts for a final solution to the dispute (Mukhopadhyay 1998). However, we find that the court's judgment about the validity of Tahira and Majid's marriage was contested by religious authority sources on the ground, and was finally resolved through social dialogue between two extended families through an active intervention of feminist workers, and stamped by the qazi in the presence of the police. The writ of the state or religion or custom does not always run supreme on the ground. At multiple levels, this dispute was discussed among the extended families and relatives, feminist organizations and local NGOs, the state court and the police, and different qazis with affiliations to different religious seminaries. This brings to light the politics and also the transformative potential of the quotidian in affecting localized change.

Nazia's story

At the same meeting, I met with Nazia, who also told her story. It's more elaborately told and I have tried to capture the flavor of the narrative.

Nazia was married to her husband when she was 17 years old. She lived in a small village in western India; she was the only sister among three brothers and had a very protected childhood. She moved to Mumbai after her marriage. She had three children by the time she was 24 and her life revolved around them.

"I didn't know much of the world," Nazia said. "I was only familiar with the street we lived in, and had never traveled anywhere along in Mumbai or outside without my husband and it was only when the children were a little older that I started walking them to the neighborhood school."

Her husband was an inspector in the Brihan Mumbai Municipal Corporation (henceforth BMC). He was very corrupt; and rather than hoarding cash, he tended to convert it into other assets, such as land, which are called *benami* property. In order to launder the black money that he received in bribes, and to evade taxation, he bought the tenancy rights of a small room apartment in a BMC-owned old building in south-central Mumbai in Nazia's name. The rent was paid regularly and the receipts were in her name, as was all documentation.

Almost 12 years after her marriage, one day her husband had a fight with her, and dragged her out of the house. He took her near the nearby police station, and handed her a paper that he said was a fatwa from a local qazi. It was a fatwa pronouncing triple talaq; it stated that he was not liable to provide maintenance to her under the Muslim Personal Law and that the custody of the children would be with her until they were no longer of minor age, then her husband would have custody. The fatwa stated that her husband would not pay maintenance while the children were in the mother's custody, but he would support them once they came back to live with him. He told her that because he was giving her talaq, as per provisions of Islamic laws of marriage and divorce, she was to vacate the house and go back to her parents' village with the three children, as he was marrying again and wanted to live in their house with his second wife. His choice of the venue was interesting – he did not take her inside the police station – but the divorce was granted outside, invoking the idea of the state, especially its coercive power, but not involving the state. He left her there. Nazia said that she was in such shock that it took her four hours to find her way back home; she kept walking in circles, although her home was about 15 minutes away from the police station. She finally returned home and sat up the whole night with her three children sleeping, wondering what she was going to do.

The qazi's fatwa not only relied (to some extent) on religious ideas but also on everyday commonsensical ideas about Muslim Personal Law in India, reflected occasionally in popular perceptions about law in state courts, in academic and popular writings, and in NGO reports. The popular and academic narratives on triple talaq in India often fail to mention the internal diversity of views and interests among Muslims; they claim that all Muslim men could and did divorce their wives arbitrarily, that triple talaq was routinely practiced, and that divorced Muslim women were not entitled to maintenance under Muslim Personal Law (see for instance Narain 2001; Parashar and Dhanda 2008). In doing so, academic and popular accounts have ignored legal developments in state courts as well as the politics of everyday adjudication of Islamic law in multiple forums. The social costs of asymmetric information and misinformation around triple talaq are evident here.

Nazia called her brothers and told them the news. The family was in a panic – they tried to talk to her husband to make him see reason and retract his divorce, but he was not willing to talk to anyone in her family. In the meantime, her husband sent her a notice to vacate the house, as she was no longer his wife, and stated that he will be taking steps to remove her name as tenant of the house and will add the name of his second wife. Nazia was crying the next day, and one of her neighbors came to visit and asked what was wrong. When Nazia told her the news, her neighbor told her to go see a lawyer nearby. When Nazia did so, the lawyer, who operated out of a balcony of a chawl, told her that the manner of her husband's delivery of triple talaq was not procedurally valid under Muslim Personal Law; also, her husband had no proof that he had given her the divorce. This was the first time Nazia had received an alternative viewpoint. The lawyer gave her a letter for the BMC officer in charge. The letter stated that she was the owner of the apartment; her husband was harassing her and trying to dispossess her, but she had been paying the rent all these years, and the tenancy agreement of the house was in her name and should not be transferred to another person. Her husband also wrote to the BMC stating that he was paying the rent of said premise, and that he bought the apartment in her name as a benami property.[6] He sent the BMC officer a copy of the talaq and stated that she could no longer stay there, as they were divorced.

Nazia went to the government office to meet with the officer and to deliver her lawyer's letter. This was the first time she had gone there, and she brought her

6 The term "benami property" refers to property bought by the owner under a fake name or in the name of someone else for tax avoidance. The Prohibition of Benami Property Transactions Act, 1988, was meant to regulate such properties and weed out corruption.

minor son for moral support. She met with the BMC officer and told her story, talking about the possibility of dispossession. She asked him where she would go with three children and no economic means to support her if she had to vacate this property. The BMC officer listened to her story – over the course of a year, her husband tried to officially change the ownership details in the documents, but the BMC officer denied the request, stating that Nazia had been paying the rent, her name was on the official documents, and that the BMC would only recognize her as the tenant of the room. The BMC officer further maintained that her husband had been unable to prove divorce, as there was no documentation about it from the state court. He reiterated that he could not recognize the fatwa as a valid document of divorce. What we see here is not really any religious discussion around the merits of claims in religious law, but a discretionary issue crafted by the lawyer, and the pragmatic and functional use of legal ambiguity by the BMC officer. Both the lawyer and the BMC officer relied on case precedent, legal irregularities, and procedural ambiguities to push for an optimal solution in Nazia's interests.

"I was still in a panic," stated Nazia, and "went to every forum that would listen to me." It was during this time that she heard about the Public Complaint Centre (PCC), a civic group with some ties to the Congress Party (a national party in India), which adjudicated in these matters. The group was initially formed to address civic complaints in the neighborhood – to discuss access to water, electricity, garbage and development works in the area. It worked as a citizens' group. Soon, however, they found that they were receiving complaints from women across religions who handed in complaints of arbitrary divorce, domestic violence, and other family disputes. The group members, mainly small businessmen and professionals (clerks, lawyers, public sector workers) of the area, met in an open plot (which was also being used as a garbage dump in the area). In the evening, a mat was placed over the open garbage dump, two large wooden tables were pulled up and about five to eight men from the area would sit, while women and men would line up to approach them with complaints, and matters would be discussed. The proceedings were public – people could get a sense of someone's dispute, but not all the details, as the others who were in line sat at some distance away. The smell of the garbage was overpowering for the newcomers, but others did not seem to notice. The litigants and complainants waiting in the area often talked to one another, exchanged information about their cases; pros and cons of various forums were discussed, as were local politics; neighborhood gossip was exchanged; and local campaigns and news were mulled over.

The term social worker in Mumbai is a self-described title used by many people; not all of them are trained in social work. The lower-level political party workers call themselves social workers; the label is used by slum activists who take up various matters, as do prominent people in the social sphere who intervene in intra- and extra-familial and other disputes. It is also a self-referential term used by strongmen. Fixers also employ the term, as do "big men" of localities. In this narrative context, it refers to a group of men from different professional backgrounds who are interested in addressing "social issues" of the area. The social workers at the PCC were not trained in Islamic jurisprudence, or Hindu family law or secular laws, nor were they all lawyers, but they all acquired legal skills through their "experience of social work"; they had picked up the knowledge of law through their interventions and conversations. They maintained contacts with the local police and municipal corporation officials, and worked with local NGOs and religious organizations when required (be it while planning public campaigns or in individual cases). Justice in these forums is not meted by neutral judges, though they all claim to be so; their reading of law and ideas of justice are entangled with their political interests, ideas of social responsibility, personal ambition, local concerns, and their need for social recognition.

The PCCs dealt with a variety of disputes – property- and tenancy-related disputes, disputes between family members, matrimonial cases and cases of domestic violence, elopements, community disputes and riots, harassment from strongmen, and civic-related issues (such as garbage, planning of civic spaces, and cleaning outside various area temples and mosques). However, matrimonial complaints formed the bulk of the disputes that they handled. When I interviewed the adjudicators at the PCC, the social workers told me that they did not impose their perspectives on the people. They tended to ask their Muslim litigants about their sect, and ask what law or school of Islamic jurisprudence they follow, then adjudicate accordingly. The lawyers present on that day would ensure that there was no conflict with the state law, and would help with any legal procedure that the litigant required. Similarly, they would ask or seek advice when needed from a qazi or others, but these persons did not serve on the dispute panel.

When Nazia narrated the story of her triple talaq, the social workers assured her that she would be helped. They gave her another date to come, and asked her husband to come and meet them, too. They also called the local qazi who had written the fatwa of her divorce. The husband came but said that he was going by state law, that his action was legal, and that he did not want to live with Nazia anymore. They asked him the reason behind the divorce; he said that she was not a good wife and did not look after the children. At that point, the neighborhood women and Nazia's family (who had accompanied her) protested loudly and accused her husband of being unfaithful and corrupt; not a good man. The PCC adjudicators opined that they did not believe in this kind of divorce without any cause, and that they did not recognize the divorce. They asked the husband who had written the fatwa, and he gave the name of a local qazi; the Centre adjudicator asked this qazi to be present on the next meeting date.

When the meeting took place with the clergy, the PCC demanded accountability from the qazis. They asked how the qazi had managed to give divorce without any procedure in this surreptitious fashion. The qazi replied that it was Islamic; they told him they do not recognize illegality in the name of Islam, and publicly reprimanded the clergy for not being accountable to society at large by handing out talaq in this arbitrary fashion without thinking about its consequences to the wife and the three children. This public reprimand (which could be heard by other people who had gathered for their complaints) had enormous social significance, for it challenged the religio-moral authority of the qazis and pried open the dissonance between their image and behavior, leaving little room for face-saving. This incident was also a form of communication evincing competition for power and authority between two power centers – the qazis, representing the religious sphere of authority, and the civic power centers, relying on the pragmatic aspect of justice in the wider sense. What we see here is also a form of non-compliance to religious authority. It is also a confrontational conversation in which religious principles as espoused by the qazi are matched against the intuitions and ideas of justice, and judged according to the degree of adherence or departure from them.

A year went by, and Nazia's marital status remained contested. She maintained that she was married and that she had not accepted divorce. Her lawyer's, the BMC officials,' and the PCC's views and interpretations of the law supported her claim. At the opposite end, her husband maintained that he had divorced her, and that she should vacate his apartment and move back with her parents. Some of the qazis in the area supported him. We see here how litigants use personal stories that demonstrate different pathways and strategies of justice; differing notions of legitimacy are invoked – at times, parties are held accountable by invocations to natural justice, while sometimes, stakeholders rely on instrumental strategy of not recognizing community divorce to protect women's rights in law. For instance, the BMC officers refuse to recognize the triple talaq unless declared so by state courts, and both the state officials and the social workers at the PCC question the religious clergy, employing a moral worldview that acknowledges the vulnerability of Nazia and her children in the husband's version of Islamic law. Discourses and interpretations of triple talaq are deployed in opposing ways by litigants and adjudicators.

The main issue for Nazia and her husband was her continued possession of the apartment with the children. Her husband tried multiple ways to force her out of the property. He kept serving her notices, but when that did not work (because of the BMC's stance) he took to sending hoodlums, thinking that she could be scared enough to change her mind. The goons kept knocking on her doors at night, entering in the apartment, verbally abusing her, and asking her to get out. They threatened her to vacate – after all, she was a single woman in her early 30s living along with three young children. They even tried to beat her up a bit, but the neighbors intervened. It was during this time that again, one of the women in the neighborhood told her about a new women's organization that was helping women; Nazia went to the group along with her neighbor.

She had gone to the AEN seeking help in this matter, Nazia explained. She also went to the PCC, but they had asked her husband to come and he refused. She wanted the AEN to help her to approach the police on her behalf to register her complaints so that the harassment would stop, and she also wanted advice on how to proceed further.

Many suggestions poured forth at this meeting. Nazia's neighbors had come as well; the neighborhood women talked about the harassment and non-action of the police. The NGOs offered to go with her to the police station. The PCC members confirmed her story and shared that they could not intervene further because her husband had refused to meet them. The qazis' roles were further criticized; the qazi who intervened in Tahira's case with his opinion about the validity of that divorce reiterated his stand, a common agenda of educating local women; other NGOs and the state officials and the judiciary was restated; and the stand taken by the BMC officer was praised.

Communication between laws and legal actors and bodies

The intricate interplay of various sources of law and authority cannot only be analytically understood as a question of tensions, confrontation, and conflict between customary and religious laws, and constitutional and statutory norms and laws. This chapter proposes to view these interactions through the prism of communication, as outlined by Niklas Luhmann (1992; 1995). As stated earlier, Luhmann conceptualizes communication as the "synthesis of three selections, namely information, utterance, and understanding (including misunderstanding)" (1992; 1995, 141–4). These three components refer to the intention and the content of the message conveyed, the "how" and "why" of communication, and the meaning of the communication that emerges from, builds upon, and guides each successive event. This chapter brings to light the layered interactions between various epistemic frames of law and implementation mechanisms that influence the interpretation of triple talaq in various forums, as well as in public debates between various stakeholders on the issue in India. Different conceptions of justice, equality, law, and religion form a basis for moral communication and are reiterated and challenged in micro-events of communication; these are productive, generative, productive processes that facilitate open-ended outcomes.

Furthermore, this chapter shows that the practice of adjudication in Muslim Personal Law is not practiced in isolation but in conjunction with customary and state laws. In addition, there are multiple readings of what comprises triple talaq in Muslim Personal Law in state courts as well as in society, capturing what I call the centralization and decentralization of law (Solanki 2011). The interactions between multiple actors and laws can also be mapped, as cases progress over time. As each case unfolds, it produces different interactions among varied social actors at different crossroads; each intersection becomes a meeting place of various and contested imaginations of justice and law. In each instance, the lines between religious law, customs, moral notions of justice, and state law are rethought, renegotiated and reformulated. The relationship between various sources is sometimes confrontational; in others, cooperative. There are a plethora of rhetoric techniques – some are conversations that are indeterminate, generic, and open, and other strategies that are far-extending and purpose-oriented, bringing clarity to issues and provide fodder for action. Moral disagreements abound and other options might be pursued at any juncture in the adjudication process. Multiple actors share social commitments and interests, and they come together for joint action through interactions among the various members and organizations at different points in the adjudication process; some of these shared values outlive and continue past the joint action and, thus, alliances are formed between groups and individuals.

Conclusion

Muslim Personal Law in India grants the man the right of unconditional, unilateral divorce; this form of divorce consolidates gender inequality and prevents women from speaking out against marital abuse and violence. The Indian women's movements have taken up the issue of gender equality in Muslim Personal Law and suggested that this law represents a conflict between religious law and constitutional equality. I suggest another conceptual route, instead, to capture these varied interactions. This chapter suggested that the question is not about the laws' hierarchy and conflict but about communication between laws and values and sources of authority. The chapter suggests that communication, not conflict, is the analytical tool that captures the rich array of poly-narratives by sources that are not always in agreement. Moreover, tracing the interactions between action taken at various points shows harmony as well as disjuncture among social norms, narratives, and action. The chapter also charts a field where political action co-occurs with story-telling, deliberation, and dialogue.

Bibliography

Abrams, Philip. 1988. "Notes on the difficulties of studying the state." *Journal of Historical Sociology* 1(1): 58–89.

Black, Laura. 2008. "Deliberation, storytelling, and dialogical moments." *Communication Theory* 18(1): 93–118.

Esposito, John L. 1982. *Women in Muslim Family Law*. Syracuse: Syracuse University Press.

Griffiths, John. 1986. "What is legal pluralism?" *Journal of Legal Pluralism* 24: 1–55.

Haddad, Yvonne Yazbeck and Barbara Stowasser. 2004. *Islamic Law and the Challenges of Modernity*. Walnut Creek: Altamira Press.

Hallaq, Wael B. 2001. *Authority, Continuity, and Change in Islamic Law*. New York: Cambridge University Press.

Jansen, Till. 2016. "Who is talking? Some remarks on nonhuman agency in communication." *Communication Theory* 26(3): 255–272.

Luhmann, Niklas. 1992. "What is communication?" *Communication Theory* 2(3): 251–259.

Luhmann, Niklas. 1995. *Social Systems*. Stanford: Stanford University Press.

Moore, Sally Folk. 1973. "Law and social change: The semi-autonomous social field as an appropriate subject of study." *Law and Society Review* 7(4): 719–746.

Mukhopadhyay, Maitreyee. 1998. *Legally Dispossessed: Gender, Identity, and the Process of Law*. Calcutta: Stree.

Mulla, Dinshah Fardunji. 1955. *Principles of Mahomedan Law*. Calcutta: Eastern Law House.

Narain, Vrinda. 2001. *Gender and Community: Muslim Women's Rights in India*. Toronto: University of Toronto Press.

Nussbaum, Martha C. 1997. "Religion and women's human rights." In *Religion and Contemporary Liberalism*. Paul J. Weithman, Ed. Notre Dame: University of Notre Dame Press, pp. 93–137.

Parashar, Archana and Amita Dhanda, eds. 2008. *Redefining Family Law in India: Essays in Honour of B. Sivaramayya*. New Delhi: Routledge.

Richland, Justin. 2011. Hopi tradition as jurisdiction: On the potentializing limits of Hopi sovereignty. *Law and Social Inquiry* 36(1): 201–234.
Shachar, Ayelet. 2001. *Multicultural Jurisdictions: Cultural Difference and Women's Rights*. Cambridge: Cambridge University Press.
Solanki, Gopika. 2011. *Adjudication in Religious Family Laws: Cultural Accommodation, Legal Pluralism, and Gender Equality in India*. Cambridge: Cambridge University Press.
Solanki, Gopika. 2017. "A court of her own: Autonomy, gender, and women's courts in India." In *Gender Equality and Justice in Family Law Disputes: Women, Mediation and Religious Arbitration*. Samia Bano and Jennifer Pierce, Eds. New England: University of New England Press.
Yuval-Davis, Nira. 1997. *Gender and Nation*. Thousand Oaks: Sage Publications.

14 Two legal orders and one cause

Or a way to simultaneous decision-making

Wolfgang Wieshaider

The frame

The disposal of objects classified as cultural heritage is commonly restricted under state law. The public interest to preserve them is juxtaposed with the right to ownership. Where such objects serve religious purposes, the human right of religious freedom is at stake as well (Wieshaider, 2002: 135–140; Wasmuth, 2017: D §§ 129, 152).

Liturgical disposals, modifications and the like are regulated by religious law, to be decided by religious bodies. State authorities are not competent in this realm, but they still need to judge the same facts of the case under state law. This article will explore a mode of simultaneous decision-making aiming at one single result anchored in both legal orders affected, as proposed by Austrian law.

The rule

Section 1(1) of Cultural Heritage Protection Act[1] defines monuments as man-made objects of cultural value. In principle, restrictions to dispose apply to monuments only in case they are classed as protected monuments on condition that there is public preservation interest based on the cultural value of the monument. Classification is effectuated in administrative procedures according to section 3(1) *leg. cit.* or assumed in the case of movable monuments owned by bodies corporate of public law according to section 2(1) *leg. cit.* Between the years 2000 and 2009 immovable monuments owned by bodies corporate of public law could be classed through ordinances according to section 2a(1) *leg. cit.*; the ordinances and hence the protection continue to be in force.

The primary restrictions laid down by Cultural Heritage Protection Act concern the destruction, the modification and the exportation of the protected monuments; finally the conveyance with regard to monuments of assumed public preservation interest. According to sections 4(1), 6(1) and 16(1) *leg. cit.* these dispositions are subject to a permission issued by the competent state authority.

1 *Denkmalschutzgesetz*, *Bundesgesetzblatt* no. 533/1923, as last amended by *Bundesgesetzblatt* I no. 92/2013.

The modification of protected monuments can be permitted according to section 5(1) *leg. cit.* if public or private interests in favour of the modification outweigh the public preservation interest, which the competent state authority has to scrutinise in an administrative procedure. With regard to certain monuments, section 5(4) *leg. cit.* provides for a specific procedure which will be the topic of the considerations of this article. The following quotation from the wording of the law will be explained in detail hereinafter.

> *Unbeschadet der sonstigen Bestimmungen dieses Paragrafen ist dem Antrag auf Veränderung eines dem Gottesdienst gewidmeten Denkmals (samt zugehöriger Nebenobjekte) einer gesetzlich anerkannten Kirche oder Religionsgesellschaft einschließlich ihrer Einrichtungen auf jeden Fall so weit stattzugeben, als die Veränderung für die Abhaltung des Gottesdienstes und der Teilnahme der Gläubigen daran nach den zwingenden oder zumindest allgemein angewandten liturgischen Vorschriften der gesetzlich anerkannten Kirche oder Religionsgesellschaft notwendig ist. Als notwendig gelten jedenfalls alle Vorschriften, ohne deren Beachtung die regelmäßige Abhaltung allgemeiner Gottesdienste nicht gestattet wäre und auch jene Umstände, die den Gläubigen die regelmäßige Teilnahme am Gottesdienst in ausreichendem Maße und in zumutbarer, würdiger Weise ermöglicht. Art und Umfang der Notwendigkeit ist auf Verlangen des Bundesdenkmalamtes durch eine von der zuständigen Oberbehörde der betreffenden Kirche oder Religionsgesellschaft ausgestellte Bescheinigung nachzuweisen. Um dem Bundesdenkmalamt Gelegenheit zu geben, Gegenvorschläge zu erstatten, ist in dieser Bescheinigung auch darzulegen, welche Konsequenzen sich daraus ergeben würden, wenn den Veränderungen nicht in der beantragten Weise oder im beantragten Umfang entsprochen würde und ist in dieser Bescheinigung auch zu allfällig bereits gemachten Gegenvorschlägen des Bundesdenkmalamtes Stellung zu nehmen.*

Section 5(4) *leg. cit.* applies to monuments and their accessories which are dedicated to divine service and are owned by a legally recognised religious society or one of its bodies. A legally recognised religious society is a special legal form of religious community, recognised by the state and vested with legal personality of public law (Potz, Schinkele, 2016: 87f.; Wieshaider, 2013). Section 5(4) *leg. cit.* is introduced with a formula intimating that the state authority be obligated (Anderle, 1978: 459; Helfgott, 1978, 439; Helfgott, 1979: 66 note 12) to permit a modification request if the modification is necessary for divine services to be organised and participated in according to cogent or generally applied liturgical regulations of the corresponding religious society. The necessity test is completed

- where otherwise regular divine services would not be allowed or
- where a regular participation would not be possible in a reasonable and worthy way.

Exceptional cases such as sporadic festive ceremonies are left out of consideration, as the explanatory notes to the amendment indicate.[2]

On request of the state authority, the superior religious authority (Anderle, 1978: 462) is obliged to give proof of the liturgical necessity in question. Therein the superior religious authority has to explain which consequences a refusal of the intended modifications would have. Thereupon it is the state authority's turn to suggest counter-proposals, to which the superior religious authority has to react in the aforementioned way. This latter procedure, however, sheds new light on the introductory clause of section 5(4) *leg. cit.* It can no longer viewed as an obligation to unconditionally accede to the application of the religious body, but it turns into a trigger of a specific procedure resembling a kind of negotiation (Wieshaider, 2000: 398–400; Wieshaider, 2014). By doing so, state law turns into a flexible device to consider and accommodate changes within a given religious society. Such changes may be of demographic or theological origin; the reasons must be plausibly explained to the state authority in the procedure according to section 5(4) *leg. cit.* (Wasmuth, 2017: D § 157).

The comparative assurance

A glance at parallel acts of law in the same region shows that such a regulation is not self-evident. Whereas in the Czech Republic,[3] in Slovakia,[4] Hungary,[5] Slovenia[6] and most of the Swiss cantons there are no specific rules, the results for Italy and Germany are quite different.

Section 6(3) of Basle's Cultural Heritage Act[7] as well as Art. 9 of the Italian Cultural Heritage Code[8] oblige the state authorities to reach an agreement with the corresponding religious authorities (Margiotta Broglio, 2000: 81–88). And in Germany, where each land regulates the preservation of cultural heritage independently, only one land – i.e. Bremen – does not have any provision covering similar questions (Bregger, 2003: 62–65; Wasmuth, 2017: D § 180, 190).

In a couple of lands it is provided that state authorities have to take the religious needs into consideration and decide after consultation with the religious

2 No. 1769 of *Beilagen zu den stenografischen Protokollen des Nationalrats*, 20th legislative period, p. 51.

3 *Zákon o státní památkové péči*, no. 20/1987 *Sbírky zákonů*, as last amended by act no. 127/2016 *Sbírky zákonů.*

4 *Zákon o ochrane pamiatkového fondu*, no. 49/2002 Zbierky zákonov, as last amended by act no. 125/2016 *Zbierky zákonov.*

5 Act no. LXIV/2001 (*Törvény a kulturális örökség védelméről), Magyar Közlöny*, pp. 5646–5678, as last amended by act no. XCII/2016, *Magyar Közlöny*, pp. 7292–7302.

6 *Zakon o varstvu kulturne dediščine*, no. 785, *Uradni list* no. 16/2008, as last amended by act no. 1367, *Uradni list* no. 32/2016.

7 *Gesetz über den Denkmalschutz*, no. 497.100 of 20 March 1980 as of 26 January 2014.

8 *Decreto Legislativo* no. 42/2004 *Codice dei beni culturali e del paesaggio, Gazzetta Ufficiale* no. 45/2004, *Supplemento Ordinario* no. 28, as last amended by *Decreto legislativo* no. 90/2016, *Gazzetta Ufficiale* no. 125/2016.

authorities. Section 21(1) of Berlin's Cultural Heritage Protection Act,[9] section 18(1, 2) of Saxon Cultural Heritage Act,[10] section 8(5) of Saxony-Anhalt's Cultural Heritage Protection Act,[11] section 21(1) of Brandenburg's Cultural Heritage Protection Act,[12] section 24(1) of Hamburg's Cultural Heritage Protection Act[13] and section 38 of North Rhine-Westphalia's Cultural Heritage Protection Act[14] are phrased in this spirit (Wasmuth, 2017: D §§ 188f., 191, 196, 200f.). Religious authorities bear the burden of proof as any other owner of classified monuments (Wasmuth, 2017: D § 175).

Whereas section 12(1) of Thuringian Cultural Heritage Act[15] (Wasmuth, 2017: D § 203) does not explicitly refer to consultations, it lays down that liturgical needs take precedence over preservation interests. Prime importance is likewise accorded to religious interests in regard to monuments dedicated to divine service by section 11(1) Baden-Wurttemberg's Cultural Heritage Protection Act[16] and section 29(3) of Hessian Cultural Heritage Protection Act[17] (Wasmuth, 2017: D § 192; (Heckel, 1987: 97–100).

Art. 26(2) of Bavarian Cultural Heritage Protection Act[18] (Eberl, Martin and Petzet, 1997: Art. 26 DSchG, §§ 11f.; Wasmuth, 2017: D §§ 186f.), section 10(3) of Mecklenburg-West Pomerania's Cultural Heritage Protection Act[19] and section 23 of Saarland's Cultural Heritage Protection Act[20] go a step further. There the competence is passed to the corresponding religious authority that will have to hand down the decision after consultation with the state authorities, if the state authority failed to take religious needs into account in regard to heritage dedicated to divine service. The latter's discretionary powers appear reduced (Eberl, Martin and Petzet, 1997: Art. 26 DSchG, § 10).

Based on the condition that the corresponding religious bodies have passed equivalent heritage regulations (Wasmuth, 2017: D §§ 131–144), section 18(3)

9 *Denkmalschutzgesetz, Gesetz- und Verordnungsblatt* 1995, p. 274, as last amended in *Gesetz- und Verordnungsblatt* 2016, p. 26.
10 *Sächsisches Denkmalschutzgesetz, Gesetz- und Verordnungsblatt* 1993, p. 229, as last amended in *Gesetz- und Verordnungsblatt* 2016, p. 630.
11 *Denkmalschutzgesetz, Gesetz- und Verordnungsblatt* 1991, p. 368 and 1992, p. 310, as last amended in *Gesetz- und Verordnungsblatt* 2005, p. 769.
12 *Denkmalschutzgesetz, Gesetz- und Verordnungsblatt* 2004, I p. 215.
13 *Denkmalschutzgesetz, Hamburger Gesetz- und Verordnungsblatt* 2013, p. 142.
14 *Denkmalschutzgesetz, Gesetz- und Verordnungsblatt* 1980, p. 226 and 716, as last amended in *Gesetz- und Verordnungsblatt* 2016, p. 934.
15 *Denkmalschutzgesetz, Gesetz- und Verordnungsblatt* 2004, p. 465, as last amended in *Gesetz- und Verordnungsblatt* 2008, p. 574.
16 *Denkmalschutzgesetz, Gesetzblatt* 1983, p. 797, as last amended in *Gesetzblatt* 2014, p. 686.
17 *Hessisches Denkmalschutzgesetz, Gesetz- und Verordnungsblatt* 2016, p. 211.
18 *Denkmalschutzgesetz, Gesetz- und Verordnungsblatt* 1973, p. 328, as last amended in *Gesetz- und Verordnungsblatt* 2015, p. 82.
19 *Denkmalschutzgesetz, Gesetz- und Verordnungsblatt* 1998, p. 12, as last amended in *Gesetz- und Verordnungsblatt* 2010, p. 383.
20 *Saarländisches Denkmalschutzgesetz, Amtsblatt* 2004, p. 1498, as last amended in *Amtsblatt* 2015 I, p. 790.

Saxon Cultural Heritage Act and section 11(2) Baden-Wurttemberg's Cultural Heritage Protection Act exempt heritage dedicated to divine service from the requirement of state permissions to modify them. Section 23(2) of Rhineland-Palatinate's Cultural Heritage Act[21] even extends this exemption in regard to any religious property regardless of its purpose (Wasmuth, 2017: D §§ 181–183); this extension is said not to apply to non-Christian religious communities (Wasmuth, 2017: D § 184).

The religious authorities will then decide after consultation with the state authorities, but only in case they have appropriate own authorities charged with the preservation of cultural heritage and approved by the state authorities pursuant to section 23(3) *leg. cit.* (Wasmuth, 2017: D §§ 197f.; Hönes, 1995: section 23 DSchG, §§ 8, 24f.). This regulation has incurred critique for being too extensive (Heckel, 1987: 101; Hönes, 1995: section 23 DSchG, § 9). Religious freedom does not demand such a wide exemption, a consideration of religious interests by the state authorities taking the decisions would be constitutionally compliant (Wasmuth, 2017: D § 179; Classen, 2015: § 391).

In some lands and pursuant to their corresponding contracts with the state, the Catholic Church and the Lutheran Church are vested with the decision-making competence after consultation with the state authorities, as is the case according to section 29(1) of Hessian Cultural Heritage Protection Act, section 23 of Schleswig-Holstein's Cultural Heritage Protection Act[22] or section 36 of Lower Saxon Cultural Heritage Protection Act[23] (Wasmuth, 2017: D §§ 195, 202).

In any case, norms which favour one or a few over other religious communities, appear unconstitutional (Heckel, 1987: 102; Wasmuth, 2017: D §§ 184, 195).

The kernel

Throughout the variety of rules in Germany the decision-making power is attached rather either to one or to the other side, i.e. to state or religious authorities. And even regulations, such as the aforementioned ones of Basle and Italy requiring an agreement do not exactly lay down the same idea as section 5(4) of Austrian Cultural Heritage Protection Act. In both cases no side will decide on the affairs of the other, but it is the swinging pendulum – the kind of 'administrative dialogue' – which renders section 5(4) *leg. cit.* unique. The pendulum makes clear whose turn it is to act and argue in a given moment. Ideally practised, it is a process of creative development for the sake of the preservation of common living heritage.

In this respect, it may be considered a proof of prevailing good practice that, so far, only one case pondering section 5(4) *leg. cit.* has been brought before

21 *Denkmalschutzgesetz, Gesetz- und Verordnungsblatt* 1978, p. 159, as last amended in *Gesetz- und Verordnungsblatt* 2014, p. 245.

22 *Denkmalschutzgesetz, Gesetz- und Verordnungsblatt* 2015, p. 2.

23 *Niedersächsisches Denkmalschutzgesetz, Gesetz- und Verordnungsblatt* 1978, p. 517, as last amended in *Gesetz- und Verordnungsblatt* 2011, p. 135.

administrative courts. There the state authority rejected a certain major alteration to the interior of a church building, but simply failed to properly respond to the congregation's arguments putting forth their liturgical considerations in favour of the alteration. That is why the Federal Administrative Court decided to refer the case back to the competent state authority.[24] In fact, at the second attempt, the state authority only charged with further investigations, but not obliged by the court to decide in a certain manner, finally acceded to the congregation's request. Meanwhile, the building has been modified and is accessible to both congregation members and the public. It is noteworthy to mention that a whole lot of other building measures had been discussed at the same time and had been met with general approval without detouring through the court. The overall results received acclaim.

Bibliography

Anderle, K. (1978). Kirchenrechtliche und staatskirchenrechtliche Aspekte der Novelle zum Denkmalschutzgesetz im Jahre 1978. *Österreichisches Archiv für Kirchenrecht* 29, pp. 446–464.

Bregger, H. M. (2003). Kirchliche Denkmalpflege im Spannungsfeld zwischen staatlicher und kirchlicher Normsetzung. In A. Hense, ed., *Denkmalrecht unter Denkmalschutz?* (Dresdner Schriften zum öffentlichen Recht 3). Frankfurt am Main: Lang, pp. 49–78.

Classen, C. D. (2015). *Religionsrecht*. 2nd ed. Tübingen: Mohr Siebeck.

Eberl, W., Martin, D. and Petzet, M. (1997). *Bayerisches Denkmalschutzgesetz*. 5th ed. Köln: Deutscher Gemeindeverlag.

Heckel, M. (1987). Der Denkmalschutz an den Sakralbauten in der Bundesrepublik Deutschland. Kulturschutz und Kirchenfreiheit im säkularen Verfassungssystem. In J. Chatelain, H. Beseler, L. Ray and M. Heckel, eds., *Denkmalpflege und Denkmalschutz an den Sakralbauten in der Bundesrepublik Deutschland und in Frankreich · Protection et conservation du patrimoine culturel religieux en France et en République Fédérale d'Allemagne*. Kehl, Strasbourg, Arlington: Engel, pp. 85–106.

Helfgott, N. (1978). Denkmalschutzgesetz und kirchliches Eigentum. *Österreichisches Archiv für Kirchenrecht*, 29, pp. 426–445.

Helfgott, N. (1979). *Die Rechtsvorschriften für den Denkmalschutz*. 1st ed. Wien: Manz.

Hönes, E.-R. (1995). *Denkmalrecht Rheinland-Pfalz*. 2nd ed. Köln: Deutscher Gemeindeverlag.

Margiotta Broglio, F. (2000). Articolo 19. In M. Cammelli, ed., *La nuova disciplina dei beni culturali e ambientali*. Milano: il Mulino.

Potz, R. and Brigitte Schinkele, B. (2016). *Religion and Law in Austria*. 1st ed. Alphen aan den Rijn: Kluwer.

Wasmuth, J. (2017). In: D. Davydov and J. Spennemann, ed., *Martin–Krautzberger: Handbuch Denkmalschutz und Denkmalpflege. Recht – fachliche Grundsätze – Verfahren – Finanzierung*. 4th ed. München: C. H. Beck.

Wieshaider, W. (2000). Auswirkungen der Novelle 1999 zum Denkmalschutzgesetz auf die Religionsgemeinschaften. *österreichisches Archiv für recht & religion*, 47, pp. 395–403.

Wieshaider, W. (2002). *Denkmalschutzrecht*. 1st ed. Wien, New York: Springer.

24 *Bundesverwaltungsgericht*, 8 May 2015, W176 2000769–1.

Wieshaider, W. (2013). Zu Rechtspersönlichkeit und Wesen gesetzlich anerkannter Religionsgesellschaften. *österreichisches Archiv für recht & religion*, 60, pp. 336–346.

Wieshaider, W. (2014). Die Weitergabe von Kultusbauten vor dem Hintergrund des Denkmalschutzrechtes. In B. Schinkele, R. Kuppe, S. Schima, E. M. Synek, J. Wallner and W. Wieshaider, ed., *Recht – Religion – Kultur, Festschrift für Richard Potz zum 70. Geburtstag*. Wien: facultas, pp. 923–934.

Index

For Product Safety Concerns and Information please contact our EU representative GPSR@taylorandfrancis.com
Taylor & Francis Verlag GmbH, Kaufingerstraße 24, 80331 München, Germany

www.ingramcontent.com/pod-product-compliance
Ingram Content Group UK Ltd.
Pitfield, Milton Keynes, MK11 3LW, UK
UKHW022013180926
475701UK00003B/339

* 9 7 8 0 3 6 7 5 8 9 3 3 2 *